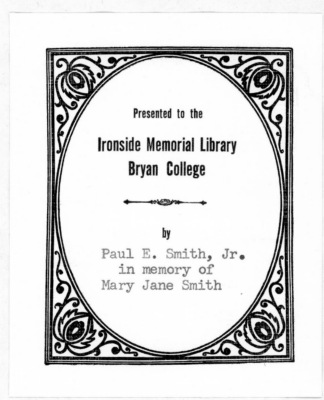

*Voices of
    American
    Fundamentalism*

Voices of
American
Fundamentalism

SEVEN
BIOGRAPHICAL
STUDIES

by C. Allyn Russell

THE WESTMINSTER PRESS

PHILADELPHIA

BOOK DESIGN BY DOROTHY E. JONES

PUBLISHED BY THE WESTMINSTER PRESS®
PHILADELPHIA, PENNSYLVANIA

PRINTED IN THE UNITED STATES OF AMERICA

Library of Congress Cataloging in Publication Data

Russell, Charles Allyn.
    Voices of American fundamentalism.

    Bibliography: p.
    Includes index.
    1. Fundamentalism. 2. Christian biography.
I. Title.
BT82.2.R87   230′.092′2 [B]   76-5886
ISBN 0-664-20814-2

To Betty, of course

CONTENTS

FOREWORD

A HALF-CENTURY has passed since William Jennings Bryan defended Fundamentalism in a sultry Tennessee courtroom during the Scopes "monkey" trial. That highly controversial Protestant movement soon passed from the center of public attention, but sharp debate about its nature and proper interpretation has continued ever since. The recent resurgence of conservative Protestant movements that in part trace their heritage to historic Fundamentalism has intensified interest in it. Some of the recent historical and theological approaches to the study of that important chapter in American religious history have been illuminating, but the leaders of Fundamentalism have often continued to be stereotyped as intransigent, anti-intellectual, misguided fighters.

Fresh, scholarly studies of the movement's central figures have long been needed, and VOICES OF AMERICAN FUNDAMENTALISM fills the gap for seven of its most conspicuous champions. The author, Prof. C. Allyn Russell of Boston University, a veteran researcher and teacher in the field of American religious history, has in every case gone back to the primary sources in these treatments of prominent fundamentalists—four Baptists and three Presbyterians. Though their common opposition to Liberalism often obscured it, they were actually a diversified lot, as this book demonstrates. They were also a colorful, confident group; much of the excitement they engendered when the movement was at its peak can be traced in these pages. They built religious empires significant in their day, yet they failed to attain their major goal—to bring their communions into the fundamentalist camp. The story of American religion and culture in the 1920's and after cannot be fully understood without attention to them.

Dr. Russell's careful biographical studies provide us with some significant building blocks for new interpretations of an important religious movement that has set its stamp not only on its own time but on ours as well. These profiles of J. Frank Norris, John Roach Straton, William Bell Riley, J. C. Massee, J. Gresham Machen, William Jennings Bryan, and Clarence E. Macartney are set in the context of contemporary historical knowledge about Fundamentalism, and make a helpful contribution to its fuller understanding.

The essay on Riley received the Solon J. Buck award for the best article to appear in *Minnesota History* in 1972.

ROBERT T. HANDY
Dean of Graduate Studies
Professor of Church History
Union Theological Seminary, New York

ACKNOWLEDGMENTS

THE AUTHOR IS INDEBTED to many individuals and several institutions for their assistance in making possible the publication of this book. Dr. Robert G. Torbet first stimulated my interest in the academic study of religion in America. Dr. Robert T. Handy served as the major critical guide to the project, giving unstintingly of his time and thought despite heavy responsibilities at Union Theological Seminary, New York City. A number of my colleagues at Boston University, as well as faculty members at other institutions, read selected chapters in manuscript form and offered helpful comments. These included Dr. Richard M. Cameron, Dr. David Hall, Dr. James D. Purvis, Dr. David K. W. Kim, and Dr. Sidney A. Burrell, all of Boston University; Dr. Paul Bechtel, Wheaton College, Wheaton, Illinois; Dr. Paul Woolley, Westminster Theological Seminary, Philadelphia, Pennsylvania; Dr. John T. Horton, State University of New York at Buffalo; Dr. Ernest R. Sandeen of Macalester College, St. Paul, Minnesota; and Dr. Carl E. Purinton, formerly of Boston University, now of Williamsburg, Virginia. Dr. Richard A. Newman, Senior Editor at G. K. Hall & Co., Boston, read several chapters and made useful suggestions, as did the Reverend Jon Zens of Fort Washington, Pennsylvania.

The Graduate School of Boston University, Dr. Robert F. Slechta, Associate Dean, provided five generous travel grants over a period of seven and a half years which made research possible in Georgia, Texas, Minnesota, Pennsylvania, New York, and the District of Columbia. Various relatives of the subjects of these biographical studies cooperated fully through interviews and, in some instances, lent valuable memorabilia and source material. Those persons are referred to in the notes of individual chapters.

Librarians and curators of historical societies who made available important primary and secondary sources included Edward C. Starr, The American Baptist Historical Society, Rochester, New York; Arthur W. Kuschke, Jr., Westminster Theological Seminary, Philadelphia, Pennsylvania; Burton L. Goddard, Gordon-Conwell Theological Seminary, Hamilton, Massachusetts; and Richard J. Crozier, then of Geneva College, Beaver Falls, Pennsylvania.

My wife, Elizabeth V. Russell, went beyond the call of duty in typing the manuscript. Prof. Franklin C. Erickson of Boston University gave both professional and personal encouragement to the project in its early stages.

The biographical chapters of this book have been re-edited since their original publication, sometimes under different titles, in various historical and theological journals. Grateful acknowledgment is hereby made to the editors of those journals who have granted permission for their inclusion in this book. The bibliographical information, including the titles of the several periodicals, is as follows:

"J. C. Massee, Unique Fundamentalist," *Foundations*, Oct.–Dec. 1969, pp. 330–356; "John Roach Straton, Accusative Case," *Foundations*, Jan.–March 1970, pp. 44–72; "J. Frank Norris: Violent Fundamentalist," *Southwestern Historical Quarterly*, Jan. 1972, pp. 271–302; "William Bell Riley: Architect of Fundamentalism," *Minnesota History*, Spring 1972, pp. 14–30; "J. Gresham Machen: Scholarly Fundamentalist," *Journal of Presbyterian History*, Spring 1973, pp. 40–69; "Clarence E. Macartney: Fundamentalist Prince of the Pulpit," *Journal of Presbyterian History*, Spring 1974, pp. 33–58; "William Jennings Bryan: Statesman-Fundamentalist," *Journal of Presbyterian History*, Summer 1975, pp. 93–119.

C. ALLYN RUSSELL
Concord, Massachusetts

CHAPTER ONE

Introducing
Fundamentalism

O F THE MANY COLORFUL CHAPTERS in the history of religion in America, none was quite so electric and acrimonious as the Modernist-Fundamentalist Controversy which focused in the 1920's. This book is about the leaders of the fundamentalist movement in that period when the struggle was at its tumultuous height. Previous studies of the conflict have been written from a topical or a strictly historical point of view, with heavy emphasis on denominational conflict. No one, however, has used the biographical method employed by the author of this volume.[1] Here the lives and thought of the ultraconservative spokesmen of that turbulent era are given central rather than peripheral emphasis. Such a study, based largely on primary sources, will reveal that these men who first went by the name "fundamentalist" (the term was coined in 1920) were a much more complex and varied group in both belief and life-style than previously has been recognized.[2] Many of the traditional stereotypes of fundamentalists (i.e., rural, uneducated, peripatetic revivalists, violent in thought and language) simply will not hold. In other instances, these traits and additional characteristics will be confirmed.

These fundamentalist leaders, with one possible exception, were outspoken religious nationalists at the same time that they were critics of American society. In the context of this paradox, attention will be given to their social as well as their strictly religious pronouncements, an aspect frequently neglected in the study of Fundamentalism. While their declarations on social issues were many, they were never proponents of the Social Gospel. Rather, they saw the solution to personal and societal needs in an individualistic ethic.[3]

These biographical studies will provide further information about other aspects of a theological tendency which, in various forms, continues to attract a large following in this country—and aspires to win an even greater number of adherents. Estimates of the number of fundamentalists range as high as seventeen million to twenty-three and a half million.[4] Ironically, considering their numerical strength, the academic works about them are relatively few. One scholar has written pointedly: "Fundamentalism remains the largest self-conscious minority group in American culture that has not been extensively studied or historically defined."[5] Furthermore, where studies have been made, they have not always been helpful. Another academician declares: "The fate of Fundamentalism in historiography has been worse than its lot in history."[6]

This book will not answer all the critical questions that surround the study of Fundamentalism. It is designed to add to our knowledge of that movement which, as yet, has no definitive, comprehensive, nonsectarian study.[7] It is also designed for individuals who wish, in a single volume, a scholarly overview of those fundamentalists who contributed substantially to the excitement of that memorable decade in American history known as the Roaring Twenties. Sydney E. Ahlstrom has observed: "The Fundamentalist controversy neither began nor ended in the twenties, but that decade did witness the climactic confrontation of American evangelical Protestantism and modern thought."[8]

The names of some of the "defenders of the faith" considered in this book are familiar—William Jennings Bryan and J. Gresham Machen, for instance. Others, such as J. C. Massee and Clarence Edward Macartney, may be less known. All, however, including J. Frank Norris, John Roach Straton, and William Bell Riley, are important. For reasons of time and space, a few—Mark Matthews, Leander Munhall, and T. T. Shields—have not been included. Seven studies, however, will introduce us to a cross section of the most outstanding fundamentalist leaders, several of whom thought that the movement which they headed was as important as the Protestant Reformation of the sixteenth century. One went so far as to classify Fundamentalism as possibly the most important religious expression since Pentecost. With the resurgence of a fundamentalist mentality in America since 1950, and an evangelical conservatism which has antecedents in Fundamentalism, it is important that we examine those strong claims and the lives of the men who held them. Before this is attempted, a brief description of the history of Fundamentalism is appropriate.

Protestant Fundamentalism surfaced in the latter part of the nineteenth century and the first two decades of the present century. Ernest R. Sandeen has traced the roots of Fundamentalism to British and American millenarianism and to the emphasis of Princeton Theology on the inerrancy of the Scriptures in the original documents.[9] Millenarianism is the belief in the physical return of Christ, followed by his literal reign with the saints upon the earth for one thousand years. Frequently the distinction is made between premillennialists and postmillennialists. Premillennialists are those who believe that the second coming of Christ will take place before the millennium. This interpretation presupposes a degeneration of society until Jesus returns to establish his kingdom. Postmillennialists of the twentieth century are those who believe that the second coming of Christ will occur after the millennium which is to come as the result of the Christianization of the world without miraculous intervention.[10] Sandeen emphasizes the frequency of the premillennial interpretation in his search to locate the roots of Fundamentalism. George Marsden acknowledges the importance of the millenarian background to Fundamentalism, but places greater stress than does Sandeen on other contributing factors. Such factors include nineteenth-century evangelical Protestantism, revivalism, the erosion of a solidly Protestant culture, opposition and antagonism to Modernism, and the emphasis on personal moral purity.[11] Of these several influences, the author believes that a major catalyst, although not the only one, which brought Fundamentalism into existence was the rise and challenge of Protestant Liberalism.

Liberalism, which cast so much fear into the conservative ranks, had known earlier beginnings but came into special prominence in the post-Civil War period of American religious life.[12] In adjusting to culture, it endeavored to hold beliefs in harmony with science while at the same time attempting to retain the core of religious truth. The proponents of this theological position stressed the immanence of God and emphasized the possibility of the progressive moral improvement of man. Moderate liberals viewed the Bible as a historical record of a people's religious development rather than an infallible collection of proof texts, direct from God. They favored Biblical criticism, convinced that the most reverent attitude toward the Bible was to take it for what the critical and scientific study of its text and history indicated it to be. Placing heavy emphasis on reason, the liberals disbelieved in the supernaturally miraculous, convinced that all elements were controlled by natural processes. They championed the Social Gospel, proclaimed freedom from theological domination by creeds, councils, or members of a religious hierarchy, and asserted that theirs was the religion of Jesus, not the religion about Jesus developed by the early church. Essentially, Liberalism was an attitude rather than a credo. William Pierson Merrill saw the liberal as one who had a controlling passion for reality, kept an open mind toward the truth, believed in the comprehensive nature and range of the true church, and trusted in truth rather than in authority and force.[13] Leaders in the vanguard of liberal theology, which cut across the major denominations, included William Newton Clarke, George A. Gordon, Phillips Brooks, Henry Ward Beecher, and somewhat later, Shailer Mathews, Walter Rauschenbusch, and Harry Emerson Fosdick. Fosdick, the founding minister of Riverside Church in New York City, popularized the movement and its beliefs with remarkable success. When the religious influence of this liberal persuasion began to infiltrate the colleges and seminaries of America, to make its impact on the thinking of denominational officials, and to take root in some of the mission fields, Fundamentalism arose in the major denominations as a responding force.

There were many differences between the liberals and the fundamentalists, but as the latter saw it, the crucial issue was naturalism versus supernaturalism. What the fundamentalists meant by the supernatural embraced the "five fundamentals" adopted by the General Assembly of the Presbyterian Church in the U.S.A. in 1910 and reaffirmed in 1916 and 1923: the inerrancy of the Scriptures in the original documents, the deity of Jesus including his virgin birth, and the substitutionary atonement, physical resurrection, and the miracle-working power of Christ.[14] It would be erroneous, however, to limit the fundamentalists to any specific quintet of beliefs. Others—the Roman Catholics, for example—also held to those same five convictions. In addition to the "five fundamentals" of 1910 the fundamentalists affirmed belief in the natural depravity of man; justification by faith alone (which Roman Catholics did not); the personal, bodily return of Christ; and, normally, a literal heaven and a literal hell. More typical and distinguishing, however, than any of the doctrines that the fundamentalists embraced was their characteristic attitude. This attitude set them apart not only from liberals but also from the conservatives who, in the Northern (later American) Baptist

Convention, for instance, comprised a numerical majority. As Robert T. Handy has indicated:

The main difference between them [the fundamentalists and the conservatives] was probably more a matter of mood and spirit than basic theological divergence. Both subscribed to orthodox Protestant theological tenets, but the fundamentalists were more aggressive, more intransigent, more certain that they had the whole truth and their opponents had none. They not only militantly asserted the plenary inspiration of Scripture, but insisted that they had correctly apprehended its meaning and their opponents not at all.[15]

In such an aggressive mood shortly after World War I the fundamentalists flung the challenge at the liberals in the major Protestant denominations in the hope that Liberalism would be routed and Christians would unite about the great fundamentals of the faith. As the fundamentalists saw it, all persons were faced with a crucial decision. They must choose either the fundamentalist interpretation of Christianity or that of Protestant Liberalism. In their judgment, there was no middle ground.

The channels through which Fundamentalism developed and expressed itself were numerous. They included so-called prophetic and Bible conferences, religious literature, Bible schools and institutes, various federations and associations of the like-minded, and the voices of prominent spokesmen. The mother of the conferences was the Niagara Conference (named after Niagara-on-the-Lake, Ontario, its most frequent place of meeting), which convened for annual summer assemblies from 1875 to 1901. Its creed, adopted unofficially in 1878 and officially in 1890, reflected a conservative Calvinistic expression including a belief in the personal and premillennial return of Christ.[16] The literature of the fundamentalist movement came to include the *Scofield Reference Bible* and, beginning in 1910, the publication of the widely disseminated *The Fundamentals: A Testimony to the Truth*.

The Scofield Bible used the King James text supplemented with notes and annotations by C. I. Scofield, a Congregationalist clergyman of Dallas, Texas. These dogmatic notes and annotations, which reflected dispensational premillennialism, a radical distinction between Jews and Christians, and a firm belief in the inerrancy of the Scriptures in the original documents, became a much-used reference for conservative Sunday school teachers, preachers, and churchgoers.[17] This reference Bible was first published in 1909, amplified in 1919, and revised in a new edition in 1966.

The Fundamentals were a set of twelve booklets, each about 125 pages, setting forth the great theological issues of the day from a conservative standpoint by a galaxy of prominent scholars from the United States, Canada, and Great Britain. Through the generosity of two wealthy laymen from Los Angeles, Lyman and Milton Stewart, these booklets were sent, over a five-year period (1910–1915), to some three million people. Every pastor, evangelist, missionary, theological professor, theological student, Sunday school superintendent, YMCA and YWCA secretary in the English-speaking world whose address could be obtained, received a copy. In the judgment of Sydney E. Ahlstrom, the significance of *The Fundamentals* was twofold. Initially, a great interdenominational witness was achieved with "dignity, breadth of subject matter, rhetorical moderation, obvious conviction, and considerable intellectual power." [18] Secondly, the project created a kind of uneasy entente between two fairly incompatible conservative elements: a denominational, seminary-oriented group and a Bible institute group (e.g., Moody Bible Institute and the Bible Institute of Los Angeles) with strong premillennial and dispensational interests.[19] Despite differing theological interpretation of various passages of Scripture, the authors of *The Fundamentals*, reflecting these two groups, were generally united on belief in the Bible's literal inerrancy. Some scholars feel that the dissemination of *The Fundamentals* marks the beginning of Fundamentalism as a movement.

The developing conflict between the liberals and those of conservative theological belief was interrupted by World War I, which absorbed the interest and time of many Americans. After the war, however, and partly because of the emotions aroused by it, the religious controversy resumed with increased intensity. The spokesmen of Fundamentalism who are described in this book served in their various areas of responsibility prior to the "war to end war," but the height of their influence was reached in the postwar period. These men were linked with the Baptist and the Presbyterian denominations, where the Modernist-Fundamentalist Controversy was most severe.

Despite some common denominators in belief and life-style, there are noticeable contrasts and differences among the seven subjects of this study. One leader shot and killed an unarmed man in his own study; another was the epitome of propriety, wearing his Geneva pulpit robe even in his coffin. In the battle against Liberalism, some of these fundamentalists left their denominations in angry protest, while others remained stubbornly faithful to their churchly ties. Some welcomed the title "fundamentalist"; others sought to be disassociated from the term. Most affirmed their belief in the verbal inerrancy of the Scriptures, although one believed that the Bible was infallible in its purposes but declined to use the word "inerrant." Millenarian interpretations varied widely among these leaders. Four came to a millenarian or premillennialist position, while the remaining three inclined toward other views. All believed in the doctrine of original sin, yet one constantly taught that mankind deserves to be trusted and that the heart of mankind is basically sound. Some would admit to the table of Communion only those who had been baptized by immersion, while another, and a Baptist at that, would welcome all persons to the Lord's Supper, including non-Christians. Several of these seven were outspoken in their criticism of the Roman Catholic Church; one declined to criticize Catholicism publicly; and another, after early criticism of Catholicism, was received by the pope, in personal audience, at Vatican City. Several were ardently opposed to granting women further "rights" in church and society, while one was a strong proponent of women's suffrage, believing that when it became a reality, it would lead to the outlawing of both war and the legalization of intoxicating beverages. It may be surprising to those who hold preconceived notions about the social attitudes of the fundamentalists that one of these spokesmen declined to support the cause of prohibition, and on the subject of smoking he sometimes expressed the regret that he had never taken up the practice because he regarded it as an aid to friendship and Christian patience. There were also marked dissimilarities in life-style. One was a scholar; another was a statesman-politician; a third was a pastor-revivalist known for his tent meetings, including a "five-poler"; and a fourth was a minister but never a revivalist.

Differences such as these among the colorful champions of Fundamentalism will make for more interesting reading in the ensuing chapters than otherwise would be the case. These same differences also make more difficult the scholar's attempt to define Fundamentalism. A biographical approach, however, is one valid way to come closer to the heart of the issues.

CHAPTER TWO

J. Frank Norris
VIOLENT FUNDAMENTALIST

ONE OF THE MOST CONTROVERSIAL FIGURES in American religious history was J. Frank Norris, of Fort Worth, Texas. He was a leading, although cantankerous figure among Baptists of the South in the 1920's. There was little of moderation about either his life or his thought. An account of ultraconservative religion, and perhaps right-wing politics, in this country would be incomplete without a knowledge of his career. A review of his turbulent seventy-four years is important because of the extent of his influence, the illustration he provides of variation within the ranks of fundamentalist leaders, and the case study in violence he affords for a nation that increasingly is analyzing its own stormy backgrounds. In addition, there is need for a critical essay on Norris, since, to this author's knowledge, the only two published works about him have been written by former associate ministers and are highly laudatory.[1]

It is difficult to comprehend the turmoil that engulfed the man who claimed to serve the largest churches in the world. It began early in his life. J. Frank Norris was shot and wounded at the age of fifteen. During his years in college (Baylor), he led a student uprising that contributed to the resignation of the president of the institution. In the midst of his ministry he was indicted and tried for arson, perjury, and murder. Nourished in the free-church, autonomous tradition of southern Baptists, the independent Norris later fought indefatigably the "denominational machine" both before and after his successive expulsions from a local pastors conference, the county association of which his church was a member, and the Baptist General Convention of Texas. The churches that Norris served suffered major splits, one of them losing six hundred members in a single year. Beset by

Homer Ritchie, First Baptist Church, Fort Worth, Tex.

J. Frank Norris

enemies without and harassed, it would appear, by psychological problems within, he was a hardworking pastor-evangelist, publisher-editor, radio preacher, world traveler, and perennial politician. He became the leader simultaneously of two huge congregations, twelve hundred miles apart, as well as the head of a "seminary" and the founder of his own Fellowship of churches. A self-appointed foe of alleged social evils, theological Liberalism, Roman Catholicism, and political communism, Norris toured the nation and the world. In his wake he left, in addition to thousands of converts, a record of acrimony, strife, and division. Ironically, his public ministry began in a place called Mount Calm, Texas. That was the closest J. Frank Norris ever came to serenity.

At the conclusion of his tumultuous career, Norris' friends hailed him as a great preacher of unmatched courage, an incisive modern prophet, and a reformer of his own denominational family. His opponents no doubt agreed with Ralph McGill, editor of the Atlanta *Constitution*, who declared on one occasion that "The Rev. J. Frank Norris, and others like him, is one good, sound reason why there are 50,000,000 Americans who do not belong to any church at all." [2] A review of Norris' ministry and the violent controversies it precipitated will indicate why men held such opposite interpretations. Few persons could appraise Norris objectively. He was loved or hated, with equal passion. This chapter reviews the highlights of Norris' life and ministerial characteristics, and then gives primary attention to his role as a man of controversy—in his local church, in the various denominations to which he belonged, and in wider areas.

I

J. Franklyn Norris was born on September 18, 1877, at Dadeville, Alabama, seventy-five miles southeast of Birmingham, the son of James Warren and Mary Davis Norris. Eleven years later, with the promise of cheap land and new beginnings on the frontier, the family moved to Hubbard, Texas. Norris' sharecropper father gave more heed to alcohol than to agriculture. Poverty, punishment, and pain characterized the lad's youth and appear to have molded his personality significantly. The parents and three children lived in a dilapidated, unpainted shack, where they eked out a minimal existence. On one occasion Norris' father disciplined his son so severely that the boy's nose was broken and his body severely lacerated.[3] Yet when horse thieves threatened his father's life, young Frank went to his aid—and was shot three times. Gangrene set in, followed by inflammatory rheumatism which left Norris voiceless and paralyzed. Three years of recuperation ensued, two of them in a wheelchair. During this trying time, Norris' mother nourished his nascent faith. He had been converted at the age of thirteen at a brush arbor revival service. She instilled in him the conviction that he was "someone of great worth who would be a leader of men." [4]

After a brief experience as a teacher, Norris felt called to the ministry. Accordingly, assisted by a loan from the family doctor, Norris enrolled as a student at the Baptist-operated Baylor University in Waco, Texas. To the consternation of his classmates and some members of the faculty, Norris announced that his goal in life was "to preach in the greatest church and pulpit in the world." With a conservative theology given him by B. H. Carroll of the university and a talent for speaking and persuasion that appeared to be inborn, Norris set himself toward the attainment of his objective. At the age of twenty-two he accepted the pastorate of the country church in Mount Calm. Serving this parish until he was graduated from Baylor, Norris spent his weekends making innumerable visits to homes of prospective members and preaching his dramatic sermons to as many as eight hundred people, twice the number who lived in the township.[5]

Norris' aggressive spirit was also revealed in the midst of a tragicomedy of errors at the university. The president at the time was O. H. Cooper, a former Yale professor who was respected in the academic community. Several prankish students smuggled a howling dog into the midst of a chapel service that was being conducted on the third floor of the administration building.[6] Infuriated by the interruption, the president seized the animal (instead of the students!) and hurled it through a window to the ground below. The embarrassed Cooper apologized the next day for his regrettable loss of control, but Norris would not let the matter lie. He led a student revolt which informed the Society for the Prevention of Cruelty to Animals as well as the trustees of the university concerning the unhappy incident. Other issues may also have been at stake, but it was this event and the protest which followed that forced the resignation of the president.[7] Thereafter, young J. Frank Norris was a person "to be reckoned with."

After his graduation from Baylor in 1903, Norris enrolled as a student at the Southern Baptist Theological Seminary in Louisville, Kentucky. He completed the three-year course in two years, and then launched upon his full-time professional career.[8] He pastored the McKinney Avenue Baptist Church in Dallas until 1908, driving himself to near-exhaustion in building its attendance from thirteen members to nearly a thousand.[9] While serving this congregation, Norris became the business manager of *The Baptist Standard*, the voice of Texas Baptists, although not owned by them.[10] When tension developed between Norris and the editor, Joseph Martin Dawson, the latter resigned and Norris assumed full leadership of the journal.[11] He introduced sensational articles and conducted a bold campaign against alleged social evils, especially racetrack gambling in the Lone Star State.[12] Despite an increase in the journal's circulation, Norris failed to receive the support of denominational leaders who disapproved of his showmanship. In turn, he felt that these men were "mechanical" in their spiritual expression, devoid of imagination and vitality. Disgruntled and disillusioned, Norris resigned his editorial post in 1909 and gave serious thought to pursuing secular work. Later in the year, however, he accepted a rather surprising call to the rich and influential First Baptist Church of Fort Worth.[13] Drawing what was purported to be the largest salary of any pastor in the South, Norris carried on a perfunctory ministry for two years until his own spirits were revived at a series of meetings that he conducted in Owensboro, Kentucky, for the Reverend Charles Carroll, the son of his former professor at Baylor. Thereafter he became the flamboyant, aggressive, controversial minister of what grew to be the largest Protestant church in the United States. He served it until his death forty-three years later, brandishing "not a little pearl-handled knife, but the broad axe of John the Baptist." [14]

During his pastoral career, Norris edited his own tabloid newspaper, *The Fundamentalist* (earlier known as *The Fence-Rail* and *The Searchlight*). This publication, which proved to be a fierce competitor to *The Baptist Standard*, developed into the religious journal most widely circulated in the South, with approximately eighty thousand subscribers. As a pioneer radio preacher, Norris, at the peak of his ministry, conducted weekly broadcasts over twenty-seven stations, reaching most of the nation with his rhetoric.[15] In 1931, when separated from the Southern Baptist Convention (for reasons to be discussed later), Norris founded the "Premillennial, Fundamental, Missionary Fellowship," a loosely knit organization which sponsored an enthusiastic program of foreign missions and a Bible Institute designed to prepare young men for ministries in fundamentalist churches.[16] Early in 1935, Norris became pastor of the Temple

Baptist Church in Detroit, and served that congregation simultaneously with his church in Fort Worth for sixteen years.[17]

In addition to these many responsibilities, Norris journeyed overseas seven times, usually on behalf of the missionary program of his rapidly growing Fellowship. He also traveled widely in the United States, conducting revivals in forty-six states and speaking as a debater and preacher on behalf of fundamentalist causes and conservative politics. His most dramatic successes as an evangelist were in Houston and San Antonio in 1924 when some two thousand converts were added to the churches. Speaking in Georgia in the late 1930's, Norris influenced a student at Mercer University, John Birch, to become a missionary to China. Young Birch followed Norris to Forth Worth, joined his church, studied one year in his seminary, and in July 1940 left for China under his personal sponsorship and the auspices of his Fellowship.[18]

Exhausted by his labors and controversies, the ubiquitous fundamentalist monarch died of a heart attack on August 20, 1952, while at a youth rally in Keystone Heights, Florida. The funeral service, attended by five thousand people, was broadcast from his home church in Fort Worth. He was buried in a red tie, a white shirt, and a blue.suit; and an escort of eighteen policemen led the miles-long procession to the cemetery.[19] There was a bit of color to the very end.

II

An analysis of the ministerial characteristics of J. Frank Norris reveals him to have been many things to many men. In perspective, it seems accurate to view him as a fundamentalist, a sensationalist, a politician, and always a controversialist. He was many things more, but these at least.

Norris' fundamentalist stance must be set within the context of religious trends in the nation as well as in the region of which he was a part. At the opening of the twentieth century, with the gradual rise of urbanization, industrialization, and the growth of theological Liberalism, traditional religious emphases were being challenged. Modifying factors came more slowly to the South—if they came at all—than to other sections of the country. Kenneth K. Bailey has pointed out that, at the turn into the twentieth century, religion in the South—especially among the predominant Southern Baptists, Methodists, and Presbyterians—had these characteristics: orthodoxy of belief, a preoccupation with individual repentance rather than

social change, a tendency toward overt expression of intense religious
emotions, ecclesiastical independence, racial segregation, and an
all-pervading poverty which made difficult, in many instances, the
training of an educated ministry.[20]

Where religious Liberalism did make its impact—in both the larger
nation and the South—it was met frequently with fear, opposition,
and hostility. J. Frank Norris personified such a response. He feared
the encroachments of Liberalism and opposed them by emphasizing a
particular set of ultraconservative beliefs. More importantly, he
manifested an aggressive and a militant attitude which became
synonymous with his name and church. In both instances—theology
and attitude—Norris fitted the fundamentalist mold.[21] Not only did
he fit the mold—in large measure he helped to create it.

The cornerstone of Norris' theology lay in his belief in an inerrant,
verbally inspired Bible. This crucial conviction as well as his
"either-or" mentality was reflected in words to a friend: "The big
issue is the verbal inspiration of the Scriptures and if there is no
verbal inspiration we have no inspiration." These Scriptures he
interpreted literally, declaring:

> Whenever you find a preacher who takes the Bible allegorically and
> figuratively . . . that preacher is preaching an allegorical gospel which is
> no gospel. I thank God for a literal Christ; for a literal salvation. There is
> literal sorrow; literal death; literal hell; and, thank God, there is a literal
> heaven.[22]

Central to his understanding of the Bible, literally interpreted, and
crucial to his preaching was Norris' firm belief in the premillennial
coming of Christ. Early and briefly in his ministry he had been a
postmillennialist, but Louis Entzminger, his ministerial associate,
persuaded him of the error of this position. Thereafter, Norris
stressed the premillennialist aspect of the second coming of Christ,
especially during the depression years when discouragement with the
human condition was rife. Although not a dispensationalist in the
usual sense of the word ("Law and grace are enough dispensations—
keep them simple," advised the defender of the faith),[23] Norris did set
forth quite specifically what he believed to be the essence of Biblical
eschatology.

> The Scriptures are very clear that before Armageddon there will be the
> first resurrection, the translation of the living saints, and the marriage of
> the Lamb, and then for a period of time, the duration of which we do not
> know, the great tribulation will be on earth, the beast or the anti-Christ

will hold sway, and at the close of the tribulation, Armageddon, and then the second stage of His return, the Revelation in glory and power with His saints, the overthrow of the beast and his armies, the conversion of the Jews, the chaining of Satan and the establishment of His throne.[24]

Holding this view, Norris felt it was the purpose of the church to prepare individuals for the bodily, personal, visible, and premillennial coming of Christ. He minimized any effort to reform society, asserting that "our motive is not to redeem America, China, or Russia, it is to get ready the Body of Christ, the Bride, . . . for the coming of the Bridegroom. . . . It [the premillennial view] is the only missionary motive . . . not to clean out the stables, but to redeem the individual man and woman." [25]

Norris' views on Biblical inspiration, premillennialism, and personal rather than social salvation reflected the beliefs of other fundamentalists. He differed with some of his contemporaries in his espousal of Zionism, his ecclesiology, his Calvinistic attitude toward the security of the believer, and in the personalization he brought to the doctrine of retribution.

Norris' Zionism was more religious than political as it tied in with his understanding of Biblical eschatology. Contrary to those who accused him of being anti-Semitic, Norris had a high evaluation of the Jew in Biblical history, contemporary society, and future events. He envisioned the conversion of the Jews as part of the divine plan and spoke specifically against anti-Semitic propaganda, believing this to be dangerous (because of God's judgment upon those who disseminate it), unchristian, and un-American.[26] In his outspoken support of Zionism, Norris differed markedly with his fundamentalist colleague from Minneapolis, William Bell Riley. Norris also held that the Scriptures taught that there would be an Anglo-Jewish alliance in the final days. Here his hopes were probably better than his hermeneutics.

On the important subject of ecclesiology, Norris affirmed the complete independence of the local church to a greater degree than many of his ultraconservative colleagues. As a body of baptized believers, the church had, in his judgment, the absolute right of self-government, free from the interference of any hierarchy of individuals or organizations. It might voluntarily cooperate with other similar bodies, but each congregation was the sole judge of the measure and method of this cooperation.[27] On all matters pertaining to membership, polity, discipline, and benevolence, the will of the local group was final. Repeatedly, Norris taught that the one and only superintendent of the church was Christ through the Holy Spirit. In turn, Christ worked his will through the human agency of the pastor. This interpretation gave Norris justification for his rejection of denominationalism in general and the Southern Baptist Convention in particular. It also gave him an independent hand in his own congregation, free from the checks and balances of official boards.

Like John Calvin, Norris asserted the eternal spiritual security of the true elect. In popular parlance this meant, "Once saved, always saved." When obvious backsliding occurred, Norris interpreted this as either temporary or reflecting that true salvation had not taken place originally. To deny the everlasting security of the Christian, he affirmed, was to place in doubt the efficacy of the atonement itself as well as the power of God to keep the individual.[28]

When it came to retribution, Norris not only held this doctrine but saw it working effectively in his own life. He believed that his own causes were being vindicated and he also held that punishment was being meted out to his personal enemies. When the district attorney who pressed charges against Norris in 1912 died in a violent traffic accident in Forth Worth, Norris interpreted this tragedy as an expression of divine judgment. A half-broken bottle of liquor, found near the scene of the crash, was brought to Norris. He took this into the pulpit, using it as an object lesson as he preached on the text: "Thou art weighed in the balances and art found wanting." [29] Such tactics made several of Norris' sermons all the more dramatic to some—and all the more repulsive to others.

Norris was a fundamentalist in attitude as well as in belief. He was dogmatic, aggressive, stubborn, and distinctly more militant than most of the leaders of his theological stripe. Furthermore, he was a fundamentalist in the company he kept, especially with men like William Bell Riley, John Roach Straton, T. T. Shields, Mordecai Ham, A. C. Dixon, and, to a lesser extent, Billy Sunday.[30] For a time, Norris courted the friendship of Gerald B. Winrod, the pro-Nazi, anti-Semitic evangelist of Wichita, Kansas, and Gerald L. K. Smith, the Christian nationalist leader. Norris' position on Zionism led him to break with Winrod, and he repudiated Smith on the grounds that the latter had little genuine interest in the gospel.[31] Norris joined several of his fundamentalist colleagues in founding the World's Christian Fundamentals Association in 1919, and he was a charter member of the Baptist Bible Union, established in 1923. Despite Norris' efforts, few Baptists in the South joined the latter organization. The

Modernist-Fundamentalist Controversy was less intense in the South than in other sections of the country because of the relative paucity of liberal Christians with whom a fundamentalist might disagree.[32]

Any doubts about his own high evaluation of the fundamentalist movement were dispelled when "the Texas cyclone" stated in the midst of his ministry:

> I believe with all my soul that future generations will write about this Fundamentalist Movement as historians now write up the Reformation and [the] Wesley Revival and other great awakenings. And as revolutions have rent and torn to pieces all political alignments and governments of the world, so we are now in the greatest religious revival that time has ever witnessed since, perhaps, Pentecost.
>
> What if the present-day denominations are smashed to smithereens? It [sic] ought to be. They are unscriptural.[33]

In addition to being a fundamentalist, J. Frank Norris was perennially the sensationalist. This attribute of showmanship was probably innate, but he also cultivated it shrewdly. It kept the crowds flocking to the growing churches under his colorful leadership. Norris was as unorthodox in his pulpit conduct, places of meeting, and general methods of "churchmanship" as he was fundamentalist in his theology.

His sermon titles illustrate this flair for the dramatic. When America moved close to active participation in World War II, Norris' subject was "Shall Uncle Sam Be Made an Ass Again?" An early topic at Forth Worth bore the peculiar homiletical caption: "If Jim Jeffries, the Chicago Cubs, and Theodore Roosevelt Can't Come Back, Who Can?" Norris' pulpit mannerisms matched his bizarre sermon topics. With a newspaper in one hand and a Bible in the other, he roamed the platform, gesturing with conviction, shouting to emphasize a point, and weeping—on occasion—to move the emotions of his listeners. Then frequently he would leap from the pulpit platform to the level of the congregation, there concluding his discourse by inviting members of his audience to join him in an act of dedication.

Norris held services wherever people would gather—theaters, taverns, night clubs, schools, street corners, and baseball parks. During his ministry at Fort Worth he conducted 103 open-air and tent revivals, and the largest tent meeting of his career (a five-poler!) was held at Cadillac Square in the heart of downtown Detroit, with the mayor of the city and the governor of the state attending one of the services.[34] Norris also conducted outdoor baptismal rallies—from

the Detroit River (with forty thousand present) to the banks of the
Jordan and the Mediterranean Sea.

Norris' methods on special occasions were as unique as his pulpit
mannerisms and places of meeting. During the controversy over
evolution he brought monkeys and apes onto the pulpit to introduce
his members to the "kinfolk" of those who accepted Darwin's thesis.
When the World's Christian Fundamentals Association met in his
church, Norris turned the sanctuary into a courtroom and placed
three Methodist institutions on "trial" for teaching evolution.[35] When
the Eighteenth Amendment was passed, Norris conducted a public
funeral for John Barleycorn, actually burying an unvarnished pine
casket filled with empty whiskey bottles. The church band played
"Dixie" and other lively tunes at the committal service. When a
famed cowboy "champion of the world" was baptized by Norris, his
trick horse watched the proceedings from inside the church auditorium. When European dictatorships seemed to threaten American
democracy, Norris burned Nazi and Soviet flags at outdoor rallies.[36]
Stunts such as these accounted in large measure for the turnover in
the congregations at both Fort Worth and Detroit. The pastor-
preacher justified the histrionics by the number of people drawn by
them and the conversions resulting. At the same time, some church
members were revolted by such theatrics, resented the types of
persons they attracted, and left the church—including the six
hundred members at Fort Worth in 1911.[37] Norris, however, never
wavered. He viewed their departure as a purifying process enabling
him to carry on a greater—and larger—work!

There was no question about the increase in numbers. Norris'
church at Fort Worth grew from 1,200 members in 1909 with an
average attendance of 500 on Sunday mornings to over 12,000 in 1928
with an average attendance of 5,200. At Detroit, he began with 800
members late in 1934 and counted 8,597 in 1943. When Dallas
Billington's mammoth Akron Baptist Temple finally surpassed the
First Baptist Church at Fort Worth in the 1940's as the "largest
church in the world," with 21,000 members, Norris worked a little
harder and by 1946 boasted that his two congregations totaled a
membership of 25,000 persons, "the largest combined membership
under one minister in the world." [38] Norris' statistical triumphs were
not limited to the membership of his churches. His Sunday school at
Fort Worth was claimed to be the world's largest, frequently
surpassing 5,000 in attendance. The enrollment of the Baptist Bible
Institute came to exceed 500 students, and estimates of the churches

in his Fellowship ranged from "several hundred" to 3,000. Furthermore, Norris claimed that his radio broadcasts "reached more people
than all the daily newspapers of Texas combined." [39]

These numerical successes did not come by accident. Many
persons, of course, were drawn by the sensationalism and personal
magnetism of this champion of the fundamentalist way of life.
Norris, however, shrewdly followed up with a thorough and persistent program of home visitation. Teams of men and women from his
congregation frequently made as many as 1,000 calls weekly in each
of the cities in which he served. One person in Fort Worth said with
conviction: "The only way to get rid of that First Baptist Church is to
join it." [40]

Norris' influence as a preacher-politician was wider than most of
his enemies cared to admit. He cast his weight on issues of national
importance. He had contact through correspondence and personal
interviews with many of the prominent leaders of the world. He
jockeyed his own followers to the advantage of the causes he
espoused, and developed a particular strategy of his own.

The aggressive role that Norris played in the presidential election
of 1928 illustrates his involvement with politics at the state and
national levels. He campaigned arduously against Al Smith and on
behalf of "that Christian gentleman and statesman, Herbert Hoover." He spoke 119 times in thirty cities over a span of three and a
half months. Although he opposed Smith because of his "wet" record,
"pork barrel" politics, and Tammany Hall associations, Norris, unlike
John Roach Straton, boldly asserted that the basic issue was the
Roman Catholic question.[41] Norris feared "foreign control," the destruction of religious liberty, and the threat to the morals of the
people which he thought a Roman Catholic president would bring.
When Texas voted for Hoover, the Republican, despite a Democratic
majority of 400,000, political leaders credited Norris as primarily
responsible for the victory.[42] A Democrat from Wichita Falls, Texas,
writing to a friend, declared that the members of his party had the Al
Smith campaign going fine until "that damn Norris came up here and
[made] it three-to-one for Hoover." [43] The exultant clergyman
attended the inauguration ceremonies in Washington at the invitation of the President-elect himself. Recent studies, however, have
indicated that there was more to southern restiveness than religious
prejudice against Smith and the so-called liquor and metropolitan
issues. The Democrats had to struggle against Hoover's personal
popularity. Their own party was in chaos when Smith assumed

leadership. Most of all, the economic prosperity of the time worked to the distinct advantage of the Republicans. Additional factors included the high-tariff policy of Hoover's party at a time when the textile industry was moving south and the inability of the Democratic candidate to find a good issue.[44]

As a preacher-politician, Norris appeared to relish his contact with the world's great men. He carried on correspondence with numerous individuals of influence in Washington, although one gains the impression that it was largely at his own initiative. He did have personal contacts with Presidents Hoover, Roosevelt, Truman, and Eisenhower; and, while overseas, he held interviews with such foreign dignitaries as David Lloyd George, Winston Churchill, the Grand Mufti of Jerusalem, the Lord Mayor of London, Benito Mussolini, and Pius XII. As Norris sought these men, so a host of individuals looked to him, requesting a variety of favors to meet personal needs. His papers include records of officeholders and would-be officeholders requesting his support; the poor asking for money, prisoners seeking parole, men and women desiring counsel, the unemployed seeking employment, relatives hunting for missing persons, businessmen advertising their products, pastors wanting churches, and churches wanting pastors.

It was as a preacher-politician that Norris developed a few basic principles by which he governed his own strategy. He learned early in his career to emphasize only his successes; he remembered his friends with adulation and gifts; he practiced the wise use of his victories; he appealed to his people's sympathy, frequently picturing himself as the tired, persecuted, lonely prophet of God, whose legs would hardly carry him, whose head was about to burst, and whose nerves were ready to give way; and he taught himself and others not to worry. Concerning this latter axiom, Norris once declared: "If you want good health, don't worry—go to bed, pull up the windows, and let the world go to hell until daylight." [45]

Norris succeeded so well as a preacher-politician that in 1929 a member of the state legislature introduced a bill prohibiting a minister from becoming governor of Texas. This was a thinly disguised slap at the pastor from Fort Worth. Norris replied with customary acidity that the step would not have been necessary if "those little peanut politicians, . . . those little simlin-headed, sawdust-brained grafters, . . . had stood like they ought to have stood." [46]

III

Of the many aspects of the life of J. Frank Norris on which one may choose to concentrate, certainly his place as a man of controversy is the most obvious. The coalescence of his other roles—fundamentalist, sensationalist, and preacher-politician—kept him constantly in the spotlight. This self-proclaimed prophet created controversy in the local church, in the community, at the denominational level, and on the national scene.

When Norris was called to Fort Worth, one of the members who opposed his coming said: "This church is not in condition for his type of ministry. If he comes there will be the all-firedest [sic] explosion ever witnessed in any church. We are at peace with the world, the flesh, and the devil, and with one another. . . . I just want to warn you." [47] Norris saw to it that the placid state of the congregation did not last long. The immediate causes of the disturbance were his sensational methods, his dictatorial qualities, his unrelenting attacks on the vices of the day, and the personal charges that he brought against "corrupt" city officials.

Believing that a congregation patterned after the New Testament should not be run by the church boards or "any official clique," Norris early assumed complete control at both Forth Worth and Detroit. In each congregation he dismissed the chairman of the board of deacons for what he termed "interference" with his work, replacing each with an individual loyal to his own cause. Boards, committees, and organizations among women and young people ceased as these congregations became little else than a preaching post for Norris.[48] A dramatic illustration of his spirit is contained in his own account of opposition at Fort Worth:

> We had a nice little choir—one woman who would start in G and end away up on Gee Whiz, and a beer-guzzling Dutchman for a choir conductor—he had hair as wide as the top of this desk, and he would shake it to the right and to the left. He had been there twelve years. . . . [One night] the crowd [at the evening service] had gotten there ahead of time, and I started them to singing some old songs, and this Dutchman came and he couldn't get in, and he wrote me a note and said: "Please open the way so the choir can get in." I wrote on the bottom, "Wait until I send for you." If he had waited he would have been standing there yet. The next morning that beer-guzzling bunch of hair came around and he shook that head of hair east and west, and north and south, and up and down. . . . I stood there and watched him shake and tell me what he wasn't going to stand for until the old windmill run down, and I said, "Are you through?"

And I said, "Professor, so we can understand each other, you have resigned." He said, "I will take it up with the deacons." [49]

The deacons held a secret meeting to consider the situation. Norris learned of it and fired the deacons! He told them heatedly: "We will understand whether or not I am going to be pastor or janitor." [50] The larger church voted to accept the "resignations" upon Norris' recommendations. Such arbitrary actions by Norris resulted in large and quick turnovers in membership. Other people, usually of lower social and economic backgrounds, were speedily drawn to the message and church of the fiery fundamentalist.[51]

When Norris aggressively attacked the evils of alcohol, prostitution, and municipal corruption, the tensions began to encompass the larger community. They reached a boiling point one Sunday evening in 1911. Before an overflow congregation, the preacher spoke on the subject "The Ten Biggest Devils in Fort Worth, Names Given." The ten men, notified in advance, were invited to dispute the charges, but only one of them, a lawyer, appeared. He was hooted off the platform upon admission that the liquor interests controlled a share in one of the city's newspapers. The opposition, however, could not remain silent long. Angered by their minister, church officials sought to dismiss him—but in vain. Community leaders, including the mayor, met to determine strategy to force Norris out of town—unsuccessfully. One attempt was made to blackmail him; another to assassinate him. Merchants refused Norris credit and clerks declined to wait on him. Newspapers refused to print his name, even in reports of weddings and funerals. Norris responded by printing and distributing weekly thousands of handbills advertising his services.[52]

Eventually, physical violence broke out. Fire of undetermined origin caused damage amounting to $10,000 to the auditorium of the First Baptist Church of Fort Worth in January 1912. One month later, the church was totally destroyed by fire. Norris, through spirited attacks, charged that his enemies were responsible. Following an investigation by a private detective, the district attorney of Tarrant County accused Norris of committing arson in order to build a larger church. A grand jury agreed and Norris was tried for perjury and arson in April 1912, and was acquitted.[53]

Such events failed to dim the ardor or change the methods of "the Texas cyclone." Norris refused to mute his message or to accept invitations to other fields of service. In the 1920's he drove himself with renewed energy and became more dogmatic than ever, especially in his anti-Catholic statements. Late in that decade occurred the most memorable and tragic event of his stormy life.

In the spring and summer of 1926, Norris increased his verbal attacks against "Rum and Romanism" which, he asserted, formed a conspiracy designed "to elect a Catholic president to overthrow the Constitution, and control this government."[54] Norris personalized the charges in Fort Worth against H. C. Meacham, Roman Catholic mayor of the city and owner of a large department store. His words on Sunday, July 11, were especially inflammatory. He accused Meacham of misappropriating city funds for the benefit of Roman Catholic institutions. He also attacked the mayor's personal integrity, claiming that some years earlier the businessman had been forced to pay a young woman employee $12,500 in order to avoid further charges. Norris concluded his impassioned discourse by shouting, "He isn't fit to be manager of a hog-pen."[55] That same day Norris introduced from the pulpit six members of the First Baptist Church who had worked at Meacham's store but had been dismissed because of their membership in the First Baptist Church. Norris' newspaper, The Searchlight, dated Friday, July 16, carried a full account of both the sermon and the testimony of the former employees. Copies of these papers were distributed widely throughout the city and to customers entering Meacham's store. Norris announced his plans to continue the exposé the following Sunday. That intention, however, was dramatically interrupted.

While Norris was preparing his sermon on Saturday afternoon, July 17, D. E. Chipps, a lumberman-friend of Meacham, made a threatening telephone call to the fundamentalist leader. Shortly thereafter Chipps entered Norris' second-floor study. Sharp words were exchanged. Soon four shots rang out and Chipps fell mortally wounded. A biographer of Norris has stated, "The life of one man was gone, the life of the other [was] never to be the same."[56]

J. Frank Norris was taken to the office of the district attorney, where he told his account of the tragedy. After he was released on bond, the preacher offered his resignation to officials of his church, but they speedily declined to accept it. Then he returned home to revise his sermon for the next day. The following morning a capacity congregation, some of whom had come as early as dawn, heard the sober pastor preach on the subject "There Is Therefore Now No Condemnation to Those Who Are in Christ Jesus" (Rom. 8:1). Norris made no reference to the calamity of the previous day, although The Searchlight of that week stated that it was not strange, "in view of the series of sermons that Dr. Norris had been preaching against Romanism and bootleggers [,] that certain parties should desire to prosecute him." A front-page announcement declared that "Dr. Norris acted in . . . necessary self-defense and did nothing but what any other reasonable, sensitive man would be compelled to do." One week later the same publication charged that "every Roman Catholic church in the city raised money for his [Norris'] prosecution." [57] In all of the excitement Norris' congregation stood by him loyally, crowding his services and, on a single Sunday, raising $16,000 for his defense.[58]

A grand jury indicted Norris for murder. In January 1927, after a change of venue, he was tried in Austin. The state charged that Norris' rabid sermons had provoked the confrontation with Chipps and that the clergyman had shot—as he had—an unarmed man. His attorneys argued that Norris had shot in self-defense when a stranger of unsavory reputation, under the influence of alcohol, provided an "apparent danger." [59] The only witness to the deed was one of the deacons of the church, L. H. Nutt, a bank teller and a devoted follower of Norris. The jury that tried the case deliberated only forty minutes. They found Norris not guilty, on the first ballot.

The controversial fundamentalist returned immediately to Fort Worth to be greeted by eight thousand persons who gathered spontaneously in the big gray stone church to welcome their leader. Congratulatory telegrams were read from William Bell Riley, Billy Sunday, Congressman William D. Upshaw, and others. Then dramatically

> the throng stood and cheered as the Rev. Mr. Norris, clad in a business suit and dark overcoat, walked across the platform, his light gray Fedora hat in his hand. As he peeled off his topcoat, he seemed to be undergoing an emotional storm. There were tears in his eyes. He asked his hearers to join him in prayer. He asked . . . that each member . . . refrain from holding malice against anyone, no matter who had persecuted him. He then requested his flock not to applaud him, but they interrupted his talk with handclapping, being unable to constrain their joy at having their pastor back after three weeks' absence.[60]

Despite Norris' effort to prevent a celebration, a reporter from the New York *American*, one of thirty who had covered the trial, wrote that "it was a jubilee, no question about that." [61]

Trouble was not over, however. Two years later the massive church building in which the Texas fundamentalist preached was totally destroyed by fire of undetermined origin.[62] In the depression it took Norris years to rebuild. The trial and the second fire left him personally exhausted but undaunted as far as the public was concerned, and more controversial than ever.

The controversy of J. Frank Norris with the Southern Baptist Convention was lengthy, bitter, and, as usual, spectacular. The roots were deep, dating from 1909 when Norris, as editor of *The Baptist Standard*, felt that he did not receive the support of denominational leaders in his showy, but victorious, campaign against racetrack gambling in Texas. Norris had also disturbed denominational leaders by advocating, successfully, through *The Baptist Standard*, and with the support of B. H. Carroll, the transfer of the theological seminary at Baylor University to Forth Worth.[63] In Fort Worth it came to be known as Southwestern Baptist Theological Seminary, with the largest enrollment of any seminary in the world. The overt reasons for Norris' vigorous and noisy opposition to the Convention were basically twofold. Initially, he charged that the denomination failed to respect the complete independence of the local church. Repeatedly he emphasized that there is no authority, ecclesiastical or otherwise, which has the right to interfere with any church or even advise a New Testament church how to order its own affairs.[64] In "The Gospel According to Norris," the denomination had violated this ideal through its cooperative programs. He resented, for instance, the "inclusive policy" whereby monies given to the denomination supported "secular education" (he had in mind schools like Baylor University) as well as the direct preaching of Christianity.[65] Norris was especially incensed by the Seventy-five Million Campaign, sponsored by the Convention in 1919. This major effort was a carefully planned financial drive designed to liquidate all the indebtedness of the Southern Baptist Convention and simultaneously to launch a program of advance in every area of work. Ninety-two million dollars was subscribed, but only fifty-eight million was actually raised. This was accounted for in part by a postwar reaction to missionary outreach.[66] Norris characterized the campaign as "dictatorial, unscriptural, [and] a foolish waste of hard-earned Mission money." The fundamentalist pastor declined to accept an apportionment of $100,000 to be raised by his own congregation. Years later he took great delight in telling the story of his rejection of this suggested sum.

> They sent out this unscriptural demand, dictating to the churches how much money they should raise, in a large envelope. . . . I had received that

letter some few days before the excathedra demand of this coterie of . . .
ecclesiastical dictators. I reached over on my desk and took the envelope
with this demand and tore it to pieces without saying a word, and then
crumpled the pieces in my right hand and cast the pieces at the feet of
these dictators, and said, "That's my answer to your papal demands." [67]

Holding to his belief in the extreme independence of the local
church, Norris castigated any efforts of the Southern Baptist Convention to cooperate with the Northern Baptist Convention, the Federal
Council of the Churches of Christ in America, and the Baptist World
Alliance. He referred to such actions as "unionizing" tendencies and
sarcastically called the latter organization the "Baptist World Entan-
gling Alliance" and "the biggest cuckoo framework ever known
among Baptists." [68] Even in the free-church, autonomous tradition,
Norris found too much control from the "hierarchical" leaders of the
Southern Baptist "machine" whom he consistently called "The
Sanhedrin."

The second major reason for Norris' firm opposition to the
Southern Baptist Convention was the supposed existence of modernism in the denomination, especially among its leaders. These men, in
Norris' judgment, were drifting away from evangelism and spiritual
power and needed to be freed from the "graveclothes" of Liberalism.
Norris felt himself called to bring this about. He aggressively
charged Baylor University, an institution controlled by the denomination, with teaching heresy, by which he meant Darwinian evolution.
He conducted such an arduous campaign that he claimed credit for
crowding out of that institution eight "anthropoid apes" (professors)
for their purported teaching of "animal ancestry." [69] His attacks on
individuals were angry and many, but the denunciation of Joseph M.
Dawson as "the Fosdick of the South" was the most persistent.[70]

Dawson was Norris' associate as editor of *The Baptist Standard*,
later minister of the First Baptist Church at Waco from 1915 to 1946,
and a strong spokesman for the Convention. He read a paper at a
meeting of Texas Baptists in 1925 in which he affirmed belief in the
inspiration rather than the verbal inerrancy of the Scriptures.
According to this view, the ideas of the Bible, rather than the
individual words, were inspired. Norris asserted that this was no
inspiration at all and accused Dawson of denying the faith. Dawson's
interpretations of the destruction of Sodom and Gomorrah and the
turning of Lot's wife into a pillar of salt were not as literalistic as
Norris believed they should have been. This gave the crusading

fundamentalist additional ammunition for his vocal warfare. Norris further criticized Dawson for his position as a contributing editor to *The Christian Century* and his public expression of appreciation for Toyohiko Kagawa, the Japanese evangelist. Norris asserted that *The Christian Century* was "the rankest modernistic paper on the American continent" and alleged that secret archives in Tokyo had revealed Kagawa to have been an official spy of the Japanese military machine. Norris' campaign against Dawson reached its height in 1945 following the latter's review in the Dallas *Morning News* of a book by John Erskine, *The Human Life of Jesus.* Erskine, a professor at Columbia University, had written a liberal interpretation of the life and teaching of Jesus which Dawson noted might "dominate the future judgment of mankind." [71] By a skillful selection of portions of Dawson's review, Norris made it appear that Erskine's views belonged to Dawson. As a result, Norris charged Dawson with "an endorsement of infidelity," the kind taught at Columbia, "where professors openly advocate companionate marriage." [72] The stormy petrel of the Southwest was so persistent with his attack that eventually the Sunday School Board of the Convention withdrew Erskine's volume from active distribution in order to still the storm.

Norris' sharp-edged tongue, however, kept the controversy simmering. He referred to George W. Truett, distinguished minister of the First Baptist Church of Dallas, as "the Infallible Baptist Pope," "His Allhighness," "The Great All-I-Am," and "The Holy Father." [73] He called the Reverend Wallace Bassett of Dallas "The Old Baboon"; and labeled F. M. McConnell, one of his successors as editor of *The Baptist Standard*, "The Old Woman Who Does the Best She Can." When Louie D. Newton, minister of the affluent Druid Hills Baptist Church in Atlanta, Georgia, became president of the Southern Baptist Convention, Norris proclaimed loudly: "The Prophecy of Isaiah is fulfilled—'children shall be your leaders and babes your rulers.' We no longer have statesmen in the Southern Baptist Convention." [74]

The denomination and allied groups felt forced to take early and stern action. A number of its important leaders resigned their membership in the First Baptist Church of Fort Worth, including Lee R. Scarborough and B. H. Carroll.[75] Norris claimed this was the result of denominational pressure. The Pastors Conference at Fort Worth expelled Norris in 1914 because of his radically independent spirit and his constant criticism of fellow ministers. The Tarrant County Baptist Association excluded him in 1922 for being a threat to the "peace, harmony, and unity" of that body.[76] The Baptist General Convention of Texas censured Norris in 1922, declined to seat his delegate the following year, and in 1924 ousted both minister and church from the state organization. The basic reasons given were Norris' "unBaptistic and non-cooperative" actions. By "unBaptistic" they meant the admission of non-Baptist clergymen to his pulpit and the "alien immersion" of certain members of his congregation.[77]

Norris basked in the publicity which the controversy with the denomination brought, and in addition he developed his own strategy of response. He declined to use the literature of the denomination in his Sunday school and proudly announced far and wide that his church would teach "the Bible only." Each week Norris spent an hour instructing 250 of his own teachers in an exegetical study of the Scriptures. They in turn taught their pupils without any lesson helps.[78] Norris held rallies and preaching services simultaneously with the annual meetings of the Baptist General Convention of Texas and the Southern Baptist Convention. He rented halls, theaters, or churches, wherever he could gather a crowd, and then would denounce the denomination and its representatives. Eventually, in 1931, with all hope gone of any kind of amiable relationship with the Southern Baptist Convention, Norris organized his own loosely bound "Fellowship" of churches. The original name of this group was the "Premillennial, Fundamental, Missionary Fellowship." Later it assumed the title "Premillennium Baptist Missionary Fellowship." In more recent years, the movement divided into the "World Baptist Fellowship" and the "Baptist Bible Fellowship." [79]

His antipathy to denominationalism was not limited to the Southern Baptist Convention. One month after assuming his pastorate at Detroit he withdrew that church from the Northern Baptist Convention, claiming interference by the "communistic, unscriptural, and socialistic leaders" of that body and of the Detroit Baptist Union.[80] In fact, Norris affirmed that it was precisely because of such intrusion that he was led to accept the pastorate of the Temple Baptist Church. The disdain that he felt for representatives of denominations in general and for the Southern Baptist Convention in particular was expressed forcefully in 1931: "Once I had a contempt for them, then I had a pity for them, and now as they cut and lance themselves, tear their hair and froth at the mouth, I feel sure the Lord gives me permission to enjoy a good laugh at them." [81] With such an attitude Norris created a chasm between himself and Baptist denominations that was never bridged throughout his turbulent career.

J. Frank Norris saw no need to limit himself to local and denominational matters. From his own pulpit in Texas and from various platforms throughout the country he waged war on broader issues. In the last decades of his ministry the colorful Norris gave less attention to Liberalism and increased attention to Russian Communism, vilifying the movement itself as well as those whom he believed to be Communist sympathizers. By Norris' definition, this latter group was exceedingly large.

Norris saw Communism as denying the Scriptures, ruling God out of the universe, leading men to immorality, and advocating a "mongrel race." [82] He preached passionately that Communists had filtered into the federal and state governments, labor unions, educational institutions, and even churches, thereby threatening the stability of society and destroying traditional values. The "answer" that the apostle of Fundamentalism brought to combat such an influence was fourfold. He suggested the cutting off of appropriations to schools that tolerated Communistic professors, the sending of "the commies back to Russia where they belong," the separation of "true" Christians from those who taught the "Social Gospel," and a return to the simple but effective preaching of "old time, personal religion." [83]

As in his verbal warfare against other isms, Norris personalized his charges. He believed that Franklin Delano Roosevelt had "sold out" at Yalta, and referred to his fellow Baptist President Truman as "Harry S. Truman and his crowd of Communists in Washington." Norris declared that the Northern Baptist Convention, of which Albert W. Beaven was president at the time, "comes with the hands of 'Baptist orthodoxy,' but with the voice of Russian Sovietism." [84] The impatient preacher was especially incensed that ministers like Edwin T. Dahlberg should dabble in the social, political, economic, and international questions of the age. On one occasion he drew laughter from his right-wing congregation and wrath from his opponents when he asserted:

> These preachers who masquerade under the livery of heaven—I don't care how many degrees they have after their names—LLD's, DD's, Asses, they are infidels when they deny the Word of God. . . . I have more respect for Tom Paine in his grave, and Bob Ingersoll—at least they had self-respect enough to stay out of the church and out of the pulpits—they were not like these little modernistic, lick-the-skillet, two-by-four aping, asinine preach-

ers, who want to be in the priest's office so they can have a piece of bread, and play kite tail to the Communists. . . . "Oh!" some sister will say, "I don't think that's the Christian spirit."—Honey, you wouldn't know the Christian spirit, any more than a bull would know Shakespeare.[85]

By such tactics, Norris cast his mantle of condemnation over Samuel McCrea Cavert, general secretary of the Federal Council of the Churches of Christ in America; Bishops G. Bromley Oxnam and Francis J. McConnell of the Methodist Church; Ralph McGill, editor of the Atlanta *Constitution*; and Louie D. Newton, president of the Southern Baptist Convention. Most men endeavored to ignore his accusations, but at times this was difficult. The case of Newton provided a classic example.

Newton, minister of the prosperous Druid Hills Baptist Church in Atlanta, along with a group of six other distinguished Americans visited Russia during the summer of 1946 on behalf of the American Society for Russian Relief. Upon their return, Newton, who also served as president of the Southern Baptist Convention, reported favorably concerning some of the conditions he found in that country. Specifically, he noted that there was a wide degree of religious freedom in Moscow and that Baptists along with people in the Soviet Union agreed in the renunciation of, and resistance to, coercion in matters of belief. Religiously, he added, we should regard Russia as an ally. Newton's remarks gained wide publicity and were circulated by the American Russian Institute. All of this infuriated Norris, who cried out that Newton was either naïve or a cold-blooded propagandist.[86]

The day before the meeting of the Southern Baptist Convention at St. Louis in May 1947, Newton arose in the Second Baptist Church to address one thousand ministers about his visit to Russia. As he did so, up stood J. Frank Norris, who had "purchased" his way as a messenger to the Convention, the result of a $250 donation, which met the denominational requirement. The craggy-faced Norris, in a penetrating voice, began reading a list of seventeen embarrassing, intimidating questions. The presiding minister, M. E. Dodd of Shreveport, Louisiana, raised a forbidding hand, but Norris continued undaunted. In desperation Dodd led the ministers in the singing of a hymn, but grinning, heckler Norris was right with them on the second verse, bellowing the words louder than anyone. When Norris resumed his interruptions at the conclusion of the song, various members of the clerical congregation shouted, "Throw him out." At the same time "a menacing knot" of young ministers gathered around Norris. Eventually several policemen appeared, explaining that they had been summoned to quell a riot. By that time the uproar had quieted. Newton continued his report, and Norris proclaimed he had achieved his objective: the exposure on the spot of "Newton and his henchmen as a bunch of appeasers with Moscow." [87] One of Norris' followers claimed later that Norris' actions prevented "poor old Louise" (Louie D. Newton) from being elected president of the Baptist World Alliance.[88]

Ralph McGill, editor of the Atlanta *Constitution*, rose to Newton's defense. He characterized Norris' charges as cheap and false, and called the latter a "Ku Klux yelper and a loud-mouthed shouter in many demagogic political and hate rallies." He also termed Norris a "pistol-toting divine" who needed to be shouted down ("I regret I could not be there shouting with them, and I am a calm man"). Norris brought charges against McGill for referring to him as a "pistol-toting divine," forcing the Atlanta *Constitution* to make a public retraction and apology. When paying his lawyer's fee of $500 for handling the case, Norris wrote: "I consider this the best investment I ever made." He then proceeded to secure 35,000 to 40,000 photocopies of the retraction made by the newspaper, and sent one to every pastor in both the Northern and the Southern Baptist Convention.[89]

The unrelenting fundamentalist continued his flagellations at Rochester, New York. He had harsh words for both Toyohiko Kagawa and the Federal Council of Churches. He assailed Kagawa as an "Apostle of Socialism and a Duke's mixture of every 'ism,' " and he charged that the Federal Council was led by a small coterie of men who labored hand in glove with the Communists of Russia.[90] When Norris was invited to address the Texas legislature at an open session in April 1949, he ripped into American educational institutions, especially condemning their practice of "academic freedom." He said of the latter that it was "the greatest misnomer and the most dishonest thing" ever perpetrated on the American people.[91] Norris suggested that one must "fight fire by fire," not giving an inch to the professors with Communist sympathies who had filtered into the schools. It was on this occasion, to the accompanying applause of the legislators and their friends, that he proposed the severance of state and federal funds from those institutions which tolerated subversive teachers.

In the late 1940's Norris viewed Communism as the great rising power threatening the very existence of Western democracies and the Christian religion. The man who two decades earlier had been so critical of Roman Catholicism now had words of praise for the hierarchical head of that faith. He referred to Pius XII as "the only power in Europe standing like Gibraltar against communism." If it hadn't been for the pontiff, Norris asserted, "Joe Stalin would be at the English Channel." Sensing that he might be criticized for such warm words of approval (as he was by T. T. Shields, fundamentalist leader from Toronto), Norris added: "Never mind the religious side of it—I will make an alliance with the devil if he is going my way and when he gets through I will say, 'This is as far as you and I go.' " [92]

Such an attitude was typical of the peripatetic pastor, whether on local, denominational, or wider issues. He was an outspoken, hard-hitting, ruthless leader who employed almost any means to champion his particular position. In the end, this severity boomeranged. Before his death in 1952, his Fellowship had broken over his dictatorial policies and his church at Detroit had severed all relations with him by an overwhelming vote of 3,000 to 7. [93] It was a melancholy, although perhaps deserved, conclusion to the career of the preacher from Fort Worth, the most colorful figure in the history of the Modernist-Fundamentalist Controversy.

IV

In retrospect, the friends of J. Frank Norris, while recognizing his eccentricities, viewed him as a courageous man of God with obvious strengths. They honored him as a preacher of great ability and with remarkable powers of persuasion and imagination; a perennial critic of personal and social wrongdoing who spared no one in his denunciation of evil; and an administrator with unmatched promotional and fund-raising talents. [94] Others interpreted Norris as a self-centered, inflexible, impatient, hot-tempered, and belligerent dictator who maligned those persons who differed with him, divided churches, disrupted denominations, and castigated a variety of movements with equal acidity. They remembered him as an exceedingly poor representative of religion, one who gave to Fundamentalism much of the odium associated with it. The combination of these negative qualities caused Ralph McGill to write on another occasion: "I would be willing to wager the good Lord winces every time J. Frank Norris mentions His name or climbs up in a pulpit." [95]

This author sees Norris as an independent spirit whose stubborn individualism, nourished by his mother on the Texas frontier during the early years of his life, never left him. This individualism set him apart even from his fellow fundamentalists in selected areas of belief and also manifested itself in his personal style of ministry.[96] While most of his fundamentalist contemporaries were outspoken and forward, Norris outdid them all in aggressiveness. A born fighter, he craved and loved controversy. He spent much of his time deliberately stirring up strife, with or without provocation.[97] In so doing, Norris became a master of acrimonious and caustic tirades. Whatever validity there was in Norris' criticisms of theological Liberalism, denominational organization, political communism, and other subjects, the constructive possibilities were usually smothered by his vituperation. When linked with his theological dogmatism and dominant personality, this made for a perilous combination. But it did not frighten Norris, who became the suspicious, accusative, inquisitorial "defender of the faith," the religious Joseph McCarthy of his generation.

The extent of Norris' influence is as debatable as his person. It is recognized that he built a sizable following about the cornerstone of his own personality.[98] The number he frightened away because of his extremism is more difficult to gauge. The exodus of six hundred members from his church in 1911 is probably representative of a larger throng isolated by his tactics. Some individuals attributed to his pressure the revision in a more orthodox direction of the Articles of Faith in 1925 by the Southern Baptist Convention. A contemporary fundamentalist historian notes that "the Norris blasts slowed down the Southern Baptist capitulation to out-and-out Liberalism" and declares that since Norris' death, "the pace of surrender to liberal thought has accelerated." [99] Others claimed that the strong appeal of the militant minister to ordinary people gave a new voice to "folks from the fork of the creek," part of the needful transition for those moving from rural to urban settings.[100] And even today, the fact that substantially over 50 percent of the Baptist churches in Fort Worth are not members of the Southern Baptist Convention is attributable in part to Norris' antidenominational invectives.[101]

These factors, however, do not obliterate the disturbing evidence that the ministry of J. Frank Norris was a one-man show. The preacher who castigated denominations for failing to respect the autonomy of the local church completely dominated his own congregation and the Fellowship he established. At the level of the local church this prevented the development of a responsible laity. At the

level of the Fellowship it hindered his own brand of Fundamentalism
from exercising a more effective influence. And at the level of wider
conservative concern, Norris' self-absorption undercut any enthusiastic support of other prominent conservative leaders. For example,
when it was announced that Billy Graham would conduct a campaign
in Fort Worth in 1951, Norris wrote languidly: "I am very happy over
Billy Graham's coming because he is preaching the same gospel that I
preached before he was born." At the conclusion of Graham's
crusade, Norris commented wryly: "It was quite encouraging that
Billy Graham took a month in confirming the confession of faith that
we hold at the First Baptist Church." [102] With such attitudes Norris
hurt the very movement he claimed to love and provided men like
Sinclair Lewis, who once visited his church, with additional ammunition for their criticism of religion.[103]

In conclusion, one suspects that (1) the problems of J. Frank Norris
were more psychological than theological, rooted in the deprivations
of his own unfortunate childhood; (2) Fundamentalism was undercut,
not only by the incoming tide of theological Liberalism but by the
refusal of its independent leaders to work more closely together as a
team; (3) Norris' ministry is painful evidence of the price of a certain
kind of Baptist "autonomy" and, in the judgment of some, an
argument for relinquishing some of that self-government; (4) part of
the strength of religion in America has been its ability to absorb the
kind of blatant extremism that was generated by the personification
of fundamentalist extremists, the colorful but irascible J. Frank
Norris.[104]

CHAPTER THREE

John Roach Straton
ACCUSATIVE FUNDAMENTALIST

As SCHOLARS GAIN PERSPECTIVE on the Modernist-Fundamentalist Controversy, new evaluations of the struggle and of the persons who participated in it are being made. One of the best-known fundamentalists, and certainly one of the most outspoken, was John Roach Straton, pastor of the Calvary Baptist Church, New York City, from 1918 to 1929, a time that closely paralleled the height of the struggle between the two theological tendencies. Recognized then as a highly dramatic pulpit orator, loquacious debater, militant leader of the ultraconservative forces, perennial center of heated controversy, and a critic of American society, Straton has been interpreted by some scholars as a "prophet of social righteousness." [1]

The author of this book brings qualifications to that viewpoint.[2] He does not question Straton's importance. Along with Harry Emerson Fosdick and S. Parkes Cadman, Straton was among the most prominent ministers of New York City in the hectic 1920's. He was an active participant in the presidential campaign of 1928 when Gov. Alfred E. Smith sought the highest office in the land. His acrimonious sermons of wrath and judgment castigated a generation in the midst of social change and doubtless provided thousands with "the vicarious enjoyment of wickedness, . . . the nearest thing to indulgence in what he denounced." [3] An inveterate enemy of theological Liberalism wherever it was found (local church, denomination, and wider religious community), he was frequently proclaimed the successor to William Jennings Bryan as head of the fundamentalist movement. In the judgment of some literary critics, Straton also provided source material upon which Sinclair Lewis relied in part for the writing of *Elmer Gantry*.[4] Although he was certainly influential and possessed several overt characteristics of the ancient spokesmen of Israel, it appears misleading to think of this colorful champion of conservatism as primarily a "prophet of social righteousness." Admittedly, Straton had many things to say about social issues, especially early in his stormy ministerial career, but he seems best interpreted as a pastor-evangelist with an emphasis on personal conversion and correct doctrine as the answer to individual and societal needs.

This chapter will survey Straton's life and thought, giving particular attention to his social and theological declarations—subject matters that are sometimes neglected in the study of Fundamentalism because of greater attention to the struggle for political control in the various denominations. Upon this foundation, an endeavor will be made to test the claim that Straton was a social prophet.

I

John Roach Straton, the third son of Julia Rebecca Carter and Henry Dundas Straton, was born in Evansville, Indiana, April 6, 1875. His father, a Baptist minister serving the First Baptist Church of Evansville at the time, had migrated to this country from Scotland ten years earlier.[5] After spending his formative years in small towns in Georgia and Alabama, where his father's pastorates had taken him, young Straton entered Mercer University in 1895, soon distinguishing himself as a public speaker. He won the Georgian and Southern Intercollegiate Oratorical Championships with an address entitled "Breaking Up the Solid South, the Salvation of the Section," an ironical subject in the light of his later conservative religious beliefs and the nature of his appeal to the South during the important presidential contest of 1928. The early death of his father made the financing of his undergraduate education increasingly difficult. This problem, linked with what was probably a deficiency in foreign languages, prevented his graduation, although after three years as a full-time student at Mercer, Straton was promptly appointed in 1899 to the position of teacher of oratory and literary interpretation.

Straton's conversion in the Baptist Tabernacle, Atlanta, Georgia, under the preaching of the Reverend James Boardman Hawthorne, a well-known southern revivalist, started him on the trail toward the ministry.[6] Baptized by Hawthorne and also influenced by him to become a preacher, Straton attended the Southern Baptist Theological Seminary (1900–1902).[7] While there (the second institution from

John Roach Straton with Uldine Utley

which he did not graduate), Straton was ordained in 1900 and served his first pastorate at the little Baptist Mission Church in Highland Park, a suburb of Louisville. His marriage to Georgia Hillyer at Atlanta was solemnized on November 2, 1903. He and his young bride journeyed to Waco, Texas, where he held another position as teacher of oratory and literary interpretation at Baylor University (1903–1905) and served in a pastorate at Hubbard City, Texas.[8]

The voice of John Roach Straton cried in the "wilderness" of four American cities: in Chicago, Second Baptist Church (1905–1908); in Baltimore, Seventh Baptist Church (1908–1913); in Norfolk, Virginia, First Baptist Church (1914–1917); and in New York City, Calvary Baptist Church (1918–1929). Between his churches in Baltimore and Norfolk, Straton was executive secretary of the Social Service Commission of the Interchurch Federation of Baltimore (1913–1914), a position in which he was unhappy since his interests and training were basically homiletical rather than administrative. In addition to his ministerial responsibilities, he was frequently a guest speaker and debater on college campuses, lecturer at Bible conferences and summer assemblies, evangelist at revival services, and a regular contributor to newspapers throughout the country.

The accumulated tensions of his stormy career, the strain of his campaign in the South against Alfred E. Smith, and the exertions of his demanding labors in New York led to a paralytic stroke. He died at a sanitarium in Clifton Springs, New York, October 29, 1929, the day of the calamitous stock market crash. An era had neared its end in both religious and secular America. Men varied in their appraisal of the tall, gaunt, severe, country-bred clergyman. Some saw him as a fearless, dedicated prophet, granitelike in his defense of revealed truth. Others viewed him as "the relentless fighter, the lean crusader of the White Lights, . . . a bizarre figure in the big city, like Oliver Cromwell in a night club, or Bishop Asbury at the Saratoga races."[9]

II

The general characteristics of the ministry of John Roach Straton included an unreserved devotion to Fundamentalism, sensational methods and techniques which constantly kept him in the headlines, and an outspoken opposition to what he felt were the personal and social sins of a corrupt society.

Straton's Fundamentalism was cradled in the orthodoxy of his father's religious convictions and the generally conservative environment of the South, including the schools that he attended. Straton, however, attributed his emphasis upon the supernatural to experiences gained in his first pastorate in Highland Park, Kentucky. When he began his responsibilities at the Mission Church, where his members were primarily railroad and factory workers, his preaching, according to Straton, emphasized moral reform and personal idealism. This pulpit content, however, brought neither converts nor changed lives; consequently he was driven back to revealed religion and the "glories" of the miraculous. "When I began preaching the Cross and the power of a risen Savior, results immediately followed." [10] Here it is likely that considerable allowance must be made for reading back into this early series of events a theological position of later years as well as remembering that a clearly defined orthodoxy would undoubtedly produce, more easily than other systems of belief, the kind of numerical results for which Straton was looking.

Central to Straton's orthodoxy was a persistent stress upon sin and judgment, both made exceedingly real by the preacher's vivid word descriptions. Of sin, he said: "It is lecherous and loathsome. It is foul and fearful, slimy with the wriggling nastiness of Satan and dripping with the foul refuse of ingratitude, disobedience, selfish desire, lust and shame." [11] Of judgment, he saw a direct connection between the tragedies that befell the American people (for instance, the San Francisco earthquake) and the "insufferable wickedness" of her people.[12]

At the heart of Straton's Fundamentalism there came to be an emphasis on the infallibility of the Christian Scriptures, not simply their inspiration, and a belief in the second coming of Christ.[13] More significant, however, than any theological belief or set of beliefs was Straton's fundamentalist temperament. He was aggressive, dogmatic, outspoken, and militant. For those who disagreed with him, the fundamentalist par excellence had severe words which were as indigenous as they were sharp. He referred regularly, for instance, to liberal preachers as "animated question marks . . . [who] are trying to heal the awful cancer of human sin with soothing syrup; they are sprinkling cologne water upon the putrid iniquities of a rebellious race." [14] He charged them to declare God's message—by which Straton meant the faith as he understood it—rather than setting forth the folly of their own subjective speculations.

Straton belonged to several fundamentalist organizations where he associated with persons of similar beliefs and attitudes. He was a charter member of the World's Christian Fundamentals Association, the Fundamentalist Federation of the Northern Baptist Convention, and the Baptist Bible Union of North America. His greatest energies, however, were devoted to the Fundamentalist League of Greater New York and Vicinity for Ministers and Laymen. Straton founded this group in 1922, served as its president, and led its members in seeking to dismiss "unsafe" teachers from denominational schools and to place conservative individuals in positions of denominational leadership. Despite Straton's affiliation with these various fundamentalist organizations, he remained within the fold of the Northern Baptist Convention until 1926, although his efforts admittedly were for the purpose of strengthening the fundamentalist cause within that church body.

The militant leader drew the attention of the nation in 1923 when at the annual meeting of the Northern Baptist Convention in Atlantic City he rose to protest personally the appearance of W. H. P. Faunce, president of Brown University, as keynote speaker. His opposition was based on Faunce's "radical and revolutionary" teachings, by which Straton meant the educator's denial of the virgin birth and the second coming of Christ as well as his espousal of liberal social views.[15] The president of the Convention overruled the protest to the cheers and applause of the delegates, who originally had hissed and jeered Straton. The latter defended his action in a lengthy article in *The Watchman-Examiner*, claiming the right of protest and letting the "world" know that the president of Brown University was not typical of all Baptists. In justifying his position in regard to Dr. Faunce, Straton wrote: "My action, in entering a respectful protest, was not as discourteous to Dr. Faunce as was his action toward our Savior in 'casting aside' some of his holiest teachings like a worn out garment, and in endorsing the evolutionary hypothesis, which contradicts the Bible teaching that Jesus Christ was the 'Son of the highest,' and makes him a half brother of the apes." [16] It was also under Straton's aggressive leadership that the denomination was "forced" to examine the orthodoxy of its own missionaries, although the means of gaining knowledge of their beliefs and those of denominational leaders were highly questionable.[17] A study commission, after investigation, expressed emphatic approval of the overwhelming majority of its missionaries. Only four individuals were recalled from their posts because of unsound doctrine and three of them gained speedy appointments elsewhere. Frustrated once again in exercising his influence on the Northern Baptist Convention, Straton finally announced in 1926 the withdrawal of his church in New York City from the denomination and its affiliated agencies. He used the occasion to criticize "one very wealthy layman and a certain brilliant but erratic young modernist who is now this wealthy young layman's pastor." [18] This was a thinly disguised reference to John D. Rockefeller, Jr., and to Harry Emerson Fosdick, whom Straton once labeled "a Baptist bootlegger . . . a Presbyterian outlaw . . . the Jesse James of the theological world." [19]

Sensational methods and techniques comprised a second characteristic of the ministry of John Roach Straton as he disseminated his brand of ultraconservative Christianity. Evangelistic and revival services were commonplace, but Straton kept himself and his churches in the public eye by the use of renowned and sometimes notorious leaders. Among these were J. Frank Norris, the extreme fundamentalist from the South, and Uldine Utley, a fourteen-year-old evangelist. Norris was frequently violent in language and on several occasions inaccurate in his reporting, a fact that drew even Straton's chastisement. After a series of revival meetings which Norris had led at Calvary Baptist Church in 1922 he returned to Texas and boasted in his newspaper that there had been five hundred conversions at the services in New York. With singular bluntness and courage, Straton wrote him: "Brother Frank, why don't you stop lying? It is not good for your health and it confuses the brethren, especially when you put it on too heavy. Stop lying and learn simply to handle the truth economically." [20]

Straton remained loyal to his friend, however, even when Norris was charged with murder in the shooting of D. E. Chipps. At the time of the tragedy Straton telegraphed Norris, making plain that he had "always admired . . . and loved him" and pledging to stand by him "in all possible ways." [21] Straton's loyalty to Uldine Utley was equally as pronounced. He saw her as a true prophetess and referred to her as "one of the greatest Bible preachers to whom I have ever listened . . . the most extraordinary person in America today . . . the Joan of Arc of the modern religious world." [22]

Throughout his ministry Straton leaned heavily on newspaper publicity and in the later years on radio broadcasting as effective means of reaching the wider community. He assisted generously by providing verbatim copies of his melodramatic sermons for the press and operating his own station (WQAO) at Calvary Baptist, the first church in New York City to broadcast regularly. Straton's efforts were not limited to these means. He held revivalistic tent meetings in the suburbs and street meetings in the city—from slum neighborhoods to the wide plaza of Columbus Circle, the latter on Sunday afternoons.[23]

John Roach Straton also confronted the forces of evil personally. In both Norfolk and New York he led delegations comprised of clergymen, deacons, and a private detective to the "red light" districts for the purpose of gaining firsthand knowledge of existing conditions of evil. He attended the Dempsey-Carpentier prizefight in 1921, reporting his reactions for a national news service. The editor described his article as a "whizzer." [24] He viewed the controversial play *Aphrodite* to learn, according to Straton, the precise nature of the stage on Broadway. He was a courtroom spectator at the infamous Hall-Mills and Snyder-Gray murder trials of 1926 and 1927, writing daily editorials for the press in which he pointed out the "moral and spiritual lessons" to be derived from such crimes.[25] He engaged prominent individuals, such as Prof. Kirtley Mather of Harvard University, in memorable public debates on contemporary issues, including evolution, the nature of the stage, and various theological subjects.

In addition to unusual methods in the present, Straton had unique plans for the immediate future. He proposed the building of a thirty-five-story church-hotel complex (what eventually became the Salisbury Hotel) on the West Fifty-seventh Street site of Calvary Baptist Church in New York City. The intention was to produce extra funds for religious purposes. With the advent of the depression, however, this project dumped into the lap of the church an indebtedness of two million dollars, an indebtedness under which Straton's former parish still labors. Late in his career, the flamboyant minister purchased a sixty-room hotel at Greenwood Lake, New York, where he founded a summer Bible conference similar to that at Ocean Grove, New Jersey. Within five months of acquisition the structure was destroyed by fire, which Straton charged—possibly correctly—was incendiary in nature.[26] Finally, in the last years of his life, Straton added to his ministry an emphasis upon healing. This was the result of what he claimed to be Biblical teaching, his own experience, the healing of one of his relatives, and successful services of healing in his own church.[27]

Because of such methods and techniques Straton lived almost constantly in the midst of storm. Charges of "hippodrome" tactics and the commercialization of religion were frequently lodged against him. Although some were attracted to his churches by the excitement, others resigned in protest. In Baltimore, Straton broke with his Sunday school superintendent, who was also a leading politician of the city, because they did not see eye to eye on the prohibition issue.[28] Some of the trustees at Calvary Baptist in New York resigned as the result of policy in general (publicity stunts) and the building program in particular.[29] When the fundamentalist clergyman preached on the "Fatty" Arbuckle–Virginia Rappe case, two hundred of his members resigned, convinced that Straton's daring "word pictures" were more alarming than the evils he assailed.[30] In 1922, Robert S. McArthur, president of the Baptist World Alliance and pastor emeritus of Calvary Baptist Church in New York City, where he had served as minister for forty-one years, severed all connections with the congregation in protest of Straton's antidenominational policies and his covering of the Dempsey-Carpentier fight for a syndicate of newspapers.[31] On one occasion, smarting under criticism, Straton snapped: "I do not believe they really want a preacher. They ought to have called a phonograph." [32]

Lawsuits with their charges and countercharges were almost commonplace. In one court case, Charles Smith, president of the Atheists Association of America, endeavored to have Straton arrested as a danger to the health of New York City because of his views on healing. Straton replied by bringing charges against Smith for sending into his home a letter and atheistic literature that he deemed blasphemous, sensuous, and seditious.[33] Justice Crain of the New York Supreme Court, in ruling on the clergyman's charges, ordered them dismissed. Crain declared that Smith's correspondence was "silly and ill-natured, but not criminal. . . . The letter and the . . . literature . . . should have been thrown into the waste basket instead of making it the subject of criminal proceedings. . . . The recipient of the letter has been sensitive rather than sensible." [34]

Through it all, the unwavering John Roach Straton and the fundamentalist cause he championed remained perennially in the headlines—as did the evil he condemned.

III

Straton's early stance on social problems was set forth in an address delivered to a joint meeting of the Baltimore and Washington Ministers Conferences at Washington, D.C., April 6, 1908. Speaking within a year of the publication of Walter Rauschenbusch's *Christianity and the Social Crisis*, Straton declared that the Christian faith makes for itself a wider claim than previously men had recognized—

specifically, social as well as individual salvation.[35] Like Rauschenbusch, he stressed the kingdom of God on earth, but he differed with "the prophet from Rochester" in defining the purpose of that kingdom and the means of establishing it. For Straton the goal of the kingdom was the improvement and perfection of our present world so that "our fellowmen may be more easily prepared for the better world beyond" (an emphasis upon immortality not found with corresponding stress in Rauschenbusch's thought).[36] The means of achieving this social goal was to be through the application of Christian love by individuals in such areas as the business world of friction and strife, the realm of labor and capital, and even in politics. Such love could be applied, however, only following the redemption of the separate units of mankind, since Straton believed that personal, moral evil was the source of all social unrighteousness.

> We must bring the truth of individual salvation and that of social salvation into their right relationship. The leaven of individual regeneration and righteousness must finally leaven the entire social lump. The main point of emphasis, therefore, must continue to be *regeneration, not reform; soteriology, not sociology*. [Italics added.] We may reconstruct society on the most ideally perfect lines, but we are still confronted with the sad fact that the human heart is "deceitful above all things, and desperately wicked," and that it must be changed before even ideally perfect social machinery will work, because "out of the heart are the issues" of social as well as individual life.[37]

This posture led Straton to emphasize the need for an "enlightened, aggressive and blood-earnest evangelism." [38] Through every person reached, Straton proclaimed, another stride would be taken "toward the social salvation which shall heal our moral desolations and cause our political wilderness to blossom in new beauty." [39] The role of the church in Straton's analysis was a vital one. It needed to assume the position of leadership in social and political reforms, not by making the church a political machine, but by insisting that every individual within the church shall apply his religion to practical affairs. When this is done, a commendable Christian public opinion will be created and eventually enacted into law.[40]

The crux of the fundamentalist's position was the conversion of the individual. Rauschenbusch also believed in the importance of personal regeneration—in fact, he made it primary. But his plan for social change after conversion was more developed than Straton's. He favored, for instance, the restructuring of life on a more fraternal basis, including abolition of the "capitalistic" and "working" classes in favor of a single class that would unite the qualities of both.[41] Until this should become a reality, he suggested a working alliance between Christianity and the laboring people.

Early in his career, Straton, like Rauschenbusch, shared the optimism that was characteristic of the first two decades of this century. He envisaged humanity moving forward, growing better day by day, led by the hand of God. He recognized the reality of modern sins and evils but concluded that, as bad as they were, they should be only added incentives to service. His words in 1908, when he believed in the gradual coming of the kingdom, were in noticeable contrast to those during the last decade of his turbulent life.

It [the future] will be a time of individualism so far as individualism is essential to progress, yet a time of more cooperation and less strife. It will be a time of less injustice and more truth, . . . of easier conditions of life through the perfecting of machinery and the discoveries of scientific truth, . . . a time of . . . renewed inspiration to the romancer, the poet, and the seer. A time of a deeper, stronger, braver trust in God. . . . And over it all shall be the cross of Christ, glorifying the heavens above, but also illuminating the earth beneath. . . . We shall add to the great dynamic of our old Christianity—faith in Christ and hope for the future—a new dynamic, a noble enthusiasm for human service, born of faith *in man* [!] and hope for the present.[42]

Consistent with this optimism and a crusading spirit in an America that loved the word "progressive," Straton in his first pastorates gave himself to campaigns against alcohol and sexual vice. While at Baltimore he tabulated the cost of drinking and came to the speedy conclusion that its price was too high. Morally, he declared, the liquor traffic cost self-respect and opened the door to other problems, including domestic discord. Physically, alcohol was a poison to the human system, not a stimulant or a food. Mentally, imbibing brought personal anxiety, disappointed hopes, and blasted ambitions. For those unmoved by his line of reasoning, Straton's clinching argument was a financial one. The cost of the care of alcoholics plus the monies lost through industrial inefficiency far outweighed revenues received through license money and tax receipts.[43] Straton's antipathy to intoxicating beverages extended throughout his lifetime. When in New York he disclosed to the authorities infractions of the prohibition laws that led to the first conviction for violation of the Volstead Act. Late in his ministry, the pastor-evangelist's vehement opposition to Alfred E. Smith, whom he called "the deadliest foe in America today of the forces of moral progress and true political wisdom," was based not on the latter's religious affiliation but primarily on his "wet" record and his desire to bring about modifications in the Eighteenth Amendment.

Straton's drive against commercialized vice, especially in Norfolk, assumed importance not only as it reflected his opinions on sexual mores but also as it revealed the most progressive social thinking of his ministry when dealing with a major social problem. To combat the existence of organized prostitution in a seaport city, where it frequently had the protection of political officials, Straton initially urged a renewed emphasis upon the home and a rigid enforcement of existing laws. In addition, righteous public opinion, he felt, should be backed by the process of education, including the teaching of sexual hygiene, beginning in the lower grades. Straton also advocated additional laws, born of social vision, that would aim at equalizing more adequately the opportunities and privileges of human life (thereby, it was hoped, keeping some women out of the tenderloin districts because of financial need). Specifically he had in mind minimum wage laws, mothers pensions, profit-sharing plans, the heavier taxing of inheritances and large incomes, and, most surprisingly, public ownership of industry.[44] The following words illuminate Straton's thought during this early phase of his career:

No store has the right to demand that a young woman shall stand upon her feet practically for ten hours a day, six days in the week, for the pitiful sum of five dollars a week. The wrath of God will be lodged against any social order that tolerates such wrongs as that. Apart entirely from the question of wages, any corporation that does not grant its women workers at least one day's sick leave in a month, without docking their pay, is a covetous, unchristian and inhuman thing. . . . The time has passed when any man can claim to be a Christian, or even a decent human being and thus enrich himself and flourish through the sweat and tears and shame and agony of women and girls who are toiling upon a pittance that will not keep them alive in purity and decency.[45]

Straton also favored the granting of suffrage to women so they could register their vote against "disgraceful and ruinous conditions," and, in the local situation, he favored the election of a new chief of police, someone not on the force at the time and therefore freed from control by the existing administration. Not all his suggestions were followed, of course, but through preaching, through the publication of a sixty-four-page booklet on the problem of prostitution in Norfolk, through continuing pressure on the city officials, and through personal visits to the blighted areas with a delegation of concerned leaders, Straton eventually was instrumental in bringing about the abolition of the tenderloin districts.[46] To that extent his efforts in Norfolk were successful. This appeared to mark the apex of his social concern. As the years progressed and humanity seemingly did not, Straton grew more conservative in his social views and appeared increasingly critical, negative, and individualistic in outlook.

The growing influence of liberal theology and a revolution in manners and morals provided the catalysts responsible for the changes in Straton's outlook. By 1918, the year Straton began his ministry in New York City, Edward Scribner Ames was speaking of modernism as the "new orthodoxy."[47] Basically, this theological tendency sought to restate the essence of Christianity in terms compatible with contemporary knowledge, which frequently meant, to the consternation of the fundamentalists, a rejection of traditional religious authority. Diverse influences combined to bring about the new folkways in the country. These included, in the judgment of Frederick Lewis Allen, the postwar disillusionment, the growing independent status of women, the circulation of the Freudian "gospel" among the lay public, prohibition and its evasion, the increased production of automobiles, and the wide circulation of "confession" magazines in which the publishers "practiced the delicate art of arousing the reader without arousing the censor."[48] These various factors created an upheaval in values as modesty, reticence, and chivalry were replaced by modernity, sophistication, and smartness. Signs of this alteration were a new frankness in literature and in the theater, a pervasive obsession with sex, manners that were not only different but unmannerly, the rapid acceptance of the cigarette, and a change in women's dress and appearance.[49] The latter reflected a new understanding of the American feminine ideal ("they wanted to be . . . men's casual and light hearted companions; not broad-hipped mothers of the race, but irresponsible playmates").[50] Such were a few of the social causes and products that ushered in what some called "the lost generation"; others termed it the day of "joyful pioneers."[51]

Straton fought the changes. He was not alone, of course, but he seemed to struggle more vehemently and more caustically than many other clergymen. His hope in the rising tide of human betterment faded. In 1920 he wrote, "We are witnessing the widest wave of immorality in the history of the human race." [52] His social program largely disappeared, and, while his condemnation of what he called "lawlessness" did not originate at this time, it now received primary attention. In Straton's judgment, this lawlessness was the crucial problem in the nation, whether in the home, in the larger society, in the church, or in the state. He attacked it with the conviction of the fundamentalist that he was and the showmanship of an actor on Broadway which many felt him also to be.

Straton bewailed the breakdown of parental authority in the home and the signs of moral anarchy in the rising generation. He directed stern words against the lack of discipline in children, the upswing in the rate of divorce, and changes in style of dress. Of the latter he affirmed that he had no quarrel with woman's instinctive desire to make herself as attractive as possible but the trouble was with those who made of dress a fetish and of style a god. He charged that there was a conspiracy between the dressmakers and the merchants to change the patterns as often as possible to keep the prices high. "Now we have a mixture of . . . styles, and every conceivable color of feather and flower has been pressed into service, until the sanctuary on Easter Sunday looks like a head-on collision between a flower garden and a poultry show." [53] As a solution that would emphasize the true object of dress (utility and beauty, not sexual appeal), the pastor of Calvary Baptist Church proposed a national costume which would serve the cause of common sense and true economy as well as the cause of art and beauty.[54]

At this point in his ministry, Straton became particularly pronounced in his opposition to such popular pleasures as dancing, theater attendance, and boxing shows. In his view these practices undermined personal piety and further contributed to the overthrow of the canons of modesty and decency in both the home and the larger community. Unlike dancing in Biblical times, which, according to the fundamentalist leader, was an expression of religious joy limited to groups and individuals (never by couples), dancing in contemporary life was an expression of degeneration.[55] It appealed to the lower instincts of the race for the sake of profit. Straton quoted approvingly the Episcopal bishop of Vermont, who viewed dancing as a waste of time, the interruption of useful study, the indulgence of personal vanity and display, and a practice leading to the premature excitement of the passions.[56] Consistent with his pulpit flamboyancy, as well as his Pauline attitude toward sex, the colorful conservative

usually included this oratorical flourish in his denunciation of dancing:

> It may be that a fossilized octogenarian, or a self-complacent mollycoddle
> with ice-water in his veins, or a dandified dude, or a society sissy, or a
> pleasure cloyed Don Juan, or a vitiated fop, who doesn't know whether he
> is a man or a woman—such a character as one of these, I say, may be able
> to hold a girl under such circumstances and still maintain a philosophical
> calm, and experience only saintly emotions, and have nothing stronger
> than Sunday School maxims running through his mind, but I do not
> believe that any real man, any youth with red blood in his veins and with
> the elemental forces of nature operating in him, could pass through such
> an experience without the natural reaction which heredity and every
> masculine instinct demands from such conditions.[57]

The Baptist leader went even further. He interpreted dancing as
having done more to corrupt the morals of his age than any other
single force.[58] His answer for the mania, as he called it, was to
destroy it root and branch ("not . . . regulation but strangulation").
While undeniably dance halls in his day carried an unsavory reputation, and clergymen far more liberal than Straton opposed the
practice, his diagnosis and proposed remedy revealed the limitations
of his own concept of morality.

After his attendance at the Dempsey-Carpentier fight, the militant
fundamentalist proclaimed that boxing was a relapse into paganism
which glorified brute power, a "moral carbuncle," which "naturally
came to a head at the weakest spot in our body politic—the state of
New Jersey, with its pro-liquor, anti-Constitution, anti-Sabbath
governor." [59] The pastor, whom some of his contemporaries remembered for his own "in-fighting," was especially irritated at the
circumvention of the law. Legislation in New Jersey banned prizefights, but by calling them "boxing matches" the pugilistic encounters
were allowed. Straton also had accusing words for the "Manassa
Mauler" (Jack Dempsey), who "when the real fight was on [World
War I] . . . ducked and dodged and failed his country in the hour of
her crisis." [60] He reserved his sharpest admonition, however, for the
five thousand women who attended the fight.

> I . . . rebuke . . . these women for their presence at this disgraceful orgy
> of blood and beastiality [sic]. . . . The early Christians were often in the
> arena of paganism and heathenism, but always as victims and never as
> witnesses of the brutality and butchery that made such a popular
> holiday. [61]

Convinced that the nation was shooting "like a rocket . . . down the greased ways toward hell" as it reveled in these popular pleasures, Straton pleaded for a return to the realities of religion, the strength of "old-time Americanism" and the discipline of Puritanism —those forces which "made our fathers great and our mothers good." [62]

When it came to criticizing lawlessness in society, Straton had a broad field to cover. He continued his earlier opposition to alcohol and prostitution, but by the 1920's his progressive social suggestions had largely fallen by the wayside. He vigorously supported the Eighteenth Amendment and castigated not only the persons who broke this law but the politicians who failed to enforce it. In New York, as in Norfolk, the Protestant "pope," as one columnist called him, led a committee to investigate those areas where prostitution flourished and the liquor laws were openly defied. He named streets and places and presented his facts to the grand jury. A few arrests were made, but the segregated districts continued their operations. Straton reserved his strongest broadsides for the people of a society in which sensualism had become commonplace. He found the increase in clandestine immorality staggering and condemned it wherever it existed. He was particularly unhappy with the declining birthrate among the well-to-do classes; consequently, it was natural for him to unite with a leading Roman Catholic against a bill proposing to legalize the giving of contraceptive information to married persons. The fundamentalist leader and the Reverend Father William J. Duane, president of Fordham University, stood side by side in 1929 battling against what they described as "artificial interference with the sources of life." [63] Straton charged that the Birth Control League of New York City was a "chamber of horrors." A woman officer of that organization asked him if he had ever visited the clinic. "I have not," retorted the fiery divine, "but I have heard about it and I have read the sort of literature you send out. I may visit it sometime—if my stomach is strong enough." [64] The opponents of the bill applauded for minutes, and the bill itself died aborning. Straton's ire had prevailed.

The breaking of the laws governing gambling likewise provoked Straton's displeasure. He saw gambling as illegal and immoral. It was illegal because lotteries and gaming were prohibited by both the penal law and the constitution of New York State.[65] It was immoral because it undermined self-reliance by leading its devotees to depend for support upon luck and fortune instead of upon courage and effort.[66] Straton's major answer to the problem was the honoring of the steady, self-reliant, plodding worker above the more spectacular type of man who endeavored to reach his goal by the shortcut route of questionable methods.

Straton's own record toward the laboring man, however, left much to be desired. He saw greed among the owners but also a wrong spirit within the ranks of labor. At a time when workers were striking for necessary benefits the clergyman asserted that the true object of all labor is not to get as much as possible, but to give as large a contribution to the commonweal as is humanly possible.

When the great captains of industry in our country get away from their selfish viewpoints, they will no longer be willing to exploit the mass of the people for their personal gain, but will strive to help their fellow men; and when the millions of laborers in the country catch the same ideal they will stop striking and get together with the capitalists, and all of them will solve these vexed problems like sensible men and patriotic Americans. All of this spirit of strife and contention and selfishness and bitterness . . . on both sides is from the Devil. It is un-American, un-Christian, and diabolical. . . . When we . . . get back once more the spirit of fellowship, . . . brotherhood, . . . love and service, all will be well.[67]

Straton's idealism without a clearer recognition of the obvious disparity in justice between capital and labor, plus his lack of specific suggestion as to how brotherhood might be brought about between these two groups, hardly qualified him as a sympathizer of labor. He went even to the extreme of chiding workers for making demands concerning minimum hours of employment and salary increases. The Baptist minister did this by satirically imagining the ministers going on strike.

We ("The Amalgamated Association for the Protection and Promotion of Progressive Preachers") . . . declare to our churches and to the general public, that unless we are given immediately an "eight hour day" and a fifty per cent boost in salary . . . will go on strike and let them [the churches and the general public] all go to Hell.[68]

The reason that clergymen did not go to such lengths, the pastor affirmed, was that there still lingered in their hearts some glimpse of the ideals of altruism and service, the same kind of attributes he was seeking to inculcate in the workmen of America. What Straton apparently did not realize was that increasing industrialization with its corresponding depersonalization made more unlikely than ever in most factories the spirit of benevolence and humanitarianism.

To Straton's credit, he spoke out sharply against racial and religious prejudice in the early 1920's. His remarks were triggered by the illegal activities of the Ku Klux Klan, which he boldly repudiated. The Baptist minister of southern background affirmed there was no place in America for the man in the mask.[69] Secret societies setting up a superlegal power of terrorization and vengeance, he asserted, must be checked, because they led only to anarchy. "The way to correct evils is not by organizing to go over the law, but by enlightened and courageous political action under the law." [70] Straton also suggested further means of handling discrimination. Initially, he proposed that people recognize the admirable qualities and contributions of minority groups. Then he pleaded for a spirit of goodwill, elemental justice, and mutual helpfulness. This, he felt, would be brought about most effectively by a fuller application of the principles of "true Americanism" and the spirit of Jesus Christ.[71] Here again, in Straton's mind, was the linking of nationalism and religion.

Straton, in two particular sermons, spoke well of the Negro, the Jew, the Catholic, and the "foreigner." He saw the black man as peculiarly lovable, naturally industrious, good-natured, obliging, warmhearted, hospitable, friendly, and loyal, with an innate talent for humor, music, oratory, and tact.[72] He confessed the sin of the white forefathers in bringing blacks to America as slaves. Such injustice, he taught, must not be perpetuated in the present by practicing injury and wrong upon the defenseless and the poor. Straton reminded his congregation of the major contributions of the Jewish community to statesmanship, science, literature, music, and art. Furthermore, he commended them as a law-abiding, home-loving people, with a remarkable record of obedience to law.[73] In a decade when considerable anti-Catholic feeling was manifest, Straton praised the Catholics for their sturdy battle against the evil of "race suicide" (birth control), their opposition to divorce, and their contributions to spiritual devotion through the composition of great hymns and the authoring of noble books. For those fearful of Catholicism's political power and the "threat" they posed to the public school (Straton was among them), Straton reminded them that love was still the most potent weapon of opposition.

In the realm of racial tensions, as elsewhere, Straton was strong on theory and weak on the "how" of realizing the ideal; nevertheless, his pronouncements in this area were among the most praiseworthy of his ministry. It is frustrating, therefore, not to find these sermons printed among his books, pamphlets, and church publications, while those dealing with popular pleasures, for instance, are constantly in the foreground. In the judgment of some, this reflects the propensity of Fundamentalism to keep secondary issues in the foreground and primary concerns in the background. It is this emphasis which caused Daniel B. Stevick to write critically:

> There is a long heritage in Fundamentalism of inflamed attacks on the theatre, John Barleycorn, tobacco, dancing, cardplaying, and other sinful indulgences . . . a long heritage of fiddling while Rome burns. Fundamentalists are . . . becoming increasingly aware that this preoccupation with the external and the trivial misses the whole heart of the Christian ethic. . . . Such preoccupations are escapist, irresponsible, out of touch with the great elemental moral realities of our time. . . . Fundamentalism isolates itself from the world where it ought to be ministering. In so doing they "pass by on the other side." [74]

IV

Unable to hold back the tide of change, Straton increasingly held theological Liberalism responsible for the new social and doctrinal trends in American life. Through the rejection of revealed religion and the enthronement of man through vanity and pride, the modernists, in his judgment, had brought lawlessness into the church. As irritated as he was with lawlessness in the home and in society, nothing matched Straton's unhappiness with what he believed to be anarchy in the church. The roots of such difficulty Straton traced to the German higher critics, but his severest words were reserved for the leading proponents of the movement in this country, especially Cornelius Woelfkin and Harry Emerson Fosdick.

In 1923 Straton preached a sermon in which he attacked "unbelieving" college and seminary professors, singling out Fosdick as one who posed in the garb of a Christian preacher on Sundays but during the week taught ideas at Union Theological Seminary that were "utterly revolutionary and subversive of the fundamentals of the Christian faith." [75] Shortly after Straton's sermon, the fundamentalists held a series of mass meetings in Calvary Baptist Church, New York City, under the auspices of the Baptist Bible Union and the Fundamentalist League of Greater New York and Vicinity for Ministers and Laymen. The sharp-tongued J. Frank Norris, pastor of the First Baptist Church, Fort Worth, Texas, castigated the liberals at the opening afternoon session before nearly a thousand people. He likened their leaders to "Judases and lepers." He promised to drive out liberal teachers from their posts. He shouted that after the conflict between the modernists and the fundamentalists the latter would be able to dictate their own terms. Above all else, he minimized the possibility of a revival of faith among the liberals. To illustrate the latter absurdity, he referred derisively to King's Chapel in Boston, a Unitarian church with an Episcopal service. Norris brought laughter to the conservative crowd when he charged that the New England church had an endowment of twenty million dollars but a membership of only seventeen.[76]

Charles Francis Potter, minister of the West Side Unitarian Church of New York City, who was in the congregation at the time as an observer, was not amused. Keenly resenting the inaccuracy of Norris' statements, he checked by telephone with the pastor of King's Chapel to ascertain the true facts. That evening, from his own pulpit, Potter publicly denounced Norris' statement as "grossly and maliciously untrue" and demanded a public apology from both Norris and Straton. When this was not forthcoming, Potter, feeling that liberals should no longer remain silent to fundamentalist charges and misrepresentations, challenged Straton to a public debate on the "fundamentals" of Christianity. Straton welcomed and accepted the challenge, believing it would serve as a means of affirming the "blessed gospel" to a larger community.[77] A committee of three was appointed to select the judges and to make other necessary arrangements. On this committee, Justice William H. Black of the New York State Supreme Court, and a member of Calvary Baptist Church, represented Straton; Colonel Robert Starr Allyn, another lawyer, who was president of the Metropolitan Conference of Unitarian Churches, represented Potter. The first debate was held in Calvary Baptist Church, the remaining three at Carnegie Hall. Radio stations WQAO and WJZ carried the polemics to a larger audience, while thirty reporters, to that time the largest number to cover a religious event in the country, kept the debates on the front pages of the nation's newspapers.[78] The Straton-Potter confrontation reflected a crisis in American theology by representatives who took their faith with great earnestness; it was a joining of Fundamentalism and Liberalism a year and a half earlier than the memorable Scopes Trial at Dayton, Tennessee.

Twenty-five hundred people overflowed Straton's church on December 20, 1923, to hear the protagonists argue the first proposition: "Resolved, that the Bible is the Infallible Word of God." Accompanying the debaters as they appeared on the pulpit platform were the three lawyers who had agreed to serve as judges (former Justice Almet F. Jenks, Judge Ernest L. Conant, and C. Neal Barney, Esq., onetime mayor of Lynn, Massachusetts).

A little side drama occurred prior to the first debate. Part of the audience sang gospel hymns before the service, led by the choir of Calvary Baptist Church. Potter protested that Straton had not kept his promise that the organist would play no hymn tunes but only classical music. Straton pointed out that he had kept the agreement to the letter, because the organist had played no hymns, merely giving the choir the pitch. Straton spoke to the organist, who announced to the assembled throng that inasmuch as some hymns had been sung, he would play something for the modernists. With that he swung loudly into "The March of the Toys" from *Babes in Toyland*. Potter believed the whole thing to have been planned for the purpose of irritating him before the debate.

Tension and expectation filled the air as Straton arose to defend orthodoxy in general and Fundamentalism in particular. His own followers, who had been seated strategically in a reserved section in the front center of the sanctuary, greeted him with waves of applause. Straton began shrewdly. He paid tribute to Potter as a man of honesty since once he had accepted liberal views he had moved from the ranks of the Baptists to the Unitarians, something Straton had suggested for a long time that Fosdick and Faunce and their kind should do. Then the fundamentalist plunged into the heart of his arguments. Initially, he considered extra-Biblical "facts" in support of the Book's infallibility. He pointed to the Bible's "miraculous" preservation and increase, its universal appeal to the human heart in every age, its remarkable unity in diversity, and its fulfilled prophecies (Biblical criticism had made no impact on his thought, since he referred to prophecy as "the foretelling of events before they happen").[79] From evidence outside the Scriptures, Straton then shifted to the Bible's own claims concerning itself. He quoted a number of verses showing the Scriptures to be the Word of God, then, on his own, quickly, naïvely, and matter-of-factly, took the long step from inspiration to infallibility.[80] It was reasoning of this sort that caused a contemporary scholar to write:

Fundamentalists apparently assume that if God is really going to reveal himself to men his revealing work must be errorless. Somewhere, in the midst of our imperfection and uncertainty, there must be an objective, perfect something. But every presumption is against this view that in one place—the Bible—God has declared himself unambiguously and infallibly. . . . God does not conduct His rivers, like arrows to the sea. . . . Yet it is felt in Fundamentalist circles that to question anything in the Bible—the historicity of any event, the validity of any teaching—plunges one into a shoreless sea of uncertainty and subjective judgments.[81]

As further evidence of infallibility Straton pointed to the vast moral influence of the Christian writings as they directed the way to religious salvation and ethical development. The defender of the faith did bring two qualifications to infallibility: the Scriptures were inerrant only in the original documents (Potter reminded him that none existed) and they were infallible only to those who accepted them. Fundamentalism's representative concluded by warning that if man rejects Biblical authority, the result is complete anarchy.

Potter carefully assured his hearers that he believed in God and recognized the great moral influence of the Scriptures. It was another thing, however, to claim infallibility for the Bible. That idea he firmly rejected because of historical and scientific inaccuracies, contradictions, and misrepresentations, especially morally degrading ideas of God.[82] As an illustration of the inaccuracies, he referred to the Old Testament account of the sun standing still (if this really had taken place, not only would the Amorites have perished but Joshua and the Israelites as well). By a contradiction, he meant irreconcilable accounts in different Gospels (in Mark, Jesus goes into the wilderness immediately after his baptism and remains forty days; in John, the third day after his baptism Jesus is in Cana of Galilee, and the wilderness temptation is not mentioned). More objectionable for Potter were such concepts of God as One who commands the Israelites to stone to death disobedient children without trial, on the accusation of their parents. The Unitarian reasoned that God was too great and too good to be included between the covers of any printed book. "The aspirations toward goodness within the heart of man are a better evidence of God than all the books ever written." [83] The enlightened conscience of man, Potter concluded, was really the final and only guide.

The judges, after deliberating thirteen minutes, decided 2 to 1 in favor of Potter and the negative position. Judge Jenks, in announcing the decision, expressed regret that the two speakers, "both eloquent and able," had not given sufficient attention to the word "infallible." *The New York Tribune* reported that feeble applause greeted the verdict, while elderly women, who had hung on to the impassioned words of the defender of the Scriptures, wept openly.[84]

According to Potter, Straton became unusually severe in his pulpit attacks on Liberalism between the first and second debates. The Unitarian clergyman attributed this harshness to chafing from Straton's unexpected defeat in the presence of his followers, the awakening of prominent modernists to the danger of Fundamentalism, and a division in Calvary Baptist Church which led to the resignation of seventeen deacons.[85] The latter had protested their pastor's dictatorial leadership and intolerant spirit. The unwavering fundamentalist weathered the storm. In fact, he announced shortly before the second debate that he and his members were praying for Dr. Potter's conversion, "so that he might be brought to Calvary Church as associate pastor." [86] Failing that, Straton confided to the press, he would offer the position of general manager of the new church-hotel complex to the Unitarian leader. Potter, tongue in cheek, declined the offer, viewing the proposed hotel (no drinking or smoking allowed) as a dreary place of accommodation unlikely to draw even the patronage of pious out-of-town deacons.

The second debate was held in a more relaxed atmosphere at Carnegie Hall on January 28, 1924. The question on this occasion was: "Resolved, that the earth and man came by evolution," with Potter addressing himself to the affirmative and Straton to the negative. Potter argued for both the evolution of the earth and the evolution of man.[87] Referring to the former, he cited evidence of change in the past and the present. Relative to the human species he called upon paleontology, geography, comparative anatomy, physiology, embryology, and chemistry to support his claim of evolution in man. The former Baptist, who later became the founder of the First Humanist Society of New York, felt that he proved that evolution was a more reasonable explanation of the origin of the earth and man than the creation story in Genesis, but even Potter recognized that was not the question.

Straton adroitly took advantage of the wording of the proposition and repeatedly emphasized that at best evolution was a hypothesis ("a theory cannot be a science").[88] In his judgment, evolution was not a fact of science, but a dogma of philosophy which belonged primarily to the realm of subjective speculation and not to the realm of demonstrated fact. He recognized development within kinds but declared that only God could create. The central issue for Straton was whether the earth and man originated by design through the creative power of God or by chance through the "haphazard" operation of evolution. "It is the issue between naturalism and supernaturalism; between calculated planning and mere fortuitous circumstance." [89]

Humor and emotion characterized the second debate. In speaking of the "pensioners," or atavistic relics of animal ancestors which men possess as evidence of their evolution, Potter noticed that by the use of scientific terms he was not reaching many in his audience. So he changed his approach and spoke in the language of the layman.

> The coccyx or skeleton tail alone proves man's connection with the monkey family. If you were to take an x-ray . . . of the lower end of Mr. [William Jennings] Bryan's backbone, you would have proof enough of the falsity of his attitude toward evolution. There are even four vestigial muscles for wagging the tail, revealed by every dissection of a human body. We cannot deny our relationship to our animal ancestors.[90]

Old Carnegie Hall rocked with laughter, cheers, and jeers. When Straton's time for rebuttal came he replied:

> My honorable opponent [looking reproachfully toward Potter] grew almost personal about our great fellow-citizen, Mr. Bryan. I thought it was taking advantage of Mr. Bryan to bring up that matter when he is not here to defend his [own] tail.[91]

Again the crowd, which filled the main floor and four galleries, reverberated with amusement. Each man had a final retort. Potter explained that he had been more polite than to fasten the caudal appendage upon Dr. Straton, but in reality he had meant him all along. "Then," rejoined Straton, with the help of an old saw, "I must now defend my own caudal appendage. . . . I have had a good many ancestors, and it is possible that some of them have hung by their necks, but I stand here tonight staking my life that none of them ever hung by his tail." Cries of "Amen" were mingled with applause. Straton drew the greatest response, however, when he declared: "If we are merely highly developed beasts, then why should we not live like beasts? Monkey men make monkey morals!" [92]

In retrospect, that which Potter remembered best about the second encounter was the crowd's reaction to one of his statements. During the debate he announced that only the previous week the State Board of Education in North Carolina with the approval of the governor prohibited the teaching of evolution in the schools under its jurisdiction. Hearing this, a voluble woman in the front row cried, "Good, good." The larger audience gave a rousing cheer for the aforementioned Board of Education. Potter wrote reflectively: "When anti-evolution measures by educational authorities were cheered in Carnegie Hall, it was the first trumpet note of challenge—the ominous challenge of democratic education by fanatic religion." [93]

The judges on this occasion were Almet F. Jenks and Phillip J. McCook of the New York Supreme Court and the Honorable Frank P. Walsh, former chairman of the War Industries Board. Holding the speakers to the precise wording of the resolution, they decided unanimously in favor of Straton and the negative. Listeners to WJZ revealed a different judgment. The radio audience, invited to send in their votes, cast 57 percent for Potter and 43 percent for Straton. The latter saw to it there would be no radio vote again. [94]

The third debate was crucial to both sides. Not only was it a tie-breaking engagement, but it dealt with a sensitive subject. To the fundamentalists, the virgin birth of Jesus, like the inerrancy of the Scriptures, was one of the "fundamentals." To the liberals, it was a bone of contention in the ordination examinations of students desiring to enter the ministry. Already the Presbyterians and the Episcopalians had argued heatedly over the doctrine and had suffered sharp internal tensions. Therefore, another interested, capacity audience gathered at Carnegie Hall on March 22, 1924, to hear the clergymen debate the question: "Resolved, that the miraculous virgin birth of Jesus Christ is a fact and it is an essential Christian doctrine." Straton, of course, took the affirmative; Potter, the negative. The three scheduled judges did not serve, one because of illness, two because of "out-of-town engagements." The three who did act were Ernest F. Conant, Esq., of the New York Bar Association; H. F. Gunnison, publisher of *The Brooklyn Eagle*; and, Louis A. Ames, president of the Sons of the American Revolution.

Straton began with a homiletical trilogy, speaking of the possibility, the probability, and the positive "proof" of the virgin birth. [95] Parthenogenesis, he stated, was a well-known fact. Furthermore, the virgin birth was not a violation of any natural law, but an act of God according to higher laws known to him although unknown to men. By the probability of the virgin birth Straton meant the need of humanity for a redeemer and the fulfillment of ancient prophecy. The "proof" of the virgin birth for the conservative leader lay in the reliability of the historical documents (especially Matthew and Luke) as well as in the testimony of trustworthy Biblical witnesses, including Joseph and Mary themselves. Straton handled the genealogical problem in Matthew by asserting that Joseph was the legal father of Jesus but not his father according to the flesh. The silence of Mark, Paul, and John on the virgin birth was not unusual, the fundamentalist affirmed. He argued that these writers assumed the reality of this miracle; it would be fairer to say that the two Gospels dealing with the childhood of Jesus mention the virgin birth than to stress the silence of others. This belief in the virgin birth, Straton continued, had been declared an essential Christian doctrine by all the major branches of the church through their creeds, doctrinal statements, and confessions of faith. To deny it would be to question the integrity of the rest of the Bible as well as to undercut the deity of Jesus and the efficacy of his atonement. "Such a being [the God-man] demands the acknowledgement of entrance into this world, not through the channels of sinful conception but by way of the altar of a virgin's womb and through the power of the Most High God." [96]

Locking polemic horns with Straton, Potter pointed out that parthenogenesis among the lower forms of life is one thing, but that is far from proving the possibility of birth without sexual union among human beings. He reasoned that because a female codfish had been known to lay eight million eggs, that did not prove the possibility of a human mother having eight million children! [97] The Unitarian minister then concentrated upon the paucity of evidence for the virgin birth of Jesus in the New Testament itself.[98] It was important to him that neither Paul, the greatest preacher of the early church, nor Mark, the author of the oldest and most trustworthy Gospel, mentioned the virgin birth. Luke, writing some seventy years after Jesus' birth, Potter went on, did not say plainly that the miracle actually occurred. He said that the angel Gabriel told Mary that it would occur. The only verse, said Straton's opponent, that cites the virgin birth as a historical fact is Matt. 1:18. In the same chapter, however, it is stated that Jesus was the son of Joseph (otherwise there is no sense to the genealogy at all). Potter concluded that Matthew then must be ruled out as a contradictory witness, for no court of law would accept a witness who contradicts himself on the crucial point of the whole case. It was the Unitarian's belief that the few references to the virgin birth were later additions to the Gospel story. He bluntly denied Straton's affirmation that the doctrine of the virgin birth was in all the major creeds, citing as illustration the Athanasian Creed and the earliest form of the Nicene Creed. He also added in rebuttal: "The only place where it says that Joseph was the legal father of Jesus and that Jesus was Joseph's adopted son is in the Gospel According to Straton!" [99] Then Potter raised the crucial question: Can any doctrine be essential to Christianity which is never mentioned in Jesus' own teachings? He drew his argument to a conclusion by declaring that the story of the virgin birth is an insult to the marriage relationship; further, it is too materialistic to be in harmony with the spiritual character of Jesus and of Christianity.[100]

The press reported that the judges had a hot debate among themselves before coming to an opinion. Finally their spokesman announced a split verdict (2–1) in favor of Potter and the negative. Straton took the loss badly. He claimed the substitute judges had been appointed contrary to the rules of the original agreement and demanded that the subject be redebated. Even the winner did not fare well. As he was leaving Carnegie Hall he was besieged by some twenty-five irate women who hurled verbal epithets at him, calling him "Antichrist," "Satan," and "Devil." Potter was finally rescued by two private detectives hired without his knowledge by the trustees of his church.[101]

Potter claimed he had difficulty getting Straton to participate in the fourth debate. Only when several conditions were met did the fundamentalist finally agree. These included the wording of the question in such a way that the minister of Calvary Baptist Church had the negative side; the agreement again that no vote would be taken from the radio audience; and the appointment of the same trio of judges who had served at the time of the second debate (and had awarded Straton a unanimous decision).[102] Under these circumstances the fourth debate, and what proved to be the final one, was held on April 28, 1924, before thirty-five hundred people with the subject: "Resolved, that Jesus Christ was Entirely Man Instead of Incarnate Deity."

Potter reasoned that there was no warrant for the acceptance of deity in the reported words of Jesus, but rather that deity had been ascribed to him as the explanation of an ignorant age to account for an unusual man.[103] The problem with such adulation, the liberal clergyman affirmed, is that it removes Jesus from mankind and robs us of God. The moment you make him God, he becomes a theological abstraction. The Unitarian declared that we must not allow the theologians to take Jesus away from us. He is the greatest of humans and we must recognize him as such—the supreme triumphant human personality of the ages. Potter was firm in stating that nowhere in the Gospels does Jesus explicitly say, "I am God." Straton's opponent went further. He raised doubts about the sinlessness of Jesus, since the record of his life available to us covers only a relatively few days.

Responding to Straton's affirmation that one argument for the divinity of Jesus is the influence he has exerted over a vast number of individuals, Potter pointed to several prominent men who had not believed in the deity of Jesus—Emerson, Parker, Longfellow—yet had lived the life inspired by the man Jesus.

Straton's presentation stressed the impossibility of accounting for such a unique and extraordinary person as Jesus on any other ground than that he was an actual incarnation of God. He buttressed this assertion with several considerations.[104] The general teachings of the Bible set forth Christ as a divine being, one who was creator and redeemer. Furthermore, its specific teachings picture him as having all the attributes of God—wisdom, holiness, love, and power. The fundamentalist's central argument was that Jesus himself had explicitly claimed divinity and unless this claim were true, then he was either a fool or a knave. The verses upon which Straton relied for this assertion were taken largely from the Gospel of John, including the "I am" passages. The ultraconservative then underscored, as evidence of Jesus' divinity, his continuing influence over a period of two thousand years. To personalize this idea Straton concluded by giving a long, impassioned, personal testimony showing the influence of Jesus upon his own life.

The judges unanimously agreed that the negative as represented by Straton had prevailed in this fourth debate. When the decision was announced, Congressman William D. Upshaw, "dry" leader in Congress and fellow student with Straton at Mercer University, rushed to congratulate the victor. Potter was not neglected. A vivacious woman came dashing across the platform, seized Potter's elbows in her hands, shook him vigorously and snapped through clenched teeth, "Now, you little devil, now will you believe God's Word?" She repeated it hysterically until finally her friends pulled her away.[105]

A fifth debate had been proposed, to be held in the fall of 1924, but it never took place. Potter claimed that Straton would have had difficulty handling the affirmative side of the last question: "Resolved, that Jesus Christ will return in Bodily Presence to this Earth and Establish the Reign of Universal Peace and Righteousness." When Straton persistently showed no interest in this engagement, Potter claimed himself the victor of the series by default. Straton told his Unitarian foe in a telephone conversation that his real purpose for entering the debates was to convert Potter to orthodox Christianity. Failing in that objective, he was deeply disappointed and saw no reason for continuing. Potter believed this was camouflage to hide his fear of losing the tie-breaking engagement, plus the fact that Straton's deacons were uneasy because of all the publicity the Unitarians were gaining through the encounter. Actually, each protagonist could claim himself the winner, despite the fact that officially there had been two decisions for each man. Of the twelve votes cast in the four contests, Straton had garnered eight. Potter had split even in the verdicts, but secured much attention for the liberal cause. Furthermore, he appeared to have gained the sympathy of the general public as reflected through the radio vote at the time of the second debate.

V

The life and thought of John Roach Straton provide considerable evidence of his pronouncements on social issues, but paramount in his theology and in his proclamations was the conversion of the individual. A change in the nature of society was sought to make such conversions easier and to provide a more hospitable environment in which the convert might live. As early as 1908, as we have seen, Straton believed that the central emphasis for Christians must be "regeneration, not reform; soteriology, not sociology." This primary stress on the conversion of the individual supplemented by the practice of a personal piety was emphasized to the last year of his life. In 1929 he reiterated what had always been his basic posture as well as bringing an interpretation of his own role of leadership.

> I am really not a reformer. . . . I have neither faith nor hope in connection with mere reform efforts and secular agencies for the amelioration of the wrong conditions of human society and the redemption of the individual and the race. I believe in regeneration rather than reform. I believe in salvation as the only source of true social service. I believe in the prophet rather than the priest, and in divine power instead of human influence, to transform the world. . . . Instead of trying to reform . . . I have earnestly called upon the members of Christ's church at least, not to be "conformed to this world, but transformed by the renewing of their minds." [106]

When a man denies that he is a reformer, does not as a general rule offer social answers for social problems, vehemently opposes a theological tendency (Liberalism) that does stress the social application of religion, and persistently emphasizes personal regeneration as the solution to both individual and societal problems, it is difficult to think of him as primarily a social prophet. How, then, did Straton view himself? He saw himself as a prophet, without the adjective "social," as if the two could be separated.[107]

John Roach Straton did possess some of the overt characteristics of the ancient spokesmen of Israel. He had a driving compulsion to preach; like the prophets, he was lonely as the result of his words of criticism which isolated him from individuals and groups; he was harsh on contemporary evils; and his messages were sometimes dramatically illustrated in enacted parables. But there were also differences between Straton and the men of the prophetic tradition. Unlike the prophets, Straton frequently did not give major attention to the weightier matters of the faith. While one may argue that at various times he favored adequate wages for all, religious liberty, woman's suffrage, the political wisdom of the two-party system, and racial justice, these did not receive the proportionate attention that his opposition to alcoholic beverages and popular pleasures did. In the midst of war, poverty, disease, and dehumanization, continuous condemnation of such personal practices as dancing and attending the theater seemed trivial and irrelevant, even for his generation.

Theologically, there were misplaced emphases as well. The debates with Potter made clear that Straton was more concerned with an infallible Bible than with the doctrine of the incarnation. This devotion to the inerrancy of the Scriptures was crucial to Fundamentalism. It led to a legalistic concept of religion and, in large measure, accounted for Straton's charges of lawlessness in the home, society, and the church.

Furthermore, many of his so-called social "answers" were a call to return to an impossible past rather than an invitation to a living, viable future. This was evident in his invitation for metropolitan New Yorkers to return to a nineteenth-century (rural) observance of Sunday with the "plow resting in the furrow and the sweet Sabbath bells [sounding] across the silent fields and the quiet cities." [108] Straton also went beyond the enacted parables of the prophets with his sensational techniques, bringing upon him the charges of being overly dramatic. More important, his concept of God was unduly severe. In all their firmness, the prophets, with the possible exception of Amos, championed a more loving God than did the pastor of New York City's Calvary Baptist Church, who once declared: "Concerning the great white throne and the time of judgment . . . [there is] no faintest suggestion of mercy; for in that judgment day, the day of mercy will be over. . . . [There will be] only the suggestion of the austerity of divine Justice and eternal Holiness, in whose awful presence no evil thing can stand but from whom, even earth and heaven flee away in fear." [109] Straton did not confine such a God and such a judgment to the future alone. On another occasion he combined this picture of an angry deity with an appeal to fear through these words:

Have you ever thought of what a good husky tidal wave would do to "little old New York"? . . . Have you ever imagined the Woolworth "sky-scraper" butting headlong into the Equitable Building, through such an earthquake as that which laid San Francisco's proud beauty in the dust? Have you ever imagined the Metropolitan Tower crashing over on Madison Square Garden some time, when there were tens of thousands of people in there at some worldly, godless, celebration on the Lord's Day? Ah yes, don't worry about God's not having the means for judgment, even in this world.[110]

If not primarily a social reformer and if not fully a prophet, what then was Straton? He was a pastor-evangelist who made personal conversion central to his solutions for a troubled society. He was a showman who provided jaded New Yorkers, among others, with a taste of the theatrical under the flag of salvation.[111] He was a fighting fundamentalist concerned about correctness of doctrine, as his debates with Potter indicated. For Straton, in the 1920's, the greatest issues were not social but theological ones: the inerrancy of the Scriptures, the deity of Jesus, the virgin birth, and the second coming of Christ. Despite all this devotion to doctrinal Fundamentalism, however, Straton undoubtedly hastened its discreditation. Potter wrote:

The most apparent . . . result of the debates was the waking up of the country to the real menace of Fundamentalism and its literal interpreta-tion of the Bible. No educated person could sit through those long sessions or listen on the radio or read the accounts the next day without realizing that Straton's beliefs, shared as they were by many thousands of Americans, constituted a growing menace to the culture and education and scientific viewpoint we had been building up and fostering for decades. The Fundamentalists . . . proposed that we return to the ideas, thought forms, frames of reference, theology, unscientific philosophies and superstitions of the pastoral nomads of the age of Abraham or Moses.[112]

Although this charge came from Straton's adversary, it appeared to be true. Consequently, scholars may point to the beginning of the triumph of Liberalism over Fundamentalism, at least in the popular mind, from late 1923 and early 1924, rather than waiting for the histrionics of the Scopes Trial of 1925.

John Roach Straton is also another example of the truth that fundamentalists should not be relegated exclusively to the small town and a rural environment. Although one cannot deny a natural kinship between the old-time religion and the rural mind, it was in the great urban centers where Fundamentalism had its birth and carried on its strongest program. It was in Chicago, Baltimore, Norfolk, and New York City that Straton became the defender of the faith "once delivered unto the saints." It was in the cities that a country-bred boy won the admiration of his friends for his sincerity, fearlessness, dedication, and zeal. It was in the cities that a product of the South tilted his lance in the North drawing the criticism of his enemies for his theological inflexibility, his perennial showmanship, and his sharp-tongued attacks. It was in the cities for those of rural background and rural mentality that the very name Straton "conjured up pictures of [rural !] campmeetings, the mourner's bench, the Sankey and Moody hymnbooks, fiery gulfs and burning lakes, winged angels with golden harps, Jonah and the whale, Joshua and the sun, and Satan with his full complement of hoofs, tail, and pitchfork." [113] And when individuals in our own day of social and theological change are tempted to look condescendingly at this leading fundamentalist of the 1920's who added so much color to that roaring decade, the tumultuous life of John Roach Straton may remind them of the importance of religious positions that have some flexibility to them, of central rather than secondary issues, and of Biblically correct concepts of God.

CHAPTER FOUR

William Bell Riley

ORGANIZATIONAL FUNDAMENTALIST

O N A HOT AFTERNOON in August 1947 an ailing eighty-six-year-old religious warrior summoned an energetic young evangelist to his bedside. The aged man was the retired minister of the First Baptist Church in Minneapolis, the president of three educational institutions known as Northwestern Schools, and the doughty champion of militant Fundamentalism over several decades. The young man, without a theological education, was pastor of a church of fewer than a hundred members, but he was prominent in youth evangelism and was vice-president of Youth for Christ International. The veteran defender of the faith turned to a dog-eared Bible, his source of authority, and read the account of Samuel anointing David king. While thunder rattled all around and lightning streaked through the premature darkness, William Bell Riley pointed a bony finger at Billy Graham and said: "Beloved, as Samuel appointed David King of Israel, so I appoint you head of these schools. I'll meet you at the judgment seat of Christ with them." [1]

Overawed by the determination of the dying man, and doubtless against his better judgment, Graham agreed to serve as interim president in the event of Riley's imminent death.[2] When Riley died in December 1947, Graham kept his promise, eventually serving as head of the schools for three and a half years while simultaneously continuing his commitments to evangelism. But Graham realized that the dual arrangement was not a good one, and he resigned in June 1951 to devote full time to his rapidly developing crusades. What has become of Graham since is well known. Less familiar today are the life and thought of Riley, the crafty, stalwart, aged Baptist clergyman who sought unsuccessfully to lay his mantle on younger shoulders. That failure may have been a portent of the inability of anyone really to succeed Riley, the independent, strong-willed fundamentalist war-horse whom William Jennings Bryan once called "the greatest statesman in the American pulpit." [3]

Riley's significance for both Minnesota and the nation is being increasingly recognized as scholars gain perspective on the development of religion in America, especially that phase of it known as the Modernist-Fundamentalist conflict. His labors as preacher, pastor-evangelist, administrator, debater, author, evangelical educator, civic leader, and social critic led some academicians to hail him as "the ablest leader of orthodox reaction during the early part of the twentieth century," "the ablest executive that Fundamentalism produced," and the founder of "the only inclusive fellowship of fundamentalists in America." [4] (The latter referred to the World's Christian Fundamentals Association, the organization that retained Bryan for the famous Scopes Trial in Tennessee in 1925.) Riley's friends went beyond even these accolades to acclaim him as "the country's foremost and ablest controversialist," "the second Martin Luther of Protestantism," and worthy of being compared with evangelical leader Charles H. Spurgeon "in the largeness of his work." [5] Others, however, viewed him in less flattering terms as an irritating, rigid interpreter of Christianity whose excessive claims for the Bible contributed to the religious polarization of American culture. Nevertheless, both friend and foe could agree with the tribute of Harry A. Ironside, pastor of Moody Memorial Church in Chicago, at the time of Riley's death: "We need to remember that God never repeats Himself. . . . He will raise up others to carry on, but there will never be a second man of Dr. Riley's stamp." [6] Riley's disciples lamented this fact; his enemies rejoiced that it was true. A review of Riley's life and thought may assist readers in making their own evaluations of this gifted, ultraconservative leader.

I

William Bell Riley was born in Green County, Indiana, on March 22, 1861, less than a month before the outbreak of the Civil War.[7] Shortly after hostilities began, his father, Branson Radish Riley, a Democrat of Scotch-Irish descent and a proponent of slavery, moved his family to Kentucky, where he felt there would be greater sympathy for his political position. The ancestors of Riley's mother, Ruth Anna Jackson, were English and Dutch Quakers of some

William Bell Riley

prominence in the early history of Pennsylvania. The young Riley spent his first eighteen years in Kentucky. To earn money for his education he obtained a loan from a friend and also raised tobacco on a farm rented from his father (a bit ironical in view of the condemnation of smoking by many fundamentalists). After attending Valparaiso (Indiana) Normal School for a year he transferred to Hanover College in Indiana, Presbyterian in origin and one of the oldest educational institutions west of the Ohio River. He received his A.B. degree in 1885, ranking fourth in his class, and, significantly, first in debate. Converted to Christianity with little outward show of emotion at the age of seventeen, Riley originally planned a legal career. But a persistent call to the ministry hounded him, until one day, on his knees in the black loam between two rows of ripening tobacco, he "surrendered" and thereafter devoted his life to religious service. In 1888, Riley was graduated from Southern Baptist Theological Seminary in Louisville, Kentucky, although he had been ordained while in college. In fact, he had preached his own ordination sermon, thereby demonstrating a self-assertiveness that characterized him throughout his long and stormy life.[8]

Several brief pastorates in Kentucky, Indiana, and Illinois followed.[9] While at Lafayette, Indiana, on December 31, 1890, Riley married Lillian Howard, a Methodist graduate of Purdue University. Six weeks after the wedding he baptized his young bride into the ranks of the Baptists. Six children were born of this union. His first wife died August 10, 1931, and some two years later Riley married Marie R. Acomb, dean of women at the Bible and Missionary Training School that he had founded in Minneapolis.

From 1893 to 1897, Riley served as minister of the Calvary Baptist Church in Chicago and then was called to the First Baptist Church in Minneapolis, where he remained for forty-five years (1897–1942). Under his persuasive leadership this congregation grew from 585 to more than 3,550 members in an area that was a stronghold for Lutherans on the one hand and for Roman Catholics on the other. Also an educator, Riley founded the three schools he entrusted to Graham's direction: the Northwestern Bible and Missionary Training School (1902) to provide pastoral leadership for neglected small-town and rural churches; the Northwestern Evangelical Seminary (1938) to meet the needs of urban congregations seeking orthodox leadership; and Northwestern College (1944) to provide a liberal arts education under evangelical auspices. Upon retirement from an active pastorate, Riley spent the last years of his life promoting these institutions.

A tall, strikingly handsome man with a commanding presence, a resonant voice, and a sense of humor, Riley was known not only in Minnesota but also throughout the nation as an evangelist, speaker at Bible conferences, and tireless leader of fundamentalist forces. He also wrote more than sixty books and countless articles and published his own religious magazines under such titles as the *Baptist Beacon*, *Christian Fundamentals in School and Church*, the *Christian Fundamentalist*, and the *Northwestern Pilot*. Near the end of his life, as president of the Minnesota Baptist convention, Riley led that body in a virtual break from the parent denomination. In the last year of his life, Riley was still fighting as he endeavored to sever all personal association with the Northern Baptist Convention, the denominational body to which his church belonged and in which he had been such a contentious figure.

Riley died at his Golden Valley home in suburban Minneapolis on December 5, 1947, bequeathing a heritage that probably made him the most important fundamentalist clergyman of his generation. This claim is supported not only by his theological position but also by his role as pastor-evangelist, social critic, and ecclesiastical politician.

II

Riley's commitment to orthodoxy emerged early in life. The pietistic faith of his parents, the revivalistic tradition of Kentucky, the religious atmosphere of the schools he attended (he claimed, for instance, that every member of the Hanover faculty was "a fundamental believer"), and the forceful impact of frequent exposure to the witness of famed evangelist Dwight L. Moody all coalesced to provide a strong conservative foundation upon which the future architect of the fundamentalist movement would build.[10] This orthodoxy as well as his polemical spirit was evident by the time of his senior year in seminary when he delivered an address to the graduating class castigating those who deviated from traditional Christian belief as "freaks of faith" who had little appreciation for the historical triumphs of orthodoxy.[11] Under the further stimulation of personal contact with liberal leaders, supplemented by his own intense study of the Scriptures, Riley crystallized his personal understanding of the "fundamentals" of the faith.[12] Of these, two were especially crucial to his thinking—a belief in the verbal inerrancy of the Scriptures in their original writings and the imminent, personal, premillennial return of Jesus.

To Riley the Scriptures were an explicit revelation of God to man, without historical, ethical, or moral error.[13] Their purpose was to reveal the nature of God, to provide man with a knowledge of himself, and to indicate the way of peace and love between the two.[14] Riley accepted these writings as inspired on the basis of internal evidence and external proofs. By the former he meant what he believed to be the Bible's matchless code of morals, its supernatural revelations, and its unity of teaching and purpose. He also felt that the Bible began in Genesis on such a lofty plane that only inspiration and not evolution could account for its height.[15] By external proofs he had in mind the experiences of men that verified Biblical promises, the fulfillment in history of Scriptural prophecies, and the support of archaeological discovery. The latter led him to see an absolute agreement between science and the Scriptures. He came to believe not only in inspiration but in the verbal inerrancy of the Old and New Testaments. Early in his career he accepted the New Hampshire Confession of Faith, which affirmed that the Bible has "truth without any mixture of error," and by 1921 he went so far as to declare that "one who rejects the verbal inspiration of the Bible rejects the Bible itself." [16] Riley felt that such verbal inspiration was important because "the record of the Saviour must be completely trustworthy if the Saviour is to be trusted, since the latter faith is based on the former record." [17]

Holding such a rigid posture, Riley differed sharply with liberals who advocated alternate approaches to the understanding of the Scriptures. To those who reasoned that the meaning of much of the Scriptures depended on the interpretation of the individual, he responded that when men depart from the plain Biblical text they have nothing to interpret. He felt that contemporary translations of the Bible distorted its meaning, and he criticized liberal scholars who, building on the research of Biblical critic Julius Wellhausen (1844–1918), postulated a multiple authorship of the early books of the Old Testament. When the authors were referred to by the letters J, E, D, and P, Riley summoned some of the clever scorn that became one of his trademarks.

> When 4,000 years from now the living critics exhume the First Baptist Church of Minneapolis and find my library, they will take my books and prove that they are composites. Wherever I speak of God, they will find one author and name him "G"; wherever I speak of the Heavenly Father, they will find another author and call him "H.F."; wherever I call him Lord, they will find a third author and name him "L"; and wherever I

speak of Christ, they will name a fourth author, "C"; and they will have the exact basis to prove that my books were produced by four men that they have applied to the composite theory of the Pentateuch.[18]

Riley's other convictions followed quite naturally from his start with an infallible book as his standard of religious authority. Using the proof-text approach, he came to regard as absolutely essential Christian truth such ideas as the trinitarian concept of God; the deity of Jesus; the sinfulness of man; the vicarious atonement, the bodily resurrection, and the personal return of Jesus; justification by faith; and the bodily resurrection of all men.[19] Later in his career Riley guided the World's Christian Fundamentals Association toward incorporating these beliefs into its doctrinal statement.[20]

In a statement published after his death, Riley asserted that his premillennialist convictions came to him through independent study a year after his graduation from Southern Baptist Seminary.[21] Like other premillennialists, Riley believed that society was characterized by decadence rather than by progress. To him, "the putrid condition" of humanity was reflected in "the most banal of all evil sources: the demoralizing effect of college philosophy . . . Darwinism, applied to every branch of learning," plus what he described as the great trinity of iniquities: the saloon, the gambling den, and the brothel.[22] Further evidences of the sorry condition of humanity were to be seen in lascivious dancing, the lewdness of the theater, suggestive movies, juvenile delinquency, divorce, suicide, the breakdown of the home, the abbreviated dress of women, and the general opulence of the day.[23] Where admirable traits persisted in contemporary culture they were due, in Riley's judgment, to the influence of Christianity rather than the forces of evolution. To illustrate such influence, Riley cited with approval a missionary friend who had "seen a filthy, almost nude, ignorant Asamese [sic] woman, with the juice of the beetle [sic] nut running from each corner of her mouth, transformed in five short years into a woman of genuine refinement, with habits of tidiness, clothed as a westerner, worthy to be spoken of as civilized." [24]

"The Gospel According to Riley" did not present a utopia resulting from human endeavor. In this age there were to be only dire judgments upon the mistakes, sins, wars, and world tragedies that men have brought about. Yet blessedness remained for the children of God. This was promised in the millennium and the ensuing kingdom of heaven, both of which would be established by God rather than by sinful man.[25] A special characteristic of Riley's version of the millennial rule was its material nature. There was to be a literal throne, a literal king (Jesus), a literal location (Jerusalem), and literal subjects. The millennial kingdom would be inaugurated at the time of Christ's second coming, which Riley felt was imminent. He saw the signs of Christ's coming in several Biblical paradoxes that purportedly were being fulfilled in modern life: the proclamation of peace and the simultaneous preparation for war, "the search for truth and the acceptance of lies" (like evolution); and the profession of godliness amid the practice of godlessness.[26] In keeping with this dispensational scheme, a final judgment would follow the millennium, and then the kingdom of God (also with its material aspects) would reach its fullness with the coming of the new heaven and the new earth mentioned in the twenty-first chapter of Revelation. At that time, the adversaries of God and men would be banished forever, the present earth would be regenerated, and the new Jerusalem—literally 1,500 miles (12,000 furlongs) long, wide, and high; every street one fifth the length of the diameter of the earth; its avenues 8,000,000 in number (all these figures in keeping with the book of Revelation)—would be the inheritance of the saints for all ages. In the meantime, the crucial mission of the church was to be the salvation of men and women, introducing them to the marvels of the kingdom, at least in its embryonic form.[27]

One further concept in Riley's Fundamentalism should be stressed. He believed strongly that correctness of doctrinal belief alone was insufficient. There was such a thing as an orthodoxy too anemic to advance the cause of Christianity. It must be supplemented by aggressive, militant action. Riley himself was a striking exemplar of this "orthodoxy plus" philosophy, as a pastor-evangelist, a critic of society, and a religious politician warring against theological Liberalism.

III

Riley became embroiled in controversy early in his Minneapolis pastorate, but in the light of his convictions, forceful personality, and aggressive leadership no one should have been surprised. Initially, he reduced the church roll from 662 to 585 members by eliminating the names of those who were inactive. Then, within a brief span of time, he preached on several polemical issues. He opposed the practice of renting pews, because he believed it created class distinctions and to that extent was unchristian.[28] He advocated tithing as a Biblical method of supporting the church and expressed dissatisfaction with bazaars, suppers, and other forms of raising money employed by many women of his congregation. He condemned such amusements as dancing, cardplaying, and theatergoing and thus isolated himself from some of the young people and their parents. The new minister also took a hand in the polity of his congregation. He guided the consolidation of the government of the local church by dissolving many of the separate boards and set up a single governing body with powers limited to advising the larger congregation.

As a result of these policies, an anti-Riley faction arose in the socially conservative congregation. Some of the members resented the newcomer's leadership and reportedly even went to the extent of putting a detective on Riley's trail for the purpose of discrediting him.[29] The early tensions came to a climax during the Spanish-American War. Several hundred people attended a rally at the Lyceum Theatre in Minneapolis to protest the annexation of the Philippines by the United States. Riley, who had expressed concern that war in the Philippines would lead to a conflict with Japan, was asked to offer the invocation. He prayed as follows: "We cannot ask Thee that our soldiers . . . may be victorious, for we do not believe that this is Thy will; but we do ask that their lives may be preserved and that they may return to their homes and friends."[30] At a time when most American people heartily supported the conflict, it seemed to many— including the press of the Twin Cities—that Riley's words were treasonable. His opponents capitalized on this situation to bring additional pressure on their minister. Unsuccessful in forcing Riley's resignation, they called two ex parte councils, each of which recommended that the church request the pastor's resignation. The congregation tabled both recommendations. A "solution" to the difficulties was at last reached at a church business meeting in 1903 when Riley demanded the exclusion of forty members who had withdrawn their contributions. The opposition came up with a larger list of about 140 names in this same category, and without further discussion a motion was passed that they be dismissed to form a new church.[31] The departing members founded Trinity Baptist (now Community) Church in Minneapolis.[32]

Freed of the "faction," Riley proceeded to build his own kind of congregation, placing considerable emphasis on evangelism. He believed that the normal condition of the church should be a state of perennial revival and set himself and others to the winning of souls. Every Sunday service concluded with an invitation for members to

accept Christ. In addition, "protracted meetings" and Bible conferences were held regularly each year, led by prominent evangelical
personalities. Numerical results followed. An average of 140 new
members a year joined the First Baptist Church during the first
decade of Riley's leadership. He claimed that the congregations were
the largest in the recent history of the church and attributed this to
"the position which we have taken for the authority and integrity of
the Word of God and the effort we are making for a church separate
from the world." [33] One should not overlook the fact, however, that
Riley had a flair for publicity and was skilled in the techniques of
drawing and handling crowds. At Sunday evening services, for
example, he introduced "attractive rather than sensational" sermon
subjects, initiated an appealing musical program featuring a choir of
more than one hundred voices and a fifteen-piece orchestra, and relied
upon the leadership of young people whenever possible.[34] Moreover,
Riley kept the church building open seven days a week from 8:00 A.M.
to 10:00 P.M., although he was careful to make a distinction between
his program and that of the more typical institutional church;

> There is an institutional church that dotes upon ice-cream suppers,
> full-dress receptions, popular lectures, chess-boards, bowling-alleys, the
> social settlement, not to speak of the occasional dance and amateur
> theatricals; and there is the institutional church that expresses itself in the
> organization of prayer-meetings, mission circles, Bible study classes,
> evangelistic corps, and multiplied mission stations. . . . This latter
> institution repeats the essential features of apostolic times, and enjoys the
> essential spirit of the apostolic power.[35]

The growth of Riley's congregation was such that Jackson Hall, a
four-story educational building with forty-six classrooms and seven
offices, was constructed in 1923. A year later the church itself was
rebuilt, and Riley preached the rededication sermon. The enlarged
sanctuary is still in use. It seats more than 2,200 persons and has a
huge balcony with aisles that slant to the front level of the main
auditorium. Designed after a similar arrangement in the First
Baptist Church of Dallas, the purpose of the slanted aisles was to
facilitate the "coming forward" of individuals at the time of public
invitation. The presupposition was that a change of mind might take
place if such persons were detoured by a network of stairs at the rear
of the sanctuary.

Riley's expository, Biblical preaching went hand in hand with his
constant stress on evangelism. Beginning in July 1923, he preached

his way through the entire Bible—a series of Sunday morning sermons lasting ten years and eventually published in forty volumes under the title *The Bible of the Expositor and Evangelist*.[36] The combination of Riley's preaching, evangelism, and aggressive leadership accounted in large measure for the addition of some 7,000 members (4,000 by baptism) to his church during his lifetime. At the time of Riley's retirement, one tenth of the Baptists of Minnesota belonged to his congregation.[37]

By arrangement with his church, Riley spent four months of every year as an evangelist in various sections of the country. In his evangelistic role he revealed many of the characteristics of revivalists of the late nineteenth and early twentieth centuries. There was the standard set of sermons (example: "Is Any Sin Unpardonable?"), the special delegations that bolstered attendance, the separate Sunday afternoon meetings for men and women, the castigation of modern amusements, the singing of sentimental hymns written by Fanny Crosby and others, the tender evangelistic appeals, the inevitable "love offering," the published words of appreciation for the evangelist's work, and the criticism of other religions, especially Unitarianism, the Bahai faith, theosophy, Christian Science, and Mormonism. In the criticism of religions, Riley was an expert. He attacked the Unitarian faith, for instance, as "a degenerating religion, an enemy in the evangelical camp, a deadly ecclesiastical infection, a conscienceless church, and an ape in theory and in practice." [38]

One way in which Riley's "union meetings" appeared to differ from those of others was in the personal style of the evangelist himself. Riley apparently did not resort to the usual mannerisms and theatrics of the conventional religious barnstormer. A reporter observing his campaign in Seattle, Washington, in 1913, wrote that Riley

upsets all the usual notions of an evangelist. He doesn't look the part and he doesn't act the part. He dresses like a prosperous banker. When he moves about the platform, which is seldom, he does not do so to the accompanying of flapping coat tails. His collar is of the latest style, and his suit of the most modern cut." [39]

The reporter continued:

When he steps out on the platform, he looks like a bank director about to address a meeting of the board of directors. And, save for the unusual earnestness of his speech, his tone of voice is that of the same banker. He doesn't rave and he doesn't rant. He doesn't wail and he doesn't weep. He has never wilted a collar in all his years of preaching. He has never torn an ounce of hair from his iron gray pompadour.[40]

This businesslike approach was in direct contrast to the style of Riley's contemporary, evangelist Billy Sunday. Although he supported Sunday's orthodoxy, Riley was the first to admit that he differed with the flamboyant, tub-thumping Iowan in method and in cultural expression. One scholar has pointed out that Riley's kind of evangelism may have made an impact on Billy Graham, helping him to bypass some of the extravagances that plagued Billy Sunday.[41]

Riley's converts in a particular city during a campaign of three or four weeks normally ran into the hundreds and reportedly exceeded a thousand on at least two occasions—at Duluth, Minnesota, in 1912, and at Dayton, Ohio, in 1915. During a Riley campaign in Fort Worth, Texas, before the pastorate there of J. Frank Norris, some 352 individuals were converted, many of them reputed to have been cattlemen who joined the First Baptist Church.[42] More important than statistical reports, however, were the contacts Riley made with evangelical leaders throughout the United States during his campaigns. These connections helped Riley in his scheme of creating an interdenominational fundamentalist movement. And his travels enabled him to see the country apart from the provincial confines of the Old Northwest. This led him to speak with greater conviction than ever on the social issues of the day.

IV

Although Riley believed in social reform, at least by his own definition, in practice his premillennialist philosophy of history and his own ultraconservative stance on various social issues militated against such reform. To Riley, Jesus was "the social reformer of all ages" whose mission was the most revolutionary the world ever saw.[43] Riley also felt the church had a social mission. Specifically, this was to save the individual from sin, to construct a new society, and to preach and practice social righteousness.[44] One must understand, however, what Riley meant by the construction of a new society. To him, it was the formation of a circle of Christian converts within a circle (the larger world) whose influence for good would make for a better, if not perfect, social order. The church, said Riley,

should form a circle within a circle. The way to correct society is not to begin at the rim, and try to set it all right, from circumference to center, by a single enactment. One must work from within outward. . . . That Jesus meant to build up a society within a society is evident in his speech concerning his own disciples [John 17:9, 14–16]. . . . It is a circle within a circle, a company working from the center to the circumference, a society instituted of God to set things to rights.[45]

Reviewing history, Riley believed that the true church had approximated this goal. Through converted individuals it had exerted a civilizing influence; it had contributed to the rising consciousness of a common brotherhood; and it had brought about increased justice among men. The key to continuing this pattern, in his judgment, was a spirit of revival in the church out of which social reform would follow.

In practice, Riley was exceedingly strong on revivalism, and there is little doubt that he created his own "circle within a circle." The social reform of which he spoke was not so evident, owing at least in part to Riley's own conservative posture on social issues. Prof. Ferenc M. Szasz has written: "He was a social radical when he arrived in Minneapolis in 1897, on the left, and a social radical when he died in 1947, but on the right. Riley went from radical to radical by standing still. For fifty years he stood on the corner and the parade passed him by." [46]

It is true that Riley was a social radical on the right when he died, and many would agree that the parade passed him by, but to call Riley a social radical on the left in 1897 seems an excessive claim. What Szasz had in mind, of course, was Riley's democratization of worship in opposing the pew rental system. Riley's position on social issues at the beginning of his ministry in Minneapolis, however, hardly supports Szasz's unqualified statement. Prior to that time, Riley had gained a reputation for stern opposition to gambling, drinking, and prostitution by such successful actions as securing 250 convictions against gambling in Bloomington, Illinois, and curbing the selling of liquor at illegal hours in Chicago. These emphases alone would not have made Riley a conservative, since the leading figures in the Social Gospel movement were also opposed to gambling, drinking, and prostitution. And it should be remembered that the progressive movement itself gave strong support to prohibition prior to World War I. Riley, however, had other convictions, too. Near the beginning of his Chicago ministry he spoke against the Sunday opening of the World's Columbian Exposition of 1893. He was unable to prevent the start of the fair on a Sunday but rejoiced that it was not a financial success on that day.[47] Further, his firm criticism of dancing, the theater, and divorce reflected nineteenth-century religious viewpoints. His disapproval of these various practices, as well as his opposition to a more liberal observance of Sunday, hardly qualified him, in 1897, as a proponent of the liberal left. His belief in the "open pew" seems to have been an exception to his otherwise conservative—or, at very best, middle-of-the-road—position.

That Riley continued to be basically conservative in his social attitudes after he arrived in Minneapolis may also be seen in his various declarations. He opposed the legalized saloon, alleging that it had caused greater degradation and more inhuman deaths than had the institution of slavery. He expressed disapproval of the more relaxed sexual practices of the day by referring to free love as the exaltation of animalism that reduced man to the condition of a brute, denied children permanent parenthood, and displayed utter disregard for God, his laws, and the highest sentiment of home life.[48] He favored the requirement of a strict loyalty oath for citizenship and spoke on behalf of the wisdom of capital punishment, reasoning that the death penalty was not half as inhuman as the work of a murderer. In the struggle between capital and labor, Riley declared that greed was common to both sides, as "sinful, self-seeking, idol-worshipping" men were found in each. Riley also had simple answers for other complex problems. With a firmness matched only by naïveté, Riley proclaimed during the depression years of the 1930's that repentance and renewed spiritual faith would bring about financial recovery.[49]

These opinions and his remitting stands against socialism and communism kept him on the conservative side of most issues. His basic answer to the social needs of the day was individual conversion "through the cross of Christ." The extent of Riley's particular contributions to social reform appears to have been limited largely to his provision of food in Chicago for some eighty needy families (the breadbasket approach) during the winter of 1895–1896, his support of prohibition, and his backing of reform mayoral candidates in Minneapolis. Having differed in part with Professor Szasz on one point, the author finds himself in hearty agreement with him in the following assessment: "The whole impetus of Riley's social message seems to have been based on his own personal experience. Hardworking and poor, he had . . . made it to the very top of his profession. He could not understand why his pattern could not be universalized." [50]

This stress upon the individual was never more evident than when Riley discussed the possibility of unemployment insurance and old-age benefits. He taught that he could find nothing in Scripture "suggesting that a healthy man is justified in living at government expense." [51] Rather, to the surprise of few and the applause of many, he preferred the Biblical injunction: "In the sweat of thy face shalt thou eat bread." Financial aid from Washington, he feared, would be welcomed by intemperate men, who would "retire to a continuous round of guzzling and sleep." [52] Riley's literal interpretation of his religious source of authority, linked to his own energetic example of personal initiative, was the root from which he derived his philosophy of social reform, such as it was. In the meantime, souls had to be won, the millennial kingdom of God had to be anticipated, and the continuing struggle against Liberalism had to be waged.

V

Of the various emphases in the life of Riley, the one that seemingly occupied him the most, on both a local and a national scale, was his firm opposition to theological Liberalism. This resistance permeated his ministry and called forth his qualities as a religious politician. His struggle against the teaching of evolution and his endeavor to gain a victory for fundamentalist Christianity within and without his own denomination must be seen in this context.

Darwinian evolution was a basic part of the modernist structure and a concrete target of fundamentalists. As Willard B. Gatewood, Jr., has pointed out, "to discredit evolution would destroy the underpinnings of modernism." [53] Riley entered into the fray with typical vigor. His primary grievance concerning Darwinism was that it represented, in his judgment, an assumption unsupported by facts. He declined "to cackle with every discoverer of dinosaur eggs ten million years old [or] . . . to enthuse over 'science falsely so-called.'" [54] He did not deny development, improvement, or varieties within species but, rather, was arguing against the development of one species from another. Riley also argued that the hypothesis of the evolution of civilization out of barbarism was not borne out by the facts of archaeology. Instead of the progress we should expect, there is retrogression and decay—in individuals, nations, and continents. Where civilization does exist, it is the result of Christian influence.[55] And, of course, Riley believed that the idea of evolution contradicted the Biblical account of man's origins, thereby invalidating the whole basis of the doctrine of sin. "Lacking a sense of sin," he wrote, "man reverted to the brute morality of his monkey ancestors." [56]

In the 1920's Riley engaged in one of his most spirited controversies over the question of the teaching of the theory of evolution in Minnesota's tax-supported schools.[57] Riley not only preached against evolution to overflow congregations in his own church for ten consecutive Sundays in 1926 but he also personally rented the Kenwood Armory in Minneapolis and told a throng of fifty-five hundred that Minnesotans should insist on "no State atheism" as well as "no State religion." [58] In addition, Riley was instrumental in bringing in "outside" speakers like William Jennings Bryan, whom he hailed as "the greatest and most godly layman that America has produced, and a statesman whose name history will link with that of Abraham Lincoln." [59]

The Anti-Evolution League of Minnesota, which was directed by Riley, concentrated on opposing the teaching of evolution at the University of Minnesota. After some wrangling, Riley finally presented the fundamentalist position in four lectures there late in November 1926. In the same year, Riley inspired an antievolution bill in the state legislature and with a squad of "flying fundamentalists" (Harry Rimmer, Gerald B. Winrod, Arthur I. Brown, and others) campaigned widely on its behalf. They covered two hundred cities and towns in the state, with Riley speaking in sixty-five of these communities.[60] He concluded his role in this endeavor with an address before the combined state legislatures emphasizing the Bryanesque theme that "the hand that writes the paycheck rules the school." [61] When the bill met defeat, Riley blamed the loss on the legislators, who were frightened by the "scholars" of the state. Riley called the latter "Darwinized . . . Germanized . . . deceived and faithless professors." [62] This was typical of the emotional overtones that surrounded the controversy as well as the tendency of fundamentalists, in a postwar atmosphere, to place heavy blame on the country from which many of the professors and higher critics had come.

In addition to his antievolution labors in Minnesota, Riley traveled widely, participating in numerous series of debates in the major cities of the country. His opponents included Maynard Shipley, the president of the Science League of America; Edward Adams Cantrell, field secretary of the Civil Liberties Union of America; and Charles C. Smith, president of the American Association for the Advancement of Atheism.[63] Although—perhaps even because—the debates were earnest and heated, many persons who attended seem to have done so for entertainment rather than for enlightenment. The debates, to which admission was charged, were normally decided by vote of the audience rather than by a small panel of judges. On one occasion such an arrangement was announced through the local newspaper. "The decision on who wins the debate will be on the loudness of the applause. It [the debate] will be in the Calvary Baptist Church, and many church members are expected to attend." [64] Such a format makes more understandable the fact that the crusading fundamentalist won all but one of the engagements. In fact, Riley, religious politician that he was, freely admitted that he went to considerable effort to pack each house with advocates and friends.[65]

In Riley's battle with Liberalism there was a second phase besides his antievolution endeavors which accentuated his qualities as a religious politician. This was his ardent endeavor to impose religious orthodoxy upon the Northern Baptist Convention. In his judgment, an unbridgeable gulf existed between Liberalism and orthodoxy; consequently Baptists must make a choice between the two. They could not have both.[66]

Riley believed that the roots of religious Liberalism were to be found in the rationalism and higher criticism of German scholars and included the "poison gas" of evolution which was but one manifestation of this "naturalistic, Bible-rejecting philosophy." [67] According to Riley, Liberalism made its impact on Baptists in America through the University of Chicago near the turn of the twentieth century. Largely responsible for this, he said, were industrialist John D. Rockefeller, whose wealth had supported the reorganization of the university in a liberal direction; William Rainey Harper, the school's president who had required no theological tests for its professors; and Prof. George Burnham Foster of Chicago's divinity school who had disseminated liberal ideas contrary to traditional Baptist teaching.[68] Gradually, in Riley's view, the theological virus had spread to other ministers, administrative officials, and a number of influential laymen. He bitterly resented not only the theology of Liberalism but also the "centralization" and "dictatorship" which liberal leaders supposedly brought to the nascent Northern Baptist Convention, organized in 1907.

As early as 1908, Riley suggested that the only solution to the tension between orthodoxy and Liberalism within the Baptist family was separation, which was preferable to constant quarreling.[69] The liberals were the ones who ought to leave, Riley thought, because they were intruding in the historical evangelical heritage. They were free to accept any theological conclusions they wished, but, once having adopted what Riley viewed as un-Baptistic and unbiblical beliefs, these "Unitarian Baptists," as he characterized the liberals, should depart to found a denomination of their own.[70] The liberals, of course, declined Riley's invitation. In fact, by 1914, even Riley admitted that they had captured the denominational schools and were threatening to control the convention. Thus, the battle lines were drawn.

At a preconvention conference on "Fundamentals of the Faith," convened by 150 clergymen and laymen at Buffalo, New York, in 1920, Riley was inordinately critical of liberal teachings in Baptist colleges and seminaries. He stated that three beliefs were endangered in these institutions: an inspired Bible, the deity of Jesus, and the fact of regeneration.[71] Riley's presentation led the conference to request the larger denomination to examine the beliefs of faculty members and trustees in Baptist schools concerning the cardinal doctrines of the faith. A committee appointed by the convention president, however, gave the schools a generally favorable report.[72] It was recommended that where there were legitimate grievances, complaints be addressed to individual institutions, because the larger denomination could not serve as a heresy court.

Rebuffed on the school issue, the fundamentalists sought to impose a doctrinal statement upon the denomination. The persistent Riley recommended in 1922 that the New Hampshire Confession of Faith, which he contended was both historical and Biblical, be adopted as an expression of Baptist views. A liberal spokesman, Cornelius Woelfkin of New York, shrewdly introduced a substitute motion affirming that "the New Testament is an all-sufficient ground for Baptist faith and practise and they need no other statement." [73] This motion won a resounding victory over Riley's, 1,264 votes to 637. Unhappy with the parliamentary victories of the liberals, and irritated even more by the moderation and lack of a program of such fundamentalist colleagues as J. C. Massee and J. Whitcomb Brougher, Riley gave increased support to the militant Baptist Bible Union—an international organization that included the United States and Canada—while still remaining in the denomination in order to continue his struggles there.

In 1924, Riley suggested unsuccessfully that a vote on denominational matters should be taken away from salaried servants of the Northern Baptist Convention.[74] He also failed in an attempt to impose a tighter doctrinal test on missionaries and to separate the Northern Baptists from the Federal Council of Churches, which they had joined in 1908. In 1926, Riley tried to make baptism by immersion a prerequisite to membership in churches of the denomination. Again he was defeated. Although Northern Baptists recognized that the Bible teaches baptism of believers by immersion only, they refused to legislate at this point, because they also believed strongly in the freedom of the local congregation.[75]

As fundamentalist frustration and factional bitterness grew, J. C. Massee, leader of the moderate fundamentalists, proposed observing a six-month truce between liberals and ultraconservatives and placing an emphasis on evangelism during that time. Riley would have no part of it. "This is not a battle," he emphasized. "It is a war from which there is no discharge." [76] Convinced that nine tenths of the laymen in his denomination were still within the evangelical camp, Riley continued the conflict, although by 1931 the peak of the initial phase had been reached.[77]

VI

During the time of the denominational encounter, Riley carried out the most ambitious project of his career. This was an attempt to unite the fundamentalists of the world on a theological rather than a denominational basis to propagate the orthodox faith and fight the inroads of Liberalism. This grandiose union, which came to be known as the World's Christian Fundamentals Association (WCFA), was founded in Philadelphia in 1919 but had its beginnings earlier. In the summer of 1918, Riley and other Biblicists met at Reuben Archer Torrey's home in Montrose, Pennsylvania, to establish a world fellowship of concerned evangelicals.[78] A new organization was formed, but there was no implementation of the original plans in the months that followed. The disappointed Riley, at this juncture, took matters into his own hands.

Working skillfully through the prophetic conference of 1918 which met in New York City, Riley laid the groundwork for the charter assembly of the WCFA by changing the emphasis of the next scheduled conference from prophecy to the great fundamentals of the faith. Some six thousand conservatives from the United States, Canada, and eight foreign countries gathered in Philadelphia from May 25 to June 1, 1919, for the meetings that gave birth to organized Fundamentalism. They heard the tall, eloquent Riley declare in his convening address: "The importance of this occasion exceeds the understanding of its originators. The future will look back to the World Conference on Christian Fundamentals . . . as an event of more historical moment than the nailing up, at Wittenberg, of Martin Luther's ninety-five theses. The hour has struck for the rise of a new Protestantism." [79]

A galaxy of other conservative spokesmen preached on major doctrinal subjects, making the conference, in the judgment of one writer, sound like "a latter-day version of *The Fundamentals*." [80] Several specific decisions were made. The association adopted a nine-point Confession of Faith drafted by the irrepressible Riley and put in its final form by a committee headed by Torrey. The affirmation included a belief in the verbal inerrancy of the Scriptures and the personal, premillennial, imminent return of Christ, although Riley insisted that no theological "hobby horses" were being ridden. Other affirmations were: one God in three persons, the deity of Jesus, the sinfulness of man, the substitutionary atonement, the bodily resurrection of Jesus, justification by faith, and the bodily resurrection of the just and the unjust.

Membership in the WCFA was to be open to individuals and organizations alike provided they, or their representatives, signed the doctrinal statement and made an annual gift of one, five, or ten dollars. The one-dollar fee enabled a person to become an associate member; the five-dollar contribution gave voting and office-holding rights; and the ten-dollar sum granted membership to a Bible conference, Bible school, church, or similar organization, with one vote for every one hundred members or fraction thereof.[81] Riley was elected president of the newly organized body, and a board of directors, never to be less than eleven members, was created.[82] Several standing committees were also established to correlate the work of Bible schools, theological seminaries and colleges, religious magazines and periodicals, missionary societies, and Bible conferences. At the conclusion of the initial meeting, Riley led a group of fourteen speakers and singers on a seven-thousand-mile, cross-country tour of three-to-six-day conferences in eighteen of the major cities of America and Canada. This kind of outreach through Bible conferences, under team leadership, proved to be one of the major accomplishments of the association. In the first six years of the life of the WCFA, Riley arranged no less than 250 such meetings to propagate the fundamentalist cause and, in so doing, raised some $200,000 to support the work of the federation.

Within two years after the founding of the association, however, the spirit of optimism that had characterized the earlier days began to decline, and Fundamentalism entered into a defensive posture.[83] This was reflected in the new stance of the association. Originally concerned with setting forth the evangelical faith, it became increasingly absorbed with the controversy over evolution. It supported several excursions into the South that were designed to outlaw the teaching of Darwinism in tax-supported schools, with Riley leading the way. He encountered the advocates of evolution in Tennessee, Kentucky, Texas, and Virginia. Between 1921 and 1929, antievolution measures were introduced in twenty state legislatures but were approved only in Oklahoma, Florida, Tennessee, Mississippi, and Arkansas.[84] The WCFA devoted much of its annual meeting in Fort Worth in 1923 to a "trial" of three Methodist institutions for teaching evolution and, significantly, appointed William Jennings Bryan as its attorney at the famed Scopes Trial in Dayton, Tennessee, in 1925. Bryan, like his celebrated opponent, Clarence Darrow, chose to serve without remuneration.

Although the distracting controversy over evolution appeared to monopolize the attention and strength of the WCFA, it was also active in other areas. It formed several state organizations as well as regional headquarters in nine different sections of the United States and Canada to provide a measure of cohesiveness for the loosely knit assembly. It also printed a series of Sunday school Bible courses, prepared a reading list of "orthodox books" on vital subjects of the Christian faith, and published a list of fifty-one "safe" fundamentalist schools and colleges.[85] Other WCFA plans failed. These included establishing a system of conservative colleges in every state and every Canadian province; a Fundamentalist Foundation for the advancement of fundamentalist education comparable in another sphere to the Rockefeller Institute; and a gift of two million dollars from some wealthy layman for the purpose of establishing a premillennial theological seminary. In perspective, the most obvious results of the WCFA were the vast number of Riley-directed Bible conferences, the antievolution forays, and the well-publicized annual meetings attended for the most part by the already convinced.

By 1927, attendance at the annual WCFA gathering had begun to decline, reflecting in part the loss of early enthusiasm as well as a prior loyalty given their own denominations by many conservatives, especially Southern Baptists. Riley resigned the presidency two years later but continued as executive secretary. Thereafter the association went steadily downhill, notwithstanding the fact that it continued to function into the early 1950's. Among the several reasons for this loss of influence was the general nature of American society in the 1920's. It was marked by disillusionment, the impact of naturalism, and the sort of skepticism represented by H. L. Mencken and Sinclair Lewis. Robert T. Handy has pointed out convincingly that in this decade a serious spiritual depression came to American Protestantism before any shadow of economic depression had been raised.[86] The failure of the WCFA must be interpreted within this context.

In addition, the association itself was beset with particular problems. In the first place, despite attempts to the contrary, the organization never lived up to its promise of being a world movement. Its base of operations and membership was in the United States, with limited assistance from some Canadians like T. T. Shields and his disciples. This was supporting evidence that Fundamentalism was essentially an American phenomenon with limited missionary influence in other countries. Secondly, even in this country the federation itself was more of a goal in the mind of founder Riley than a reality that actually bound all fundamentalists together. Some postmillennialists did not join, for example, and during the conflicts of the 1920's a larger number of premillennialist fundamentalists gave their loyalties to conservative groups within their own denominations rather than to the more inclusive but less tangible WCFA.

In the third place, some fundamentalists resented the fact that Baptist leaders came to dominate the organization, although a number of Methodists and Presbyterians played responsible roles. Fourthly, the identification of the WCFA with the evolution controversy tended to damage its long-range effectiveness. When the crisis over Darwin's hypothesis had passed, there appeared to be no unifying cause (although an attempt was made to draw the members together through prayer for a worldwide revival). Furthermore, despite several technical victories, the fundamentalists came out of the struggle over evolution with a tarnished image, partly because of Riley's defeat in the Minnesota legislature.

Fifthly, and most importantly, the excessive individualism of the leaders of the WCFA undermined the general cause. Strong-willed, independent, stubborn men, masters of their own domains, they frequently found it difficult to cooperate with one another. Even Riley regretted what he called "a guerilla method of warfare" and commented that "men of strong conviction are often men of independent action. Independence leads to leadership, and leadership to division." [87] Nevertheless, Riley broke with J. Frank Norris, criticized J. C. Massee for his moderation, grew cool toward T. T. Shields, had limited contact with John Roach Straton, and never met J. Gresham Machen.[88] When illness laid him low for seven months in 1924, Riley found it increasingly difficult to exercise control over some of his provincial colleagues. And the death of William Jennings

Bryan in 1925 increased the sectional emphasis and division as each of several contenders for his top fundamentalist mantle struggled to champion his own cause.[89] The organization that had aspired to world influence now had trouble securing a united fellowship in one country among its own leaders.

Finally, with the arrival of the depression, new issues arose that diverted the attention of the nation and its people to more immediate needs. What remained when Paul W. Rood of Turlock, California, succeeded Riley as president of the WCFA was a rapidly diminishing mailing list. In 1935, the seventy-four-year-old, once-optimistic Riley drew upon his familiar source of authority to remark wistfully, "I even I, only am left." [90]

Frustrated by his unsuccessful attempt to pull the Northern Baptist Convention toward Fundamentalism, and unhappy with the ineffectiveness of the WCFA, Riley still continued to struggle for the ultraconservative cause in his later years. He opposed a minimal educational requirement for ordination as set forth by leaders of his denomination. To him this was another threat to the independence of the local church and an attempt to undermine the influence of Bible schools like his own Northwestern.[91] Riley believed that competence, character, and a call from God were the basic qualifications for ordination. He emphasized repeatedly that Dwight L. Moody was not ordained and that such evangelical leaders as Charles H. Spurgeon, G. Campbell Morgan, and George W. Truett were not highly educated men.

Riley also advocated bipartisan elections in the Northern Baptist Convention, suggesting that for every office there be a liberal candidate and a conservative candidate. He was persuaded that, by such a procedure, there would be a return to orthodoxy within five years.[92] As late as 1938, Riley wrote that Modernism was breaking down and liberal schools existed only because of endowments by orthodox backers of earlier years.[93] But this was whistling in the dark. Five years later Riley capitulated in his attempts to control the denomination, recognizing that his theological opponents had gained control of offices, properties, and publications.[94] Thereafter he concentrated almost exclusively on his interests in Minnesota.

Through the influence of the many graduates of Northwestern Schools who held Baptist pastorates in the state, as well as through local application of his bipartisan policy, Riley was elected president of the Minnesota Baptist convention in 1944 and 1945. Under his direction this body severed its working relationship with the Northern Baptist Convention, eventually necessitating the creation of another organization to represent denominational interests in Minnesota.[95] Riley threw his weight behind the establishment of the Fellowship of Minnesota Conservative Baptist Churches, supported the work of the Conservative Baptist Foreign Missionary Society, and in 1947 looked with favor upon the creation of the Conservative Baptist Association of America. Although his own church technically remained in the Northern Baptist Convention, in actuality it became an independent congregation, dividing its missionary and denominational gifts in a variety of directions.

Disturbed, however, that he belonged to a church which nominally was a member of the Convention, Riley in the last year of his life wrote to its president to relinquish his personal membership in the Northern Baptist Convention. The self-appointed defender of the faith declared that the only alternative to the reformation of an apostate body was separation from it. He wrote: "I should be ashamed to die in the fellowship that seemed to me un-Biblical, and consequently un-Baptistic. . . . I believe this to be divinely inspired direction." [96]

Having concluded his pastoral labors, and having settled his business with his denomination, Riley spent his last days dreaming of a prosperous future for his schools. It was in such a mood, and again convinced of divine guidance, that Riley called Billy Graham to his side on that hot afternoon in August 1947.

VII

Viewing the life of William Bell Riley in perspective, one is impressed at first by the qualities of independence and indefatigability. Here was a man who earned his own education, preached his own ordination sermon, delivered the address at the dedication of his rebuilt church, shaped his congregations in his own image, founded his own schools, fought his denomination, edited his own magazines, chose his own educational successor, and, for all practical purposes, wrote his own biography. Some might equate such independence with self-centeredness. For Riley, however, it was merely fulfilling the goals to which he believed God had called him. This independence in a dominant personality made it difficult for others to work with him—a difficulty not uncommon among leaders of Fundamentalism.

Boundless energy was perhaps Riley's most remarkable trait. At one time in the mid-1920's, for example, he was simultaneously minister of a large downtown church that had just completed a half-million-dollar building program, president of a growing Bible school, preacher in cities far removed from Minneapolis, debater on a popular lecture circuit, editor of several religious publications, would-be reformer of his denominational family, vice-president of the Baptist Bible Union of which he was a charter member, and president, executive secretary, and chairman of the conference committee of the WCFA. His unquestioned sincerity and deep belief in conservative causes undoubtedly moved him to such arduous and persistent effort. His psychological motivations, however—like those of most of us—may also have been mixed. For instance, he may have had the need to dominate others.

However one may react to his zealous, austere, but also sometimes kindly, personality, Riley did much to point the nature of Protestantism in Minnesota in a conservative direction, especially among the Baptists. His influence as a forceful, perhaps even great, preacher was considerable, but the most tangible conservative impact he made was through the graduates of his schools who came to hold pastorates in the state. By the year of Riley's death there were nearly two thousand alumni of the three institutions he had founded. No less than 70 percent of the 125 Baptist churches in Minnesota at the time were served by pastors trained at these schools.[97] This leadership had enabled Riley to control the state convention. Since he had moved that body away from the larger denomination, emphasizing the independence of the local church and charging the Northern Baptist Convention with centralization and dictatorship, Riley also was largely responsible for the fragmentation of the Baptists that followed. The path of independence led to the division of Minnesota Baptists into six groups: American Baptists; the Fellowship of Minnesota Conservative Baptist Churches; the New Testament Association of Independent Baptist Churches (a split from the previous group), supplementing the previously existing General Association of Regular Baptists; the Baptist General Conference (Swedish Baptists); and the North American Conference (German Baptists).[98] The latter five groups share a common conservative theological denominator but possess varying attitudes toward cooperation with those of differing Christian beliefs. Ironically, much of the problem of "separation" or "nonseparation" centers in attitudes toward Billy Graham. The ultraconservative New Testament Association of Independent Baptist Churches, for instance, condemns him for his "ecumenical evangelism." [99]

This marked division among the Baptists of Minnesota also contributed to the decline of Riley's schools, although other factors were also involved. These included the fading agrarian-rural nature of the Upper Midwest, with an attendant emphasis on higher-quality education, and the resignation of Billy Graham. Riley's schools reached their peak enrollment just before Graham's departure. Students in this upsurge represented a broad spectrum of evangelical, Youth for Christ types rather than individuals with strong Baptist connections. Literally hundreds wanted to learn to be evangelists like Graham. When he left, there was no comparable charismatic figure to draw such young people.

At any rate, of the old Northwestern Schools, the Bible and Missionary Training School and the Seminary have ceased to exist. The former property of Northwestern College was sold to the state and now houses the Metropolitan State Junior College. The new Northwestern Bible—Arts and Sciences—Vocational Training College, founded in 1972, is located in Roseville, a suburb of St. Paul, with an enrollment of approximately seven hundred students.

While admittedly Riley did much to move Protestantism in a conservative direction in Minnesota, he must also be held largely accountable for the present division and confusion that exists among American and various shades of conservative Baptists of the state. In evaluating Riley's contributions, some would also point to areas of influence upon Billy Graham: the religious and social conservatism, depth of conviction, businesslike approach to evangelism and concern for evangelical education. At the same time it must be recognized that Riley and Graham knew each other only three years at the most in the mid-1940's, and their personal contacts during that period were limited. Furthermore, there were differences between the two men, the most notable being Graham's willingness to cooperate with people of various Christian beliefs. Part of this is due to Graham's need to gain a broad base of support for his successful crusades.[100] Riley worked with men of other denominations but normally only with those who were theologically fundamentalist. Riley was publicly critical of other religions in ways that Graham has not been. Although Graham liked Riley and was encouraged by him early in his career, the evidence suggests that any influence Riley had on Graham was not significant in reference to Graham's success in or approach to evangelism. Any influence would have to be measured in some other respect. In a letter to the author, Graham confirms this evaluation:

In my judgment Dr. W. B. Riley was a man of great integrity, high principles, and deep religious convictions. He was head and shoulders above many of his contemporaries in the fundamentalist movement. Contrary to what some people may think, I did not know him very well. I heard him preach a number of times. I talked to him privately on several occasions. It is true that he chose me to be his successor but I think quite largely on the basis of having heard me preach at various conferences. I do not think that his impact on me was very significant in regards to evangelism. However, I do think that I learned a great deal from some of the mistakes I thought he had made. I learned something from him concerning uncompromising convictions, courage, and above all, personal integrity.[101]

R. S. McBirnie, writing in 1952, expressed his belief that the most enduring result of Riley's labors was the conservative nature of the Minnesota Baptist state convention.[102] Although this achievement may have been the most tangible product of his life, the most consequential seems to have been his vision of an inclusive fellowship of fundamentalists on a world basis. He was unable to realize his dreams for reasons that have already been considered, but Riley awakened ultraconservatives to the possibility of a united strength upon which others might build. In 1941, when the WCFA had reached a low point, Carl McIntire organized the American Council of Churches (ACC). A year later Harold J. Ockenga, J. Elwin Wright, and Carl F. H. Henry led in establishing the National Association of Evangelicals (NAE). These two organizations agreed doctrinally but were divided in method. The former required members to separate from denominations or churches affiliated with the Federal Council of the Churches of Christ in America; the latter did not.[103] While these were national rather than world organizations (as the WCFA proved to be in reality), they had caught the vision of a union of conservative forces. Riley had laid the foundation; others built upon it.

This contribution, along with his other influences, helped make Riley the most important fundamentalist minister of his generation. His impact was more extensive than that of the flamboyant John Roach Straton, whose outreach was primarily limited to the New York City area; he was less vituperative and more respected than the violent J. Frank Norris; he offered a program of administrative leadership that surpassed that of the warmhearted moderate, J. C. Massee; and his popular following and national contacts excelled those of the more scholarly J. Gresham Machen. Only the prominent layman, William Jennings Bryan, eclipsed Riley as the personification of Fundamentalism in his day. Indeed, upon the death of Bryan, Riley was widely considered his unofficial successor.

Despite this high standing among fundamentalists, Riley had limitations that hindered his own cause. He possessed an inflexible theology, a censorious spirit, a dominating personality, and misplaced emphases, causing one of his contemporaries to write: "Fundamentalists of the Riley brand are our best infidelity road-builders and guideposts." [104] More crucial than such limitations was the fact that Riley was moving against the strong tide of theological and social change. His aims were often vetoed by the choices and decisions of a more liberal society.

CHAPTER FIVE

J. C. Massee

MODERATE FUNDAMENTALIST

IN THE WRITING of American religious history, J. C. Massee has been notably neglected. This is deeply ironical because Massee claimed to know more about the origin, progress, and outcome of the Modernist-Fundamentalist Controversy in the Northern (later American) Baptist Convention than any other individual.[1] Whether or not one agrees with Massee's claim (a strong case exists to support it), many aspects of his life and thought are extremely important, especially since they reflect a pronounced individualism within the fundamentalist ranks. Such individualism has not been sufficiently recognized by the historians and theologians who have dealt with the turbulent days of religious controversy in the early decades of this century. The temptation has been to stereotype the fundamentalists, to identify them with ignorance, hatred, emotional excess, doctrinal conformity, and violence in thought and language without qualification. Massee's life illustrates the danger of such categorizing. While he was certainly a fundamentalist, he was not a "wooden literalist" whose response could always be predicted. This was no more dramatically true than in the heat of the denominational conflict when his leadership of the conservative forces took some unexpected turns. Such surprises demonstrated the distance between Massee and men like Norris, Straton, and Riley.

I

The life of Jasper Cortenus Massee spanned a full ninety-three years.[2] He was born on November 22, 1871, in Marshallville, Georgia (Macon County), the last of thirteen children, ten of whom lived. He died on March 27, 1965, in Atlanta, after a varied career in the North and the South as pastor-evangelist, revivalist, author, teacher, and the denominational leader who served as the first general of the organized fundamentalist forces. When he began his pastoral ministry in a small church, his salary was thirty-five dollars a month plus rent and fuel; when he concluded his labors, he retired to a new suburban home made possible by a farewell gift from his last congregation, one of the largest Baptist churches in the country. When he began his service as denominational leader, he was hailed as the hope of the fundamentalist cause; when he concluded his work, there were some who viewed him as an apostate to the movement, to be classed with the archenemy, Harry Emerson Fosdick. Between such contrasts of life and interpretation, this controversial figure went about his business contending for the faith "once delivered unto the saints." Although he was a quiet man personally, his life was rarely placid.

Massee's parents, Drewry Washington Massee and Susan Elizabeth Bryan Massee, came from eminent families in Marshallville, a rural town in west-central Georgia known for its camellias and for the richness of its neighboring cotton plantations. Both the Massee and Bryan clans emanated from Scotch-Irish backgrounds, although the Massees pointed to even earlier beginnings in England and France. The ancestors of each family settled in North Carolina following the Revolutionary War and moved into Georgia early in the nineteenth century. J. C. Massee's father "read" medicine in his hometown and gained repute as one of three physicians at Andersonville, the notorious Confederate military prison just twenty-three miles from the family homestead. His mother, daughter of a prosperous businessman-politician, a woman of culture and charm, was a distant relative of William Jennings Bryan.

Conservative influences in town, home, and church played steadily on Massee's early life. Economically, the community depended on Negro labor and the plantation system. Politically, the people of Marshallville were Whigs who followed John Calhoun rather than Andrew Jackson, although after the days of Reconstruction, like countless communities in the South, they supported the Democratic Party. Religiously, the faith of Massee's parents had its source not only in the orthodox Christian tradition but also in that of the Primitive (Hard Shell) Baptist variety.[3] Later they became Southern Baptists, and it was in a church of this persuasion that the last of the

R. Quinn Pugh, Bel Air, Md.

J. C. Massee

children of the Drewry W. Massees made his first public profession of faith.

J. C. Massee was converted at the age of nine or ten in the Marshallville Baptist Church. He "went forward" at a Sunday morning service conducted by a visiting minister, probably one of the peripatetic revivalists so familiar to that section of the country. His mother, thinking him too young for such a decision, initially held him back. But an uncle intervened and persuaded her to let the boy make his own response.[4] It was his first significant independent decision. As a country boy, Massee was self-conscious, sensitive, and shy, frequently depressed by the monotony and the toil of farm work. But his developing intellectual abilities and the sacrifices of his parents provided him with the cherished opportunity of gaining a college education. He entered Mercer University, forty miles to the north of his home, in 1888. There his public-speaking abilities came to the fore and he served as anchor man on the school's debating team. Although he then had no plans for the ministry, his religious interests continued to expand. It came, therefore, as no surprise to his closest friends when he declared his intention to become a preacher. Upon graduation in 1892 he spent a year as teacher and principal of the school in Abbeville, Georgia, probably with the hope of earning money for a seminary education. Ordained and married in December 1893, he served the Baptist Church in Kissimmee, Florida, until 1896. Following the early death of his first wife, Massee remarried in June of 1896, and with his family, moved that fall to Louisville, Kentucky, where for a single year he attended Southern Baptist Theological Seminary.[5]

The year at the seminary was a hectic one. The Whitsitt Controversy, then at its height, brought Massee into touch with religious conflict for the first time. William H. Whitsitt, the seminary's third president, was being assailed for an article he had written declaring that "Roger Williams was probably baptized by sprinkling rather than immersion and that immersion of believers among English Baptists was 'invented' by Edward Barbour in 1641." [6] Many of the Baptists of the South arose in a fury of protest, although the faculty, led by John R. Sampey, steadfastly defended the president, stressing his integrity, scholarship, orthodoxy, and right to carry on research.[7] A leading protagonist against Whitsitt was E. E. Eaton, editor of *The Western Recorder*, the Baptist paper of Kentucky. One day in a class taught by Sampey, Massee ingenuously presented a news item from Eaton's publication. He was astounded when this made him the object of Sampey's verbal wrath before his fellow students. Until that time he had naïvely believed that all Baptists loved and agreed with all other Baptists. He did not know that at a meeting of the Long Run Association, Sampey had run across the church floor, shaken his fist under Eaton's nose, and shouted, "When Greek meets Greek, then comes the tug of war, and you now meet your Greek." Thereafter, in true gladiatorial fashion, they continued their "fraternal discussion." [8]

Unhappy in the midst of such an atmosphere and hard pressed financially, Massee accepted a call to the Baptist Church in Orlando, Florida, where he served for two years. This was the beginning of a long, uninterrupted pastoral trail, which led him to prominent churches in both the North and the South, concluding with an influential ministry at Tremont Temple Baptist Church in Boston from 1922 to 1929. In addition to the congregations mentioned, Massee served the following churches: The Baptist Church, Lancaster, Kentucky, 1899–1901; Park Avenue Baptist Church, Mansfield, Ohio, 1901–1903; Tabernacle Baptist Church, Raleigh, North Carolina, 1903–1908; First Baptist Church, Chattanooga, Tennessee, 1908–1913; First Baptist Church, Dayton, Ohio, 1913–1919; and Baptist Temple, Brooklyn, New York, 1920–1922.

After his pastoral career, Massee spent nine years as a Bible conference speaker and an evangelist-at-large at a time when revivalism on a national scale was at its lowest ebb. He traveled widely throughout the country, especially in the North and the West. During this time Massee held "union meetings," primarily in the great urban centers of the nation. These services were characterized by interdenominational sponsorship, prearranged attendances (special groups on given nights), an emphasis on music (his son, William C. Massee, was his song leader for several years), interest-provoking sermon topics, evangelistic pleas, and the signing of cards by members of his congregations promising to forsake "unchristian" practices (e.g., dancing and cardplaying). He also regularly invited young people to pledge themselves "to Christ and to purity," usually at the conclusion of his oft-preached sermon, "What Is Wrong with Petting Parties?" On the Bible conference trail, Massee was well known at Winona Lake, Indiana, where he was a regular platform speaker for twenty years.

Massee concluded his full-time public ministry by holding a guest lectureship in homiletics at the Eastern Baptist Theological Seminary in Philadelphia from 1938 to 1941.[9] He spent his retirement years in his attractive suburban Atlanta home. At the age of eighty-seven, in December of 1958, he returned to the Marshallville Baptist Church for a service celebrating the sixty-fifth anniversary of his ordination. After a ministry that had taken him to forty-one states, all sections of Canada, and several countries in Europe, the fundamentalist warrior had come back home to give an account of his stewardship.

II

Several emphases characterized the long and varied ministry of J. C. Massee. Initially, he was a fundamentalist in theology, with a thoroughgoing insistence upon the supernatural that set him apart doctrinally from those of liberal persuasion. His own belief was simply stated:

> I believe that all that is involved in and revealed through the Old Testament was fulfilled in Jesus Christ, my Savior and Lord; that the New Testament scriptures reveal every essential fact about His person, His ministry of reconciliation with God and His Lordship in the life of the believer and of the church. I believe that He was born supernaturally, lived sinlessly, died vicariously, arose bodily, ascended into heaven, sent forth the Holy Spirit and will surely come again according to His promise. I accept final authority concerning the inspiration of the scripture in its own statement, II Timothy 3:16. I crave and rejoice in the fellowship of all like-minded believers in Christ Jesus as Savior and Lord.[10]

Such a completely evangelical declaration, however, did not mean that he agreed in every detail with his conservative brethren. While in general he accepted the famous five points of Fundamentalism adopted by the General Assembly of the Presbyterian Church in the U.S.A. in 1910, he placed a different emphasis on the crucial matter of Biblical authority. He never referred to the Scriptures as inerrant, and only on rare occasions did he speak of them as infallible. His view of inspiration was more pragmatic in nature. For him the Bible served the purpose for which God gave it to men, that is, it revealed the nature of God and the longings of man in such a satisfactory way that man might find God and hold conscious, personal communion with him.[11] Consequently, Massee believed that the Scriptures were authoritative in life, not as a mechanical tribunal of judgment, but as a vibrant source, profitable by their own declaration for teaching, reproof, correction, and instruction in righteousness.[12] To assert more than this was to run the risk of claiming more for the Bible than it claimed for itself. When once asked if even a fundamentalist then did not necessarily accept the Bible from cover to cover exactly as it was written, Massee replied: "Fundamentalists differ somewhat even among themselves. There are some, perhaps, who are not quite as liberal as I am. . . . I say that it is inspired as to what it records. . . . That record is perfect for the purpose for which the record was given. The purpose is declared in II Timothy 3:16." [13] Because he held this basic conviction, it was natural when Massee set forth his own five Baptist fundamentals of the faith that initially he should declare his belief in "the inspiration of the Bible, a real revelation of God to be interpreted by the individual and adapted to all sorts and conditions of men." [14] Significant were the absence of the words "inerrancy" and "infallible," the stress on a real revelation, and the central place left for personal interpretation. Massee's other Baptist fundamentals were: the essential deity of Jesus Christ; the spiritual nature of the church, composed only of those who have been born again by the Holy Spirit; the divine call to the ministry; and the emphasis on evangelism. In other theological areas, Massee was a pronounced premillennialist; a Calvinist, but not of the Princeton variety, as his theory of inspiration attests; and a Chalcedonian in Christological belief who nevertheless so stressed the oneness of God's nature that he found it necessary to defend himself against the charge of Sabellianism.[15]

A second characteristic of Massee's ministry, and certainly the dominant one, was a consuming passion for evangelism which precluded for him, at least, a major emphasis upon a social gospel. Whether in the local church, at Bible conferences and summer assemblies on the evangelical Chautauqua circuit, or in the midst of "union meetings," his whole program was geared to win people to the Christian faith. His evangelism was different from that of many of his fundamentalist contemporaries, not so much in its theological essence (although he did have a greater doctrinal stress than they) as in its noncondemning note of pleading.

> The ministry to which we are committed . . . is a ministry of reconciliation not of denunciation or condemnation. . . . For me there is an instinctive drawing away from any gospel of threats, of appeal to fear, to harsh judgment, to the accompaniment of harsh voice, pounding of pulpits, clenched fists, and glaring eyes. My gospel has a different flavor. . . . In the Book I do not find a single instance . . . when Jesus ever exposed any sinner's sin to anyone except to the sinner himself; and that exposure was always scented with the radiant fragrance of love and forgiveness.[16]

Also because of this conviction, Massee spent a minimum of time in the pulpit berating the "heresy" of either men or institutions, such as the Roman Catholic Church, or of religious movements, including Liberalism itself. He stated: "I am unwilling to close the door between me and them [Roman Catholics] by any attack or any system of organized opposition by which Protestantism shall be arrayed against Catholicism." [17] Furthermore, there was less emotion in Massee's meetings than in those of such flamboyant colleagues as J. Frank Norris and John Roach Straton. Emotion was there, of course, even by Massee's own admission (how could one experience forgiveness and not be joyous?), but he sought to steer a sane, middle path between "the Moody-Sankey type of emotional evangelism and the so-called social service type." [18]

Massee's desire to reach as many people as possible with the message in which he believed resulted in a distinctive attitude toward those who might receive the ordinance of Communion. He confessed he was utterly at variance with the tradition of excluding the non-Christian from the observance of the Lord's Supper. "I'd fill the galleries of every church . . . with men and women to partake of his body and blood. I would let them partake of it until they asked the question 'Why?' and heard the story of the revealed love." [19] This was an unusual attitude for one who had known the practice of "closed Communion" in the religiously conservative South. It was also remarkably akin to Stoddardeanism in late seventeenth-century and early eighteenth-century New England.[20]

The most obvious result of Massee's evangelistic outreach was a large number of converts wherever he served. At Tremont Temple, for instance, some twenty-five hundred joined the church during his seven-year ministry, raising the membership to nearly four thousand, the highest in the congregation's history.[21] When the pulpit committee invited Massee to Tremont Temple, he said he could not promise to fill the second balcony. They replied, "If you will keep the baptistry filled, that is all we ask." Actually, he did both. His Sunday morning and evening congregations consistently averaged between two and three thousand persons, and during his seven-year ministry, 2,489 individuals joined the church, 1,414 coming by Baptism. Furthermore, substantially over a million dollars was received through freewill offerings.

Although he was successful in evangelism, there were times when Massee's assumptions about his converts appeared naïve. On one occasion, for instance, his description of their Christian life seemed unrealistic: "When the penalty of sin is paid the practice of sin is discontinued." [22] Taken literally, that statement would place Massee within the camp of Christian perfectionists, although that was never his actual theological location. He was precise, however, as to where he stood on the Social Gospel. Massee said: "The regeneration of the social order . . . can be accomplished only by the regeneration of . . . the human units who make up the social body. . . . The preachers who are going about preaching the gospel of social service are preaching foolishness. . . . Before industry can be Christianized, man must be Christianized." [23] Such an attitude was typical of fundamentalist leadership despite frequent statements on a variety of social issues.

Whatever chance existed for Massee to link a broad social gospel with his emphasis on evangelism was rudely dispelled in the early days of his pastorate in Raleigh in 1903. While exegeting the Book of Job at his midweek service, Massee came upon a passage in which Job declared he had never oppressed a wage earner. Applying this portion of Scripture to contemporary life, Massee stated boldly:

> I think the people of this country have a whole lot to answer for the way they treat the negro [sic]. . . . The black man should be treated as a human being. I don't wonder that they steal when they are paid such small salaries, not enough to support a family; it is grinding that man down, and in the sight of God one stands condemned who does it.[24]

Massee's people took his remarks quietly, but the editor of one of the local newspapers, Josephus Daniels, later Secretary of the United States Navy, gave the comments front-page coverage, accusing the clergyman of making incendiary remarks.. The headlines read: "Preacher Says He Does Not Blame the Negro for Stealing," while news accounts declared that never in the history of the city had the utterance of any minister called forth such universal condemnation. An editorial concluded: "His [Massee's] language is an outrage upon them [his congregation] and the community. If the Tabernacle Church does not want another pastor very promptly we shall be disappointed." Massee held his ground although provoked by the published statement of another clergyman who made it clear that "this is what happens when a minister goes outside of his mission to preach the gospel." [25]

The newspaper attack on Massee continued editorially for several weeks. His name was never spelled "Massee" but "M. Asse." When Dr. Bassett of Trinity College wrote in the *South Atlantic Quarterly* supporting Massee's position, an editor of the *News and Observer* commented: "Strange that the two southern white men who have made the biggest fools of themselves in the last ten years have the same three letters in the middle of their names." [26]

On the Sunday after that significant midweek service, Massee went to church not knowing whether the doors would be open or closed to him. They were open. An overflow crowd had gathered, and Massee conducted the morning service without reference to the controversy. At the conclusion of the worship experience, the chairman of the deacons publicly assured Massee of his full trust, support, and love. He then invited others of a similar mind to come to the front of the sanctuary to tell the minister so. Hundreds came forward to pledge Massee their loyalty. Years later Massee called this day the real beginning of his ministry. Nevertheless, despite Massee's insight and courage on this occasion, despite his raising of funds while in Boston to build a new school for blacks in Marshallville, and despite his continued friendship for individual members of the black community (although he declined to eat with them), this was the closest he ever came to a significant social application of the faith that he loved.[27] It was this lack in many fundamentalists which caused Edward J. Carnell to write:

> In due time fundamentalism made one capital mistake . . . the fundamentalists failed to develop an affirmative world view. They made no effort to connect their convictions with the wider problems of general culture. They remained content with the single virtue of negating modernism. When modernism decayed, therefore, fundamentalism lost its status. Neo-orthodoxy proved too complex for it to assess. It became an army without a cause. It had no unifying principle.[28]

A pietistic morality in his own life as well as in his preaching content was a third characteristic of J. C. Massee. If he did not regularly condemn broad economic, racial, and political injustices, he did have firm words of criticism for selected personal practices. This made him an outspoken opponent of those who smoked tobacco, drank alcoholic beverages, played cards, attended the theater, wore gaudy apparel, or engaged in what he felt were sins of sexual promiscuity. His opposition to smoking and drinking was based on the physical harm he thought these practices caused the body.[29] Furthermore, in his judgment, intoxicating beverages disrupted homes and contributed to the breeding of crime. He regarded as mistaken, however, those zealous "reformers" who insisted upon substituting grape juice for fermented wine in the Communion service.[30] He also declined an invitation from William Jennings Bryan to head a movement in Massachusetts to organize all Christians in signing a pledge not to purchase liquor from bootleggers. Massee replied naïvely: "I refused on the ground that I do not think it necessary for Christians to sign any kind of a pledge. The spirit of God within them would make buying liquor of a bootlegger or from any other source impossible." [31]

Cardplaying, to Massee, was a waste of time and a temptation to gambling, and he claimed that the theater, through sordid commercialism, idealized immorality, self-indulgence, and worldliness. During his pastorate at Raleigh, Massee engaged in animated correspondence with a former pastor of his church in that city, Thomas Dixon, Jr., who had become a playwright. Dixon protested a sermon of Massee's that condemned the modern drama. In replying, Dixon referred to Massee as "my benighted little brother" and a "purveyor of ignorance," the majority of whose uneducated church members needed the theater most—the world of dreams, poetry, beauty, and idealism—to balance their hard, colorless lives. Massee replied firmly that it had been twenty years since Dixon visited Raleigh, so what did he know about the constituency of the congregation! Furthermore, asked the opponent of the theater, what kind of stage idealism was it that led one of its actors to declare flippantly, "Damned if it ain't good to be decent!" [32]

Massee's heaviest broadsides were reserved for "sins" of a sexual nature. Dancing, petting parties, birth control, and especially divorce were his favorite targets. Dancing was sensuous; petting parties, referred to by Massee as "America's favorite indoor sport," cheapened and robbed marriage of its romance and mystery; birth control for the deliberate purpose of refusing to have children was "legalized concubinage"; and divorce was the greatest of all social evils. Massee declined to marry divorced individuals unless they were the innocent parties in separations brought about by adultery. He preached that "caressing, kissing, hugging become familiar pastimes of many young men and women who should be put in straightjackets until they learn some sense of decency . . . and modesty." [33]

Massee's perennial solution to avoid indulgence in such personal sins was the familiar call to conversion followed by a stress on the centrality of the home, regular devotional experiences, the avoidance of clandestine associations, and, above all, the "practice of the presence." "Whatever, in the light of the Scriptures, you can do with a good conscience as in the [bodily] presence of Christ it is safe and right to do." [34] This he saw as the acid test of all friendships, associations, and indulgences. Even in practicing the presence, however, the individualistic nature of Massee's Christianity came to the fore. An enthusiastic church member came to him and proposed that they organize a society around Charles M. Sheldon's famous question, "What would Jesus do?" Massee declined, convinced that this was an individual matter and an organization would quickly turn it into both an inquisition and a ritualistic form of piety.[35]

A fourth trait of Massee's ministry was a remarkable preaching ability linked with a flair for the dramatic and that indefinable quality known as showmanship. Whatever one felt about the theology of Massee's sermons, they were carefully prepared and skillfully delivered, reflecting earnestness, sincerity, and eloquence. The minister, of course, could not be separated from his messages. Big, straight, well proportioned, weighing 225 pounds, standing six feet two inches tall beneath a heavy flock of snow-white hair (after middle age), the ruddy-complexioned Massee made an imposing impression. In the pulpit his black cutaway coat, gray striped trousers, and dark four-in-hand tie added to this appearance of distinction.[36]

When Massee came to Boston, Samuel Lindsay, who had known him as a fellow pastor in Brooklyn, commented that although Massee was devoid of sensational features ("he talks quietly and smiles quietly"), he viewed him as the greatest religious publicist in the country. "He knows how to sell religion." [37] Selling religion for Massee meant skillfully handling the large congregations drawn by his person and message. With these throngs he could be alternately thought-provoking and dogmatic. One moment he would stimulate reflection by stating, "God is supreme and absolute personality"; another moment he would declare with conviction, "The devil would never have repealed the eighteenth amendment, the politicians who are more devilish than the devil did that." [38] Selling religion meant, for Massee, linking it with good music. His services invariably featured great choirs, song leaders such as Homer Rodeheaver ("the man with the 'orange blossoms' in his voice"), professional vocalists and instrumentalists, and organ concerts before and after the stated hours of worship. Selling religion meant, for Massee, giving it front-page newspaper coverage (he cultivated the press shrewdly), and he was one of the first clergymen in New England to broadcast his services when radio came into vogue.[39] Selling religion meant, for Massee, responding to special occasions with special emphases. When, for instance, a group of thirteen underclassmen at the University of

Rochester formed an atheistic club called The Society of Damned Souls, Massee arranged a "college night" at Tremont Temple. The auditorium was decorated with banners from the major educational institutions in Greater Boston, voices from college glee clubs augmented the choir, and the vice-president of the Harvard Glee Club led the congregational singing. Before hundreds of students, Massee characterized the society as "either perverted thought, a foolish effort to be funny at the expense of the old people, or just the braying of a few asses who had escaped from their father's fields." [40] When Carson-Newman College at Jefferson City, Tennessee, wished to honor Massee in 1926 with a Doctor of Laws degree, the recipient saw that it was conferred at a Sunday evening service in Tremont Temple after he, the president of the honoring institution, and various religious officials had walked the length of the main aisle to the pulpit platform.[41] Massee probably loved the crowd more than the degree that recognized him as "a painstaking scholar, an eminent author, an eloquent lecturer, and an outstanding preacher of the gospel." If the academic community was not impressed, another standing-room-only congregation was. For a man who throughout his lifetime consistently opposed the theater, Jasper Cortenus Massee put on a remarkably good show.

III

It was as a denominational leader and general of the fundamentalist forces in the 1920's that Massee experienced his greatest triumphs, suffered his most obvious defeats, and manifested most clearly his sense of individualism. At this time his fundamentalist theology, pietistic morality, and preaching ability with a flair for the dramatic coalesced to make him one of the most loved and one of the most hated of the religious personalities within the Northern Baptist Convention.

When Massee came to Brooklyn from Dayton in 1920, he was welcomed at his service of installation by John Roach Straton, minister of the Calvary Baptist Church, New York City.[42] Soon thereafter, twenty-five pastors in the metropolitan area of New York City, including Massee, met for a day of discussion and prayer. Out of this meeting a committee was appointed to provide for a conference prior to the annual meeting of the Northern Baptist Convention in Buffalo.[43] These leaders, among them Curtis Lee Laws and Frank Goodchild, were ready to challenge what they felt to be dangerous liberalizing tendencies in the denomination. Massee's association with such men seemed like a natural partnership, but the future relationships were to disappoint that hope.

Like others of similar persuasion, Massee believed that the crucial issue between the liberals and the conservatives was the central issue of naturalism versus supernaturalism. He wrote: "The issues are clear and simple. . . . Fundamentalists are contending for the supernatural element in Christianity as against the modernists who seek for every known means to discredit and reject the supernatural element in Christianity." [44] It was with this conviction and in a mood of aggressiveness which became typical of the fundamentalists that over 150 clergymen and laymen issued a call to action, with Massee heading the list.[45] Alarmed by the influence of rationalism in the churches and the schools, as well as the growing "worldliness" of many in their own constituencies, these leaders extended an invitation to all Baptists within the denomination to a preconvention conference on "Fundamentals of Our Baptist Faith" at the Delaware Avenue Baptist Church, Buffalo, New York, June 21–22, 1920. The purpose of the conclave was "to restate, reaffirm, and reemphasize the fundamentals of our New Testament faith." [46]

J. C. Massee presided at the conference, where eleven prominent conservatives delivered addresses, most of them centered on the historic principles of the Baptists.[47] It remained, however, for the venerable William Bell Riley, minister of the First Baptist Church of Minneapolis, to attack aggressively the opposition and to portend coming events. In a blistering message entitled "The Menace of Modernism," he stated that three beliefs were endangered in the present situation: an inspired Bible, the deity of Jesus, and the fact of regeneration.[48] Riley's presentation, which was inordinately critical of liberal teachings in the schools and the seminaries, stirred up a great deal of emotional fervor. At its conclusion, the conference voted to request the Convention to investigate the schools and report at the annual meeting of 1921 on the attitudes of faculty members and trustees concerning the cardinal doctrines of the faith. In fact, the preconvention group audaciously suggested the individuals who should pursue the investigation.[49] Then the struggle was thrust into the conference itself. The stage was now set for conflict between the fundamentalists and the liberals on the main battlefronts of the orthodoxy of denominational schools and missionaries, and the formulation of a creedal statement.

The question of the schools was central at the Buffalo convention of 1920. Massee, who had been elected president of the newly formed Fundamentalist Federation at the preconvention conference, presented the resolution that asked for a committee of nine "to inquire into the loyalty of our Baptist schools to Jesus Christ and his gospel . . . and their efficiency in producing men and women of Christian character and capacity for service . . . [and] . . . to investigate the method of election, or appointment of trustees, . . . and report on the entire question of the control of these institutions."[50] The schools themselves were asked to examine their work, to correct evils that they might discover, and to set forth a statement of their purpose that might give assurance of their fidelity to the gospel. In the discussion that followed, pandemonium arose when men such as John Roach Straton and Milton G. Evans, president of Crozer Seminary, clashed over the presence or absence of orthodoxy in the academic institutions of the Baptists. The motion passed overwhelmingly, however, and the Committee of Nine began its difficult task.[51]

In retrospect one may say that the fundamentalists at Buffalo won the initial skirmish. They had successfully brought about an investigation of the educational institutions of the denomination, and Massee had been elected first vice-president of the convention. But it was a costly victory. A deep feeling of tension and bitterness had arisen, the result of political conflict, theological accusation, and harsh words. Even Curtis Lee Laws, editor of *The Watchman-Examiner* and a strong advocate of the conservative forces, commented in an editorial:

> The [school] resolution . . . created the wildest disorder. A sober, reverential body of men and women was transformed into a shouting, hissing, applauding bedlam. . . . The disgraceful scenes witnessed at Buffalo should never be repeated. We must acknowledge that every man has a right to think for himself and publicly express his thoughts if he does not transgress the amenities of a public gathering. . . . In contending for the faith men should have and should manifest the spirit of their Master.[52]

Massee himself had been disturbed by the behavior of his compatriots. He placed the blame for the poor spirit among the fundamentalists squarely on the shoulders of John Roach Straton and Cortland Myers (Massee's immediate predecessor at Tremont Temple). Their speeches at the preconvention conclave, Massee believed, "were abusive, almost scurrilous attacks on the convention, shockingly bad taste as well as a complete disregard of the announced purpose to 'reaffirm, restate, and re-emphasize the historic faith of Baptists.' "[53]

It would appear that a heresy of spirit was beginning to manifest itself, far more dangerous than heresy of belief. And the worst was yet to come.

Between the conventions of 1920 and 1921, Massee left little doubt about his position on the schools. Initially, he felt their management was undemocratic and anti-Baptistic because the colleges and seminaries, almost without exception, were governed by self-perpetuating boards of trustees subject to neither direct nor indirect control of the denomination or the state conventions. In addition, the Board of Education operated under an independent charter. Secondly, there was an absence of any authoritative uniform statement of belief to which the teacher must subscribe. Thirdly, Massee, very much the fundamentalist, feared the danger arising from the so-called scientific study of the Bible, especially by teachers who themselves were not Christians. With considerable emotion he asked: "What has our educational Rehoboam [rationalism] to say to the servants of the King? . . . What have we to do with this new tyrant of modernism? What part have we in this new dynasty of rationalistic intellectualism? To your tents, O Israel!" [54] Massee's tent at this time was Brooklyn, where he declined to give either his money or moral support to the denomination's educational program, nor would he encourage his church to do so. He took one further step. Early in 1921, apparently on his own, he sent questionnaires to all the graduates of Baptist schools (class of 1920) related to the convention, inquiring about the attitude of faculty members toward the Scriptures. Massee was alarmed that of the "hundreds" of answers received, only 40 percent of the graduates had been definitely convinced that their teachers accepted the Bible as a direct revelation from God.[55] Buttressed with this information, Massee proposed as a partial answer the separation of the educational and missionary budgets. The unified budget, he was persuaded, helped to support unworthy individuals and institutions in the academic field and also led to the depersonalization of the missionary cause.

The Committee of Nine shared neither the depth of Massee's anxiety nor his proposed solutions. At the convention in Des Moines in 1921, this group reported that for the most part the Baptist schools were ones of which the denomination could be proud. Where there were legitimate grievances, these matters were referred to the trustees of the local institutions. The committee did affirm, however, that "it is the duty of the Baptist communities throughout the country to displace from the schools men who impugn the authority of the Scriptures as the Word of God and who deny the deity of our Lord." But it added quickly that "they must do it in the prescribed ways . . . and . . . in such a method as will conserve the well-being of the churches . . . and in such a spirit as will extend and strengthen his [the Lord's] work at home and abroad." [56] Massee, leaning heavily on that aspect of the committee's judgment which suggested the removal by local officials of those who denied the Bible and the divinity of Jesus, expressed satisfaction with the report, although it was quite evident that the liberal forces had captured the victory in this engagement. The denomination, as a denomination, had declined to take action against schools in general or teachers in particular. Frustrated here, the fundamentalists shifted the conflict to the creedal field.

The possibility of a confession of faith about which Baptists might unite was considered at the preconvention conference of fundamentalists in Des Moines in 1921. There the Fundamentalist Federation adopted a statement known as the Des Moines Confession. Written by Curtis Lee Laws after consultation with J. C. Massee, Floyd Adams, and Frank Goodchild, it contained the essence of the Philadelphia and New Hampshire Confessions of Faith (a Calvinistic and pietistic Protestant orthodoxy) plus an emphasis on the Baptist distinctives of believer's baptism and the autonomy of the local church.[57] The framers of this confession were careful to distinguish between a creed to which agreement was required and a confession of faith designed to set forth the essence of Scriptural truth to others—in this instance, the liberals of their own denomination.

While the Des Moines Confession was not presented to the convention in 1921, the executive committee of fundamentalists of which Massee was the head hoped this might be the case at Indianapolis in 1922. They gladly abandoned this expectation when it appeared likely that a confession of faith called the Columbia Proposal would be formulated by a joint commission from the Northern and Southern Conventions.[58] To their surprise, however, representatives of the Southern Baptists repudiated the proposal at a late hour, leaving the fundamentalists without a carefully developed plan of action. Under these circumstances, the executive committee decided not to recommend a confession of faith at Indianapolis.[59] Other fundamentalists, among them Riley and Joshua Cravett of Denver, disagreed, insisting the time had come for the denomination to take a stand. At one of the preconvention strategy sessions these men rejected the Des Moines Confession because of its "humble origin" and persuaded the group, over Massee's protest, to offer the New Hampshire Confession to the denomination for adoption.[60] William Bell Riley was asked to make the presentation, and for the sake of a united front Massee reluctantly went along. At the convention of 1922, therefore, Riley read the New Hampshire Confession of Faith and moved that the denomination recommend it to the churches as an expression of Baptist views, contending it was both historical and Biblical. Immediately, Cornelius Woelfkin of New York City, the leader of the liberal forces, shrewdly offered his substitute motion: "Resolved, that the Northern Baptist Convention affirm that the New Testament is an all-sufficient ground for Baptist faith and practice and we need no other statement." [61] After three hours of spirited debate, during which time Massee argued against the substitute motion because he viewed it as a parliamentary maneuver, the Woelfkin resolution was adopted by a margin of 1,264 to 634. To this day the denomination has successfully resisted attempts to change this basic posture, which represented another triumph for the liberal forces.

Various analyses have been made of the groups at the Indianapolis convention of 1922. The most familiar is a threefold division: the fundamentalists, the liberals, and the large bloc of middle-of-the-road conservatives. Prof. Frederick L. Anderson saw no fewer than five different "parties": the fundamentalists; the conservatives who were not fundamentalists; the great middle-of-the-road group which both fundamentalists and radicals ignored; the liberals of whom there were only a few real radicals; and the nontheological group, composed mostly of lay men and women, who did not understand what the controversy was about. With some notable exceptions, Anderson believed all these groups, except the fundamentalists, voted against the New Hampshire Confession of Faith and for the New Testament as the all-sufficient ground of faith and practice. Robert T. Handy also viewed five theological parties but with a different arrangement: modernists, evangelical liberals, conservative evangelicals, strict conservatives, and fundamentalists. There seems to be near-agreement that when the controversy was keen, members of these different groups went to one or the other extreme, thereby undercutting the middle ground.[62]

In addition to the attractiveness of the Woelfkin motion, which left abundant room for personal interpretation of the Scriptures, several factors had contributed to the defeat of the fundamentalists. Their inability to agree among themselves undercut the possibility of strong, united action in the time of conflict. While circumstances linked with the Columbia Proposal had worked to their disadvantage, even more damaging was the extremism of their own members who antagonized not only the liberals but many of the numerically large middle-of-the-road group. Writing just prior to the convention, the obstreperous William Bell Riley declared that modernists were controlling the denomination in part because few of them were busy in their pastorates. "The degree of their success seldom burdens them. They have time, therefore, for denominational demands and reveal a spirit of utter readiness [for denominational leadership]. . . . The consequence is, liberals govern a conservative people." [63] And of the middle-of-the-roaders, he proclaimed they were either incapable of thinking or unwilling to take the consequences of decision.

Massee, unhappy with both the liberals and the ultrafundamentalists, found himself in that awkward position where he was caught in the cross fire between the two groups. The liberals disliked his theology and his opposition to centralizing tendencies within the denomination, and the ultrafundamentalists charged him with offering no program for them to follow. The latter group by this time had run out of patience. Smarting under another setback, irritated by Fosdick's sermon, "Shall the Fundamentalists Win?" (he pleaded for a church inclusive enough to embrace both groups), and displeased with Massee's lack of leadership, they founded in 1923 the more radical Baptist Bible Union. The result was that now there were officially two brands of fundamentalists contending for the faith, although in reality they spent a great deal of time contending against one another.

One major struggle in the denomination remains to be considered. This was the question of the orthodoxy of missionaries on the home and foreign fields. Although the fundamentalists believed in the evangelical loyalty of most of the missionaries of the Northern Baptist Convention, they still feared the influence of modernism in this phase of their work. Education, the healing of physical disease, and social service, they believed, must not be allowed to serve as a substitute for evangelism.[64] There was also a widespread feeling that the whole missionary program was becoming depersonalized as the result of administrative centralization as well as resentment of interdenominational cooperation, lest Baptist distinctives be compromised.[65] Massee urged a more direct tie between the local church and missionaries on the field, but for many of his contemporaries this answer was too mild and impractical.

The Fundamentalist League of Greater New York, under the assertive leadership of John Roach Straton, took the situation into its own hands. Suspicious of the orthodoxy of Baptist missionaries, as well as of the officers who appointed them, Straton, joined by thirty ministers and laymen, personally requested permission of the Board of Managers of the American Baptist Foreign Mission Society to examine correspondence files for the purpose of verifying or disproving the theological soundness of missionaries and secretaries.[66] The board, of course, denied the request on the ground that such correspondence was confidential and frequently personal in nature.[67] It did, however, affirm its desire to send out only individuals who were evangelical in faith and spirit. This did not satisfy Straton, who called for an investigation by an impartial group outside the board and its officials. The place had now been reached where Massee, unable to control the ultrafundamentalists, joined forces with the liberals in political strategy. Fearful of the influence of the Fundamentalist League and its continuing pressures, Massee, representing the moderate fundamentalists, accepted an invitation from C. Wallace Petty, representing the moderate liberals, to support a motion at the Milwaukee convention of 1924 calling for a commission of seven individuals "to investigate the conduct, policies and practices of the Board of Managers of the American Baptist Foreign Mission Society." [68] The motion, made by Massee himself, provided for the appointment of the members of this commission by the president of the convention, thereby excluding the extremists. This maneuver successfully kept the investigation within denominational control.

The width of the breach among the badly divided fundamentalists was further evidenced at Milwaukee when the Baptist Bible Union held a two-day preconvention conference of their own on the fundamentals of the faith. Of course, it severely upstaged the usual preconvention meeting of the Fundamentalist Federation.[69] At the Bible Union sessions, spellbinders such as T. T. Shields, William Bell Riley, and John Roach Straton castigated German philosophy, the Social Gospel, and the substitution of education for evangelism, while simultaneously the Federation held two quiet prayer services in the same building. First on the Federation's prayer requests was "the cleansing of all our hearts from personal bitterness which has led to the estrangement of brethren." [70] Curtis Lee Laws tried to minimize the obvious split, but his words carried a distinctly hollow ring: "Let not the rationalists conclude that apparent differences among the fundamentalists will cause the war on rationalism to cease. Fundamentalists and Bible Unionists may disagree about methods and policies, but they are absolutely and indissolubly one in their hostility to rationalism." [71] This appeared to be a defensive gesture at best.

The commission of seven presented a thoughtful, moderate report at the convention in Seattle in 1925. It mentioned some cases of unsound belief among missionaries but expressed emphatic approval of the great majority.[72] Only four individuals were recalled from their posts as the result of the commission's work. Dissatisfied that the denomination, in accepting this report, had not imposed a tighter doctrinal test on its missionaries, some fundamentalists, led by W. B. Hinson of Oregon (an associate of Riley), again sought to impose a creedal requirement. The delegates rejected this proposal by a close vote, once more reaffirming the Indianapolis decision of 1922 that the New Testament alone would be their standard of faith and practice.[73]

As a member of the commission of seven, Massee supported the report, which further increased his unpopularity with many fundamentalists. When he did not attend the sessions at Seattle, dissatisfaction with his leadership continued to grow. Then Massee took decisive action. He resigned the presidency of the Fundamentalist Federation, a post he had held for five years. Shortly thereafter he left the political ranks of the fundamentalists completely. His resignation might have been expected. The moderate fundamentalists were clearly losing to the liberals and they were being shelled by heavy criticism from the outspoken members of the Baptist Bible Union. Furthermore, Massee's duties at Tremont Temple, the largest church in the denomination, were admittedly heavy, and the care of his invalid wife a constant concern.[74] But for the general of the forces to leave the ranks completely was a major surprise. Even more startling was the reason he gave for such a move. Massee had once said, "If the time comes when I find my heart being possessed by bitterness toward the brethren and estrangement from them, I shall withdraw from this 'fundamentalist' movement." [75] The time had come for him to fulfill his promise, and he did just that. Writing shortly after his departure, Massee commented: "I do not believe in the wisdom or the righteousness of denunciation, misinterpretation, the imputing of motives and the widespread directing of suspicion toward men who declare their conservatism and their faithful adherence to the Word and to the Christ of God." [76] Years later, Massee candidly reiterated the cause of his action:

I left the fundamentalists to save my own spirit, they became so self-righteous, so critical, so unchristian, so destructive, so incapable of being fair that I had to go elsewhere for spiritual nourishment.[77]

The fundamentalist leaders, moderates and extremists, were shocked and embarrassed by Massee's declarations. They charged him with betrayal of the cause, compromise, lack of courage, and even bribery.[78] With the storm swirling about him, Massee managed a discreet silence, although he remained active within the larger denomination, endeavoring to serve as a reconciling agent between the moderate fundamentalists and the evangelical liberals. There was one arrow left in his quiver of dramatic actions. This he released at the annual meeting of the Northern Baptist Convention in 1926.

At the convention in Washington that year, when tensions were near the breaking point again between the fundamentalists and the liberals (this time the issue was whether or not a church practicing open membership could send delegates to the convention), Massee was asked to deliver a major address. The white-haired patriarch, in a sermon entitled "The Laodicean Lament," after extolling the virtues of an evangelistic ministry, dramatically pleaded for a six months' armistice between the opposing forces. During that time there would be a moratorium on fund raising and a rededication of the denominational machinery and agencies to the task of evangelism. He further suggested that one hundred cities be centers for such united efforts and that to conserve the results a permanent Commission of Evangelism be established to function under the Home Mission Board.[79] While Massee's proposals did not deal with the theological issues involved, psychologically they came at the right moment. The delegates (with the exception of some fundamentalists), weary of controversy, enthusiastically accepted the suggestions and Massee was hailed as one of the men responsible for bringing a moderate solution to the problems of the Northern Baptists.

Massee's former allies, however, were far from satisfied. Frank Goodchild, his successor as president of the Federation, announced that their members would agree to a truce "when all the denomination's colleges and seminaries cease perverting the scriptures by teaching modernism, and when our preachers will return to the simplicity of the gospel and to the preaching of the cross." [80] Riley and Straton were even more severe. At a caucus meeting of the Bible Union forces, they confessed in sorrow the spiritual collapse of their erstwhile colleague. Disapproving Massee's recommendation for a truce, Riley exclaimed: "This is not a battle. It is a war from which there is no discharge." [81] Massee was considered an apostate, to be classified with Fosdick, while the Baptist Union renewed its pledge to a militant orthodoxy.[82] Despite the truculence of the radical fundamentalists, Massee's sermon in 1926 proved to be an important contribution to the cause of peace. The strife thereafter never seemed so acrimonious, intense, or widespread. Other factors, as well, added to the return of a relative harmony by the time of the convention in Chicago in 1927. These included the tolerant attitude of the president of the denomination, J. Whitcomb Brougher; the devotional talks of George W. Truett of Dallas; the absence of the leaders of the Bible Union; and the official recognition of conservative men like Massee, who preached the convention sermon on the subject "The Vicarious Atonement." [83]

After 1926 the fundamentalists carried on their defense of the faith within their own groups, although periodically there was wider sniping and guerrilla warfare in the denomination itself. This latter action continued until the 1940's. In 1944, when a strategy meeting of fundamentalists was held in Atlantic City, presided over by Earle V. Pierce, Massee was excluded because of his refusal to sign the Des Moines Confession as a test of faith.[84] This was doubly ironical because Massee had been one of the original framers of the statement. Massee's forced departure from that meeting, brought about by the "young Turks" of Fundamentalism, left a deep impression on those who were present as observers. After having seen the white-haired, stoop-shouldered, elder statesman of Fundamentalism exiled from his own fellowship, some of these observers vowed never to support the fundamentalist movement.[85]

Once more repulsed in their endeavor to impose a creedal test on the convention, the fundamentalists withdrew from the Northern Baptist Convention and in 1947 formed their own denomination, the Conservative Baptist Association of America. Massee protested the establishment of this new body of Baptists by withdrawing his membership from a Warsaw, Indiana, church (near Winona Lake) and transferring it to Tremont Temple.[86] When he was extended the right hand of fellowship to the Boston congregation, the aging warrior reviewed his thirty-year effort to hold the denomination together in spite of theological differences. He deplored the divisiveness which had crept into the ranks, suggesting at the same time that there was room in any Baptist body for differences of opinion provided there was agreement on three broad principles: (1) the competency and responsibility of the individual in relation to God; (2)

the sufficiency of the New Testament in faith and manner of life for Christians; (3) the authority of the local church.[87] That was his pulpit valedictory.

Massee's literary valedictory came through an article in *The Chronicle* in 1954 in which he analyzed the controversy of thirty years.[88] In retrospect he saw much good emanating from the years of struggle. Appearing to rationalize, he pointed to the elimination of "radicals" from control of the convention; the recognition of minority groups within the denomination; the founding of conservative seminaries (Central, Northern, Eastern); the creation of a Commission of Evangelism; and the development of a conservative scholarship and literary expression.[89] He pinpointed the ill-timed and ill-fated Baptist Bible Union as being responsible for the division of the conservative forces and thereby weakening their voice of protest. In an apparent melancholy mood, Massee wrote: "Thus we came to Boston in 1950 [for the annual meeting of the Northern Baptist Convention] and 'they went out from us,' and we had not enough grace left to weep. We had argued together, but prayed apart." [90] The patriarch added quickly that it was still better to separate and live in peace than to be bound together only by a spirit of discord.

Reviewing the new splinter denomination, Massee saw accurately that the distinction between the convention conservatives (moderate fundamentalists) and the Conservative Baptist Association was not one concerning the authenticity and authority of the Bible as the Word of God or the character of Christ and the gospel of reconciliation. The real distinction was made by the millennial emphases and eschatological programs of the latter and by their demand for the adoption of a creedal confession by the American (formerly Northern) Baptist Convention.[91] With Massee, however, there was no turning back.

Fellowship cannot be coerced. . . . No human being has either the right or the power to select a vocabulary in which my faith is to be expressed. . . . No ecclesiastical coercion requiring me to sign can be tolerated. . . . The effort to force an exclusively creedal statement upon the Northern Baptist Convention has failed and will fail because it is inquisitorial in character and is, therefore, divisive and disturbing.[92]

Marshallville's son, conservative though he was, had come a long way.

IV

Jasper Cortenus Massee typified the contribution of the South to the Fundamentalism of the North in the early decades of the twentieth century. It is a historical fact that Fundamentalism, which had its birth and early concentration in the metropolitan areas of the Northeast (especially Philadelphia, New York, and Boston) in the late nineteenth century, came—in the early decades of the present century—under the leadership of men like Massee, John Roach Straton, William Bell Riley, Curtis Lee Laws, and J. Frank Norris, whose backgrounds were in the South. Ernest R. Sandeen states that "fundamentalism was not a sectional controversy, but a national one, and most of its champions came from the same states as their opponents." [93] This assertion appears to need qualification. There were many fundamentalists below the Mason-Dixon line, but the conflict there was minimal because there were so few liberals with whom to contend. It may have been true that most of the fundamentalist leaders came from the same states as their opponents, but if so, Massee, Straton, Laws, Norris, Riley, and Machen were notable exceptions. This is not to claim a southern origin for Fundamentalism; rather, it is to point out that Fundamentalism in the North in the early 1900's was markedly influenced by several prominent leaders whose background and training had been nurtured in the religiously conservative South.

Although Massee was better read and less emotional than most of the fundamentalists, his life still evidenced several strains of anti-intellectualism, thereby supporting Richard Hofstadter's thesis that in America there was "a resentment and suspicion of the life of the mind and of those who are considered to represent it, and a disposition constantly to minimize the value of that life." [94] Such an attitude was typical of fundamentalist leaders who normally scorned academic standards, believing unashamedly that much learning led to skepticism and atheism. [95] In Massee's life this anti-intellectualism was seen in the Primitive Baptist background of his family which taught that lack of education was no deterrent to the ministry; in his own words when he declared, "All the theology I needed I received from my mother and father"; in the limitation of his theological training to a single year of study; in his perennial preaching emphasis that character is more important than learning; in his "either-or" mentality which polarized the theological alternatives of his day without cultivating real, meaningful dialogue; and in his whole evangelistic outreach, with its stress on numerical dividends and evangelical piety rather than rational analysis, despite the evangelist's claim that part of his appeal was to the mind of man. The fundamentalist posture itself, with its insistence on accepting what

God has revealed rather than the encouragement of man's thought, also contributed to this depreciation of the mind.

Despite a certain anti-intellectualism, Massee's exaltation of faith over reason, his belief in a transcendent God, his emphasis on the sinfulness of man with the necessity of a crisis conversion experience, and his refusal to be a Scriptural literalist may have contributed to the climate of opinion in which neo-orthodoxy would find receptivity. Although this latter movement is considered by some scholars to be antirational, nevertheless it brought to American religious life a greater sophistication of expression and a more relevant religious language than Fundamentalism had done, as well as a deeper appreciation of the Social Gospel and Biblical criticism. It is possible that unwittingly Massee served as a connecting link between the two movements. If not making a contribution in this direction, he surely was laying the groundwork for the coming of neo-evangelicalism.[96]

By his relatively moderate position Massee did much to prevent an earlier and potentially greater break in the Northern Baptist Convention. The vast majority of Baptists in the 1920's originally were neither fundamentalists nor liberals. They comprised a numerically large conservative group who in the heat of battle chose between the contesting factions, thereby undercutting the middle ground. The extremism of the ultrafundamentalists encouraged many conservatives either to vote politically with the liberals, without changing their theology, or to stay with Massee's moderate kind of Fundamentalism. Many, although not a majority, took the latter alternative, influenced in part by Massee's conservative theology, practical piety, and willingness to remain within the denominational fold. This political strength of the moderate fundamentalists when joined with the power of the liberal forces made for an unbeatable combination, thereby reducing the possibility of a wider division among the Northern Baptists and making the liberals more indebted to Massee than frequently they realized. To express it another way, the inability of the fundamentalists to agree among themselves prevented any real chance of a significant political or theological victory, which, if one or both had taken place, would have sundered the denomination in a major way. The Baptists were fortunate that Massee chose to throw his influence in the direction of the moderate (evangelical) liberals rather than toward the ultrafundamentalists. Freedom of personal interpretation, a cherished belief among the spiritual descendants of Roger Williams, profited thereby.

Massee's greatest personal success was as a pastor-evangelist. He had failed as president of the Federation. He could not keep a united house; his program was weak, as Riley charged; he had naïve answers for difficult problems; and he was resisting inevitable theological change. It is possible, but not likely, that a leader other than Massee might have welded the fundamentalists together. Their history, however, has been one of constant separation, causing Edward J. Carnell to remark about them that "divisions in the Church are considered a sign of virtue. And when there are no modernists from whom to withdraw, fundamentalists compensate by withdrawing from one another." [97] But as a strong, if not a great, man of the pulpit, Massee combined charm, culture, compassion, wit, sincerity, diligence, and drama to present successfully a simple faith, full of comfort and inspiration to countless people. While his fundamentalist theology and moralistic piety probably turned some away, many others, whom the liberals had not been reaching, were attracted by his message and person.

Lastly, Massee's life provided obvious evidence of "gradations" among the fundamentalists. The gulf was especially wide between Massee, on the one hand, and Riley, Straton, and Norris, on the other. Independent man that he was, Massee refused to be crowded into a creedal mold. This rugged individualism and the reasons for it made him stand out among his peers:

> I cannot pronounce the shibboleth of any creed, nor meet the demands of any group that would enslave me to the tyranny of another's opinion. It seems to me that such a fellowship prevents intellectual honesty, moral initiative, and spiritual growth. It develops a censorious habit of mind and life and a critical attitude that alienates its real friends and grieves the Spirit of God. If we be teachers of the truth we should be seekers after the truth. Within the charmed circle of the New Testament gospel message there is indeed place for difference in conception of details of procedure and no place for a censorship of others that does violence to the whole intent of Christian fellowship and to the Spirit of Christ. . . . That closed circle includes too few and excludes too many of God's children. An interpretation for example of Daniel's prophecy is no proper test of faith or fellowship in Christ.[98]

Massee was not as literalistic in his interpretation of Scripture as many of his own theological stripe. He was kinder in spirit and less abrasive in language toward his opponents than many of his colleagues. In the pulpit he pleaded with men rather than condemned them. He was loyal to his denomination in a way that Straton and Riley were not. He was sufficiently mature to admit shortcomings and adopt new positions. Occasionally, in the realm of thought, he saw grays between black and white absolutes (sometimes even reds!). Despite being frequently in the center of debate, he still loved people more than a fight. In a word, he sought to make his a constructive rather than a destructive Fundamentalism. Massee himself recognized these differences among the religiously conservative when he declared to personal friends, "There are fundamentalists and damn fundamentalists." He left little doubt to which group he belonged. To recognize Massee, however, as one of the better fundamentalists is lukewarm praise. Sincere and colorful man that he was, he still opposed the social interpretation of the gospel, reflected an anti-intellectual attitude, and was tied to a debatable theology. The independent man was there, but so also was the influence of culture.

CHAPTER SIX

J. Gresham Machen

SCHOLARLY FUNDAMENTALIST

STUDENTS OF THE MODERNIST-FUNDAMENTALIST struggle have long
recognized J. Gresham Machen as one of its most unusual and
important leaders. The multitalented Presbyterian clergyman-
professor deserved this acknowledgment. Showmanship and rhetoric
were not his forte, in contrast to several of his noisy contemporaries.
He was important rather because of his erudition, the depth of the
controversy that he precipitated, the nature of his apology for an
ultraconservative Christianity, and the manner in which he declined
to be crowded into previously established molds—even fundamentalist ones. Despite Machen's significance, only one major book-length
work has appeared dealing with his life, and that by an enthusiastic
and contemporary disciple who wrote twenty years ago.[1] It is fitting,
therefore, with the greater perspective brought by time, as conservative theology is constantly reevaluated, and as Presbyterians and
others continue to face important doctrinal and ecumenical decisions,
to take another look at this staunch heir of the Hodge-Warfield
tradition at Princeton Theological Seminary.[2]

I

Unlike many fundamentalists, Machen had a family tradition
characterized by wealth, culture, a marked intellectual ability, and a
pronounced social influence. John Gresham Machen was born in
Baltimore, Maryland, July 28, 1881, the second of the three sons of
Arthur Webster and Mary (Minnie) Gresham Machen.[3] His parents
were of English ancestry by way of Virginia and Georgia. Machen's
father became a prominent lawyer who read five languages, including

Italian, which he learned after the age of eighty.[4] His mother, to whom Machen was especially attached throughout his lifetime, possessed many interests, namely, religion, poetry, nature, botany, and astronomy. She wrote a book entitled *The Bible in Browning*, and kept a close personal friendship with Gertrude Lanier, sister of the famous poet Sidney Lanier.[5] Machen's maternal grandfather, John Jones Gresham, illustrates the interest that members of the Machen family took in political and educational matters. Twice he served as mayor of Macon, Georgia, in addition to being a member of the state legislature and, for various terms, a trustee of the University of Georgia, Oglethorpe University, and Columbia Theological Seminary.[6] The father of Woodrow Wilson, who taught at the latter institution, was in his older years a frequent visitor to the Machen home in Baltimore.[7]

In such a cultured atmosphere Machen's early religious training took place. It consisted primarily of a knowledge of the Scriptures and the Westminster Shorter Catechism. Recalling the nature of his spiritual upbringing, Machen wrote near the end of his life: "I had acquired a better knowledge of the contents of the Bible at twelve years of age than is possessed by many theological students today." [8] After instruction in a private school, the future fundamentalist entered Johns Hopkins University at the age of seventeen. There he majored in classics and was graduated as valedictorian and elected to Phi Beta Kappa in 1901. He lingered at Johns Hopkins for a year of graduate study before beginning his long relationship with Princeton Theological Seminary by enrolling as a student in the fall of 1902. His study at Princeton Seminary brought him into contact with Benjamin Breckinridge Warfield, theological successor to Charles Hodge, a defender of Calvinism and a leader whom Machen called, on the occasion of Warfield's death in 1921, "the greatest man I have known." [9] Machen earned his B.D. degree from the seminary in 1905, a year after receiving an M.A. degree from Princeton University.[10]

Eager to continue his theological education, Machen traveled to Germany for further study at Marburg and Göttingen. There he worked with several of the world's leading Biblical scholars—among them Adolf Jülicher, Johannes Weiss, Walter Bauer, Wilhelm Bousset, and, above all others, the brilliant Ritschlian theologian, Wilhelm Herrmann. It was a time of perplexity and doubt for Machen as he studied under able scholars who rejected the supernatural, but who nevertheless made deep impressions on him. Such impressions were the result not only of intellectual acumen but, especially with

Photo by Marceau. Presbyterian Historical Society, Philadelphia, Pa.

J. Gresham Machen

Herrmann, of convincing religious commitment. In time Machen came to believe that there was a moral contradiction in the "reconstructed Jesus" of Herrmann's theology, but he remained greatly moved by the depth of Herrmann's personal fervor and moral earnestness.[11]

When Machen returned from Germany in 1906, he accepted an appointment at Princeton Seminary, the beginning of a twenty-three-year period as a member of the faculty. He served initially as instructor from 1906 to 1914, then as assistant professor of New Testament from 1914 to 1929. Somewhat surprisingly, Machen was not ordained until 1914. This delay was due to an intense personal struggle with intellectual doubt plus a feeling of deep personal unworthiness to be a minister of Christ. His doubts, which had originated prior to his studies in Germany, were intensified there. They were finally resolved through a renewed trust in the "Christ [who] keeps firmer hold on us than we keep on him." [12] Commenting later on this phase of his life, Machen wrote:

> The question is not merely whether we can rest in our faith, but whether we can rest in the doubt that is the necessary alternative of faith. It is all very well to toy with the thought of a Christless world, but when we once imagine ourselves living in it we see that really . . . we have not given up our Saviour after all. . . . We ought to distrust our moods. . . . Faith is often diversified by doubt, but a man should not desert the conviction of his better moments because the dark moments come.[13]

During his professorial years, Machen's erudition was manifested through his prolific writings. His *New Testament Greek for Beginners* (1923), eventually published in some forty editions, came to be used widely in colleges and seminaries. His classic study, *The Virgin Birth of Christ* (1930), is considered the ablest treatment of that subject, from an orthodox standpoint, in the field of New Testament studies.[14] Other prominent books that he wrote included *The Origin of Paul's Religion* (1921); *Christianity and Liberalism* (1923); *What Is Faith?* (1925); *The Christian Faith in the Modern World* (1936); and *The Christian View of Man* (1937).

If Machen's views had been limited to his books, he probably would have escaped much of the trouble that centered about his person. But his denunciation of Liberalism took on an even more specific character in classroom and pulpit, in the press, and in denominational circles, as he condemned what he felt to be a growing apostasy in his own church and a trend away from Calvinism and toward theological inclusiveness at Princeton Seminary. His criticisms precipitated a conflict of major proportions, one that was resolved at the seminary only by a reorganization of that institution in 1929. Because this reorganization led to a policy that he could not support, Machen withdrew and led in the establishment of Westminster Theological Seminary in Philadelphia in the same year. He taught there as professor of New Testament until his death.

Various crises continued to characterize his latter years. In 1933, in protest to supposed liberal theological tendencies among the missionary authorities of his denomination, Machen became the chief organizer of the Independent Board for Presbyterian Foreign Missions. In response, his own Presbytery of New Brunswick, after a formal trial, found him guilty of being a schismatic and suspended him from the ministry on March 29, 1935. Undismayed, Machen led in the formation of the Presbyterian Church of America, later known as the Orthodox Presbyterian Church. Machen died in Bismarck, North Dakota, January 1, 1937, while visiting several churches of his recently established denomination. Technically, the cause of his death was pneumonia; it is likely, however, that the deterioration of his health was related to overwork and disappointment in failing to achieve several of his basic goals, as an account of his activities will reveal.

In his personal life, the five-foot-eight-inch, stocky, dark-haired, heavy-jowled bachelor took an interest in literature, painting, and the theater. When time permitted, he was also a devotee of tennis, walking, bicycling, and mountain-climbing.[15] Although he made many friends and was especially devoted to his students, "by nature he was not gregarious and he continued all his life to enjoy the liberty and relaxation of privacy and solitude." [16] In this respect, as in many others, he was a strange compatriot of most fundamentalists.

There was, however, one very close bond in Machen's life. That was his intimate tie to his mother. While Machen had called Benjamin B. Warfield the greatest man he had known, he reserved for his mother the title "the best and wisest person" he had ever known.[17] The depth of this relationship was reflected in the fact that during a period of thirty years she wrote him over one thousand affectionate letters and he responded in kind and number.[18]

Machen's opponents thought of him as an adamant, impatient, censorious, frequently bitter, ultraconservative leader. His friends viewed him as a scholarly defender of Biblical faith whose sincerity, courage, integrity, and completeness of dedication "sometimes evoked heroic responses." [19] This author views him as a reluctant and "independent" fundamentalist whose work as an apologist was more successful than were his labors as an ecclesiastical politician.

II

The theology of J. Gresham Machen was centered in what he believed was the truthfulness of the Christian religion as set forth in the Scriptures and summarized most accurately in the creeds of the Reformed (Calvinistic) faith, especially the Shorter Catechism.[20] He thought that such Christianity required and was susceptible to scholarly defense. Machen the apologist was the first to admit that argument alone was insufficient to win individuals to Christianity, but he reasoned that it does not follow that argument is unnecessary. "You can hardly have evangelism," he insisted, "unless you have Christian scholarship." [21] Machen personified this conviction as he spent most of his life advancing the claims of the Christian faith and refuting those whom he regarded as its enemies. These apologetic endeavors began early in his career, as his first public speeches indicate, especially "History and Faith," an address delivered at Princeton in 1915 on the occasion of his inauguration as assistant professor of New Testament literature and exegesis.

Crucial to Machen's understanding of Christianity was the conviction that the Christian faith was based not on aspiration or exhortation but on historical facts—the birth, life, death, and bodily resurrection of Jesus—and could not be reduced to subjective ideas disconnected from history and science, as Protestant Liberalism appeared to be doing.[22] For Machen, Christianity was not a life, as distinguished from a doctrine, but rather a life founded on doctrine that was, in turn, founded on facts.

> You cannot change the facts. The modern preacher offers reflection. The Bible offers more. The Bible offers news—not reflection on the old, but tidings of something new; not something that can be deduced or something that can be discovered, but something that has happened; not philosophy, not history; not exaltation, but a gospel. The Bible contains a record of something that has happened, something that puts a new face upon life. What that something is . . . is the life and death and resurrection of Jesus Christ. The authority of the Bible should be tested here at the central point.[23]

While anxious not to let the faith be reduced to a few carefully selected doctrines, as many of the fundamentalists were doing (he preferred the conception of truth as a systematic whole), Machen focused his own emphasis "at the central point." Specifically, this was his belief in the supernatural nature of Jesus, including his virgin birth, his vicarious atonement, and his bodily resurrection. Machen appeared to give special stress to the vicarious atonement. In his judgment, the substitutionary death of Jesus made Christianity a religion of redemption and distinguished it from those faiths which found salvation in man's obedience to moral demands. Machen called the latter a "sublimated form of legalism." He had Liberalism in mind. Machen declared:

> The Bible contains an account of a revelation which is absolutely new. That new revelation concerns the way by which sinful man can come into communion with the living God. . . . The eternal Son was offered as a sacrifice for the sins of men. To that one great event the whole of the Old Testament looks forward and in that one event the whole of the New Testament finds its center and core. Salvation then, according to the Bible, is nothing that was discovered, but something that happened. . . . Christianity depends, not upon a complex of ideas, but upon the narration of an event.[24]

In Machen's theology, the Old Testament prophets looked forward to this event, while many of Jesus' disciples proclaimed it as already past. Even the meaning of that which happened was set forth. He wrote: " 'Christ died'—that is history: 'Christ died for our sins'—that is doctrine." [25] Machen believed that this was such plain Biblical truth that there was really no room for interpretation. One might accept it or reject it, but he should not try to verbalize it away by calling it "an inspiring example of self-sacrifice," as Harry Emerson Fosdick had done.[26] In this context, Machen was disturbed that the sacrifices of men in time of war (for him, World War I) could be compared to the sacrifice of Jesus. He recognized that there were crosses or trials that bring us nearer to God, but certainly this was not the gospel. He also regretted that the people on the sinking *Titanic* could not find a better hymn to sing than "Nearer, My God, to Thee" ("e'en though it be a cross that raiseth me"). Machen the theologian expressed a preference for hymns such as "In the Cross of Christ I Glory" or "When I Survey the Wondrous Cross." [27]

Machen gave considerable attention to his theory of the authority of Biblical inspiration, since the vicarious atonement and the other doctrines that for him comprised the "central point" were referred to in the Scriptures. To the surprise of very few, he concluded that the books of the Bible in the original autographs were "an infallible rule of faith and practice." Like his theological predecessors at Princeton, Machen affirmed the true individuality of the Biblical writers at the same time that he stressed the absence of any kind of error in the Scriptures.[28]

These theological convictions of Machen (the supernatural nature of Jesus' personality and the infallibility of the Scriptures), when joined with his acceptance of Biblical miracles, seemingly placed the conservative from Princeton in the camp of the fundamentalists, yet Machen was deeply reluctant to accept such a designation. If the choice was between Liberalism and Fundamentalism, then, of course, he classified himself with the latter, but he disliked the way fundamentalists summarized Christianity in a few neatly defined doctrines; he was not a Scofield dispensationalist nor a premillennialist, as many of his conservative colleagues were; and he lacked many of the characteristics found in typical fundamentalist piety.

Machen declared that if a person accepts the annotations of the Scofield Bible, "he is seriously out of accord with the Reformed Faith and has no right to be a minister or elder or deacon in the Presbyterian Church of America" (i.e., the denomination Machen founded). Even more specifically, he wrote that the "dispensationalism of the Scofield Bible seems to us to be quite contrary to the system of doctrine taught in the Westminster Standards." [29]

On the important subject of premillennialism, Machen was convinced that the Scriptures did not speak so precisely as to warrant a premillennialist conclusion:

> A large number of Christian people believe that when evil has reached its climax in the world, the Lord Jesus will return to this earth in bodily presence to bring about a reign of righteousness that will last a thousand years, and that only after that period the end of the world will come. This belief . . . is an error arrived at by a false interpretation of the Word of God; we do not think that the prophecies of the Bible permit so definite a mapping out of future events. The Lord will come again, and it will be no mere "spiritual" coming in the modern sense—so much is clear—but that so little will be accomplished by the present dispensation of the Holy Spirit and so much will be left to be accomplished by the Lord in bodily presence—such a view we cannot find to be justified by the words of Scripture.[30]

While firmly disagreeing with the premillennialists, theoretically Machen saw no difficulty in cooperating with them, because he and they held other beliefs in common, such as the authority of the

Scriptures and the deity of Jesus, including his virgin birth and physical second coming. On at least one occasion, however, Machen was excluded by them. In 1930, he declined an invitation to a meeting of the executive committee for the Philadelphia district of the World's Christian Fundamentals Association because the invitation was conditional upon the acceptance of their Confession of Faith, which included a belief in the "personal, premillennial, and imminent return" of Jesus. Machen replied:

> I do not think that the Scriptures warrant us to be so precise in our knowledge of the order of future events as is implied in your Confession of Faith. The Scriptures, I think, in accordance with the purpose of God, keep certain details in that sphere hidden from us in His wise and mysterious counsels.[31]

In addition to such doctrinal differences, Machen did not reflect, in his personal life, the piety called for by many fundamentalists. True, he was a strict Sabbatarian, owing more to his Presbyterian training than to fundamentalist influence; but on such matters as the drinking of alcoholic beverages and the use of tobacco he differed markedly from the fundamentalists. While he believed that intemperance was wrong, he declined to accept total abstinence as the only alternative. The social practices of his family, dictated in part by the circles in which they moved, linked with his own knowledge of the Scriptures (did not Paul teach that a little wine was good for the stomach and one's frequent ailments?), undoubtedly contributed to this conclusion.[32] And when it came to tobacco, Machen was even more precise. "My idea of delight is a Princeton room full of fellows smoking. When I think what a wonderful aid tobacco is to friendship and Christian patience I have sometimes regretted that I never began to smoke." [33]

Machen was, then, a Calvinist Christian who felt that the Christian religion could and should be defended. While holding many views in common with the fundamentalists, he was reluctant at best to accept the label. His doctrinal position was stated forcefully and succinctly by Machen himself when writing to a lawyer friend in 1927:

> Thoroughly consistent Christianity, to my mind, is found only in the Reformed or Calvinistic faith; and consistent Christianity, I think, is the Christianity easiest to defend. Hence I never call myself a "Fundamentalist." There is, indeed, no inherent objection to the term; and if the designation is between "Fundamentalism" and "Modernism," then I am willing to call myself a Fundamentalist of the most pronounced type. But,

after all, what I prefer to call myself is not a Fundamentalist but a Calvinist—that is, an adherent to the Reformed Faith. As such, I regard myself as standing in the great central current of the church's life—the current which flows down from the Word of God through Augustine and Calvin, and which has found noteworthy expression in America in the great tradition represented by Charles Hodge and Benjamin Breckinridge Warfield, and the other representatives of the "Princeton School." [34]

Machen's positive description of the Christian faith comprised one side of his apologetic coin; the other side was an unrelenting and perennial attack upon naturalism as expressed in Protestant Liberalism, which he considered the chief rival to Christianity. It was Machen's thesis that Christianity and Liberalism were essentially two distinct and mutually exclusive religions, not two varieties of the same faith.[35] He argued that they proceeded from altogether different roots despite the use of traditional phraseology by the liberals. In assaulting Liberalism as a non-Christian religion, Machen declared that the liberal attempt to reconcile Christianity with modern science had relinquished everything distinctive of Christianity. What remained was the same type of religious aspiration that was in the world before the coming of the Christian faith.[36]

The specific theological differences between Christianity and Liberalism were so pronounced, Machen contended, that one could not avoid the conclusion that they were separate religions. Christianity, in his judgment, stressed a transcendent God, a humanity corrupted by its own sinfulness, the infallible Scriptures as man's source of religious authority, salvation through the vicarious atonement, to which man responds in faith, pessimism about change in human institutions, and a church composed of the brotherhood of the redeemed waiting for the bodily return of Jesus. In contrast, argued Machen, there was Liberalism with its "pantheizing" concept of God, its supreme confidence in human goodness, its location of religious authority in the experience of man, its interpretation of Jesus as an example and teacher, its claim that salvation may be discovered through obedience to moral law, its optimism about the possibility of social change in this life, and its eagerness to establish the kingdom of God on earth.[37]

It was at the central point of Christology that Machen found the contrast between Christianity and Liberalism especially obvious—and odious. While Christianity viewed Jesus as the God-man, a real person into whose hands the destinies of men and nations had been cast, an object of faith rather than merely an illustration of faith,

Liberalism interpreted him in naturalistic terms—a teacher, an example ("the fairest flower of humanity"), a guide, and the founder of Christianity.[38] This "reconstructed Jesus" of Liberalism had been reached by separating the natural from the supernatural elements in his life. Machen declared, however, that this was an impossibility because the two were inextricably intertwined.[39] Furthermore, even if this were conceivable, the liberal Jesus contained a hopeless contradiction at the center of his being. This was the antithesis between Jesus' simple, humble, human qualities as a teacher and those lofty claims whereby he spoke of himself as a heavenly person who was to come on the clouds of heaven to be the instrument in judging all the earth.[40] Such a contradiction could not be handled satisfactorily, Machen reasoned, by denying that Jesus was the Messiah, for his Messianic consciousness was rooted too deeply in the sources ever to be removed by the critical process.

Machen's most trenchant criticism of the "reconstructed Jesus" remained, for him, unanswered.

> Suppose the critical sifting of the Gospel tradition has been accomplished, suppose the resulting picture of Jesus is comprehensible—even then the work is only half done. How did this human Jesus come to be regarded as a superhuman Jesus by His intimate friends, and how, upon the foundation of this strange belief, was there reared the edifice of the Christian Church? . . . Christianity never was the continuation of the work of a dead teacher. . . . According to modern naturalism, that event, which caused the founding of the Christian Church, was a vision, an hallucination; according to the New Testament, it was the resurrection of Jesus from the dead.[41]

The bodily resurrection of Jesus, Machen concluded, confirmed the belief of the disciples and apostles (including Paul) in a divine savior and further contributed to making Christianity a distinctive religion. With Liberalism, however, as Machen saw it, a belief in Jesus' continuing presence was rooted in the subjective consciousness of the disappointed disciples. Tauntingly he wrote: "It means that the Christian church is founded upon a pathological experience of certain persons in the first century. . . . It means that if there had been a good neurologist for Peter and the others to consult there never would have been a Christian church." [42]

Viewing such contrasting convictions between Christianity and Liberalism, Machen concluded that the latter was no mere heresy differing at isolated points from Christian teaching, but a totally

different religion constituting a unitary system of its own. Furthermore, Machen proclaimed that these separate faiths could not exist
within the same denomination, including his own Presbyterian
Church in the U.S.A. The liberals, he declared, should leave, and if
they would not, then the "Christians" should.[43] It was this conviction,
taught and preached aggressively, in a denomination and a seminary
that were moving toward a broadening and inclusive theological
position, which led, in the 1920's and the 1930's, to an inevitable and
exciting but painful struggle.

III

One frequently neglected aspect of Machen's thought has been his
attitude toward social issues. It is important to examine his views on
society before we proceed to the turbulent ecclesiastical struggle in
which he became involved, because they provide a further clue to
understanding both his personality and the role he played in
American religious and intellectual life.

Machen took a wide interest in the social issues of his day—a wider
interest, in fact, than most fundamentalist leaders took. While he
mentioned his social concerns occasionally in his sermons and books,
the normal channels for his pronouncements were personal correspondence, denominational and secular journals, and, above all, the
press—especially through a constant stream of letters to *The New
York Herald Tribune* and *The New York Times*.

Four convictions characterized his views on social issues: (1)
Machen was a firm civil libertarian who fought restrictions and
regulations placed on the individual. He was particularly adamant in
opposing trends of centralization in government, declaring that the
great American principle of liberty was being threatened.[44] (2)
Machen believed that the church itself, as a body (whether denomination, presbytery, or local congregation), should not take a stand on
social and political issues (e.g., prohibition) about which there was no
specific Scriptural guidance, although individuals might express
themselves.[45] There is some doubt as to whether this conviction was
consistent with historic Calvinism. (3) He held that the church of his
day was giving too much attention to the physical distresses of
mankind and insufficient regard to the spiritual needs of men and the
intellectual basis of the Christian faith.[46] (4) It was his conviction
that the true hope for social progress lay not in a modern "paganism,"
characterized by a profound satisfaction with human goodness, but

rather in Christian Fundamentalism (supernaturalism), with its emphasis on human sinfulness and the regenerating power of the Spirit of God.[47]

A survey of pronouncements by Machen on a variety of subjects illustrates his basic judgments concerning American society, especially his opposition to centralization in government.

Of the Civil War, Machen, whose uncle became a Confederate soldier and whose father declined an appointment as a United States district attorney out of fear that he would be required to prosecute those who openly adhered to the Southern cause, said: "Far from thinking that the Southern states in 1861 were guilty of treason or rebellion, I am convinced they were acting in the plainest possible exercise of constitutional rights, and that the real revolution was entered into by those who endeavored to prevent such plainly guaranteed rights." [48] This appeared to be an example of culture influencing religion rather than religion influencing culture, despite Machen's theoretical claim that the Christian church was in dire peril from a hostile contemporary culture and, in order to survive, must master such culture and consecrate it to the cause of Christ.[49]

The early proponents of women's rights found no solace in Machen's conservative views. In 1918 he spoke against a proposed amendment to the Constitution which would have granted suffrage to women. Machen interpreted the amendment as a divisive measure in wartime, an expression of "ill-timed and unintelligent feminism," and a matter which ought to be left to the individual states to decide.[50] Furthermore, he stated that there was no clear evidence that a majority of women desired suffrage as yet. `He concluded that the amendment represented an attempt to avoid a popular vote by unscrupulous suffragettes who were not representative of the women of the country.[51]

Machen's displeasure was particularly keen when state or federal authorities seemingly overstepped their jurisdiction in the field of education. He opposed the Lusk laws in New York State, which required the licensing of teachers, subject to state control and visitation, and he rejoiced when these laws were repealed.[52] Machen also took issue with a school law in Oregon (later tested by Nebraska) which provided that no language other than English should be studied in either public or private schools until the pupil had completed the first eight grades. The Supreme Court, overruling such legislation, agreed with Machen and others that families who desired to give their children some contact with the cultural and spiritual heritage of their race, at whatever age, should be permitted to do so.[53] In 1926, Machen disapproved of the creation of a federal Department of Education and appeared personally in Washington before a congressional committee to express his views. He saw the proposed uniformity as poor educational procedure as well as a threat to both personal liberty and parental authority.

> Intellectual decline comes through the development of this principle of unification and standardization to which I object. . . . In the sphere of education uniformity always means not something uniformly high but something uniformly low. . . . The aim of education is not to conform human beings to some fixed standard, but to preserve individuality, to keep human beings as much unlike one another in certain spheres as they possibly can be. . . . Standardization is an admirable thing in the making of Ford cars. But . . . a very harmful thing . . . in the case of human beings.[54]

Unlike many churchmen, Machen viewed with disfavor the National Prohibition Act of 1919 (better known as the Volstead Act), which prescribed in great detail rules for the enforcement of the law prohibiting the sale of alcoholic beverages and penalties to be imposed on persons violating those rules. His objection stemmed not only from the fact that he was not a strict prohibitionist but also from the belief that church support of the Act was unwise, convinced as he was that religious groups had no business to tell the state how to run its affairs.[55] In 1924, Machen spoke against proposed child labor legislation that was designed to give Congress power to limit, regulate, and prohibit the labor of persons under eighteen years of age. He viewed this as an extreme example of materialistic paternalism by the modern state as it attempted to usurp family prerogatives.[56] He also thought that such regulation should not be made applicable to the work of children on farms or in schools. If some legislation were needed, Machen preferred that such matters be handled by state rather than congressional powers.[57]

A typical example of Machen's fear of bureaucratization in the Federal Government occurred in 1925. The Secretary of Labor advocated the enrollment of aliens. Machen replied that if there were an enrollment of aliens, there might also have to be, in the interests of consistency, an enrollment of all citizens:

> If aliens were to be called upon, at the discretion of officials, for their registration cards, citizens must be given some means of proving that they are not aliens, and so they must presumably provide themselves with

registration cards, too. And so we shall have a full-fledged European police system established almost before we know it; the American citizen will be required as he goes from place to place to "show his papers" quite in the European style. And when that happens the real America will be dead.[58]

In the same year (1925) Machen wrote against the action of the national Phi Beta Kappa Society (of which he was a member), disputing its plan to refuse one of its chapters to any college that gave evidence of denying freedom of thought and speech. The background was the law against the teaching of evolution in Tennessee and the widely heralded Scopes Trial. Machen protested the entrance of the society into the field of political propaganda and "the destruction of its character as a society for the promotion of scholarship." [59] He also interpreted the proposal as a serious blow to denominational schools (i.e., those institutions which did not believe in evolution and desired to express themselves accordingly), as well as a threat to civil and religious liberty. Taking a rather typical ultraconservative posture on this issue, Machen argued that the right of voluntary association was denied in principle by such action.[60]

On no social subject did Machen speak more heatedly than on what he believed to be excessive appropriations for recreational purposes in the national parks. He was not opposed to conservation, but he deeply resented the implied paternalism of the national agencies in entering the field of recreation. Of the coming of the Federal Government to Mount Desert Island in Maine, his own summer home, Machen wrote bitterly:

A network of carriage roads . . . is scarring almost every mountainside. . . . The forest is being ruthlessly "cleaned up" until every bit of natural charm is destroyed. . . . The delicate beauty of those forests is being systematically forced into the commonplace mold of a city park. . . . These gentlemen regard a moss-covered rock as an eyesore which must be removed.[61]

Not all of Machen's social declarations reflected a conservative viewpoint. At the time of World War I he opposed a required military conscription, not because he was a pacifist (in fact he was not), but because he saw this conscription as one more invasion of personal rights. Again, in 1930, he looked with disfavor upon the Vestal Copyright Bill, which included, among other provisions, a ban on the importation of British editions of books by British authors whenever there was also an American publisher. He reasoned that this was a potential barrier to the interchange of ideas and in the field of publishing would erect a veritable Chinese wall of exclusion around this country.[62] A final illustration is more typical of Machen—and, some might add, reflects his insensitivity to the new age of mechanization in which he was living. This was his opposition to a jaywalking ordinance in Philadelphia. He believed that such an ordinance was an infringement on the personal freedom of the individual.[63]

On all these various issues, Machen stood unalterably against standardization, centralization of governmental powers, and what he termed "soul-killing" collectivism. In a generation marked by increasing centripetal forces, his view normally placed him in a defensive and negative position. On the "positive" side he favored the rights of the states over those of federal authorities and, ideally, favored the rights of the individual over those of the states. This pronounced individualism—already seen in his theology—reflected the nineteenth century more than the twentieth. It revealed a man more sympathetic to the Jeffersonian concept of liberty than to the Social Gospel of Walter Rauschenbusch or to the political stance of Franklin D. Roosevelt. It also left him seeking the religious conversion of all men as the crucial ingredient of true liberty in society, which, he believed, was giving more attention to the superstructure than to the foundation.[64] Furthermore, one may suggest that the identity so often noted between right-wing politics and right-wing religion is partially foreshadowed in Machen's social views.

IV

Opposed to centralization in government, Machen was equally set against administrative centralization and theological inclusiveness in religion. This leads us quite naturally to the ecclesiastical struggle in which Machen played the central role. The difficult events at Princeton Theological Seminary leading to the reorganization of that institution in 1929—and the departure of Machen—must be interpreted within the denominational context as well as the larger religious milieu of the early part of the twentieth century.

Presbyterians in America had experienced their share of theological and ecclesiastical controversy since the establishment of their faith in this country in the seventeenth century. By 1729 there had been those who favored and those who opposed a strict subscription of ministers and licentiates to the Westminster Confession of Faith and catechisms that issued in a compromise measure. Contention had been even greater at the time of the Great Awakening, when Presbyterians, like other Christians, were divided into Old Side and New Side, the former averse to the methods and beliefs of the movement, the latter supporting them. Early in the nineteenth century a Plan of Union (1801) between Presbyterians and the Congregationalists on the frontier had caused further strife. The Presbyterians became divided between New School men, who wished to keep the union, and Old School men, who resented the impact of New England theology on traditional Calvinism.[65] Other factors entered in, including differing attitudes toward the issue of slavery. The differences became so pronounced that the Old School and New School factions went their separate ways from 1837 to 1870, finally reuniting on the basis of the Westminster Confession of Faith. Princeton Seminary, in the 1830's, shifted from a moderate position to the Old School side, influenced in part by the founding of Union Theological Seminary in New York City (1836) under New School leadership and independent of the control of the General Assembly.[66] Even after the reunion of the Old School and New School factions, Princeton continued in the Old School tradition, loyal to Calvinism and the more conservative expressions of the faith. Within this broad context of previous controversy and division, Presbyterians confronted the challenge of a new Liberalism late in the nineteenth century and early in the twentieth century.

Among the Presbyterians, both the conservatives and the liberals counted their share of partial triumphs—without winning a decisive victory. The former, after several attempts, succeeded in 1893 in suspending from the Presbyterian ministry Charles A. Briggs, professor of Biblical theology at Union Seminary, for his rejection of the verbal inspiration of the Bible and his denial of the Mosaic authorship of the Pentateuch. The conservatives also crowded Harry Emerson Fosdick, a Baptist, from the pulpit of the First Presbyterian Church of New York City in 1925, although public sympathies remained with him.[67] The conservatives likewise were successful in forcing the General Assembly in 1910 to adopt the previously mentioned five-point doctrinal statement (reaffirmed in 1916 and 1923) as reflecting "essential and necessary" articles of faith. Ironically, the Assembly also declared that other unnamed articles were equally important, apparently fearing "the danger of seeming to reduce the essential faith of the Church to this brief compass." [68]

Despite such endeavors, the tide of Liberalism was coming in strongly. A modification of the Westminster Confession was brought about in 1903 that, among other things, explicitly affirmed the salvation of all who die in infancy.[69] More importantly, liberal leadership drew up in 1923 and published in 1924 the so-called Auburn Affirmation. This statement, eventually signed by 1,274 clergymen, challenged the right of the General Assembly to declare the five beliefs as special tests for ordination unless the constitution were changed by a vote of the presbyteries. It also declared that the five doctrines were not essential to the system of doctrine taught in the Scriptures and were merely theories about those facts and doctrines.[70] Despite the obvious liberal stance of this affirmation, the conservatives surprisingly took no official action against it, although their grumblings were widespread.

Because the continuing tensions between liberals and conservatives had become so acute, the General Assembly in 1925 finally appointed a committee of fifteen "to study the present spiritual condition of our Church and the causes making for unrest, and to report to the next General Assembly, to the end that the purity, peace, unity, and progress of the Church may be assured." [71] The committee in its report the following year recognized that the Presbyterian system admitted of diversity of view where the core of truth was identical, and stressed the conviction that the church had "flourished best . . . when it laid aside its tendencies to stress these differences, and put the emphasis on its unity of spirit." [72] The pronouncement satisfied neither the ultraconservatives nor the ultraliberals. It is within this framework of denominational controversy and general religious struggle that the days of crisis at Princeton Theological Seminary must be viewed and interpreted.

Eight years after Machen began at Princeton as an instructor, J. Ross Stevenson was elected president of the seminary (1914) to succeed Francis L. Patton. This event was an important watershed in the life of the institution because it marked the beginning of the end of the old "historic Princeton position." Stevenson, whom Norman F. Furniss referred to as "a man of less eminence in public life and less orthodoxy in theology" than Patton, openly declared that he desired the seminary to represent the whole Presbyterian Church and not a particular theological faction.[73] This immediately set against him a majority of the faculty, including Machen, who wished the seminary to reflect only the traditional Old School, Calvinistic theology. Actually, both Stevenson and Machen had their particular fears. Stevenson believed that loyalty to Princeton's traditional theological position would lead to religious isolation. He feared that the institution might become "an interdenominational Seminary for Bible School–premillennial–secession fundamentalism." Machen, on the other hand, dreaded the prospect of Princeton becoming a "cheap, Christian Endeavor" kind of school and eventually a Modernist institution.[74] The real point of issue at Princeton came to be, in the words of Lefferts A. Loetscher, "whether orthodoxy and tolerance were compatible." [75]

A built-in administrative factor added further fuel to a potentially explosive situation. The president of the seminary possessed broad powers, which some of the faculty resented; furthermore, there was the awkwardness of two boards governing the same institution. A board of directors was responsible for the educational life of the school, while a board of trustees governed its financial operations. The majority of the directors came to side with a majority of the faculty in supporting the conservative cause while the president, a minority of the directors, a minority of the faculty, and a majority of the trustees favored the more inclusive policy in both denomination and seminary.[76]

Specific events in the 1920's polarized the two sides almost completely. In 1920, President Stevenson, backed by Charles R. Erdman, professor of practical theology at the seminary, publicly supported a plan of union designed to unite organically nineteen evangelical denominations.[77] Machen, the opponent of what he called theological indifferentism and centralization, set himself against the plan, declaring that the language of the preamble was theologically vague and colorless and arguing that while the proposed plan had a creed, it was not one to which the clergy were required to subscribe.[78] Machen rejoiced when the plan, which he called "the most serious attack upon the character of the Presbyterian Church which has ever been made" and "a milestone on the way to complete skepticism," was defeated in the presbyteries 150–100.[79] Machen had been an instrumental force in bringing about the defeat, but the gulf between him and the president of the seminary had widened even further.

Machen's book *Christianity and Liberalism*, with its plea for a separation of the "Christians" from the liberals, appeared in 1923. In the fall of the same year, Machen accepted an appointment as stated supply of the First Presbyterian Church at Princeton. This too was a source of conflict. Henry van Dyke, professor of English literature at the university and an ordained Presbyterian clergyman, gave up his pew in the church to protest what he termed "the schismatic and unscriptural preaching of Dr. J. Gresham Machen." [80] Van Dyke claimed that Machen had devoted his sermons to a dismal discussion of the Modernist-Fundamentalist controversy rather than setting forth the claims of the gospel. Van Dyke absented himself until Machen resigned his preaching responsibility in July of 1924, giving as his reasons the pressure of his work at the seminary and his desire to be free to accept speaking opportunities away from Princeton.[81] The session "reluctantly and with the highest respect" accepted Machen's resignation.[82] Ironically, Charles R. Erdman succeeded Machen as stated supply. Erdman, a colleague of Machen's, while personally conservative in his theology, was a strong supporter of the president and an outspoken proponent of the inclusivist policy. Erdman, endorsed by Stevenson, also became a candidate for Moderator of the General Assembly in 1924 and 1925. In both years he was opposed by a majority of the faculty. He lost to Clarence E. Macartney, a conservative, in 1924, but won the office in 1925. Machen's firm public opposition to Erdman further intensified the tensions within a relatively small faculty of seventeen members.

Not unexpectedly, the continuing controversy engulfed members of the student body. In 1925 an organization called the League of Evangelical Students was formed after delegates from Princeton had come to question the doctrinal orthodoxy of an interseminary conference sponsored by the Middle Atlantic Association of Theological Seminaries. Stevenson and Erdman (the latter having served as faculty adviser to the students for twenty years) both opposed the new League, believing that its spirit was divisive, although the conservative majority of the faculty heartily endorsed the organization.[83] When the students differed among themselves as to the selection of a faculty adviser for another year (some were opposed to Erdman because of his attitude toward the League) the matter was finally referred to the faculty. With the conservatives in control, and upon Machen's motion, they selected as adviser one of their own kind, Robert Dick Wilson, rather than Erdman. The blame for the change was laid squarely at Machen's feet. Machen responded that the faculty had acted upon the matter only when requested to do so by the students, and that it had been a simple democratic choice.[84]

With a majority of the faculty and student body holding to religious conservatism at a time when the denomination was moving simultaneously toward "administrative centralization and theological decentralization," Stevenson took specific action in 1926.[85] He recommended to the General Assembly that Machen's appointment as professor of apologetics and ethics (which both boards had approved) be held up until the seminary could be investigated about conditions "subversive of Christian fellowship." [86] Speaking to the General Assembly, Stevenson said: "What I want is to have the light thrown on me, on the members of the Faculty and the whole institution. If there is to be judgment, let it fall where it will, and let the seminary go forward in the traditions of its founders." [87]

A committee was duly appointed to inquire into the situation. After lengthy considerations, which included personal interviews with members of the faculty, students, alumni, and members of the two boards, the committee reached the carefully weighed conclusion that the only solution to the existing problems was the reorganization of the seminary.[88] Machen, reflecting the urgent concern of his conservative colleagues, declared that such reorganization would have the result of "putting the present conservative majority out of control of the institution and putting into power a minority that represents, with regard to the fundamental questions of policy, a radically different point of view." [89] Having allowed ample time for reflection and measured judgment, the General Assembly in 1929 approved the plan of reorganization. The two boards gave way to a single board of trustees comprised of thirty-three members (eighteen ministers and fifteen elders), one third chosen from the board of directors, one third from the board of trustees, and one third from the church at large.[90] Very significantly, the approval of the seminary's reorganization by the General Assembly was made possible by the vote of a third "party" within the denomination, one neither extremely liberal nor extremely conservative but comprised of theological evangelicals who despite their doctrinal orthodoxy were not opposed to an inclusive policy within the church and at Princeton.[91] Machen reserved his greatest ire for these individuals, calling them "indifferentists" and "theological pacifists."

Feeling that he could not be a part of the reorganized inclusive seminary, and desiring an institution that would preserve the witness of traditional Calvinism, Machen led in the formation in the same year, 1929, of Westminster Theological Seminary, to be located in Philadelphia. Three other faculty members (Robert Dick Wilson, Oswald T. Allis, and Cornelius Van Til) and twenty students made the break from Princeton with him.[92] A total of fifty students registered for the first semester, a majority of whom came from Pennsylvania and New York with undergraduate preparation at such evangelical institutions as Wheaton and Asbury colleges and Taylor University.[93]

Carl McIntire and Harold J. Ockenga, both of whom were to become
prominent leaders in conservative circles, were members of the
original student body. Five full-time professors and three full-time
instructors supplemented by six part-time teachers comprised the
new faculty.[94] A unique arrangement for the governing of the
seminary was planned in order to avoid what some felt had
contributed to the difficult situation at Princeton. The founding
charter and constitution made no provision for the office of president
but rather allowed for a chairman of the faculty, elected by his peers.
Furthermore, three members of the faculty, elected annually, were to
meet with the trustees in an advisory capacity. In addition, nomina-
tions for the teaching staff of the seminary were limited to the
faculty.[95] The rationale behind these moves was to give the faculty a
major voice in the actual operation of the institution. Hopes were
high at the first exercises of the nascent, independent school. Machen
heralded Westminster Seminary as "the beginning of a great
movement to resist, and, if possible, overcome the tendency toward
Modernism, and one which would be a reformation like that of the
sixteenth century, with a return to common honesty and common
sense." [96]

With Machen, however, division was to become a process, not an
event, undercutting the enthusiasm of the early days at Westminster
Seminary. Shortly after the founding of the seminary, Machen,
disturbed by the influence of Liberalism on the foreign mission fields
and especially among the administrative leaders of his own denomination, the Presbyterian Church in the U.S.A., organized the Independent Board for Presbyterian Foreign Missions.[97] The General
Assembly declared this board to be schismatic and ordered all
members who were Presbyterians to withdraw from it or stand trial.
As one would expect, Machen refused to obey the mandate, was duly
tried, and in 1935 was suspended from the ministry.[98] Thereupon, in
the endeavor to maintain a "true church," he led in the establishment
of the Presbyterian Church of America (1936) and was elected its first
Moderator. When the parent denomination, the Presbyterian Church
in the U.S.A, successfully brought suit against the new denomination
because of the confusion created by the similarity of names, Machen's
faction changed its title to the Orthodox Presbyterian Church
(1939).[99] Some who had agreed with the move from Princeton to
Westminster Seminary declined to support the fledgling denomination, thereby further weakening the struggling seminary and making

more difficult the growth of the new church. One of these was Clarence E. Macartney, Machen's close friend and a member of the governing board at Westminster Seminary. He referred to the new denomination as a "cloud on the horizon" and an abortive attempt that was followed by "only a handful of sincere and courageous men." [100] By this time Machen had separated himself not only from all liberals but also from many conservatives and a few ultraconservatives as well. The "true" fellowship was to become even more select, this time the result of a division from Machen rather than by him.

Carl McIntire of Collingswood, New Jersey, joined by J. Oliver Buswell, president of Wheaton College, and Allan A. MacRae, a professor at Westminster Seminary, led a break, during the last month of Machen's life, against his denomination, which eventually led to the founding of the Bible Presbyterian Synod (1937). The issues involved concerned doctrine, Christian liberty, and church polity. McIntire and his group claimed that attacks were being made on premillennialism; they advocated complete abstinence rather than moderation in the use of alcoholic beverages, and they preferred, in some instances (e.g., in their support of the Independent Board for Presbyterian Foreign Missions) a congregational rather than a presbyterial form of church government.[101] When McIntire left the Presbyterian Church of America to form his own fellowship, he took with him thirteen ministers and three elders.[102] The new Bible Presbyterian Synod immediately announced its intention to revise the Westminster Confession of Faith "in any particulars in which the premillennial teaching of the Scriptures may be held to be obscured." [103]

Amid these winnowing events, where strangely enough Machen found himself separated from a portion of the movement he had virtually created singlehandedly (i.e., he was no longer in control of the Independent Board), he struggled manfully to defend the faith as he understood it.[104] He spoke of Gideon's three hundred and the remnant of Israel, and he labored feverishly to equate his "true church," already deeply divided, with these ideals. In such a context—exhausted and spent—he journeyed to North Dakota to try to hold together a few churches of his own denomination. There he contracted his fatal illness.[105] The body of the lifelong champion of orthodox Presbyterianism was returned to Philadelphia, where ironically his funeral service was held, not in a Presbyterian church, but in the Spruce Street Baptist Church. This was a congregation whose pastor, a graduate of Westminster Seminary, shared Machen's views.[106]

V

In perspective, several conclusions may be drawn from this study of the life of J. Gresham Machen. Initially, and partially over his own objections, Machen must still be considered a fundamentalist. Despite the fact that he had some differences with Fundamentalism in piety and doctrinal belief, as pointed out earlier, the nature of his protest against Liberalism, the attention he gave to the five "essentials" of 1910 (seemingly as much consideration as to the five points of Calvinism), and his intransigent mood and spirit—these combined to place Machen within the fundamentalist camp. And he may be considered the inspirer, certainly against his will, of an ultrafundamentalism expressed in the separatist action and thought of Carl McIntire.

Machen also illustrates another contribution of the South to the indigenous American movement known as Fundamentalism. His family roots were entwined in southern soil. His relatives were openly sympathetic to the cause of the Confederacy. His most influential instructor at Johns Hopkins reflected southern mores and thought (Professor Gildersleeve, a native of Charleston, South Carolina, had taught twenty years at the University of Virginia before assuming his responsibilities at Johns Hopkins). The city in which the Machens lived, Baltimore, preserved southern culture. The church the Machens attended was known as a congregation with southern affinities and, in fact, later became officially affiliated with the Southern Presbyterian Church. Machen's social views, nurtured as they were in his own aristocratic, elitist background, also echoed southern judgments.

Theologically, it would appear that Machen, the last great defender of the Hodge-Warfield tradition, should be remembered for the role he played as an early and scholarly critic of Liberalism. Long before Harry Emerson Fosdick's sermon of 1935, "The Church Must Go Beyond Modernism," Machen was warning of an easygoing optimism about man and society, stressing the danger of humanizing God and overadjusting to modern culture. With an emphasis on the transcendence of God and the sinfulness of man, Machen appeared to foreshadow the coming of the more "realistic" theological forces of the mid-twentieth century. And just as history appeared to discipline theological Liberalism and vindicate neo-orthodoxy (through the failure of the League of Nations, the depression, two world wars, the Korean conflict, the insights of depth psychology, and the ever-present threat of a third world war), so one might make a case that history also vindicated Machen—especially in his concept of man. Furthermore, as a critic of Liberalism, Machen early cautioned against the impossibility of "reconstructing" Jesus so as to harmonize him with preconceived rationalistic notions. He reminded religious leaders of the difficulty of separating the natural from the supernatural in Jesus, particularly when a supernatural belief such as the resurrection of Jesus was woven so deeply into the fabric of the Christian message. He also admonished those who were overly subjective in their approach to religion, sometimes creating thereby as many religions as there were subjective judgments.

If the foregoing illustrations are reflective of Machen's theological "strength," his doctrinal weaknesses may also be suggested. His contemporary opponents believed that his theological assumptions, especially those dealing with the existence of God, were greater than the evidence he provided. In addition, his concept of the church as a voluntary society (in the sense that one may join or not join, similar to a political club) has been criticized as being more Anabaptist than Presbyterian in nature.[107] But greater than his opponents' disagreement with any particular belief is the judgment that Machen doggedly made theology an "either-or" proposition. He gave the impression that truth was found only on his side—apparently to be buried in his tomb, or, at least, the tombs of his disciples. The facts of Christianity could be interpreted only his way. Such dogmatism appeared to be almost as exclusive as the aristocracy from which Machen sprang and caused more than a few to believe that while his orthodoxy may have had rational validity, it was neither flexible, warm, nor evangelical.[108]

As a theologian, Machen has been evaluated differently by different men.[109] There is no such disagreement in interpreting Machen as a religious politician. The verdict is nearly unanimous that in this area he failed and for a simple reason. The heart of politics is to know when to compromise, but the word "compromise" was foreign to Machen's vocabulary.[110] Because of rigidity in "practical" affairs Machen became the major catalyst that divided the Presbyterians, leading to an independent board of missions and eventually to the Orthodox Presbyterian Church. Such complete unyieldingness placed the ultraconservative Presbyterian in an ever-diminishing group of allies while simultaneously adding to the number of his theological opponents. Ernest R. Sandeen has effectively described this man of loneliness:

> Machen could be understood by other intellectuals, though they might not agree with him. . . . But when he stepped out of his role as the intellectual into that of the denominational politician, he proved hopelessly inept. . . . What he called faithful militant witnessing for the truth was often nothing more than perverse obstinacy and a fatal lack of openness to the truth that might (however dimly) glow in some other heart. When crossed, Machen typically cut off the former friend or ally with an irreversible anathema and proceeded on his way uncompromised but more than ever the hermit saint. The medieval anchorites may have been honored in some Christian communities, but few were ever elected pope.[111]

Even Machen's sympathetic biographer, Ned B. Stonehouse, while referring to the former's absence of political expediency and craft as a sign of strength, nevertheless admits that there was in Machen a kind of generalship which was satisfied to state and expound principles and objectives and then simply appeal to men to follow them. Little or no time was devoted to persuading his comrades of the necessity of taking the measures that he believed were required. In a classic understatement, Stonehouse concludes: "It is possible therefore that Machen contributed somewhat to the lack of harmony among the other Presbyterian leaders." [112]

Lefferts A. Loetscher implies that part of the problem of Machen's leadership—indeed, that of the conservative majority at Princeton—was the lack of pastoral experience.[113] That is a possibility, although one may also argue that men such as J. Frank Norris, John Roach Straton, and William Bell Riley were lifelong pastors whose contact with people at the grass-roots level failed to deliver them from either dogmatism of doctrine or dogmatism of spirit. What is known is that Machen's independent seminary grew to only moderate size and that "the true church" of which he was the founder has remained a small, factional group at best.[114]

A final look at Machen's contribution to American religious culture indicates that his unquestioned integrity, courage, and perseverance were countered by an individualistic, absolutist outlook on societal and theological issues, and an overabsorption with the dangers of Protestant Liberalism. This dogmatism and lack of balance, while appealing to some evangelicals, isolated a larger number of both evangelicals and nonevangelicals. His life might have been saved from such a melancholy interpretation had he recognized the importance of the judgment of the group as a check against extreme individualism, the insights of the religious experiences of others, and the fact that tolerance still remains one of the greatest of scholarly virtues.

CHAPTER SEVEN

William Jennings Bryan
STATESMAN-FUNDAMENTALIST

FUNDAMENTALISM'S best-known spokesman without doubt was
William Jennings Bryan. He was a lawyer, professional politician,
unequaled American orator, editor, social and political reformer,
self-proclaimed and widely accepted "champion of the people," and
popular lay preacher. With his national influence, in contrast to the
regional impact of other representatives of ultraconservative theology, the colorful Bryan in his twilight years brought Fundamentalism
to the attention of the masses through his relentless opposition to the
Darwinian theory of evolution.

Bryan's Fundamentalism, however, was not an appendage of his
later years. The ingredients of that theological tendency and
life-style had been with him from his earliest days. Yet this
charismatic leader, to whom the fundamentalists looked for deliver-
ance from the threat of religious Liberalism as farmers and blue-
collar workers had once looked to him for rescue from the monied
interests of the East, did not fit many of the traditional fundamentalist stereotypes. He was unique in person and emphasis as well as in
the quality and persuasiveness of his legendary voice. Following a
cursory review of Bryan's life and thought, this chapter will trace the
development of his religious posture, with particular emphasis upon
parental training; thereafter it will seek to indicate the indigenous
nature of Bryan's Fundamentalism.[1] Such a study is important
because it further illustrates the considerable diversity among
fundamentalist leaders; it also gives us a truer picture of the "Great
Commoner" (as he came to be called) than that of the aged,
out-maneuvered, humiliated antievolutionist at the Scopes Trial.
Moreover, in the present day, when many are calling for renewed

William Jennings Bryan at his desk

integrity in government, it shows us the difficulties in the application of religious principles to national and international political problems.

I

William Jennings Bryan was born of rugged Irish-English-Scotch ancestry in Salem, Illinois, March 19, 1860.[2] He received his education at Illinois College, where he majored in classical studies, and at the Union College of Law in Chicago. Bryan initially practiced law in Jacksonville, Illinois, and later in Lincoln, Nebraska. In 1884, the fledgling, impecunious attorney married Mary Baird, the educated and refined daughter of a prosperous merchant. To be of assistance to her husband, she also studied law and was admitted to the bar just four years later. She was the only woman in her class at the Union College of Law, and, scholastically, ranked third among seventeen candidates.

Bryan entered upon his political career in earnest in 1891 after failing to distinguish himself as a lawyer. Twice the people of the First Congressional District of Nebraska elected him to serve as their congressman in the U.S. House of Representatives. A campaign for the Senate followed. Although Bryan, a Democrat, captured a substantial majority of the votes, he lost the race in the midst of a Republican landslide because at that time senators were chosen by members of the state legislature rather than by popular election. Following this defeat, Bryan became editor-in-chief of the *Omaha World-Herald*, and continued as a popular lecturer on bimetallism. Then came the dramatic campaign of 1896, which was the first of three occasions when he was the Democratic Party's nominee for President of the United States.

At the youthful and unprecedented age of thirty-six, Bryan won the nomination "by a perfect blend of oratorical brilliance, political finesse, and sheer luck."[3] The key policy which he favored to handle the financial difficulties of the day was the free and unlimited coinage of silver without waiting for the aid or consent of any other nation. The emotional turning point of the nominating convention at Chicago was reached when Bryan concluded an eloquent and moving address with classical words based upon Biblical metaphors:

> Having behind us the producing masses of this nation and the world, supported by the commercial interests, the laboring interests, and the toilers everywhere, we will answer their demand for a gold standard by saying to them: "You shall not press down upon the brow of labor this crown of thorns, you shall not crucify mankind upon a cross of gold."[4]

Despite receiving a total popular vote larger than that of any previously elected president, Bryan lost his bid for the nation's highest office to William McKinley, who received 271 electoral votes to Bryan's 176. The popular vote was much closer, with McKinley drawing 7,107,822, or 50.88 percent, to Bryan's 6,511,073, or 46.77 percent.[5] While the apex of Bryan's political career had already been reached in 1896, he continued as the standard-bearer of his party for nearly twenty years. In 1900 he ran a second time against McKinley on a platform that advocated "free silver" and opposed "imperialism," applying the term to his country's annexation of the Philippines. In 1908, Bryan's opponent was William Howard Taft, supported by Theodore Roosevelt. The issue was the nature and role of financial trusts, although personal charges and countercharges beclouded the campaign.[6] In each instance, Bryan lost more decisively than in 1896, capturing 155 electoral votes out of a possible 447 in 1900 and winning 162 out of a possible 483 in 1908.

In 1898, at the time of the Spanish-American War, Bryan, the erstwhile proponent of world peace, organized and commanded a regiment of soldiers from Nebraska, holding the rank of colonel. On the day the war ended, he resigned his position in the Army as an expression of opposition to the developing imperialism of his country. In 1901, after the second of his unsuccessful efforts to gain the presidency, Bryan founded and edited a weekly journal called *The Commoner*, which became an important channel for the dissemination of his political, social, and religious views.

Frustrated three times in his own attempt to become the leader of his country, the dauntless Bryan persisted in state and national politics until destiny and political opportunism provided him the occasion to become a "kingmaker" for someone else. When the Democrats seemed hopelessly deadlocked in their endeavor to choose a presidential candidate at Baltimore in 1912, Bryan strategically switched his loyalties from Champ Clark of Missouri, speaker of the House of Representatives, to Woodrow Wilson of New Jersey.[7] This unexpected support eventually led to Wilson's nomination on the forty-sixth ballot, and ultimately to his election as President. The reward for Bryan was an appointment as Secretary of State in Wilson's cabinet, a position for which he was eminently unqualified. Bryan, however, held the office with some distinction from 1913 to 1915. The achievement in which he took the greatest pride was the successful negotiation of peace treaties with thirty foreign nations whereby these powers agreed to submit all disputes to an impartial inquiry and to delay military hostilities a full year while arbitration was taking place. Ironically, at the time of World War I, President Wilson and his cabinet were unwilling to apply this principle to Germany; whereupon, in protest, the courageous Bryan resigned as Secretary of State.[8]

During the last decade of his life, while continuing to exercise leadership in the councils of his party, Bryan gave himself increasingly to religious interests. He continued to lecture on the Chautauqua circuit, which he had been doing since 1896, and where he was widely hailed as the most inspirational of speakers. He fought tenaciously against the teaching of evolution in the public schools. He taught an immensely popular Bible class in Miami, Florida, where he had moved in 1921. In time, he rose to the defense of the fundamentalist movement both within and without his own Presbyterian denomination. The weary warrior, veteran of many a political and religious campaign, died at Dayton, Tennessee, July 26, 1925, five short days after the conclusion of the renowned Scopes Trial. Paradoxically, the intermittent pacifist was buried, at his own request, in the national military cemetery at Arlington, Virginia.

II

For many, the Scopes Trial has greatly distorted the image of William Jennings Bryan. If he had died a year earlier, the public undoubtedly would have remembered him as the political and social reformer that he was—for good or ill, depending upon one's evaluation of individual reforms—rather than as the zealous defender of a literalist interpretation of the Scriptures. As a reformer, Bryan had championed the cause of the underprivileged, especially the farmer and other laborers, endeavoring to assist them in securing equal rights with those whom he thought were the overprivileged. While living in an era that was dominated by a passion for social progress, including reform in politics, business, and morals, Bryan had been frequently in the forefront of the struggle, both in time and in program. Actually, his political and social views had been an unusual combination of progressive and conservative elements invariably intertwined with his religious beliefs.

Among the reforms that Bryan championed and that eventually became legalized in his own day were the popular election of United States senators (supported in part as the result of his own experience), a federal income tax, women's suffrage, national prohibition, the publication of the names of the owners of newspapers, the creation of a Department of Labor in the national government with its executive officer holding cabinet rank, the outlawing of contributions by corporations to national campaign funds, the publication of individual campaign contributions *before* elections, the enlargement of the powers of the Interstate Commerce Commission, tighter governmental control of such diverse groups as the meat-packing industry and the railroads, and the introduction of the initiative and referendum into contemporary voting practices.

The Great Commoner fought for other causes before their time had come, which reflected his forward-looking and crusading spirit. These included the limitation of the presidency to a single six-year term (advocated by him *prior* to each of his own three candidacies); a national primary; the abolition of the electoral college, with its replacement by direct, or popular, voting for the presidential office; a bipartisan national bulletin for the purpose of keeping the electorate informed on political issues; compulsory signing of all newspaper editorials; a referendum on war, except in the case of actual invasion; a national minimum living wage law; and a change in the Constitution to make it more easily amendable.[9] Furthermore, Bryan favored a single standard of sexual morality and, in conjunction with his support of women's suffrage, believed that the vote of women, when it became a reality, would outlaw both war and the legalized saloon.

In the realm of international politics, Bryan hailed the League of Nations as "the greatest step toward peace in 1,000 years," stressing the fact that the substitution of reason for force (as he had advocated when Secretary of State) was in itself an epoch-making advance.[10] But not even Bryan's attempt to secure world peace received more attention or reflected greater conviction than did his struggle against alcoholic beverages.

Throughout his lifetime Bryan saw intoxicants as the nation's worst enemy and the liquor traffic as its greatest evil.[11] He viewed the drinking of alcohol as a sin against the individual, against society, and against God.[12] Drink, he reasoned, brought no advantage, decreased a man's efficiency, imparted a constitutional weakness to one's offspring, was a waste of money, formed a dangerous habit, caused poverty and crime, and, from a Christian standpoint, provided a poor example.[13] Bryan did more than "preach" against the practice of drinking. He was a total abstainer who had signed the temperance pledge even before he knew its meaning. As a Bible teacher he asserted that the wine mentioned in the account of Jesus' first miracle at Cana of Galilee was, in reality, unfermented grape juice, and he used the New Testament record to attack the liquor interests.[14] When Secretary of State, with President Wilson's approval, Bryan and his wife declined to serve alcoholic beverages at social occasions, substituting instead White Rock water and grape juice. At one state dinner the Russian ambassador told his dinner partner that it was the first time in years that he had tasted water.[15]

As a politician, Bryan initially favored local option in the control of the liquor traffic. Later, in 1908, he advocated county option; in 1914 he advocated state prohibition; and, finally, he championed the cause of national prohibition. No one was a more ardent spokesman for outlawing liquor than the tireless Nebraskan who crisscrossed the country speaking with the zeal of an evangelist on behalf of the Eighteenth Amendment. To legalize alcohol, Bryan told the crowds, was insanity. "How absurd it is to license a man to make men drunk and then fine men for getting drunk . . . it [is] like licensing a person to spread the itch and then fining the people for scratching." [16]

Bryan's personal presence at the State Department when the Eighteenth Amendment was signed into law was high recognition of his leadership in making America "dry." Furthermore, the National Dry Federation (of which he was then president) presented Bryan with a silver loving cup for his gallantry in the cause of prohibition. Shortly thereafter, in his sixty-first year, Bryan optimistically predicted that within his lifetime he expected to see the outlawing of the saloon "in every civilized nation." [17]

There was no doubt that Bryan, along with Billy Sunday, had been America's foremost spokesman for the cause of temperance. Yet there was something deeply ironical about the fact that the portly Bryan with a Gargantuan appetite could be so abstemious about drink and so undisciplined about food. Overeating was a lifelong vice, for as a boy Bryan had carried extra pieces of bread in his pockets to satisfy his appetite between meals. As an adult, in the last years of his life, he carried a pith helmet filled with radishes also to satisfy his hunger. On one occasion, the constantly hungry but never "thirsty" Bryan said with deep conviction:

> I am fond of radishes; my good wife knows it and keeps me supplied with them when she can. I eat radishes in the morning; I eat radishes at noon; I eat radishes at night; I like radishes.[18]

Frequently progressive in an era known for its progressiveness, Bryan was not without his conservative counterpoints, the most notable of which was his attitude on race. For Bryan, the voice of the people was the voice of God *(vox populi vox Dei)*, but this hardly applied when it came to the voice of the Negro. The Negro's voice had been muted by centuries of slavery and, despite theoretical emancipation in Bryan's time, the black person in the South was still imprisoned by an educational qualification for suffrage which virtually left him without political expression. Because Bryan's strength came in large measure from the South, he could not afford to lose southern support by pronouncements of a too-liberal nature on racial issues. His political dilemma and personal roots compounded the situation. With the white southern vote already in his column, realism dictated that the black vote, at least in the South, was not crucially needed. Consequently, in the words of Louis W. Koenig, "Bryan faced the political task of reassuring his Southern supporters, while subtly encouraging a Negro breakaway from the Republicans." [19]

Bryan's specific statements appeared to reflect more his own southern cultural heritage than his religious idealism of brotherhood and understanding. He declared that the white man had a more advanced civilization and higher ideals than the black man; that the white people of the South, if in control, would be more apt to deal justly with the blacks than vice versa; and that the white people already realized that it was in their interest to raise the standard and elevate the condition of the black man.[20] In Bryan's judgment, the existence of an educational qualification for suffrage did not deny the natural and the inalienable rights of the black man. If he could not vote today, then he could look forward to voting tomorrow. Besides, the suffrage amendments in the South, which were introduced in self-defense and for self-preservation, were not nearly so severe as the Republican colonial policy in the Philippines! [21] Bryan added that the Republican leaders were stirring up racial antagonism in the country to keep the "colored" vote solid for the Republican Party. He concluded that the amalgamation of the races, which would be the result of social equality, was not the solution to the racial question. The solution was for the Negro to establish a reputation for virtue, sobriety, and good sense. Then he could devote himself to the building up of the society which would satisfy his needs.[22]

III

William Jennings Bryan was not a trained theologian, but he liked to speak on religion even more than on politics, and the world knew that he enjoyed doing the latter! As Bryan was progressive in his political and social outlook with a few important exceptions, he was conservative in his theological beliefs, also with a few important exceptions. Since he was not a theologian, he never set forth a systematic presentation of his religious ideas. A review of his books and speeches, however, indicates his major Christian emphases.

Bryan was an avowed supernaturalist whose religious convictions were rooted in the Bible. The Scriptures for him were so divinely inspired as to be free from error and to be an infallible authority concerning what God has said and done.[23] Bryan stated flatly that these Scriptures have never yet been incorrect on any issue. The proofs of such inspiration for him were internal ones—fulfilled prophecies, the harmony of the Biblical documents, and the unity of their structure despite the fact that they were written by many individuals whose lives spanned many centuries.[24] The Bible, for Bryan, had pragmatic advantages. It gave meaning to existence, supplied each individual with a working plan for life, and answered the longing of the heart with a satisfying knowledge of God.[25] The God revealed by these Scriptures and in whom Bryan believed was all-wise, all-powerful, and all-loving. Bryan preferred to begin with such a God and "reason down" from that high premise rather than begin with dull, inanimate matter and "reason up" to God. He argued that belief in this God was not an optional matter. It was the necessary basis of every moral code as well as the required foundation for the establishment of justice and brotherhood among nations and men.[26]

Like most religious conservatives, Bryan gave Jesus a central place in his theology. He stated that the life of Jesus, his teachings, and his death, as well as the general impression that these have made on the human race, led him to conclude that Jesus was divine. A particularly interesting argument for Jesus' divinity was Bryan's conviction that one cannot contemplate the fact of Christ's life without feeling that in some way that life is related to those now living. "Somehow," he mused, "there is a cord that stretches from the life of Jesus to modern man." [27] Acceptance of Jesus' divinity by Bryan included a belief in the virgin birth, the vicarious atonement, and the bodily resurrection of Christ. Such a supernatural Christ, Bryan declared, is the only Christ of whom the Bible speaks, and to believe his divinity is the easiest way to explain his personality and the miracles that he performed.[28]

Despite the fact that Bryan was an avowed supernaturalist, his theology had its this-worldly aspects. He did emphasize immortality, but even in this respect he stressed that a belief in the future life restrains the individual from evil deeds in this life.[29] Unlike many other fundamentalists, Bryan was not a pronounced adventist. On one occasion he commented that there were too many people who didn't believe in the first coming of Christ to worry about those who didn't believe in the second.[30] Bryan's almost complete silence on the second coming, and consequently his silence on premillennialism, tied in with his understanding of the social application of the gospel and the nature of man. Rather than expecting the world to grow progressively worse until the second coming of Christ, as the premillennialists believed, Bryan stressed the possibility of a better society in his own day through Christians who applied the teachings of Jesus to every human situation. Yet Bryan cannot be classified as a postmillennialist. In 1924 he wrote that he would give no attention to the question of premillennialism or postmillennialism. "Both schools rely upon the Bible as their authority; it is not a question of inspiration but of interpretation. Both realize that Christ's second coming depends upon His first coming." [31] Beyond that, Bryan had nothing to say about the second advent of Christ or the millennialist positions when discussing the crucial theological issues of his day.

Bryan's suggestions as to where the social applications of the teachings of Jesus should be carried out were far-ranging in their scope. He proposed the establishment of church loan societies to assist the "temporarily embarrassed"; he begged for sympathy and fellowship between capital and labor; he condemned the rich tax dodger and the "corrupter of government"; and he pleaded for a new sense of fairness, duty, and patriotism.[32] He also suggested that love, forgiveness, friendship, and cooperation be the foundation of a new world order instead of hatred, revenge, and war. In this latter context Bryan was applying to international relations the teaching of Jesus to "love your enemies" and the words of Paul: "If thine enemy hunger, feed him; if he thirst, give him drink: for in so doing thou shalt heap coals of fire on his head." (Rom. 12:20). In the bitter days that followed World War I, Bryan declared that there never was a time in the world's history when the returning of good for evil was more imperatively needed. In response to the declaration by President Lowell of Harvard University that militarism must be fought with militarism, Bryan responded: "Those who advocate the policy of 'fighting the devil with fire' seem to overlook two important facts: (1) the devil is better acquainted with fire than his adversaries; (2) being at no expense for fuel he has an economic advantage which tells powerfully in any prolonged contest." [33]

Bryan's idealism was linked with his understanding of the nature of man. He did not believe that man was perfect, but neither did he accept man's total depravity as many Calvinists have done. Between the extremes of perfection and total depravity Bryan leaned in the direction of stressing what man might become through "pure purpose and persevering diligence." [34] Surprisingly for one who was so orthodox in other beliefs, Bryan encouraged men to have faith both in themselves and in mankind. He cautioned against confidence in oneself which would lead to egotism, but also indicated that egotism was not the worst of possible faults. Bryan quoted with approval his father who had said on one occasion that if a man had a big head, it could be whittled down, but that if he had a little head, there was no hope for him.[35] Bryan's exhortation was to have faith in one's self, but a faith which was conditioned by moral, intellectual, and physical preparation. Bryan was equally realistic about faith in mankind. He reasoned that it was better to trust others and to be occasionally deceived by them than to be distrustful and live alone.

> Mankind deserves to be trusted. There is something good in everyone, and that good responds to sympathy. . . . The heart of mankind is sound; the sense of justice is universal. Trust it, appeal to it, do not violate it. . . . Link yourselves in sympathy with your fellowmen; mingle with them; know them and you will trust them and they will trust you.[36]

This high regard for humanity was at the heart of Bryan's political and social philosophy as well as being important in his theology. As early as 1888 he declared that history teaches that, as a general rule, truth is found among the masses and emanates from them. He stated: "Earth has no grander sight than the people moving forward in one compact mass, destroying evil, suppressing wrong, advancing morality. Divinity itself might look with admiration upon such a picture." [37] Those were strong words, indeed, for one who eventually enlisted in the fundamentalist political and theological camp.

As one would expect, Bryan placed a high premium on service. He believed that a wonderful transformation would occur in society when all were animated by a desire to contribute to the public good rather than by an ambition to absorb as much as possible from others.[38] Such service, Bryan stated, was the measure of greatness and happiness for both the individual and the nation. Bryan, the patriot as well as the Christian, especially hoped that the goodness associated with service would be a trait of his own beloved country. He wanted America to "destroy every throne on earth, not by force of violence, but by showing the world something better than a throne— a government resting upon the consent of the governed—strong because it is loved, and loved because it is good." [39]

A knowledge of Bryan's religious tenets makes it easier to understand his deep-rooted opposition to evolution. In his view the acceptance of Darwinism raised serious questions about Biblical authority because its conception of the origin of man differed from the account in Genesis, where it is stated that man was made by the direct fiat of God. Evolution also undercut social reform since, by this theory, life was governed by the slow, gradual "survival of the fittest," not by the deliberate application of Christian principle. Bryan also argued that this unproven hypothesis weakened faith in God, threatened the orthodox interpretation of Jesus, made a mockery of prayer, lessened the sense of brotherhood, contributed to class struggle, encouraged "brutishness," and undermined belief in immortality.[40] His "answer" to this major threat was to be found in clergymen who taught the Biblical account of creation, in trustees who permitted only Christian teachers (meaning those who rejected evolution) to teach in Christian schools, and in taxpayers who prevented the teaching in public schools of atheism, agnosticism, Darwinism, or any other theory that "linked man to the brute." [41] Finally, the hope of the world, in Bryan's judgment, lay not in the heartless speculation of the survival of the fittest, but in the conversion of society through the silent influence of a noble Christian example that returned good for evil.[42]

A last belief held by Bryan, one that is important to an understanding of his life, and that many biographers have neglected, was his firm conviction of retribution. He believed deeply in a God of justice who in this life stood behind the truth and was able to bring victory to his side. He also proclaimed the existence of a future life in which the righteous would be rewarded and the wicked would be punished.[43] Such convictions led Bryan to say: "One can afford to be in a minority, but he cannot afford to be wrong; if he is in a minority and right, he will someday be in the majority." [44] This belief in the righteousness of his causes and in that elusive "some day" when they—and he—would be vindicated, provided the Great Commoner with much of his motivation. It also made his life—especially the concluding years—all the more melancholy.

IV

The clue to understanding Bryan's religious and political convictions lies in the nature of his training as a child and youth. His parents were deeply religious people who transmitted their faith to Bryan. Consequently, by the time he left home for college their beliefs had become his and these convictions were not to change appreciably in the years that were to follow. Just as he never varied the style of his clothes from youth to old age (he wore a black frock coat), so Bryan did not deviate noticeably from the religious persuasions of his own home.[45]

Bryan's religious conditioning began with his paternal great-grandfather. William Bryan was such a prominent Christian in the Blue Ridge Mountains of Virginia, near Sperryville, that the Baptist church in his neighborhood became known as the "Bryan Meeting House." Silas Willard Bryan, the father of William Jennings Bryan, inherited such a religious tradition, gave it to his children, and, in the process, experienced religion himself. One event in his life was especially formative. Gravely ill with pneumonia, he prayed earnestly for healing, promising God that if his health were restored, he would pray three times daily the rest of his life. When he did regain his health, he kept the promise despite a demanding schedule as lawyer, politician, circuit judge, and farmer.

Bryan's father was a devout Baptist; his mother, Mariah Jennings Bryan, was a conscientious Methodist who eventually transferred her church membership to her husband's congregation in 1877 at the age of forty-three. The parents conducted family devotions regularly as well as faithfully attending church, Sunday school, and prayer meeting. The piety of the family was evident in the practices of Bryan's father, who had once used tobacco and snuff but eventually became convinced that these were harmful and gave them up just before the birth of his son. One biographer wrote of the Bryan family: "The Protestant [evangelical] religion—the gospel service, the revival, the emphasis on missions, and the appeal to the heart rather than to the mind in soul-winning—amply sufficed for them, their community, and the Middle West." [46]

While loyal to the Baptist and Methodist churches, Bryan's parents were not rigid denominationalists. Annually they invited the ministers of the churches in Salem, including a Catholic priest, to their home for a social occasion, and annually a load of hay was sent at harvesttime to each of the same clergymen from the Bryan farm. Of these various churches and their representatives, Bryan indicated that there was agreement upon the "fundamentals" and charity regarding all the nonessentials.[47]

Reflecting upon the richness of his own heritage, Bryan commented in his Memoirs:

I was born in the greatest of all ages. No golden ages of the past offered any such opportunity for large service, and therefore, for the enjoyment that comes from [the] consciousness that one has been helpful. I was born a member of the greatest of all races—the Caucasian Race, and had mingled in my veins the blood of English, Irish, and Scotch. . . .

I was born a citizen of the greatest of all lands. So far as my power to prevent was concerned, I might have been born in the darkest of the continents and among the most backward of earth's peoples. It was a gift of priceless value to see the light in beloved America, and to live under the greatest of the republics of history.

And I was equally fortunate in my family environment. I cannot trace my ancestry beyond the fourth generation and there is not among them . . . one of great wealth or great political or social prominence, but . . . they were honest, industrious, Christian, moral, religious people—not a black sheep in the flock, not a drunkard, not one for whose life I would have to utter an apology. The environment in which my youth was spent was as ideal as any that I know.[48]

With such a high evaluation of his heredity and environment, it is no surprise that Bryan's beliefs did not change during his lifetime. In his opinion he had received the best—he was beginning at the highest level—and therefore there was little, if any, room for growth. The challenge was not to grow; the challenge was to share the legacy of one's good fortune.

The shaping of Bryan's own religious fortune, in addition to the influence received at home, centered in the churches of Salem, Illinois. He attended the Methodist Sunday school in the morning with his mother and the Baptist Sunday school in the afternoon with his father. Bryan was converted at the age of fourteen at a revival service in the Presbyterian church, after which he joined that congregation with seventy other young people. His father had secretly hoped that his son would become a Baptist, but he declined to interfere with his decision, stating: "I am thankful that my son's convictions are sufficiently deep that he has a preference." [49] Although his conversion necessitated no change in patterns of thought or personal habits because of the prior training in his own home, Bryan declared that it had more influence for good upon his life than any other experience.[50] Following his conversion, young Bryan continued to live an exemplary pietistic life. He did not smoke, swear, drink, dance, play cards, or gamble. Furthermore, at the conclusion of his second year in high school, he already believed in the superiority of faith over reason.

Following two years of high school, with his head full of politics, fortified with a protecting insulation of conservative religion and armed with his church letter of transfer, Bryan prepared to meet the "mind worshippers" at Whipple Academy, the preparatory school of Illinois College.[51] At Whipple and at Illinois, he increased his knowledge, majored in classical studies, but clung to earlier convictions. The Bible remained his primary source of authority. Other books that he came to value, in the order of their importance, included the works of Thomas Jefferson, Tolstoy's essays, Fairchild's *Moral Philosophy*, Carnegie Simpson's *The Fact of Christ*, the poems of William Cullen Bryant; Plutarch's *Lives*, the writings of Shakespeare; Homer's *Iliad* and *Odyssey*, and the novels of Charles Dickens.[52]

While at college, Bryan joined the Presbyterian Church at Jacksonville and remained a member there until 1917, when he transferred his membership to the First Presbyterian Church of Lincoln, Nebraska. Bryan faced a major vocational decision during collegiate days. As a boy he had given some thought to entering the ministry, but when he learned that to become a Baptist minister (this was before his Presbyterian days) one had to be immersed in water, he quickly gave up the idea of that profession![53] Later, as a lad whose family was about to move to a 500-acre farm, he considered the possibility of becoming a farmer himself and raising pumpkins.[54] Eventually, he settled upon a career as a lawyer, influenced by having heard his father successfully argue cases in court. Finally, he chose to become a politician, motivated largely by the desire to please his mother and to compensate for a narrow political defeat suffered by his father. Bryan's daughter, who may be supposed to have written from intimate knowledge, declared: "I have no doubt that the desire to please his mother, to give her the satisfaction of seeing her son in the position that her husband failed to reach [he had lost a campaign for Congress by a scant 240 votes] greatly influenced my father in his decision to accept his first nomination to the House of Representatives." [55]

One may conclude that early in his career Bryan had adopted a way of life consistent with what Fundamentalism later came to be.

The Bible, literally interpreted, had become his central religious authority; there was agreement in his family on the basic doctrines of Christianity; faith was already recognized as superior to reason; and the pietistic life was being followed. Furthermore, Bryan was highly motivated by love for his mother and respect for his father to win an influential Congressional seat. Undoubtedly he also felt that the God of retribution was on his side.

Bryan continued his devout religious stance during the years of his professional political career. In so doing he combined the socially progressive and the personally conservative in a unique way. As a public servant, Bryan's endeavor to bring about international peace and his specific condemnation of war were based on loyalty to Jesus, the Prince of Peace, and a literalist interpretation of Jesus' teaching as found in the Bible. For the same reasons, Bryan opposed what he believed was American "imperialism" in the Philippines.

> If true Christianity consists in carrying out in our daily lives the teachings of Christ, who will say that we are commanded to civilize with dynamite and proselyte with the sword?
>
> Imperialism finds no warrant in the Bible. The command, "Go ye into all the world and preach the gospel to every creature," has no gatling gun attachment. Compare . . . the swaggering, bullying, brutal doctrine of imperialism with the Golden Rule and the commandment "Thou shalt love thy neighbor as thyself."
>
> Love, not force, was the weapon of the Nazarene; sacrifice for others, not the exploitation of them, was His method of reaching the human heart.[56]

Bryan also found support for numerous progressive causes in the Scriptures, even for Populism itself; in fact, he was fond of quoting the text that said of Jesus: "The common people heard him gladly." [57] Invariably, whatever his audience, Bryan's speeches and addresses were saturated with Biblical quotations, expressions, and metaphors. Probably no politician in American history quoted so copiously from the Scriptures as did Bryan. For this reason, some taunted him for being a dreamer and a visionary, but even for these Bryan had a Biblical rejoinder—as well as a touch of humor. He replied that it was not so bad being a dreamer so long as, like Joseph in the Old Testament, one had the corn! [58] For others who could not be handled so easily, Bryan manifested love, forbearance, and the turning of the other cheek.

Throughout his public career, Bryan also showed a great deal of moral courage, no more so than at the national convention of his party in San Francisco in 1920. To delegates who were "wet" in their attitudes toward prohibition and altogether hostile to his principles, Bryan pleaded with deep conviction:

> Are you afraid that we shall lose some votes? O, my countrymen, have more faith in the virtue of the people! If there be any here who would seek the support of those who desire to carry us back into bondage to alcohol, let them remember that it is better to have the gratitude of one soul saved from drink than the applause of a drunken world.[59]

There were other occasions when Bryan's impassioned opposition to the "money men" of the East drew such belligerent responses that his life was threatened—yet Bryan, the politician of moral stamina, declined to retreat from his position and, at the same time, refused physical protection.[60]

In his personal life during the years of his political leadership, Bryan, who believed that religion and politics were entirely consistent, kept the simple, pietistic faith of his fathers. Until his children grew up and went their own separate ways, Bryan led his family in daily devotions, comprised, as they had been in his own home, of Scripture, prayers, and the singing of hymns. To find time to do this was not easy, since Bryan worked a twelve- to thirteen-hour day—but it was normally done. The Bible was also at Bryan's bedside at night and instinctively, in the time of trial and indecision, he turned to it and to personal prayer for guidance.

Another important facet of Bryan's religious expression was his strict Sabbatarianism, both in theory and in practice. Theoretically, Bryan reasoned that it was natural and proper that the day which is observed religiously by the general public should be selected as the day of rest also, with respect still being shown to those who conscientiously observe another day. He made allowance for variation of practice in different communities on Sundays, but declared that his own experience led him to two basic propositions (1) every citizen should be guaranteed *time* for rest and for worship, and (2) every citizen should be guaranteed the *peace* and *quiet* necessary for both rest and worship.[61] In practice, Bryan endeavored whenever possible to spend his Sundays at home. He declined to accept speaking engagements of a political nature on Sundays; what few addresses he did make were religious talks or "sermons" delivered without compensation.[62] Normally, Bryan was at home on Sundays—whether in Nebraska, Washington, D.C., or Florida.

While at home, the members of the Bryan household regularly attended public services of worship. When Bryan moved in 1902 from Lincoln, Nebraska, to his country home in nearby Fairview, he transferred his membership to, and attended, the Westminster Presbyterian Church, where he was elected a ruling elder.[63] Bryan remained a member of this congregation until he took his letter to the First Presbyterian Church of Miami in 1921, although he frequently attended the neighboring Methodist church as well.[64] When in Washington, the Bryans worshiped at the New York Avenue Presbyterian Church, the church where his funeral services were to be conducted in 1925. While traveling, Bryan visited churches of several faiths—reflecting the denominational-ecumenical pattern established by his parents.

V

Loyal to his religious beliefs both in public and in private, it was a natural move for Bryan, the Christian statesman, to join the fundamentalists and for them initially to welcome his leadership. The issue that drew them together was a strong mutual dislike of religious Liberalism, including the espousal by many of the liberals of the theory of evolution. Psychologically, this union between Bryan and the fundamentalists was beneficial to both sides. Bryan needed the Modernist-Fundamentalist Controversy as the subject matter for another crusade, after his seemingly successful espousal of women's suffrage and prohibition (as well as after his earlier failures to gain the presidential prize). The fundamentalists, on the other hand, were pleased to have a spokesman of such obvious prominence as Bryan who would support their views and give their cause national visibility.

With typical flourish and zeal, Bryan attacked theological Liberalism through his books, speeches, and popular "Bryan Bible Talks." [65] The latter were delivered on Sunday mornings at the First Presbyterian Church of Miami, Florida, the city to which the Bryans had moved in 1921. These talks reflected Bryan's fundamentalist theology and eventually drew such large crowds (two thousand to six thousand people) that it became necessary to hold the meetings outdoors on the edge of Biscayne Bay. The talks were also syndicated in many newspapers throughout the country, reaching thereby an estimated fifteen million people.

Bryan accused the religious liberals of disturbing the harmony of the church and robbing Christian theology of its true meaning. In a

sermon with the intriguing title "They Have Taken Away My Lord,"
Bryan affirmed that the modernists "have robbed our Saviour of the
glory of a virgin birth, of the majesty of His Deity, and of the
triumph of His resurrection . . . and are attempting to put in His
place a spurious personage, unknown to the Scriptures, and as
impotent to satisfy the affections of Christians as a painted doll would
be to assuage the sorrow of a mother mourning for her first born." [66]

Bryan touched base on the issues to which the fundamentalists
were giving attention. The great question of the day, he affirmed,
surpassing all national and international questions, was whether the
Bible was true or false. If the Bible is not true, he reasoned, then
Christ ceases to be a divine character and his words are no longer
binding upon man. Bryan declared his own belief in the verbal theory
of inspiration in the original Biblical manuscripts.[67] The proofs of
such inspiration, he declared, were not only the words themselves but
the influence that these words had exerted on the hearts and lives of
millions of people.[68] Of the virgin birth of Jesus, Bryan argued that
no writer in the Scriptures denied it and the only ones who mentioned
his birth [Matthew and Luke] mentioned his virgin birth. Bryan
stated that there was nothing more mysterious about the birth of
Christ than the birth of anybody else. "The birth of every person is a
mystery. Christ's birth was simply different." [69] Defending the
vicarious atonement of Jesus, Bryan said that winning hearts
through love expressed in sacrifice is a natural way of redemption.[70]
On the subject of the resurrection, Bryan, in a typically graphic
presentation, asserted that Christ, by his resurrection, had made
immortality sure. "He has transformed death into a narrow, star-lit
strip between the companionship of yesterday and the reunion of
tomorrow." [71] Bryan believed in the power and willingness of God to
perform miracles and in the actual performance of miracles in
Biblical and modern times. Of modern miracles, he declared that the
feeding of the five thousand with a few loaves and fishes was not
nearly so great a mystery as the cleansing of a heart and the
changing of a life today.[72] He was particularly incensed that the
liberals sought to allegorize the Biblical miracles. "Give the modernist the words, 'allegorical,' 'poetical,' and 'symbolical' and he can suck
the meaning out of every vital doctrine of the Christian Church and
every passage of the Bible to which he objects." [73]

Within the context of the Modernist-Fundamentalist Controversy,
Bryan had harsh words to say about the Biblical scholars known as
the "higher critics." [74] He referred to the average higher critics as

"men without spiritual vision, without zeal for souls, and without any deep interest in the coming of God's Kingdom." Their opinions, Bryan was convinced, were formed before their investigations. Like many other liberals, in their handling of the Scriptures they were "tampering with the main spring" and mutilating the inspired Biblical books. In Bryan's judgment, they lacked the "spiritual fluids" to digest the miraculous and the supernatural in the Bible. Furthermore, Bryan pointed out, they were opposed to revivals! Such a position prompted Bryan to defend revivals, in general, and the methods of Billy Sunday, in particular.[75]

Politically, Bryan's fortunes with the fundamentalists were about as frustrating as they had been in national politics. Most of his endeavors were within his own Presbyterian denomination, although in 1922 he spoke to the Southern Baptist Convention and the Fundamentalist Federation of the Northern Baptist Convention. The latter appearance brought the accusation that he was an "outsider" meddling in a serious family quarrel.[76] Among the Presbyterians, Bryan attended several General Assemblies. In 1923 he ran for Moderator of that body in hopes of turning the attention of its delegates to his particular concern—evolution. He was defeated on the third ballot by Charles F. Wishart, probably because "his policy of coyly concealing his desire for office placed his supporters in a disadvantageous position." [77] This was Bryan's last major bid for elected office. A year later, in 1924, Bryan nominated and supported Clarence E. Macartney in a close and successful bid for Moderator of the General Assembly. In appreciation, Macartney appointed Bryan Vice-Moderator, primarily an honorary position, in the hope that "in a year or two" he might become Moderator apart from the conflict and tensions of recent elections.[78] In the General Assembly of 1925, Bryan broke with the extreme fundamentalists when he supported the candidacy of W. O. Thompson, president of Ohio State University, who advocated the settling of denominational problems engendered by the Modernist-Fundamentalist Controversy through peaceful means. Thompson humiliated Bryan by rejecting his support.[79] Thompson's defeat by Charles R. Erdman, a theological conservative, did little to salve Bryan's wounded feelings. By this time, Bryan's political and religious-political fortunes were at an all-time low and the God of retribution seemed embarrassingly far off. Bryan continued to battle, although a certain testiness, unusual for him, was beginning to show. At a meeting of the Men's Fellowship of the General Assembly in 1925 he criticized both major political parties "for their failure in their platforms to say 'a single word about the greatest need of the world—religion.' His criticism was unsparing. 'One candidate in particular,' he added, 'I should have expected to recognize this need, but he did not. That was my brother.' " [80] Bryan's shrewd brother, Charles, had assisted him in editing *The Commoner* and had held office first as mayor of Lincoln, Nebraska, and later, with Bryan's active support, as governor of the state.

At this low ebb in his career, Bryan needed a victory badly. He sought it through his sincere and continuing opposition to evolution. Like many of his other convictions, Bryan's opposition to the theory of evolution had come early in life. While in college he had experienced a low-keyed struggle about the origin of man but quickly resolved the difficulty in an act of faith in a personal God who was the creator of all. This subject matter of evolution and creation lay relatively dormant as far as Bryan was concerned until the last five years of his life (1920–1925), when he campaigned ardently against Darwinism with much of his old-time fervor and wit. The catalyst which brought about the change was not only Bryan's need of a cause but the belief that the teaching of evolution as fact rather than theory was destroying or chilling the faith of many college students. It also tied in naturally with Bryan's opposition to Liberalism, because he firmly believed that evolution was the basis of Liberalism.[81] Evolution, carried to its logical conclusion, he argued, would annihilate revealed religion. In colleges and universities, in state legislatures and religious assemblies, Bryan's theme was much the same:

> Let the atheist think what he pleases and say what he thinks to those who are willing to listen to him, but he cannot rightly demand pay from the taxpayers for teaching their children what they do not want taught. The hand that writes the paycheck rules the school. As long as Christians must build Christian colleges in which to teach Christianity, atheists should be required to build their own colleges if they desire to teach atheism. . . . Modernist teachers, . . . by endorsing unproven guesses, undermine confidence in the Bible as a divine authority. . . . With from one to three millions of distinct species in the animal and vegetable world, not a single species has been traced to another. . . . Why should we assume without proof that man is a blood relative of any lower form of life? [82]

On several occasions, Bryan said that he was not certain whether man was an improved monkey or whether the monkey was a degenerate man. The Bryan antievolution crusade, with thoughts such as these, and with fundamentalist support all along the way, led in 1925 to Dayton, Tennessee, the village that became the Waterloo of the religious politician from Nebraska. The facts about the Scopes Trial are so well known that they need not be repeated here.[83] A few observations, however, are in order.

One letter to Bryan indicates that earlier, at least in an indirect way, he had contributed to the events that brought about the Butler Act, which banned the teaching of evolution in Tennessee. A Nashville lawyer, W. B. Mann, informed Bryan that a lecture of his entitled "Is the Bible True?" delivered in the state, had been published and distributed generally. Five hundred copies were sent to the members of the state legislature, including John Washington Butler. Mann theorized that "evidently this caused Mr. Butler to read and think deeply on this subject and prompted him to introduce his bill." [84] After the bill was introduced, the pamphlets containing Bryan's talk were sent once again to the members of the state legislature. Admittedly, this link between Bryan and Butler was a tenuous one, but it shows at least that Bryan did contribute to the general atmosphere out of which the Butler Act arose.

In perspective, there appeared to be two highlights to the trial itself. One was the persuasive speech of Dudley Field Malone, a member of the team of defense lawyers, and, ironically, the third Undersecretary of State under Bryan during the years 1913–1915. Malone, in what was generally considered the most eloquent speech of the trial, declared that the actual effect of the Butler Act was the declaration by the legislature that the truth must not be taught in the schools of the state. For his part, Malone reasoned that the denial of the truth of nature is atheism disguised as religion. He pointed out that truth is of the most imperishable order. "It may inconvenience us, it may disturb us, it may completely upset many of our scientific ideas, it may run counter to our religious views; our duty is not to avoid the consequences of the truth but to face them and overcome them." [85] Malone concluded by declaring that truth, imperishable as it was, needed neither governmental support nor the support of Mr. Bryan. "We feel we stand with fundamental freedom in America. We are not afraid. Where is the fear? We deny it!" [86] When Malone finished his oration, women shrieked their approval and men cheered. After the courtroom had cleared, a sober Bryan said to his former colleague in the state department: "Dudley, that was the greatest speech I ever heard." "Thank you, Mr. Bryan," Malone replied, gathering up his papers. "I am terribly sorry that I was the one who had to do it." [87]

The second highlight of the Scopes Trial was the result of Bryan's unfortunate decision to permit himself to appear on the witness stand to be cross-examined as an authority on the Bible. It was surprising that Bryan, untrained in theology, would subject himself to the merciless and persistent questioning of Clarence Darrow, because just three years earlier he (Bryan) had written:

> I know of no reason why the Christian should take upon himself the difficult task of answering all questions and give to the atheist the easy task of asking them. Anyone can ask questions, but not every question can be answered. If I am to discuss creation with an atheist it will be on condition that we ask questions. . . . He may ask the first one if he wishes, but he shall not ask a second one until he answers my first.[88]

Going contrary to his own advice, Bryan permitted Darrow (an agnostic, not an atheist) to crowd him into an embarrassing corner where, among other things, he admitted that the Biblical days of creation mentioned in Genesis were not necessarily six days of twenty-four hours, but lengthy periods of time—possibly encompassing six million to six hundred million years. Such an opinion ran directly contrary to a literalist interpretation of the Scriptures held by the fundamentalists and, therefore, did much to discredit Bryan in their eyes. This was ironical because, on at least one previous occasion, Bryan had expressed the same judgment in a letter to a friend, although, it had not, of course, received such widespread publicity as his expression at Dayton.[89] More ironical was the fact that Bryan, who had supported many a fundamentalist cause, and who had been used widely by the fundamentalists to champion their programs, was practically boycotted by the fundamentalist leaders at the Scopes Trial. J. Frank Norris wrote Bryan shortly before the trial telling him that he (Bryan) was engaged in the greatest work of his life, "and [you] are rendering ten thousand times more service to the cause of righteousness than a dozen presidents." [90] Norris also volunteered to provide a court stenographer at his expense to cover the trial. But when the trial began at Dayton, Tennessee, Norris, together with T. T. Shields, and William Bell Riley, the president of the World's Christian Fundamentals Association (the organization that had asked Bryan to prosecute John Scopes), was in Seattle, Washington, for the battle royal between the fundamentalists and the liberals at the annual meeting of the Northern Baptist Convention. John Roach Straton originally had agreed to be present at Dayton but later found his vacation retreat in the Adirondacks too attractive to leave. J. C. Massee, in the midst of his own defection from the fundamentalists, was not present at either Seattle or Dayton. J. Gresham Machen wrote Bryan that he did not consider himself a specialist on the subject of evolution. James M. Gray, president of Moody Bible Institute, declined Bryan's invitation because of "summer conference work which will keep me on the go until September." [91] P. H. Welshimer, minister of the First Christian Church of Canton, Ohio, asserted that he would be unable to attend because his congregation was in the midst of constructing a new building.[92] Alfred W. McCann, a Roman Catholic author whose books dealt with the subject of evolution, refused to become a witness because he disapproved of the entire procedure ("men will go on thinking their thoughts regardless of any inhibition or dictum to the contrary").[93] Billy Sunday wrote Bryan indicating that he could not be present, but he sent a few "ideas" that he thought might be used (e.g.: "If man evolved from a monkey, why are there any monkeys left? Why don't they all evolve into humans?"). So Bryan, who came to Dayton in failing health, with an invalid wife, and who had not been in a courtroom in twenty-eight years, was left to dangle alone on Darrow's cruel and inescapable hook. While technically the decision of the Bible-reading mountain folk who constituted the jury favored Bryan's side, the verdict of the public went strongly against him. The Great Commoner had lost his final battle.

VI

William Jennings Bryan was a strange and fascinating combination of the conservative and the progressive, a union of what Sydney Ahlstrom has called the nostalgic and the forward-looking.[94] Bryan's conservatism was rooted in his rural, Protestant, evangelical background, including a firm grounding in a literalist interpretation of the Scriptures. The seeds of Bryan's progressivism were found in Jeffersonian thought; in the democracy of the American frontier where his ancestors became prominent self-made men and women; and in the application of the same Scriptures, again literally interpreted, to new and broad-ranging social problems. The influence of Bryan's parents was crucial in shaping his religious beliefs and helping him to become America's foremost Christian layman. Furthermore, Bryan's conviction of the superiority of his inheritance, his religion, his country, and the era in which he was born, gave him considerable motivation but also prevented noticeable growth and led beyond patriotism and pietism to a dangerous chauvinism and a marked expression of self-righteousness.

A sense of melancholy surrounded Bryan during his concluding years. After 1896 the trail led downward as the Great Commoner seemed finally deserted, not only by politicians and fundamentalist leaders, but by the God of retribution as well. As people viewed Bryan in perspective, few were neutral about his person or contributions. Most agreed that he was America's leading orator, but after that opinions varied widely. His friends saw him as an idealistic, sincere, honest, courageous champion of the masses, the real leader of progressivism in his generation. Some termed him the John Bright and the William Gladstone of American politics; others, in the field of religion, went so far as to call Bryan the greatest lay preacher in the history of America and the St. Paul of the twentieth century.[95]

Bryan's enemies emphasized his lack of originality, called him variously a buffoon, a demagogue, and a deceiver, and stressed his dogmatism, opportunism, self-centeredness, and superficiality. H. L. Mencken wrote that Bryan was "a charlatan, a mountebank, a zany without sense or dignity . . . a peasant come home to the barnyard." [96] Another person wrote: "When I reflect upon what this Nation and perhaps the World escaped through his [Bryan's] successive defeats for the Presidency, I am almost persuaded that there is a Providence which looks after fools, drunkards, and the United States." [97] Bryan's opponents even taunted him about his oratorical skills. Joseph Foraker, a Republican, when asked if he thought that Bryan's title, the Boy Orator of the Platte, was an accurate one, replied that it was, because the Platte River was six inches deep and six miles wide at the mouth.[98] The truth probably lies somewhere between such polarized extremes. One individual wrote:

> No one wants to be remembered for his old age, while the rest of his life is ignored. A fairer label would be based upon all the years of his life rather than those at the end when the flame flickered out of a core of hardened dogma, and that label would have to be neither martyr nor buffoon. Bryan was, like most of us, an individual who had contributed both good and bad, and a fair man would pity him for the bad he brought to the world, and love him for the good.[99]

That interpretation seems even more impressive when one realizes that it came from John Scopes in his own older years. In the category

Bryan *(right)* and Clarence Darrow at the Scopes Trial

of the "good" mentioned by Scopes, it seems more fitting to remember Bryan for his attempts to gain international peace through arbitration and his opposition to nationalistic imperialism—long before others (including many liberals) sought such worthy goals or made such needed protests—than for his excessive claims for the Scriptures in Dayton.

Finally, as a fundamentalist, Bryan provides one further classic illustration that there is no single stereotype into which one or all of the ultraconservatives may be placed. William Jennings Bryan was one of a kind, primarily because the sphere of national politics in which he worked was different from that in which other fundamentalist leaders found themselves. His influence was national; theirs was mostly regional in impact. The company he kept was much more cosmopolitan than that known by other fundamentalists, as he associated with both the humble and the great, the conservative and the liberal. The champion of the common man crossed paths with presidents and counts; the defender of the faith who was linked with the World's Christian Fundamentals Association also spoke at the famous World Missionary Conference at Edinburgh in 1910 and once called the Federal Council of Churches "the greatest religious organization in our nation." [100] Bryan, as we have seen, also gave more attention to political and social reform than did other ultraconservative leaders. Despite his belief in original sin, Bryan possessed more faith in the ability of human nature to bring about such reform than did most fundamentalists. It was confidence in the average person that led Bryan to oppose what he felt to be elitism in politics, in religion, and in education. Bryan was also more pacifistic in his leanings than were his contemporary conservative stalwarts. One would hardly expect the latter to declare, as Bryan did, that "war is not necessary. It is the philosophy of Nietzsche, not the doctrine of the Nazarene." [101] Furthermore, despite being a fighter for the faith as he understood it, Bryan seemed less hostile to his enemies than did his fellow fundamentalist leaders, many of whom were widely known for their bitter invectives.[102] Lastly, Bryan was neither a millenarian nor a dispensationalist. He preferred to emphasize proper conduct in this life and a general belief in immortality based upon a belief in retribution—that elusive retribution which seemingly had failed to reward Bryan during his own earthly career. One, however, should be careful not to suggest that the God of retribution was to blame for Bryan's mundane defeats. More likely, notwithstanding his cosmopolitan associations, Bryan was too closely identified with the farmer and the farmer's religion in an age when America was becoming increasingly urbanized and industrialized. More likely Bryan was ahead of his time while Secretary of State but behind his time at Dayton. More likely his ideals were stronger than his organizational abilities to realize them.

While Bryan was thus a unique fundamentalist, let it be said clearly that he remained a fundamentalist to the end—in belief and in attitude. The last words of his last prepared speech were these:

> Faith of our fathers! living still . . .
> We will be true to thee till death.[103]

Quite properly, therefore, they carved the words on Bryan's gravestone at Arlington Cemetery: "He kept the faith."

CHAPTER EIGHT

Clarence E. Macartney
PREACHER-FUNDAMENTALIST

THE TREND TOWARD RELIGIOUS conservatism in the 1970's provides a natural context in which to examine the life and influence of Clarence E. Macartney. He was a dignified and eloquent spokesman of the Presbyterian fundamentalists in the early decades of this century.[1] A study of Macartney's life seems important for several reasons. He and his churches furnish an excellent case study for scholars like Dean M. Kelley who are currently analyzing the strong appeal of traditional religion.[2] Macartney also illustrates an aspect of the great diversity among ultraconservative leaders for all who are interested in taking a fresh look at historic Fundamentalism in this country. Furthermore, Macartney is important in his own right as a stalwart defender of the faith and a man of considerable influence. He served large urban churches; wrote fifty-seven books; initiated the charges that crowded Harry Emerson Fosdick from a Presbyterian pulpit; and held the highest office in his own denomination, Moderator of the General Assembly. Most important of all, he earned the reputation of being one of the great preachers of his generation. Macartney also seems significant because he struggled throughout his career with the issues confronting contemporary religious leaders—the tensions between liberal and conservative theology, church unity and denominational loyalty, personal religion and social religion, denominational authority and fidelity to the local church, and traditional approaches versus new methods of communication. In the light of all this it is somewhat surprising that the only significant published work about Macartney appears to be his autobiography, printed posthumously in the form of memoirs and uncritical in nature.[3]

After examining his life and beliefs, this chapter will present a

G. Hall Todd, Philadelphia, Pa.

Clarence E. Macartney

critical appraisal of Macartney, showing him as the indefatigable pulpit champion of a particular kind of orthodoxy, despite the storms and changes that perennially swirled about him.[4]

I

Clarence Edward Macartney, the strong-willed Presbyterian who brought dignity and propriety to the fundamentalist ranks, was born in the little isolated village of Northwood, Ohio, September 18, 1879, the last of seven children in a home characterized by culture, knowledge, piety—and modest means. His father, John Longfellow McCartney,[5] whose family pointed to Irish backgrounds, was a clergyman-professor who served in Northwood as minister of the First Miami (Reformed Presbyterian) congregation and later as a member of the faculty at Geneva College, the small denominational school of the same faith. His mother, Catherine Robertson McCartney, the dominant influence in the family, came to this country from a well-to-do background in Scotland, where her father owned the largest cotton factory in the world.[6] A woman of considerable refinement, she also was a member of the Reformed Presbyterian Church (Covenanter), a strongly Calvinistic group whose members sang only the psalms in worship, prohibited instrumental music, observed closed Communion, and were opposed to taking oaths in court, to joining secret societies, and to participating in civil affairs.[7]

When the fledgling Geneva College experienced financial difficulties, it was moved in 1886 from Northwood to Beaver Falls, Pennsylvania, thirty miles north of Pittsburgh, in order to be nearer the center of its Covenanter constituency.[8] The McCartney family made its hegira to western Pennsylvania at the same time, Clarence Edward, aged nine months, being carried on the train ride by "Alabama Mary," a black nurse. The new family home was established on the campus of Geneva College overlooking the Beaver River; Macartney's father, once a student of Louis Agassiz, the famous Swiss naturalist, became professor of natural science; and the children grew up in this industrial community amid both strong educational and conservative religious influences.[9] Macartney experienced a quiet conversion at the age of eleven, largely the result of family influence. He then joined the Covenanter Church in Beaver Falls and participated in a Communion service for the first time, an especially solemn event among Reformed Presbyterians.

In 1894, when Macartney was in his teens, the family moved to

California, then later to Colorado, in the endeavor to find a climate that would be beneficial to the failing health of the father. This change did much to broaden young Macartney's cultural and intellectual horizons. He completed his work in high school at Redlands, California, and in the preparatory department of Pomona College at Claremont. His first year in college was spent at the University of Denver. When his family returned to the East, Macartney transferred to the University of Wisconsin, one of the great intellectual centers of the expanding Midwest, from which he was graduated in 1901.

At Wisconsin, while majoring in English literature, Macartney came into personal contact with several distinguished scholars who also stirred his interest in history and oratory. Among these were Charles Kendall Adams, the president of the university and author of important works in European history; Frederick Jackson Turner, professor of American history, known for his "frontier thesis"; Charles Homer Haskins, an authority in medieval studies and later dean of the Graduate School at Harvard; and David Bower Frankenburgher, professor of public speech, who made the deepest impact on the future fundamentalist.[10] At Wisconsin, Macartney joined the oldest of the debating societies, Athena, and represented the university in the Northern Oratorical League, made up of several major Midwestern universities. He was coached personally by Robert M. LaFollette, Sr., who lived in Madison only a block away from Macartney.[11]

Despite his developing skill in public debate, Macartney experienced at Wisconsin an unusual and, as he later acknowledged, painful timidity. This shyness, caused perhaps by diffidence and extreme sensitiveness, kept him from the usual round of social activities for a time, even with his own family. Although it eventually disappeared as mysteriously as it had come, the residue of this experience was a cautious reserve which characterized most of his adult life.

Finally, at Wisconsin, Macartney struggled with a rather mild case of unbelief. His collegiate studies had gradually led him away from the firm orthodoxy of his younger years. His graduating thesis at Wisconsin, "A Comparative Analysis of Byron's *Cain* and Shelley's *Prometheus Unbound*," reflected a note of pessimism, despair, and agnosticism. When a member of his family remonstrated with him about his attitude toward revealed religion, Macartney's curt reply was rather striking in the light of his later convictions: "It is all very well if you can believe these things. I cannot." [12]

A serious vocational struggle followed Macartney's graduation from Wisconsin. It was a time of great restlessness when he struggled with the possibility of a career in law, teaching, or, surprisingly, the ministry. This year of indecision led him briefly to Harvard (without hearing a single lecture), to the British Isles and France for a short sojourn, to his home county in western Pennsylvania where he worked as a reporter for the *Beaver Times*, to Yale (for only one class), and finally to Princeton Theological Seminary, where he enrolled as a student preparing for religious service. In none of his writings does Macartney specifically tell us what led him to take this final step. Was it the death of two young women in whom he had become romantically interested? [13] Was it a desire to find a sounding board for his oratorical abilities? Was it the example of an older brother, already at Princeton? Or were other unknown factors involved? Macartney does not share the secret. In older years, he simply wrote in true Calvinistic fashion:

> Looking back . . . over that year of indecision and restlessness . . . I firmly believe that the hand of the Lord was leading me and guarding me when I knew it not. Princeton Theological Seminary with its grand and ancient tradition of a stalwart defense of the truth, and of the glory of the Christian revelation, was the right thing for me. I had found my true place. Henceforth, there was no wavering; no halting between two opinions, but straight forward towards the goal. . . . I have never doubted for a moment that it was the hand of the Lord that led me past the gates of Harvard, Yale, Edinburgh, the newspaper office, and the professor's chair to the halls of Princeton Seminary. "There is a divinity that shapes our ends." [14]

At Princeton, Macartney came under the influence of Francis L. Patton, the president of the seminary; Benjamin Breckinridge Warfield, the distinguished professor of systematic theology; and Robert Dick Wilson, the renowned Old Testament scholar. After three years of intensive study at the seminary, during which time he also earned a Master of Arts degree at the university, Macartney embarked on his own course as pastor-preacher. Throughout his lengthy career he served only three churches: the First Presbyterian Church of Paterson, New Jersey, where he was ordained into the ministry of the Presbyterian Church in the U.S.A. (1905–1914); the Arch Street Presbyterian Church of Philadelphia (1914–1927); and the First Presbyterian Church, Pittsburgh (1927–1953).

While a clergyman, the hardworking Macartney averaged six

hours daily in his study. In addition to his pastoral and ecclesiastical responsibilities, he continued his interest in history, writing several books on the Civil War and delivering on many occasions a popular lecture entitled "Highways and Byways of the Civil War." The latter was the result of many personal visits to the various battlefields of that conflict.[15] Macartney also traveled widely, making numerous trips to the Near East, where he sought to journey to every place visited by the apostle Paul. He also lectured frequently at colleges and seminaries and participated in several public debates, one of them on the subject of evolution with the president of the American Museum of Natural History.

Personally, Macartney, a lifelong bachelor (like his contemporary, J. Gresham Machen), was a dignified, intense, somewhat dominating, Napoleon-like individual.[16] The five-foot-eight-and-one-half-inch, self-assured Presbyterian enjoyed the company of the upper classes of society as well as the privilege of preaching to—and receiving the fealty of—the common man.[17] A study of his life will reveal that he was a remarkably successful preacher with a devoted following, an aloof although faithful pastor, and a frustrated ecclesiastical leader who became isolated, on the one hand, from the developing liberal forces of his own denomination and, on the other hand, from the ultraconservative constituency which he once had headed.

After an illustrious and controversial career that had catapulted him into national prominence, Clarence Edward Macartney, the dignified Presbyterian leader, died on February 19, 1957, at the family homestead in Beaver Falls, Pennsylvania. At the beginning of his ministry he had gone to churches near Princeton wearing a high hat and a black tailcoat, and he remained the personification of propriety to the very last. In his coffin he was attired in his doctoral robe.[18]

II

The pulpit was Clarence E. Macartney's throne. He used it to express his oratorical talents, to proclaim the truth in which he believed (not to search for it), and to build his churches in his own image. Other phases of his ministry, including pastoral visitation, Macartney carried out dutifully, but with neither the enthusiasm nor the ease that characterized the delivery of his sermons—four of them every week.[19]

As a preacher, Macartney was a talented craftsman. He brought to his discourses careful organization, excellent diction, vivid imagination, superb illustrative ability, a thorough knowledge of the Scriptures, depth of conviction, and supremely important for holding the attention of his "subjects," a freedom from all notes and manuscripts.[20] The confident Macartney preached without the latter from the second Sunday of his ministry. He said on one occasion to theological students at Princeton: "If you can trust the Lord for your salvation, for eternity, surely you can trust him for twenty-five minutes for your sermon the next time you preach." [21]

In his sermons Macartney employed a variety of approaches. He delivered doctrinal, historical, prophetic, topical, and, occasionally, exegetical messages, but his forte was biographical sermons. He was also a strong proponent of serial preaching, believing that such a method sustained interest and prevented a haphazard approach to a study of the Scriptures. Macartney's best-known sermon, an exhortation on opportunity entitled "Come Before Winter," was delivered every fall in his churches and frequently on the lecture circuit.[22] Macartney first preached this sermon in Philadelphia, on October 18, 1915. It became to him what "Acres of Diamonds" had become to Russell H. Conwell.[23] In addition to other strong homiletical features, this sermon illustrated Macartney's ability to be dramatic, if not theatrical. Emphasizing the importance of repentance in the present rather than at some future time, Macartney declared: "The Holy Spirit, when he invites men to come to Christ, never says 'Tomorrow' but always 'Today.' If you can find me one place in the Bible where the Holy Spirit says, 'Believe in Christ *tomorrow*' or 'Repent and be saved *tomorrow*,' I will come down out of the pulpit and stay out of it—for I would have no gospel to preach." [24]

Macartney believed strongly that the purpose of preaching should be evangelistic, yet he was not a revivalist as were many of his fundamentalist contemporaries. During a concluding prayer and hymn following his sermons, the dignified Presbyterian allowed time for "decisions" or "commitments" of a personal nature but rarely extended a public "invitation" or altar call.[25] In part, this may have contributed to the size of his congregations, because individuals knew in advance that the respectful Macartney would play no tricks with their emotions nor manipulate them into artificially contrived judgments. Even so, Macartney was a skilled leader in the art of public relations. He spotlighted the entrances to his churches, advertised his services widely, employed "street" pulpits and the radio to reach a maximum number of people, and made a deliberate, perennial appeal to the members of other congregations through his Sunday evening services and Tuesday noon meetings for men.[26] At Pittsburgh, the Tuesday Noon Club alone eventually drew a membership of substantially over two thousand men representing thirty-one denominations and 656 churches.[27]

Although Macartney employed highly authoritarian channels of communication (the pulpit, the radio, and the printed page) over which he maintained tight control with a minimum of feedback from his listeners, his congregations grew markedly or maintained a high numerical level under his leadership.[28] The membership of his church at Paterson increased from 258 in 1906 to 506 in 1913. The Arch Street Church in Philadelphia jumped from 481 members in 1914 to 708 in 1926, while the evening service vaulted from an average attendance of 100 to over 1,000. At Pittsburgh, despite the movement of population toward the suburbs, Macartney's wealthy downtown congregation kept a high plateau of membership, totaling 2,476 members in 1952, eight more than when he had begun his ministry in 1927.[29] Few urban churches of comparable size in America could match such holding power. The one major area that did not prosper under Macartney's leadership was the Sunday school at Pittsburgh, where Macartney served as his own superintendent. The membership dropped from 1,509 in 1927 to 940 in 1952.

Macartney's ability to proclaim and to defend effectively his understanding of truth was recognized early. In 1925 the directors of Princeton Seminary elected him to the chair of Christian ethics and apologetics, with the expectation of transferring him to the chair of homiletics, for which he was better fitted. Macartney declined the offer, however, feeling that he preferred to preach himself rather than to try to teach others how to do so.[30] Near the end of his life, the clergyman who made preaching central rather than peripheral and who "triumphed through monologues rather than dialogues" had not regretted that decision.[31]

III

It was more than Macartney's obvious talent as a preacher that made him a man of influence. Primarily it was his immutable devotion to a particular kind of belief that gave content to his sermons and created for him, in the minds of his followers, an image of the "defender of the faith."

Macartney's belief was a nineteenth-century orthodoxy but with a particular loyalty to the Reformed tradition as shaped by Princeton Theology.[32] In general, it may be said that Macartney was not an innovator, but one who energized existing truth as he understood it. In the words of one of the deans at Princeton Seminary, Macartney "put fire into the veins of anemic Christians." [33]

When Macartney began his twenty-six-year ministry at Pittsburgh, he declared: "I have no theological knickknacks, novelties or sensations, but a profound and experimental faith in the power of the gospel." [34] For Macartney that gospel centered in the "grand particularities" of the Christian religion—a sovereign, loving God responding to the plight of rebellious, disobedient men through the incarnation of Jesus.[35] This incarnation included Jesus' virgin birth, his miracles, vicarious atonement, bodily resurrection, bestowal of the Holy Spirit, and ultimate bodily return. Without such an objective, historical foundation, Macartney believed that the Christian religion had no power and the church possessed no reliable base. He placed special emphasis on the vicarious atonement, which he considered "the grand central truth of our . . . faith" as well as the fountain of Christian morality and ethics.[36] The atonement, in Macartney's judgment, made Christianity, unlike Protestant Liberalism, a redemptive religion.

The influence of the Reformed, or Calvinistic, tradition upon Macartney was seen, among other theological influences, in his espousal of predestination and in his belief in the Westminster Confession of Faith. He asserted that "back of all our histories and biographies and heredity and environment and education lies the almighty purpose of God." [37] He was careful to point out, however, that predestination without the accompanying Biblical doctrine of personal freedom and responsibility results in fatalism. Macartney, as a Presbyterian minister, subscribed to the definitive statement of Presbyterian doctrine embodied in the seventeenth-century Westminster Confession, and he expected others to follow suit. His stance explains why the example of a liberal Baptist clergyman preaching doctrines contrary to the Westminster Confession in a Presbyterian pulpit drew Macartney into the tumultuous religious conflict in the 1920's.

The effect of Princeton Theology on Macartney was particularly evident in his view of the Bible. He considered it credible, inspired, authoritative, and inerrant. In this, Macartney seems to have been influenced by Archibald A. Hodge and Benjamin B. Warfield. Hodge and Warfield wrote in the *Presbyterian Review* in 1881, at a time when the advocates of Biblical criticism were putting pressure on traditional interpretations of Biblical inspiration: "The historical faith of the Church has always been that all the affirmations of Scripture of all kinds, whether of special doctrine or duty, or of physical or historical fact, or of psychological or philosophical principle, are without any error, when the *ipsissima verba* of the original autographs are ascertained and interpreted in their natural and intended sense." [38] This Princeton emphasis on Biblical inerrancy was precisely the position Macartney adopted, although Ernest R. Sandeen has pointed out that the Princeton doctrine of inspiration went beyond the more limited claims of the traditional Reformed faith.[39]

When writing to G. A. Johnston Ross of Union Theological Seminary in 1924, Macartney set forth with particular clarity his doctrinal views about the Scriptures. He declared that his faith rested on the credibility of the Scriptures, although he had never taken the position that Christianity depended on the inspiration of the Scriptures or the mode of inspiration (also a conviction of Princeton Theology). He added that the doctrine of the inerrancy of the Scriptures was neither new nor unique but was the faith of historic Christianity. Macartney resented the dogmatic assertion frequently made by liberals that some narrow-minded Protestants were substituting an infallible Bible for an infallible pope. He concluded by asserting that the Scriptures themselves teach Biblical inerrancy, although he averred that such inerrancy applied only to the original documents.[40] It may be questioned whether his Biblical proof text, Luke 24:44, supports the claim of Scriptural inerrancy, and the limitation of inerrancy to the original documents is frustrating to some critics because none of the original documents exist.[41] Nevertheless, Macartney insisted on this kind of Biblical authority and felt that the great weakness of Protestant Liberalism was the rejection of its claims and the substitution of human reason for its revealed truth. He echoed this judgment when delivering the first commencement address at Westminster Seminary in 1930. Macartney said: "A deleted Bible has resulted in a diluted Gospel. Protestantism, as it loses its faith in the Bible, is losing its religion. . . . Men who desire such dilutions can drink de-caffeined coffee and smoke de-nicotined tobacco; and now we have on every hand, without money and without price, de-christianized Christianity." [42]

While accepting the Scriptures as his great source of authority, and feeling a responsibility both to proclaim and to defend their truth, Macartney candidly recognized some inscrutable mysteries. These included the nature of the Trinity, the fate of the heathen, the prevalence of evil, the problem of eternal punishment, and the relation between a sovereign God and man's freedom of the will. Here, as elsewhere, Macartney found encouragement in a Biblical proof text: "The secret things belong unto the LORD our God: but those things which are revealed belong unto us and to our children for ever." [43] Macartney concluded that the mysteries must be left with God but in the meantime man must be obedient to the revealed knowledge which he already possesses and about which there is no question.[44]

Holding orthodox beliefs shaped by the Princeton Theology, Macartney disliked being called a "fundamentalist." He preferred the term "conservative, evangelical Christian." [45] Nevertheless, with one important exception, it appears accurate to call Macartney a fundamentalist. He kept close company with the fundamentalists of his own denomination; these colleagues and the public press hailed Macartney as the recognized leader of the fundamentalist Presbyterian forces; and he possessed the intransigence and many of the beliefs of the fundamentalists.[46]

One major area where Macartney differed from many of his ultraconservative contemporaries was over eschatological matters, especially the second coming of Christ. While many fundamentalists stressed the imminent and premillennial return of Christ, Macartney specifically rejected this interpretation. He believed that the premillennialists, overly sure about the future of the church and the race, had succumbed to the temptation to write history before it was made. Macartney went to great pains to point out that the event (the return of Christ) was certain but that the date was uncertain. Macartney preached positively that this second coming was to be visible, personal, local, sudden, unexpected, unpredictable, and future. He did not equate this return with the destruction of Jerusalem (as did John Humphrey Noyes), nor with the spiritual presence of Christ with his church, nor with the coming of death to a believer. Neither did he believe that the end would come by natural development or by the expansion of the church and the spread of the gospel. Rather, human history would be brought to its conclusion and redemption to its climax by the personal return of Jesus in power. Such a doctrine, Macartney taught, was a warning against sin and an impulse to holy living.[47]

The one characteristic of Macartney's theology that most impresses the interested observer is its immutability. Macartney began his ministry in 1905 with a nineteenth-century Reformed orthodoxy shaped by Princeton Theology. He concluded his ministry forty-eight years later with that nineteenth-century Reformed orthodoxy shaped by Princeton Theology. Two world wars, a devastating depression, the conflict in Korea, the development of liberal theology including the Social Gospel, the Modernist-Fundamentalist conflict, centralizing tendencies in government and religion, and the nearly incredible impact of modern technology—none of these had any noticeable effect on Macartney's belief. From his standpoint, this was not unusual. God remained the same; despite changing cultural patterns, man and his basic needs remained the same; and the gospel itself with its objective, given, "grand particularities" remained the same.[48] There was no need to change or to adapt the message. When *The Christian Century* asked Macartney in 1939 to write one article in a series entitled "How My Mind Has Changed in This Decade," the unyielding Presbyterian reflected the immutability of his own theology with great accuracy.

> I hope that during the last decade I have grown in grace and knowledge and humility, but I am not . . . ashamed to confess that as to the great underlying truths . . . I have experienced no emotional or intellectual change in the last ten years. Of course, I have had widening experiences, and perhaps here and there the emphasis has been altered; but as regards . . . the "constituent" doctrines of our faith, I am conscious of no changes. I am glad that this is so, for if at the end of every ten years I had a different point of view as to my Christian faith I would have to conclude that the Christ whom I follow is someone other than "Jesus Christ, the same, yesterday, today, and forever." [49]

This was part of Macartney's great appeal. In a world of social and theological upheaval he represented the strong foundations of traditional religion which provided needed support for many people. When frequently all else appeared to be crumbling or in the midst of flux, causing uncertainty and sometimes resentment, there was at least one constant factor for Presbyterians in Paterson, Philadelphia, or Pittsburgh. That was the imperturbable Clarence E. Macartney, fastidious in his sober black robe, climbing the steps of his authoritative pulpit and proclaiming his immutable gospel. Liberal clergymen, with their greater emphasis on reason and introspection, found this dignified herald and his fixed theology a combination difficult to match.

IV

The fundamentalists have frequently been accused of lacking any real interest in the application of Christianity to broad social problems such as disease, race, ignorance, poverty, industrialism, urbanization, and the reorganization of government. Macartney's ministry quite clearly supports this judgment. He firmly rejected a social gospel, including the kind of faith advocated by Walter Rauschenbusch (Macartney's contemporary until his death in 1918), who sought to reorganize all humanity on a more fraternal basis according to the will of God. For Rauschenbusch, this included the application of the teachings of Jesus to pressing questions of public morality, such as war, labor-management relations, politics, and government. Macartney, on the other hand, believed that the clergymen of his generation were overemphasizing the ethical and social side of religion to the exclusion of the winning of souls (the primary goal of the minister) and the proclamation of such cardinal truths as revelation and individual redemption.[50] Whether the charge of such one-sidedness was true or not, Macartney provided considerable evidence of going in the other direction, thereby illustrating the conviction held by Rauschenbusch that frequently on one side there were unchristian socialists and on the other side unsocial Christians.[51] Macartney stated his position succinctly and with typical firmness:

> You search the New Testament in vain for any record or intimation of the idea that those who established Christianity in the world were thinking primarily of changing the government of the world, or of the abolition of evil customs and institutions in the world. . . . The interest in and the passion for a better world order and a better social order is worthy and laudable in the highest sense. But let us make no mistake. The passion for a social order and a world order is no substitute for a passion for souls.[52]

Macartney also believed that it was the lack of religion which had created social problems in the first place—he saw no other causes—and the Social Gospel had not borne the fruit in solving these problems that its proponents expected.[53] What appears significant in such a position is that for all practical purposes Macartney limited religion to personal faith and so excluded the wider social dimension. Several factors may have accounted for this exclusion. Initially, there was his background in the Reformed Presbyterian Church, which taught that Christians should neither vote nor hold office until God was recognized as sovereign by the Constitution. Later, there was Macartney's own conviction that evil would continue to flourish until the end of human history, a view that did much to sever the nerve of wide-ranging social reform. In addition, there was Macartney's antipathy to theological liberals who, in his judgment, substituted the Social Gospel for "Biblical Christianity." With them he wanted no company. Lastly, it is possible that Macartney's elitist, upper-middle-class style of life undermined a meaningful exhortation to social, political, and economic change. In Pittsburgh, for instance, this distinguished Presbyterian served a socially prestigious congregation, lived at the Duquesne Club, the most exclusive men's club in the city, and began his ministry in 1927 at the munificent salary of $12,000.[54] One must be cautious, however, in making an unqualified judgment, because there were many definitely upper-middle-class clergymen who did become proponents of a social gospel and in some instances even Christian socialism (e.g., Lyman Abbott and W. S. Rainsford).

While Macartney developed no blueprint of broad social reform, he was not hesitant to condemn specific evils. The problem, however, was that he normally dealt with effects rather than causes and viewed sin in personal rather than social terms. His list of personal sins was a long one. He spoke against dancing, drinking, attending the cinema, reading the comic sheets, participating in sexual "irregularities," watching or engaging in prizefights, practicing birth control, and desecrating the Sabbath. Macartney saw dancing as death to the spiritual life of both individuals and congregations. The cinema drew his displeasure because of its emphasis on violence and "sexology." The comic sheet contained vulgarities. Prizefighting, as illustrated in the Dempsey-Tunney bout of 1927, was an "exaltation of the body over the soul and an alarming revival of paganism."[55] Some of Macartney's strongest broadsides were reserved for the practice of birth control, which he viewed as contrary to the laws of natural morality. "Where men are interested in the New Birth," he wrote, ". . . they will have little time or taste to discuss Birth Control, and will leave it to the physicians to whom it properly belongs."[56]

Macartney's customary methods of opposition to personal iniquities were his pulpit pronouncements and his books (normally his sermons in print). On some occasions, however, he took more specific action. Once Macartney attended a hearing before the state legislature in New Jersey which was considering a bill providing for local option in the selling of alcoholic beverages. When an Episcopal minister spoke against both local option and prohibition, the usually self-controlled Macartney shouted, "Judas Iscariot." He never regretted the outburst, writing in his memoirs that it was a good witness and one of the best sermons he ever preached.[57] In 1926, at Philadelphia, Macartney as a convinced Sabbatarian, resigned from various committees planning the country's sesquicentennial celebration in protest to the opening of the exposition on a Sunday.[58] In Philadelphia and Pittsburgh, Macartney took personal midnight walks through the "tenderloin" sections of each city to investigate the conditions of vice which were rampant in these areas. He also spent some time counseling the men who had been apprehended by the authorities in such sections and taken to neighborhood police stations.[59] There is no record that he sought to counsel the women involved.

Despite his far greater concentration on personal religion and personal shortcomings than on broad social problems, Macartney did speak out on a few social issues from the conservative side. He favored capital punishment, declaring that such a penalty possessed Biblical authority.[60] He supported those who would bring some limitation to the practice of academic freedom lest that freedom be abused. He also spoke firmly against the role of women in society, including the possibility of women becoming elders or ministers in the Presbyterian Church. In his judgment there was no authority in the Scriptures for ordaining women. He felt that such a practice would tend toward the more complete feminization of the church, would increase the occasion for "satanic church quarreling," and would further widen the gulf between Protestantism and Roman Catholicism.[61]

More significant than a few specific pronouncements by Macartney were notable omissions or silences in his social declarations. One reads his sermons in vain for comments on racial matters, although his father had been a leader in the abolitionist movement, participating actively in the Underground Railroad; a black nurse had carried him as an infant from Northwood to Beaver Falls; a black houseman lived in the attic of the family homestead; and, during his pastorate in Pittsburgh, Macartney served on the Mayor's Council of Amity.[62] More notably absent from his declarations, since he served in major manufacturing cities, are references to the problems of capital and labor. When industrial strife was brewing during his pastorate in Paterson, the best suggestion Macartney could offer was that the agitators of such violence "and all others who say the United States is no better than Russia" should be sent to that country "for a season." [63] Throughout his career the only "liberal" positions seemingly taken by Macartney were successful support of an antifraternity cause at Wisconsin in order to democratize those societies and, in Philadelphia, a firm opposition to the Monroe Doctrine and war with Mexico.[64] Macartney's attitude toward fraternities was consonant with his church's position on secret societies; and, concerning war with Mexico, he reasoned that if that country could not govern itself, then it should receive the assistance of the great powers of the world, not the assault of one.

Despite the evils that Macartney saw in his own country, he was an ardent patriot throughout his career.[65] With the exception of the Mexican war, Macartney supported the military conflicts in which America was engaged.[66] From his Geneva (street) Pulpit in Pittsburgh, in 1944, he invoked the blessing of God upon American soldiers, sailors, and airmen and told the throngs gathered on Sixth Avenue that the Allied soldiers were representing a great and sacred cause. This cause was "the emancipation of the enslaved, the redemption of mankind, the overthrow of tyrants and despots, and the vindication of the great truths of our Christian faith." [67] When the war continued with heavy losses Macartney cautioned the soldiers not to doubt the final victory, "for the stars in their courses are fighting against Sisera." [68] At the same time, he took a hard line against pacifists, warning them that neither the Bible nor common sense justified their position.[69]

As Macartney grew older, his criticism of American society accelerated. He lamented the increase of juvenile crime, the abandonment of religious instruction in the home, and the growing emphasis on material success.[70] Yet the immovable fundamentalist came no closer to the Social Gospel. Macartney believed that parishioners were weary of hearing about problems. They wanted to have "their hearts warmed and their faith steadied." He specialized in doing that, but when even a Macartney could not avoid confrontation with social problems of a ubiquitous nature, his "solution" remained personal in nature. His "answer" to an America in the midst of social change and moral decline was personal conversion and religious commitment, instruction in the articles of the faith, a renewed emphasis on immortality, and a demand of political leaders that they act "in behalf of morality and religion." [71] If some thought this was half a gospel at best—a nineteenth-century answer to twentieth-century problems—it was difficult to argue against Macartney because by the very materialistic standards he condemned, Macartney succeeded. Week after week, and year after year, his churches were thronged by large congregations comprised of those same people who wanted "their hearts warmed and their faith steadied."

V

As an ecclesiastical politician, Clarence E. Macartney achieved two early and related successes which cast him into national prominence as the standard-bearer of the Presbyterian fundamentalist forces. Thereafter, although his characteristic independence remained—in fact, perhaps because of it—the star of Macartney's leadership fell rapidly, causing him to place nearly all his emphasis on the local church and his first love of preaching and writing.

In 1922 it was Macartney who initiated charges that were successful in crowding Harry Emerson Fosdick from a Presbyterian pulpit. Fosdick, a Baptist, was serving as associate minister of the First Presbyterian Church of New York City, with preaching responsibility only. This was a deliberate experiment in interdenominationalism and had been approved by session, presbytery, and synod.[72] Through his preaching, Fosdick distinguished between the ancient thought forms of early Christianity and the abiding core of spiritual truth.[73] For instance, he rejected the virgin birth of Jesus but affirmed a belief in the uniqueness of Jesus' person, the result of complete moral obedience. Fosdick denied the existence of angels, but believed in a personal providence. He did not accept the idea of a personal devil, but he did give credence to the destructive forcefulness of evil. He denied the doctrine of the physical, literal, second coming of Christ, stating that it was contrary to God's law of physical nature that men should ascend at Christ's return, for if one man should ascend from Melbourne, Australia, and another from London, England, they would be going in opposite directions. While casting aside the thought form of the second coming, Fosdick affirmed his belief in the victory of righteousness in the coming kingdom of God wherein Christ would rule in human hearts. Such ideas, of course, were noticeably contrary to the Westminster Confession of Faith and the basic beliefs of the fundamentalists.

When, on May 21, Fosdick delivered a famous sermon, "Shall the Fundamentalists Win?" appealing for a church sufficiently inclusive to accommodate both liberals and fundamentalists, this was more than Macartney could take. It was bad enough to have heresy preached from a Presbyterian pulpit; it was intolerable for a Baptist to be doing it.[74] Macartney responded with a sermon of his own entitled "Shall Unbelief Win?" In it he stressed the irreconcilable differences between historic Christianity with its "grand particularities" and theological Liberalism with its subjectivism and sub-Scriptural views. Later that year at a meeting of the Presbytery of Philadelphia, Macartney introduced an overture which requested that the General Assembly see to it that the preaching in the First Presbyterian Church of New York City conform to the doctrines of the Presbyterian Church as set forth in the Westminster Confession of Faith. Macartney made it clear that he believed in religious liberty for all, including Fosdick, but argued that it was unconscionable for a liberal Baptist to preach ideas contrary to the Westminster Confession of Faith in a Presbyterian pulpit.[75] Macartney quoted with approval the editor of a secular paper who wrote: "It is not exactly ethical for a vegetarian to accept employment from a meat packer and urge a diet of spinach upon all who come asking for meat. This is a land where anyone may worship God as he sees fit, but this does not mean that he can make people who disagree with him keep him in their house of worship." [76]

After much parliamentary maneuvering which lasted nearly two years, the Judicial Commission of the General Assembly finally directed the Presbytery of New York to see that Fosdick subscribe to the Confession of Faith and become a minister of the Presbyterian Church (which implied being subject to its doctrinal control). This, of course, Fosdick was unwilling to do. Over the protests of his own devoted congregation, he resigned his position, declaring: "I am a heretic if conventional orthodoxy is the standard. I should be ashamed to live in this generation and not be a heretic." [77] Years later, reviewing this phase of the Modernist-Fundamentalist struggle, Fosdick referred to Macartney as "very decent and dignified in his attitude . . . [one whose] theological position was incredible, [but who] personally was fair-minded and courteous." [78]

Macartney's election as Moderator of the General Assembly of the Presbyterian Church in the U.S.A. in 1924 was closely related to the Fosdick case. He had become known nationally through his initiative in that event. The fundamentalist forces hailed him as their successful leader, and the ultraconservative forces were hoping for additional victories. At the General Assembly in Grand Rapids, which resembled a national political convention in its strategy, tension, and bitterness, Macartney was nominated for the moderatorship by William Jennings Bryan. The latter, with a typical oratorical flair, presented Macartney as a conspicuous defender of the faith, saying:

It was his vigilance that detected the insidious attack made upon the historic doctrines of the Presbyterian Church; it was his courage that raised the standard of the protest about which the Church rallied; it was his leadership that won a decisive victory for evangelical Christianity and historical Presbyterianism. He was the man of the hour and linked himself with the fundamental tenets of the creed of our church.[79]

Macartney's victory was a close one. He defeated by a narrow margin Charles R. Erdman of Princeton Seminary (464–446).[80] In so doing, at the age of forty-four Macartney had become the second youngest man to be elected to the office of Moderator in his denomination's history. The position enabled him to appoint fundamentalists to several key positions within the church, and it gave him a wider sounding board than the local parish from which to proclaim his conservative views. At the conclusion of his one-year term, Macartney again bewailed the inroads of "neo-Christianity" with its lack of redemptive preaching. He also pointed out certain benefits accruing from the Modernist-Fundamentalist Controversy. These included, in his judgment, freshly found courage among many leaders, a new prominence given to the central doctrines of the faith, the furtherance of a true unity among evangelical believers, and the making of a sharp distinction between two mutually exclusive and contradictory religions.[81]

Macartney continued active in the councils of conservative Presbyterian leadership after his term as Moderator, although fundamentalist strength waned during the latter part of 1925 and throughout 1926. This was due partly to a reaction to the Scopes Trial, where William Jennings Bryan made excessive claims for a literal interpretation of the Scriptures. When Macartney assumed his new pastoral responsibilities in Pittsburgh in 1927 he appeared to be less argumentative in nature. He did, however, strongly support the cause of J. Gresham Machen in the latter part of the decade, lamenting that the crowding out of the latter from Princeton Seminary was due ironically to Machen's loyalty to the Reformed tradition. At the same time, Macartney manifested his independence of and occasional differences with Machen. In the strongest terms possible Machen unsuccessfully implored Macartney to accept a professorship at Princeton in 1926 "to strengthen the Seminary . . . and to save the day in the one great evangelical theological institution which remains." [82] In the midst of the Machen struggle at Princeton, Macartney on at least one occasion counseled Machen to make it plain that their dispute was not "primarily with persons, but with wrong principles." [83] The advice was not heeded, because Machen could not bring himself to separate the two. Another insight into Macartney's character and leadership was seen at the General Assembly of 1929, which finally settled the difficulties at Princeton by providing for a single board of control. At the close of the vote, Macartney stepped forward and said to the Moderator: "In behalf of the losing side I want to offer you thanks and gratitude for the eminent way in which you have presided over a most difficult assembly." This act was greeted with "the greatest applause accorded any event in the Assembly." [84]

Although Macartney was one of the few on the old board of directors at Princeton who was not ousted at the time of the reorganization of that institution, he withdrew from Princeton and became a director of the new Westminster Theological Seminary which had been founded by Machen. At the time of the organization of the Independent Board for Presbyterian Foreign Missions, Machen and others again sought Macartney's support—this time urging his loyalty to the separated organization. The latter not only refused to give such support but with twelve other of the twenty-eight Westminster Seminary trustees resigned his position in protest.[85] These men reasoned that support of the new mission board was contrary to the original purpose of Westminster Seminary (i.e., the restoration of Princeton to its policies and traditions prior to its reorganization in 1929) and that ordination into the denomination would be exceedingly difficult for graduates of an institution sympathetic to a separatist organization.[86]

By this time Macartney had become a rather lonely ecclesiastical figure. He had broken with his ultraconservative colleagues and friends of many years to be loyal to a denomination in which he no longer carried a significant influence and to a denomination whose leaders, he believed, had lapsed in their support of creedal Christianity.[87] In such a dilemma, Macartney, the lifelong Presbyterian, hoped for a new conservative religious fellowship that would cut across denominational lines.[88] When this did not materialize, he concentrated on his preaching and writing and the work of the local church in that community where he had become known as "the St. Paul of Pittsburgh." In older years, Macartney attended presbytery infrequently, and when he did, usually made only token appearances.[89] This was ironical, indeed, for the one who had been recognized as the unquestioned leader of the conservative forces within his church and a former Moderator of the General Assembly.

VI

Clarence E. Macartney was a talented clergyman whose abilities as a preacher surpassed his other qualities of leadership despite the fact that he experienced two early successes in his role as an ecclesiastical politician. Even as a preacher, however, Macartney tended to dominate his congregations and to preach a nineteenth-century Reformed theology in a twentieth-century world. His social views also reflected a nineteenth-century individualism minus many of the humanitarian concerns of those who lived in that age. To the extent that Macartney emphasized the personal to the limitation, if not to the exclusion, of the social, he joined others by making his own long-range contribution to the divorce in American religion between personal ethics and a broader morality. If the foregoing appears too negative a judgment, then it must be emphasized again that on a personal level the dignified, informed, hardworking, conscientious Macartney brought inspiration, comfort, and security to a large number of people from the middle and upper classes of society in the various communities where he served.

In perspective it should also be pointed out that Macartney was recognized as the undisputed clerical leader of the fundamentalist forces among northern Presbyterians. He was their standard-bearer in 1925; he was the one to whom Machen appealed in the latter half of the same decade to save the evangelical situation at Princeton; and, as late as 1933, at the time of the missionary crisis in the denomination, a leader like Wilbur M. Smith wrote Macartney: "You are the one man in the Presbyterian Church in the U.S.A. who can really command the absolute loyalty of the entire conservative side of our church." [90] Despite such confidence placed in him, Macartney could not hold back the inevitable tide of liberal theology and eventually could not prevent Machen and a coterie of other ultraconservatives from establishing their independent missionary organization and eventually their separate denomination. Macartney had been successful in initiating the train of events that crowded Fosdick from his pulpit, taking action where others did little more than complain, but even in that instance a strong case may be made for saying that this was a Pyrrhic victory. Public sympathies supported Fosdick, as they had supported Clarence Darrow. Shortly after Fosdick's resignation from the First Presbyterian Church in New York City he possessed a greater sounding board than ever before at the famous Riverside Church in New York City.

An additional conclusion must not be overlooked. Macartney's life and ministry provide one more illustration of the considerable diversity among fundamentalist leaders. While some were primarily politicians, or pastors, or pastor-politicians, or, as in Machen's case, scholars, Clarence Edward Macartney was, above all else, a preacher. As has been shown, he carried out his pastoral responsibilities conscientiously, he held an important ecclesiastical office, and he was an informed individual through a wide reading of history and literature. The fact remains, however, that the pulpit was his throne. There were other differences that distinguished Macartney from his fundamentalist colleagues. In worship he was more formal, solemn, and conservative than they. In methodology he was not a revivalist, as were many of his associates. In theology he held to the Reformed faith and disagreed with many of his religious contemporaries on eschatological matters. In polity he remained loyal to his denomination when others left it (some would call this "institutional Fundamentalism"). In personality Macartney represented a gentlemanly force among the fundamentalists, light-years removed from the shenanigans of such men as John Roach Straton or J. Frank Norris. These characteristics of the independent Macartney caution the scholar to avoid easy and neat profiles of the "typical" fundamentalist.

While Macartney differed in these several areas from his fellow ultraconservatives, he nevertheless possessed one trait common to them all. This was intransigence. He would not be moved from his immutable theological, social, or ecclesiastical positions, whatever the cost or whatever the seeming validity of new interpretations. Such intransigence appears to have been the most distinctive trait of this dignified fundamentalist, a nineteenth-century Christian living self-confidently in a twentieth-century world. Ironically, Macartney's inflexibility, joined with his tendency to dominate and his failure to adopt a more balanced gospel (between the personal and the social), tempts one to think that he, whose best-known sermon was a discourse on opportunity, missed his own chance for a wider influence.

CHAPTER NINE

Voices in Perspective

SEVERAL THEMES RECUR in these biographical studies of the colorful leaders of those who first went by the name "fundamentalist." The most constant motif appears to be the variation in belief, emphasis, and life-style which characterized these men, despite several common denominators. Certainly one would expect differences among any seven selected individuals; however, the diversities seen in these spokesmen of Fundamentalism are greater than previously has been indicated by popular and scholarly understanding.[1]

J. Frank Norris and John Roach Straton represent the radical, militant wing of Fundamentalism. Their belligerency—and in Norris' case instances of violence—did much to discredit the movement and made it extremely difficult for others, including their own colleagues, to work with them. William Bell Riley, the most conservative of the group theologically, was exceedingly aggressive in his opposition to Liberalism; however, he was not as flamboyant a showman as Norris or Straton. J. C. Massee and Clarence E. Macartney reflect the more moderate leadership, generally characterized by propriety and gentlemanliness, although still manifesting deep convictions. J. Gresham Machen is the intellectual of the fundamentalists but equally tenacious in clinging to his religious beliefs. Had he lived long enough, the denomination he founded might have been reduced to a single member. A poor politician, he saw the danger of theological heresy in others, but not the evil of anarchy caused by his own doctrinal rigidity.[2] William Jennings Bryan is the single statesman-politician of the seven. He is a puzzle in that he seems to be a typical American "booster" type, highly optimistic about man and his future, yet he affirmed belief in original sin and, late in life, allied himself with many who were pessimistic about the future of mankind. In numerous ways it appears that he was more influenced by Populism and Progressivism than by the Bible, in which he asserted such unqualified belief.

The strong sense of individuality which characterized these men contributed heavily to their diversity. Distrustful of others and convinced of the correctness of their own beliefs and causes, they built great religious "empires" more about their own personalities than about a carefully arranged theology. By so doing, inevitably they became men of controversy—a characteristic common to all of them. As controversialists, they were often instrumental in the division of churches, schools, and denominations. In fact, at times it appears as if controversy, for them, was a substitute for intellectual, theological, and Biblical content in their sermons and discourses. Consequently, those who verbally placed such unlimited confidence in the Scriptures, even in charitable judgment, seem frequently to have been noticeably unbiblical. As obstinate individualists, these fighting fundamentalists did not shy away even from possible polarization of the religious population. Many times such polarization was the result of their activities, since few people remained neutral about them and the dogmatic religion they espoused.

Despite the diversity of these independent fundamentalists, several factors held them together, even though the union was a loosely bound one. Theologically, they were united in a belief in the supernatural. Religion for them was an objective, divine "given" from a transcendent God, rooted not in human aspiration, exhortation, or meditation, but in the historical facts of the birth, life, death, and resurrection of Jesus. After that basic, supernaturalistic tie, the specific doctrine that united them more than any other was the inerrancy of the Scriptures in the original documents. There was far greater agreement on this subject—notwithstanding J. C. Massee's qualifying interpretation—than on millenarian views.

Another factor that bound them together, despite diversity, was the common enemy of theological Liberalism and what that Liberalism entailed. All of them, for instance, opposed an interpretation of man from natural categories only. All, except possibly Bryan, eschewed social means as the method of saving society, choosing evangelism instead. All opposed Biblical criticism, and all set themselves against ecumenical tendencies, fearing centralization in religion as much as centralization in government. As long as

Liberalism existed as the common enemy, the diversities of the fundamentalists were minimized by the opponent that united them in anger. When Liberalism declined, however, the fundamentalists and some of their descendants found themselves in the strange situation of an army wishing to fight but lacking an adversary. Under those circumstances, their diversities were accentuated; new opponents had to be discovered (evolution and, later, Communism); sometimes, in compensation, they fought one another. Through it all, the fundamentalists developed a harsh, arrogant attitude which came to characterize them far more than a theological position. For, in truth, these leaders were not normally doctrinal innovators. Rather, they energized existing conservative, Protestant orthodoxy and, in a few instances, unorthodox beliefs received from others. But their aggressive, acrimonious attitude came to be their hallmark, an attitude which, linked with their dogmatism, proved to be a very dangerous although distinguishing combination. The contribution of that attitude by the fundamentalist leaders of the 1920's was a major factor in the development of Fundamentalism itself.

A second motif running through these biographical studies, in addition to the diversity in belief, emphasis, and life-style, is the tension between the patriotism of these fundamentalist leaders and their criticism of society. Invariably they professed love for America (J. Gresham Machen somewhat less overtly than the others), yet they were sensitive to the sins and shortcomings of the country without normally becoming proponents of a social gospel. The most notable exceptions to this absence of a social gospel were William Jennings Bryan and John Roach Straton. Bryan, during his years in political service, supported most of the social reform movements of his day. Straton, as we have seen, advocated a number of reforms early in his ministry, but as he grew older and his country grew more corrupt, his social optimism waned rapidly.

Usually when the fundamentalists criticized the larger society, they gave their primary attention to outlawing the liquor traffic and prostitution. They (Machen excepted) directed their heaviest and most frequent broadsides, however, against "sins" of a more personal nature—smoking, dancing, drinking, and attending the movies and the theater. This caused some of their critics to proclaim that they were "majoring in minors." Ironically, the fears of the fundamentalists about the physical dangers in the use of tobacco and intoxicants have materialized to the extent that these indeed have become major social problems in America and elsewhere.[3] What irritated people, however, was not so much the correctness or incorrectness of the views of the fundamentalists in these areas as it was their dogmatic, absolutist, haughty insistence that they and they alone were right. They made no allowance for other views and they saw no gradation in the evils that they condemned. In dealing with dancing, for instance, they made no distinction between folk dancing and nightclub sensuousness. Concerning movies and the theater, no thought was given to good movies and bad movies, good theater and bad theater. The irrationality of such an attitude was pointed out some years later by an incisive critic when he wrote: "One of the unexpected blessings of television is that it lets the fundamentalist catch up on all the movies he missed on religious principles." [4]

This tendency to be long on condemnation and short on constructive suggestion applied also to the broader areas of society. In the midst of the most pressing social problems—war, industrial strife, political corruption—the answer of these fundamentalist leaders was rarely, if ever, a change in the social structure of society itself. Their perennial solution was, rather, the conversion of the sinful individual through evangelism. It was assumed that the pietistic life would follow. This overemphasis on evangelism ignored other Biblical gifts, resulted in the fundamentalist churches becoming little more than preaching stations dominated by pastor-evangelists, and, most important, contributed toward the divorce between personal ethics and a wider morality. In this regard, the fundamentalists were shaping in a negative way the very society they condemned.

The question may now be asked, To what extent were these leaders of Fundamentalism influential? The answer is that their impact on their own and future generations was wide, although, ironically, in the 1920's they lost the theological battle to their liberal opponents. The clergymen among them served large churches, in fact, among the largest in the world, but a strong case may be made that those churches were primarily preaching centers rather than autonomous or presbyterial congregations in which laypersons participated actively in significant decisions. J. Frank Norris, William B. Riley, and J. Gresham Machen founded schools from which literally thousands of graduates went out to further the fundamentalist faith. All of these fundamentalist leaders wrote books and published newspapers, periodicals, and various journals. They also disseminated their views widely by means of the radio, the lecture circuit, public debates, and Bible conferences. In addition, Norris and Machen founded fellowships or denominations of their own. Theologically, their stress on the

Scriptures served as a corrective to subjective, nebulous experience and gave many people enduring pillars of doctrine to which to cling in time of social and religious change. Their emphasis on evangelism introduced thousands of individuals to a religious experience which, in many instances, eventually led beyond Fundamentalism. Their obvious commitment to what they believed impressed others with the ardor and sacrificial quality of their lives. Their criticism of overcentralization in denominational life foreshadowed contemporary criticism of church life that seeks to shift the focus of attention from administrative headquarters to local churches. Through such means, these spokesmen influenced unnumbered people and contributed significantly to the religious climate out of which neo-orthodoxy and neo-evangelicalism arose. Furthermore, their dramatic lives (especially J. Frank Norris, John Roach Straton, and William Jennings Bryan) added color and excitement—as well as bitterness—to the decades in which they lived. Two generations of Americans have responded to them and the movement they championed in either negative or positive terms. Fundamentalism, with its appeal to literally millions of people, has become a major current in American religious life.

At the same time, however, that Fundamentalism was manifesting its strong influence in the 1920's, it suffered notable defeats. It lost the popular verdict when Harry Emerson Fosdick was forced from the pulpit of the First Presbyterian Church in New York City. It lost the public judgment at Dayton in 1925. It lost the struggle at Princeton when the seminary was reorganized in the latter part of the decade. It lost the endeavor to gain religious-political control of the mainline Protestant denominations. It lost the attempt to establish a closely knit world association of fundamentalists, despite the attempts of William Bell Riley. Perhaps these losses were not so much victories for Liberalism as they were defeats for Fundamentalism.

Several factors, reflected in the leaders of Fundamentalism, contributed to these defeats. Initially, there was the sensationalism of method and language by men like J. Frank Norris and John Roach Straton. Many people with even limited cultural sensitivity were repulsed by Norris' tactics of bringing a horse into the sanctuary to see its cowboy master baptized or by Straton's use of a fourteen-year-old child evangelist to win worldly-wise New Yorkers to a religious experience. Their feelings were much the same when Norris chose ten civic leaders from his home city and then preached an explicit sermon entitled "The Ten Biggest Devils in Fort Worth, Names Given." Straton was not far behind, calling Harry Emerson Fosdick "the Jesse James of the theological world" and declaring that Governor Alfred E. Smith was "the deadliest foe in America . . . of moral progress and true political wisdom." Actions and remarks such as these attracted some people, but alienated more.

A second reason was the theological stubbornness of the fundamentalists, both leaders and disciples. They would recognize no truth save that found in their own understanding of the essentials of Christianity. At times, in that understanding, they approached bibliolatry as they claimed a greater perfection for the Bible (verbal inerrancy) than the Bible claimed for itself. In insisting on this particular interpretation of Scriptural inspiration as one of the essentials of faith, they bordered on sub-Reformation thinking. No longer was salvation by faith alone! Thirdly, the fundamentalists hurt their own cause by a heresy of spirit more dangerous than a heresy of doctrine. Their harsh and arrogant attitude toward all who differed with them revealed their own self-righteousness and made it difficult for the majority of people to communicate with them in any meaningful way. At times this reached the ludicrous stage, as when J. Gresham Machen regretted that the people on the sinking *Titanic* could not find a better hymn to sing than "Nearer, My God, to Thee." Is it conceivable that the scholar of Fundamentalism really expected the ill-fated passengers, in the moment of crisis, to analyze the theological content of various hymns before they intoned their death song?

Fourthly, the fundamentalists failed because their leading figures were such prima donnas that they did not effectively work together for the common cause. Strong-willed and individualistic, they generally were more concerned about the success of their own programs in their own particular areas than the good of the larger movement. The most striking illustration of this lack of teamwork was the forsaken William Jennings Bryan at Dayton. His ultraconservative colleagues were praying for him—but from afar. Finally, the fundamentalists lost the religious battle of the 1920's because of one factor largely beyond their own control. This was the cultural drift of the times when life was moving in a more liberal direction. In religion, this direction was symbolized in somewhat extreme form by "A Humanist Manifesto," issued in 1933, which culminated trends that had long been developing. The Manifesto was a dramatic statement by thirty-four prominent individuals, including eleven professors, from various denominational and religious backgrounds who publicly confessed belief in a new religion, Humanism, and stated fifteen theses on which they could agree. Charles Francis Potter, Straton's opponent in debate, was one of the signers. He was convinced that "the humanization of religion would require the substitution of discovery for revelation, the replacement of salvation by education, the substitution of democracy for monarchy in religion, the replacement of the churches by free religious societies, and the supplanting of the supernatural by the natural." [5] This move toward humanism was but one manifestation of a liberal trend that sought to reconstruct religion in the light of the intellectual and technological revolutions of the last half of the nineteenth century. It was difficult to fight against such a tide.

After its confrontation with Liberalism in the 1920's, Fundamentalism continued to express itself in the conservative wings of major denominations and in the rise of some of the smaller, often pietistic, Protestant denominations such as Machen's Orthodox Presbyterian Church, the General Association of Regular Baptists, and the Conservative Baptist Association of America. Since 1950, however, there has been a resurgence of fundamentalist and evangelical strength in the United States, despite the seeming victory of Liberalism in the 1920's. Billy Graham and his well-attended crusades are indications of this revival, although "old school" fundamentalists still have difficulty in accepting his "inclusive evangelism." Liberalism, on the other hand, was disciplined early: by history which did not move in as favorable a direction as the liberal devotees had hoped; and by a neo-orthodox theology which stressed God's transcendence more than his immanence and took a grim view toward man and society. Liberalism has almost ceased to exist as a separate theological tendency, although its accomplishments remain. It brought about the wide acceptance of Biblical criticism as a method; it encouraged the broad application of a social gospel; it stimulated numerous movements in an ecumenical direction; and it still maintains control of several mainline denominations, although these groups are declining in relative strength.

One may now ask what lies ahead in the study of Fundamentalism. A long-range need is an overall history of the movement objectively oriented and academically critical. Prior research into two generally neglected areas would enrich the quality of such a definitive work. In the first place, a sociological, "quantitative" analysis of the rank and file of fundamentalists is needed. Who comprised the people of this major religious expression? What were their geographical and cultural backgrounds? From what economic strata did they come? Why were they drawn to this theological tendency and not others? Older stereotypes have pictured the fundamentalist population as comprising the poor, the dispossessed, and the disinherited segments of society.[6] Careful research, however, may reveal that the fundamentalists consisted of a much more inclusive social grouping.

A second area of needed research has already been hinted at in this book, in fact may have provided an additional motif. That is a psychological history of the fundamentalist leaders themselves. Such a study is important if one accepts the thesis that Fundamentalism is as much an attitude as a set of beliefs. That the warriors of this ultraconservative movement lived with such psychological problems seems most likely. There was the troubled, insecure J. Frank Norris whose passion for numerical success may well have been linked to the tragedies and influences of his youth. There was John Roach Straton conceivably enjoying his role of being "the accusative case." There was William Bell Riley with his possible need to dominate. There was J. Gresham Machen and his close attachment to his mother which probably made difficult other meaningful relationships. There was William Jennings Bryan seeking to compensate for his own political losses and those of his father. There was Clarence E. Macartney, unduly sensitive, frustrated in romantic hopes, and harboring a Napoleonic complex.

A trained psychoanalyst would be required for such a study, someone, for example, in the tradition of Erik H. Erikson.[7] Even then there would be the difficulty of not being able to interview the subjects of investigation, since all are now deceased. On general topics, however, it is not difficult to imagine the responses of these seven spokesmen were they alive today. All would affirm the centrality of supernatural rather than natural forces in their lives as well as in their theology. And concerning society, if John Roach Straton and his colleagues thought that humanity in the 1920's was "shooting like a rocket . . . down the greased ways toward hell," one can hardly imagine that the condition of American society fifty years later would have changed their attitude. If that leaves too negative an impression of these colorful, self-willed leaders, then it may help to remember the judgment of Edward J. Carnell that the perversion of the fundamentalists was fathered by misguided zeal, not malice.[8]

NOTES

Chapter One. Introducing Fundamentalism

1. The best-known secondary sources dealing with Fundamentalism are, in order of publication, Stewart G. Cole, *The History of Fundamentalism* (1931); Norman F. Furniss, *The Fundamentalist Controversy, 1918–1931* (1954); Louis Gasper, *The Fundamentalist Movement* (1963); Willard B. Gatewood, Jr., ed., *Controversy in the Twenties: Fundamentalism, Modernism, and Evolution* (1969); Ernest R. Sandeen, *The Roots of Fundamentalism: British and American Millenarianism, 1800–1930* (1970); Erling Jorstad, *The Politics of Doomsday: Fundamentalists of the Far Right* (1970); George W. Dollar, *A History of Fundamentalism in America* (1973).

2. The term "fundamentalist" was coined in 1920 by Curtis Lee Laws, editor of *The Watchman-Examiner*, a Baptist publication, shortly after the preconvention conference of conservative Baptists, prior to the annual meeting of the Northern Baptist Convention at Buffalo, New York. *The Watchman-Examiner*, July 1, 1920.

3. The Social Gospel was a submovement within religious Liberalism which sought to bring about the ideal age by the application of Christianity to the social, political, and economic problems of an increasingly industrialized American society.

4. Robert Campbell, *Spectrum of Protestant Beliefs*, p. 8. The lower estimate belongs to John Warwick Montgomery; the higher to Campbell. These figures do not include descendants of fundamentalists known as evangelicals. It should be stressed, however, that these are estimates and that no official census has ever been taken.

5. George M. Marsden, "Defining Fundamentalism," *Christian Scholar's Review*, Winter 1971, p. 141.

6. Sandeen, *Roots of Fundamentalism*, p. 285.

7. Dollar's book, *History of Fundamentalism*, is highly subjective in

nature, written from the standpoint of militant Fundamentalism and characterized by much sermonizing.

8. Sydney E. Ahlstrom, *A Religious History of the American People*, p. 914.

9. Sandeen, *Roots of Fundamentalism, in toto;* Ernest R. Sandeen, "Defining Fundamentalism: A Reply to Professor Marsden," *Christian Scholar's Review*, Spring 1971, pp. 227–233.

10. Amillennialists are those who deny belief in the millennium. For more on millenarianism and millennialism, see Ernest Lee Tuveson, *Redeemer Nation: The Idea of America's Millennial Role*, and Edwin S. Gaustad, ed., *The Rise of Adventism*.

11. Marsden, "Defining Fundamentalism," pp. 141–151. Erling Jorstad thinks of religious nationalism as another resource in the development of Fundamentalism. Jorstad, *Politics of Doomsday*, pp. 24–25.

12. Some of the background factors of Protestant Liberalism were medieval scholasticism; the humanism of the Renaissance period; the scientific discoveries of the sixteenth through the nineteenth centuries, including Biblical criticism; Darwinian evolution; and Deism.

13. William Pierson Merrill, *Liberal Christianity*, pp. 26–30.

14. Traditionally, historians have referred to the "five fundamentals" of Fundamentalism as emanating from the Niagara Bible Conference of 1895. The five are the inerrancy of Scripture, the deity of Jesus including his virgin birth, the substitutionary atonement, the physical resurrection, and the bodily return of Jesus. Ernest R. Sandeen, however, points out that the only time a five-point statement was made was in 1910, by the General Assembly of the Presbyterian Church in the U.S.A. (it was reaffirmed in 1916 and 1923). He feels that Cole, *History of Fundamentalism*, was responsible for the confusion, since he carelessly stated that the Niagara group had adopted such a five-point declaration; but the only creedal statement ever produced by that body was in 1878, and it contained fourteen points, not five. Sandeen further states that through uncritical acceptance of Cole's mistake generations of students have been taught to identify Fundamentalism by the five points. See Ernest R. Sandeen, "Toward a Historical Interpretation of the Origins of Fundamentalism," *Church History*, March 1967, p. 79.

15. Robert T. Handy, "Fundamentalism and Modernism in Perspective," *Religion in Life*, Vol. XXIV (1955), p. 390.

16. Sandeen, *Roots of Fundamentalism*, p. 141.

17. Ahlstrom, *Religious History*, p. 810. Dispensationalism is the belief that God has divided all human history into successive periods or dispensations, frequently interpreted to be seven in number, sometimes marked by, but not identical with, successive covenants.

18. *Ibid.*, p. 816.

19. *Ibid. The Fundamentals* were republished in 1958 under the sponsorship of the Bible Institute of Los Angeles as a part of its Jubilee Year celebration.

Chapter Two. J. Frank Norris, Violent Fundamentalist

1. The two books written about Norris are Louis Entzminger, *The J. Frank Norris I Have Known for Thirty-four Years,* and E. Ray Tatum, *Conquest or Failure?* Entzminger's volume is unsatisfactory from an academic standpoint because of its panegyrical and devotional nature. Tatum's work overstresses the maternal influence on Norris. Furthermore, there is minimal reference to the division in Norris' Fellowship in the early 1940's and, surprisingly, there is no mention of Norris' death. Norris himself wrote several books, although the reader will invariably discover that these are collections of sermons and debates stenographically recorded. These include his *Inside History of First Baptist Church, Fort Worth; and Temple Baptist Church, Detroit. Life Story of Dr. J. Frank Norris* (hereafter referred to as *Inside History*).

Four unpublished master's degree theses have been written about Norris: D. G. Bouldin, "The J. M. Dawson-J. F. Norris Controversy: A Reflection of the Fundamentalist Controversy Among Texas Baptists" (Baylor University, 1960); B. E. Burlinson, "The Ecclesiology and Strategy of J. Frank Norris, from 1919 to 1950" (Baylor University, 1960); Kenneth Connolly, "The Preaching of J. Frank Norris" (The University of Nebraska, 1960); Homer Ritchie, "The Life and Career of J. Frank Norris" (Texas Christian University, 1967). Bouldin's work is handled especially well, although all four theses and the books by Tatum and Entzminger are noticeably lacking in their references to Norris' correspondence covering the years from 1928 to 1952. This correspondence, on which the author of this book has relied heavily, is referred to in the notes as Norris Papers. The author of this study has also read extensively in Norris' newspaper, *The Fundamentalist* (earlier known as *The Fence-Rail* and *The Searchlight*), and has visited Fort Worth, Texas, for the purpose of conducting interviews and attending services in Norris' former church. Those interviewed included J. Frank Norris, Jr., Omer Ritchie, and Homer Ritchie, Norris' immediate successor.

For excellent monographs on religion in the South, see K. K. Bailey, *Southern White Protestantism in the Twentieth Century,* and Samuel S. Hill, Jr., *Southern Churches in Crisis.*

2. Atlanta *Constitution,* May 8, 1947.

3. Entzminger, *The J. Frank Norris I Have Known,* p. 34. Norris was, without question, the source of such information. He also told the story of his mother literally horsewhipping the local bartender because of his refusal to cease selling whiskey to her husband. While not denying the problem of alcohol in the Norris home, this author speculates that these stories may have been embellished for homiletical purposes.

4. *Ibid.;* Tatum, *Conquest or Failure?* pp. 27–29, 31; Bouldin, "Dawson-Norris Controversy," p. 16. The quotation is from Bouldin.

5. Tatum, *Conquest or Failure?* pp. 42, 47, 50–51, 56–57.

6. Joseph Martin Dawson, *A Thousand Months to Remember: An Autobiography*, p. 57.

7. *Ibid.*, p. 52; Bouldin, "Dawson-Norris Controversy," p. 20. Cooper later became a teacher and president of Hardin-Simmons University in Abilene, Texas.

8. Norris accelerated his study at the seminary because he had the responsibility of supporting a family. He had married Lillian Gaddy on March 5, 1902. At the time of their wedding her father, J. M. Gaddy, was the general missionary for the Texas Baptist General Convention. The Norrises became the parents of four children: Lillian, Jim Gaddy, J. Frank, Jr., and George Louis. *The Watchman-Examiner*, Aug. 28, 1952; Norris, *Inside History*, p. 23; Tatum, *Conquest or Failure?* p. 67.

9. The key to Norris' numerical accomplishment was the gaining of "decisions" in the home, and his insistence that a public declaration of faith follow—in his church, of course.

10. Ritchie, "Life and Career," p. 10. Norris purchased a controlling share of stock in the publication with the insurance money his wife received at the time of her father's death. The death of Norris' father-in-law was shrouded in mystery. Norris and J. M. Gaddy were riding on the rear platform of a train near San Marcos, Texas, in 1906, when the latter fell off and was killed. For further discussion, see Bouldin, "Dawson-Norris Controversy," p. 20.

11. The major source of irritation, according to Dawson, *A Thousand Months*, pp. 97–98, was Norris' refusal to confine himself to the business side of the paper. On one occasion, Norris smuggled to the printer a lengthy article filled with "damaging insinuations about Baptist leaders." The editor did not see it until it was in print. *Ibid.*, p. 98.

12. As the result of Norris' crusade, racetrack gambling was made illegal in Texas in 1909. *Journal of the Senate of Texas, being the Regular Session of the Thirty-first Legislature* (1909). The governor presented to Norris the pen that had been used in signing the antigambling bill into law.

13. The church had called another man, but when he accepted the invitation of a congregation elsewhere, the people turned to Norris, who had served them as a supply preacher on several occasions. Norris, *Inside History*, p. 37; Tatum, *Conquest or Failure?* p. 101.

14. *Time*, Sept. 1, 1952, p. 73.

15. Ritchie, "Life and Career," p. 2.

16. Tatum, *Conquest or Failure?* pp. 259–260.

17. *The Watchman-Examiner*, Aug. 28, 1952. This arrangement seems to be unique in American church history. Norris traveled by train and plane between his two congregations. When in one pulpit, he would send lengthy telegrams to his other congregation describing his numerical and spiritual successes. Tatum, *Conquest or Failure?* pp. 272, 275, 288. Norris actually began his work at Detroit late in 1934, but did not officially become the minister until early in January 1935. After a serious illness, Norris resigned

from his church in Detroit in November of 1948 but reconsidered early in 1949 and continued to hold that office until 1951, although with lessened responsibilities.

18. J. Allen Broyles, *The John Birch Society: Anatomy of a Protest*, p. 24. There has been much speculation about the relationship between Fundamentalism and radical-right politics. One scholar believes that while the radical-right political posture "appeals to many Fundamentalists, the identification of the two movements now seems unlikely." Ernest R. Sandeen, "Fundamentalism and American Identity," p. 63.

19. Fort Worth *Star-Telegram*, Aug. 23, 24, 1952; *The Fundamentalist*, Aug. 19, 1952.

20. Bailey, *Southern White Protestantism*, pp. 1–24.

21. Cole, *History of Fundamentalism*, pp. 52–62, 65–91, 281–297; Sandeen, *Roots of Fundamentalism*, pp. 188–232; Furniss, *Fundamentalist Controversy*, pp. 3–45; Handy, "Fundamentalism and Modernism in Perspective," p. 390. Prof. Samuel S. Hill, Jr., distinguishes between southern Fundamentalism and classical Fundamentalism. He sees southern Fundamentalism as lacking the greater doctrinal comprehension of classical Fundamentalism, less apologetical in nature than classical Fundamentalism, and more revivalistic than the standard tradition. In general, Norris fits Hill's description. Hill, *Southern Churches*, p. 26.

22. Norris to Charles Alexander, Dec. 20, 1929. Norris Papers. J. Frank Norris, *The Gospel of Dynamite*, p. 6. The second quote is from *Gospel of Dynamite*.

23. Homer Ritchie quotes Norris on dispensationalism. Interview with Homer Ritchie, June 8, 1970.

24. Norris, *Gospel of Dynamite*, p. 168.

25. *Ibid.*, p. 7.

26. *Ibid.*, p. 135.

27. *The Fundamentalist*, Jan. 25, 1929.

28. For Norris' full argument on eternal security, see *Norris-Wallace Debate, Delivered in Fort Worth, Texas, November 5th, 6th, and 7th, 1934*, pp. 164–167.

29. Norris, *Inside History*, pp. 11–20.

30. William Bell Riley served for a time as associate editor of Norris' publication, *The Fundamentalist*. Norris first met Straton when the latter was pastor of the Hubbard (Texas) Baptist Church and also served as professor of oratory and literary interpretation at Baylor during Norris' junior and senior years.

31. Ralph Lord Roy, *Apostles of Discord*, p. 355.

32. W. S. Taylor, "Norris, John Franklyn," *Encyclopedia of Southern Baptists*, Vol. II, p. 983. The Baptist Bible Union was an interdenominational society comprised of Baptist fundamentalists who aggressively fought the inroads of Liberalism in church, school, and denominations.

33. Norris, *Inside History*, p. 194.

34. Tatum, *Conquest or Failure?* pp. 264, 279–280.

35. William Bell Riley acted as the presiding judge and six students from Southern Methodist University, Southwestern, and Texas Woman's College appeared as witnesses. Norris, *Inside History*, p. 10; Furniss, *Fundamentalist Controversy*, p. 122.

36. Ritchie, "Life and Career," pp. 35, 195, 196. The cowboy was Jack "Red" Thompson; the horse, "Hogeyes."

37. Tatum, *Conquest or Failure?* p. 121.

38. *Ibid.*, pp. 116, 281; Ritchie, "Life and Career," p. 16; *Newsweek*, April 11, 1949, p. 76; Roy, *Apostles of Discord*, p. 352; Norris to Harvey Campbell, March 24, 1947, Norris Papers. The quote is from Roy. The membership at Fort Worth eventually reached 13,000; at Detroit, 12,000. In the latter city Norris drew many displaced southerners who had been attracted to Detroit by the automobile industry. Tatum, *Conquest or Failure?* pp. 5, 270.

39. Norris to Hon. Alva Bryan, May 4, 1928. Norris Papers.

40. G. Beauchamp Vick, "The How-Methods of Enlisting Members," printed as a chapter in Norris, *Inside History*, pp. 277–278; *The Watchman-Examiner*, April 20, 1922. It was not unusual for as many as one hundred persons to join each of Norris' churches on a given Sunday. A key individual in "banking the fires" which Norris lighted was Louis Entzminger, a converted lumberjack and former pastor of the First Baptist Church of New Orleans. He joined Norris at Fort Worth in September 1913 as his full-time Sunday school superintendent. Entzminger brought a measure of organization to the crowds, especially the church school which he divided into departments, classes, and groups. He also supervised the burgeoning visitation program. Tatum, *Conquest or Failure?* pp. 163–167. Aside from Entzminger's organizational efforts, the First Baptist Church of Fort Worth became little more than a preaching station for Norris.

Norris' insatiable thirst for numbers was probably evidence of his own insecurity. The teeming throngs were necessary to bolster his own ego and to prove his success to himself and to others, especially to denominational leaders with whom he had broken. Once Norris' life had run its span, without the stimulus of his leadership, the membership of his churches declined rapidly. There was also some evidence to question the veracity of Norris' numerical reporting.

41. *The Gospel Witness*, Nov. 29, 1928; Norris to W. H. Brockman, Dec. 11, 1928; Norris to J. R. Bennett, Dec. 31, 1928; Norris to H. Beauchamp, Sept. 29, 1928. Norris Papers.

42. Henry Zweifel to H. W. Buckholz, undated telegram. Norris Papers.

43. J. E. Boyd to Norris, Oct. 25, 1928. Norris Papers.

44. Ruth C. Silva, *Rum, Religion, and Votes: 1928 Re-examined*, pp. 15–49; Richard Hofstadter, "Could a Protestant Have Beaten Hoover in 1928?" *The Reporter*, March 17, 1960, pp. 31–32; Edmund A. Moore, *A Catholic Runs for*

President: The Campaign of 1928, p. 195; Roy V. Peel and Thomas C. Donnelly, *The 1928 Campaign: An Analysis*, p. 71; Richard O'Connor, *The First Hurrah: A Biography of Alfred E. Smith*, p. 225.

45. Norris, *Inside History*, p. 116; Norris, *Gospel of Dynamite*, p. 56. Norris to Mrs. A. L. Bryan, Oct. 30, 1944; Norris to J. W. Amerman, May 23, 1930; Norris to R. J. Barber, Aug. 23, 1949. Norris Papers.

46. *The Fundamentalist*, Feb. 1, 1929.

47. Norris, *Inside History*, p. 38.

48. Dollar, *History of Fundamentalism*, p. 124.

49. Norris, *Inside History*, pp. 82–83.

50. *Ibid.*, p. 83.

51. Dollar, *History of Fundamentalism*, p. 129; *The Searchlight*, Dec. 23, 1922, p. 1.

52. Entzminger, *The J. Frank Norris I Have Known*, pp. 25, 91, 95, 101, 103; Norris, *Inside History*, pp. 56, 57–58, 89, 91–92, 93, 108, 111, 113–114.

53. Tatum, *Conquest or Failure?* pp. 133–136, 137–138, 155; Ritchie, "Life and Career," pp. 47–48, 50; Norris, *Inside History*, pp. 63–65.

54. *The Searchlight*, July 31, 1926.

55. *Ibid.*, July 16, 1926.

56. *The Press* (Fort Worth), July 17, 1926; Tatum, *Conquest or Failure?* p. 221.

57. *The Searchlight*, July 23, 30, 1926.

58. Tatum, *Conquest or Failure?* p. 226. This amount of money was raised on Aug. 2, 1926, through contributions placed in a galvanized washtub located on the platform of Norris' church.

59. Ritchie, "Life and Career," pp. 172–173. For full contemporary newspaper accounts of the trial, see Austin *Statesman*, Jan. 14–28, 1927; *The New York Times*, Jan. 10–28, 1927.

60. New York *American*, Jan. 28, 1927. After the tragedy in his study in 1926, Norris was extremely sensitive about being called a "pistol-packin' preacher," "Trigger Norris," "the shooting salvationist," or words of similar description. Since the gun with which he shot Chipps was taken from the drawer of the desk used by the night watchman and there was no evidence that the minister himself ever carried a gun, Norris was successful in forcing retractions from at least five different newspapers. The Chipps affair left other scars for Norris. Of the fundamentalist leaders, only T. T. Shields of Toronto, Canada, remained loyal to him, and later even Shields expressed marked differences with Norris. Some of Norris' friends averred that after the death of Chipps, Norris could never accept being alone at night. Dollar, *History of Fundamentalism*, p. 132; Tatum, *Conquest or Failure?* p. 228.

61. New York *American*, Jan. 28, 1927.

62. This second conflagration occurred Jan. 18, 1929.

63. Tatum, *Conquest or Failure?* p. 94.

64. Norris, *Inside History*, p. 160.

65. Ritchie, "Life and Career," p. 73.

66. *Ibid.;* Joseph Martin Dawson, *A Century with Texas Baptists,* p. 88.

67. Norris, *Inside History,* p. 161.

68. *Ibid.,* p. 138.

69. For a fuller account of the controversy over evolution at Baylor, see the personal papers of President S. P. Brooks in the Texas Collection, Baylor University. For an excellent general account of Fundamentalism and evolution, see Gatewood, ed., *Controversy in the Twenties.*

70. Norris' opposition to Dawson may have been rooted in a personal slight. At the time of their graduation from Baylor in 1903, President Brooks publicly expressed words of appreciation for Dawson, the class valedictorian, but noticeably ignored Norris, the class orator, whom Brooks distrusted. "This merest incident may have accounted in some degree for the subsequent bitter hostility of Norris toward Baylor and toward [Dawson] personally." Dawson, *A Thousand Months,* p. 68.

71. Dallas *Morning News,* Nov. 11, 1945.

72. J. Frank Norris, *Infidelity Among Southern Baptists Endorsed by Highest Officials,* p. 181.

73. Truett endeavored to ignore Norris, although this was difficult to do when the latter sent accusatory telegrams designed to arrive just before Truett began important speaking engagements. There is, however, no mention of Norris in Truett's authorized biography. See Powhatan W. James, *George W. Truett: A Biography.*

74. Norris to O. K. Armstrong, June 4, 1948. Norris Papers.

75. Scarborough was president of Southwestern Baptist Theological Seminary.

76. Ritchie, "Life and Career," p. 61.

77. *Minutes of the 39th Annual Session of the Tarrant County Baptist Association,* Sept. 10–11, 1925, pp. 12–15, as cited in Ritchie, "Life and Career," pp. 93, 97; Tatum, *Conquest or Failure?* pp. 191–192.

78. *The Watchman-Examiner,* Jan. 27, 1921; April 20, 1922. Even this conservative publication felt that Norris, in reacting from a dangerous course (overreliance on lesson helps instead of on the Bible itself), had swung to a course more dangerous still.

79. Tatum, *Conquest or Failure?* pp. 198–205; see Ritchie, "Life and Career," p. 181. For more on the World Baptist Fellowship and the Baptist Bible Fellowship, see Dollar, *History of Fundamentalism,* pp. 226, 216–220.

80. Norris, *Inside History,* p. 229. See also *Time,* May 19, 1947, p. 70.

81. *The Fundamentalist,* Jan. 23, 1931.

82. J. Frank Norris, "Americanism: An Address to the Texas Legislature," p. 24. This address was delivered by Norris to the legislature in open session, April 20, 1949. Sandeen, in "Fundamentalism and American Identity," p. 63, states, "For a time . . . there was serious danger that anti-Communist hysteria might actually sweep Fundamentalism off its feet."

83. Norris, " 'Americanism,' " pp. 16, 22, 26. Norris criticized the preachers of the Social Gospel, declaring they would send the prodigal son a new suit of clothes and a ham sandwich and tell him to stay in the hogpen when he ought to come home and start a new life. Although Norris was opposed to the Social Gospel, his church provided food, clothing, shelter, shower baths, and medicinal supplies for the destitute during the bleak winter of 1932–1933. Bailey, *Southern White Protestantism*, pp. 112–113.

84. Norris, *Inside History*, p. 225.

85. *Ibid.*

86. *Time*, Aug. 26, 1946, p. 68; Ralph Lord Roy, *Communism and the Churches*, pp. 176–177; *The Fundamentalist*, April 18, 1947.

87. The account of this "confrontation," including quotes, is taken largely from *Time*, May 19, 1947, p. 70. Norris' questions included the following: "Why have you [Newton] not said one single word in defense of . . . Greek-Turk Aid to stop Communism? In all your writings and talks about Russia, why have you not said one word . . . condemning the atheistic-communistic tyranny of Joe Stalin and his Polit-Bureau of fellow-gangsters?" Norris to Louie D. Newton, May 7, 1947. Norris Papers.

88. O. K. Armstrong to Norris, Feb. 27, 1948. Norris Papers.

89. Atlanta *Constitution*, May 8, 1947; Norris to Samuel D. Hewlett, March 15, 1948, Norris Papers. The Norris quote is from the Norris to Hewlett letter.

90. Rochester *Evening Journal*, April 15, 1936.

91. Norris, " 'Americanism,' " p. 17.

92. *Ibid.*, p. 20. Norris made his comment about Pius XII after a fifteen-minute interview with the Pontiff during the summer of 1947. Shields, Norris' longtime friend and his former associate in the Baptist Bible Union, "deplored" his conduct. The Canadian Baptist wrote in his own religious paper: "We repudiate his whole action as being . . . unworthy of any minister of the gospel, who calls himself Protestant. . . . We know of no living man who can talk more nonsense in five minutes on world affairs than Dr. Norris. His action in Rome, while it will serve the purpose he had in view, namely spreading himself in the public press, in our judgment was the essence of folly." Roy, *Communism and the Churches*, p. 355. The quote about Stalin is from Norris, " 'Americanism' "; all other quotes are from Roy.

93. *Baptist Bible Tribune*, June 23, 1950, as cited by Ritchie, "Life and Career," p. 150. Other clergymen in Norris' Fellowship came to resent his completely arbitrary decisions, ranging from setting the time and place of the meetings of the organization to selecting those who would serve as the officers of the group. G. Beauchamp Vick, Norris' associate at the Temple Baptist Church in Detroit, and Norris' successor in that congregation, led an uprising which resulted in the formation of a splinter group known as the Baptist Bible Fellowship, with its own Baptist Bible College in Springfield, Missouri. Norris, in failing mental and physical health the last two years of

his life, castigated this group unmercifully, charging them with everything from disloyalty to sexual immorality. In 1948, Norris wrote a friend: "The worst enemies and critics I have are not Roman Catholics, Jews, or machine Baptists, but treacherous fundamentalists I have helped." Norris to R. J. Barber, July 24, 1948. Norris Papers.

94. Late in his life, Norris told Homer Ritchie that he regretted spending so much time on social issues (e.g., his campaigns against the liquor interests, commercialization of Sunday, prostitution, and gambling), since his efforts had effected no change. Sandeen, in "Fundamentalism and American Identity," p. 59, points out that men like Norris faced an unresolved tension between their premillenarian views and their efforts to change society. "Millenarians have consistently taught that nothing can save this world from destruction, and that attempts to ameliorate the condition of man . . . are all doomed." Norris spoke infrequently on racial matters, although he believed in the supremacy of the white race and sharply attacked other religious leaders who expressed different ideas.

95. Atlanta *Constitution,* May 8, 1947.

96. In addition to differences previously discussed, Norris' advocacy of military intervention by the United States in World War II set him apart from William Bell Riley; and his rigid antidenominational stance placed him in opposition to J. C. Massee. Riley had already broken with Norris in 1927 when the latter, in an apparent power grab, changed the name of his paper from *The Searchlight* to *The Fundamentalist.* Norris' strategy was to make it appear that his paper was the official organ of the World's Christian Fundamentals Association, of which Riley was the executive secretary. *The Canadian Baptist,* May 5, 1927.

97. Tatum, *Conquest or Failure?* p. 114.

98. Among Norris' converts was a lawyer who had become addicted to drink. After the reformation of his ways he became wealthy. In gratitude for the change in his life he gave Mrs. Norris $175,000, of which $40,000 was used for the building of the home in which the preacher and his wife lived. Norris took great delight in telling this story to his astounded congregations. Tatum, *Conquest or Failure?* pp. 264–266.

99. Dollar, *History of Fundamentalism,* p. 129.

100. Taylor, "Norris," Vol. II, p. 983; Ritchie, "Life and Career," p. 193. For a fuller discussion of the "rural mentality" in the urban environment, see Paul Carter, *The Twenties in America,* p. 81.

101. Interview with Omer Ritchie, June 7, 1970.

102. *The Fundamentalist,* Feb. 16, 1951, and March 30, 1951.

103. After visiting Norris' church Sunday morning, Oct. 31, 1937, Lewis told reporters: "I admire the eloquence and vigor of Dr. Norris and have wanted to hear him. I have never seen before so many people at church at once." Fort Worth *Star-Telegram,* Nov. 1, 1937.

104. It is interesting, although dangerous, to speculate on the motivations

and environmental factors that influenced Norris. Some factors were probably the sense of independence inherited from the frontier; the maternal influence which gave him the drive to excel; the need to compensate for three years lost to illness; the revivalistic environment in which he was raised; his ultraconservative religious training which equipped him with a rigid "either-or" mentality; the fear of change and the resulting insecurity it would bring; and the dread of becoming "anonymous" in the whirlpool of denominational activism.

Chapter Three. *John Roach Straton, Accusative Fundamentalist*

1. Walter Ross Peterson, "John Roach Straton: Portrait of a Fundamentalist Preacher" (doctoral dissertation, Boston University, 1965), p. 41; Hillyer H. Straton, "John Roach Straton: Prophet of Social Righteousness," *Foundations*, Jan. 1962, pp. 17–38.

2. Sources for this study of Straton's life include his published works, largely collections of sermons; articles by and about him in religious journals and, primarily, his personal papers. The author also interviewed the late Dr. Hillyer H. Straton on March 18 and April 11, 1969. The works about John Roach Straton include the dissertation of Walter Ross Peterson (see n. 1, above) and several articles by Hillyer H. Straton: "John Roach Straton: Prophet of Social Righteousness" (see n. 1, above); "The Straton-Brady Debate on the Theatre," *Encounter*, Autumn 1965, pp. 452–460; coauthored with Ferenc M. Szasz, "The Reverend John Roach Straton and the Presidential Campaign of 1928," *New York History*, April 1968; "John Roach Straton and the Ku Klux Klan," *Andover-Newton Quarterly*, Nov. 1968; Ferenc M. Szasz, "John Roach Straton: Baptist Fundamentalist in an Age of Change, 1875–1929," *The Quarterly Review: A Survey of Southern Baptist Progress*, April–June 1974. The article by John Haynes Holmes, "Straton, John Roach," in *Dictionary of American Biography*, Vol. XVIII, pp. 125–126, is especially valuable for its critical evaluation.

3. Holmes, in *Dictionary of American Biography*, Vol. XVIII, p. 126.

4. James Benedict Moore, "The Sources of Elmer Gantry," *The New Republic*, Aug. 8, 1960, p. 17. Professor Moore felt that there was a largely discernible amount of Dr. William L. ("Big Bill") Stidger, a Kansas City Methodist, and Dr. Straton in *Elmer Gantry* (published in 1927). Sinclair Lewis attended a Sunday evening service at Calvary Baptist Church, New York City, in 1925, after which he introduced himself to Straton and invited the minister to dine with him at a mutually convenient time. Feeling that there was no fellowship between them, Straton declined: "No, Mr. Lewis, I do not care to break bread with you, but I will stay here all night to talk with you if I can be of any help." Letters of John Charles Straton, July 11, 1961, and Hillyer H. Straton, July 14, 1961, to Professor Moore of Whittier College.

5. Henry Dundas Douglas Straton was born in Bannockburn, Scotland, about 1840, a descendant of the old Straton family of Lauriston Castle, Kincardinshire, peers of Scotland from the twelfth century. A graduate of the University of Edinburgh, he served, in addition to his pastorate at Evansville, Baptist churches in Greenville and Greensboro, both in Georgia; and Selma, Alabama. He died in 1895. Julia Rebecca Carter was born at Laurel Grove near Richmond, Virginia, about 1850. She also died in 1895.

6. Stanley Walker, "The Meshuggah of Manhattan," *The New Yorker*, April 16, 1927, p. 27. Interpreting his conversion experience in later years, Straton stressed the depth of his sinfulness prior to his public espousal of the Christian faith. When pressed as to the specific nature of his shortcomings, the fundamentalist warrior pointed to blackberry wine and an occasional game of draw poker.

7. In addition to his training at Mercer University and Southern Baptist Theological Seminary, Straton attended for one year the Boston School of Oratory and Expression (now Curry College, Milton, Massachusetts) and a summer school session at the University of Chicago. He was awarded an honorary Doctor of Divinity degree by Shurtleff College (Illinois) in 1906. *Who Was Who in America*, 1897–1942, Vol. I, p. 1196.

8. Georgia Hillyer's father was J. L. Dagg Hillyer of Atlanta, Georgia, a Baptist minister who was graduated from Mercer University. The John Roach Stratons became the parents of five children: Hillyer, John Charles, Warren, Catherine (who died at the age of twelve), and Douglas.

9. *The Fundamentalist*, Nov. 8, 1929, p. 8; Walker, "Meshuggah of Manhattan," p. 27.

10. John Roach Straton, "A Life-Changing Business," *The Christian Herald*, Dec. 28, 1929, p. 4. (Published posthumously.)

11. John Roach Straton, "What's Wrong with the World?" *The Faith (Fundamentalist)*, March 15, 1925, p. 3.

12. John Roach Straton, *The Menace of Immorality in Church and State*, p. 179.

13. Straton came to both his Biblical literalism and premillennialism relatively late in life. Szasz, "John Roach Straton," p. 62; Szasz to C. Allyn Russell, April 23, 1973.

14. Straton, *Menace of Immorality*, p. 14.

15. *The Watchman-Examiner*, June 28, 1923, p. 824; *The Atlantic City Evening Union*, May 25, 1923.

16. *The Watchman-Examiner*, June 28, 1923, p. 825.

17. A member of Straton's church was employed in 1923 as a stenographer by the American Baptist Foreign Mission Society. She spent many evenings in overtime work copying, from the files, correspondence between missionaries and officials of the Society that might be interpreted as evidence of theological Liberalism. She made such information available to the fundamentalists. This provided the background for the requests of Straton and his

colleagues to see selected correspondence from the files of the Society to ascertain whether or not the stenographer's reports were true. William B. Lipphard, *Fifty Years an Editor*, pp. 124–126; *The Watchman-Examiner*, Nov. 15, 1923, p. 1466.

18. *The New York American*, Oct. 30, 1926; John Roach Straton, "Religious Authority and the Lawless Dr. Fosdick," *The Faith Fundamentalist*, Dec. 28, 1924, p. 8.

19. Harry Emerson Fosdick, *The Living of These Days*, p. 153.

20. Straton to Norris, June 8, 1922. Straton Papers.

21. Telegram published in *The Searchlight*, July 23, 1926. Actually, the friendship between Straton and Norris was a two-way street. When the former was being criticized for his opposition to President Faunce and his role in bringing about an investigation of denominational missionaries, Norris wrote: "Old man, when the battle goes a little hard with you and they begin to shoot at you, just know this: That millions of people all over this whole country of ours are with you and are praying for you . . . all we need to do is to stand firm and give them [members of the denominational "machine"] a little more grapeshot." Letter from Norris to Straton, July 5, 1923. Straton Papers. Norris' choice of words was ironic in the light of the death of D. E. Chipps, for which the pastor from Fort Worth was brought to trial in 1926.

22. As the result of his use of Uldine Utley, some southern religious leaders charged Straton with inconsistency, lack of common sense, and denial of the authority of the Bible, which taught that "women should keep silence in the churches." Straton handled the Pauline reference through an appeal to the whole trend of the Bible instead of relying on isolated verses which, in his judgment, applied only to local situations. He further argued that the verse in question referred only to unconverted women. Editorial, "And, Now, It Is Dr. Straton," *Religious Herald*, July 1, 1926, p. 11. John Roach Straton, "Does the Bible Forbid Women to Preach and Pray in Public?" pp. 1, 7, 10, 11.

23. Straton's street meetings were conducted from an automobile. He spoke from a pulpit placed on a portable platform over the engine of the car.

24. Letter from George T. Hargreaves, editor and manager of Universal Service, Inc., to Straton, July 5, 1921. Straton Papers. Straton was paid fifty dollars for covering the prizefight, a sum that he donated to the benevolence fund of his church. Straton had also been requested to attend the match by the president of the International Reform Association so that he might later appear before the legislature in an effort to halt similar future performances.

25. *New York Evening Journal*, April 14, 1927. In 1922, the bodies of Edward Hall, minister of the Episcopal Church of St. John the Evangelist, New Brunswick, New Jersey, and Mrs. James Mills, his paramour, were found on an abandoned farm. Under the prodding of the New York *Daily Mirror*, the pastor's wife, two of her brothers, and a cousin were brought to trial for murder. The chief witness against them, Mrs. Jane Gibson

(popularly known as the "Pig Woman"), was the eccentric owner of a farm near where the bodies were discovered. The defendants were acquitted, after which Mrs. Hall forced the *Daily Mirror* to make a large out-of-court settlement. Ruth Snyder, a housewife from Long Island, with the help of her lover, killed her husband. Both were brought to trial, found guilty, and electrocuted. The tabloid newspapers, specializing in sex, violence, lurid reporting, and pious lip service to traditional morality, made much of these two cases.

26. *The New York Times*, Nov. 11, 1928, p. 1. The fire leveled the building just days after the defeat of Gov. Alfred E. Smith, a candidate for the presidency against whom Straton had waged an arduous campaign. Straton declined to charge the forces of Smith with the deed, but he was convinced that the blaze had been set deliberately.

27. Despite his stress on healing, Straton believed there was still a place for the doctor in the scheme of life, especially in the fields of diagnosis, prevention of disease, and the simpler forms of surgery. "They [doctors and drugs] seem to be primarily for the natural man and those who do not know the full truth. Divine healing, on the other hand, is for those who fully trust the Lord and have faith to walk with Him without any crutch or dependence whatsoever." John Roach Straton, *Divine Healing in Scripture and Life*, p. 80. Despite such beliefs, Straton had several nervous breakdowns and died at the early age of fifty-four.

28. *New Orleans States*, Oct. 16, 1921.

29. *The Watchman-Examiner*, May 27, 1926, p. 663.

30. *The Indianapolis Sunday Star*, undated newspaper clipping. Straton Papers.

31. *The Baptist Banner*, March 1, 1923.

32. John Roach Straton, "The Truth About Calvary of New York," *Religious Herald*, Nov. 10, 1921, p. 5.

33. Straton to Louis L. Harris, Commissionary *[sic]* of Health, New York City, Nov. 15, 1927. Straton Papers.

34. *The New York Times*, Dec. 20, 1927.

35. John Roach Straton, *The Salvation of Society and Other Addresses*, p. 9.

36. *Ibid.*, p. 12.

37. *Ibid.*, p. 19.

38. *Ibid.*, p. 20.

39. *Ibid.*, p. 22.

40. *Ibid.*, p. 23.

41. Walter Rauschenbusch, *Christianity and the Social Crisis*, p. 407.

42. Straton, *Salvation of Society*, p. 24.

43. John Roach Straton, "Licensing the Liquor Traffic, A Wrong and Wise Policy." Essay written while Executive Secretary, Social Service Commission, Baltimore, Maryland, 1913, pp. 18–23. Straton Papers.

44. John Roach Straton, *The Scarlet Stain on the City and How to Wipe It Out*, p. 59.

45. *Ibid.*, p. 58.

46. Hillyer H. Straton, "John Roach Straton, Prophet of Social Righteousness," p. 29.

47. Gatewood, ed., *Controversy in the Twenties*, p. 15.

48. Frederick Lewis Allen, *Only Yesterday*, pp. 106–122.

49. *Ibid.*, pp. 122–138.

50. *Ibid.*, p. 128.

51. Carter, *The Twenties in America*, p. 5.

52. Straton, *Menace of Immorality*, p. 12.

53. *Ibid.*, p. 39.

54. *Ibid.*, p. 50.

55. John Roach Straton, *Fighting the Devil in Modern Babylon*, p. 18.

56. *Ibid.*, p. 40.

57. *Ibid.*, p. 33.

58. *Ibid.*, p. 28. "The dance hall is the nursery of the divorce courts, the training ship of prostitution, and the graduation school of infamy."

59. *Ibid.*, p. 131.

60. *Ibid.*, p. 135.

61. *Ibid.*, p. 146.

62. *Ibid.*, p. 150.

63. *The New York Sun*, Feb. 20, 1929.

64. *Ibid.*

65. Straton, *Menace of Immorality*, p. 128; *The Watchman-Examiner*, Sept. 12, 1918, p. 1177.

66. *The Watchman-Examiner*, Sept. 12, 1918, p. 1176.

67. Straton, *Menace of Immorality*, p. 128.

68. *Ibid.*, p. 210.

69. John Roach Straton, "Our American House Divided Against Itself: The Menace of White Ku Kluxism, Green Sectarianism, Yellow Journalism, and General Blackguardianism." Sermon preached Dec. 3, 1922, p. 11. Straton Papers. Straton's praiseworthy pulpit stand on the Ku Klux Klan was clouded because of his brief membership in the Supreme Kingdom, a "religious" organization led by the nefarious E. Y. Clarke, a former Klansman. Straton spoke twice in the South under the auspices of this group before resigning therefrom after a newspaper exposé. See Hillyer H. Straton, "John Roach Straton and the Ku Klux Klan." Although Straton disowned the Klan, the latter did not disown Straton. Provisional Klan No. 7, Bay Shore, Long Island, commended him for his courageous stand against Al Smith, J. H. Fletcher to Straton, Aug. 20, 1928, Straton Papers; the Rockville Center (Long Island) Klan No. 126 sent Mrs. Straton a letter of sympathy upon the death of her husband, Oral Belflower to Mrs. John Roach Straton, Nov. 5, 1929. Straton Papers.

70. Straton, *Menace of Immorality*, p. 13.

71. Hillyer Straton felt that by "old-time Americanism" his father meant

Biblical and democratic virtues which included all men of goodwill. Hillyer H. Straton, "John Roach Straton: Prophet of Social Righteousness," p. 130.

72. John Roach Straton, "How to Fight the Negroes, the Foreigners, the Catholics, and the Jews—The More Excellent Way." Sermon preached Dec. 10, 1922, p. 2. Straton Papers.

73. John Roach Straton, "Can New York Handle the Jewish and Catholic Questions in the More Excellent Way?" Sermon preached Dec. 17, 1922, p. 2. Straton Papers.

74. Daniel B. Stevick, *Beyond Fundamentalism*, p. 59.

75. Charles Francis Potter, *The Preacher and I*, p. 193.

76. *Ibid.*, p. 146. At the time, King's Chapel membership approximated two hundred people.

77. *The Battle Over the Bible; First in the Series of Fundamentalist-Modernist Debates Between Rev. John Roach Straton . . . and Rev. Charles Francis Potter . . .* , p. v.

78. Potter, *Preacher and I*, p. 158.

79. *Battle Over the Bible*, pp. 13–31.

80. *Ibid.*, pp. 33–39.

81. Stevick, *Beyond Fundamentalism*, pp. 51–52.

82. *Battle Over the Bible*, pp. 58–64.

83. *Ibid.*, p. 65.

84. Potter, *Preacher and I*, p. 179.

85. *Ibid.*, p. 181.

86. *Ibid.*, p. 182.

87. *Evolution Versus Creation; Second in the Series of Fundamentalist-Modernist Debates Between Rev. John Roach Straton . . . and Rev. Charles Francis Potter . . .* , pp. 14–29.

88. *Ibid.* For a fuller account of Straton's presentation of the second debate, see pp. 30–85, 107–109. Potter claimed in his autobiography (*Preacher and I*, p. 241) that the lawyers for the prosecution in the Scopes Trial, including William Jennings Bryan, used Straton's research, arguments, and documentation.

89. *Evolution Versus Creation*, p. 36.

90. Potter, *Preacher and I*, p. 188.

91. *Ibid.*; also *Evolution Versus Creation*, p. 59.

92. Potter, *Preacher and I*, p. 188.

93. *Evolution Versus Creation*, p. 184.

94. According to Potter, Straton thought up the rationalization that the people who owned radios were mostly rich wastrels whose opinions didn't count.

95. *The Virgin Birth—Fact or Fiction? Third in the Series of Fundamentalist-Modernist Debates Between Rev. John Roach Straton . . . and Rev. Charles Francis Potter . . .* , pp. 11–52, 70–87.

96. *Ibid.*, p. 52.

97. *Ibid.*, p. 56.

98. *Ibid.*, pp. 54–69, 89–95.

99. *Ibid.*, p. 92.

100. *Ibid.*, pp. 68–69. By the materialism of the virgin birth, Potter meant the fact that it places the emphasis on a method of physical conception rather than on the spirit of Jesus.

101. Potter, *Preacher and I*, p. 216.

102. *Ibid.*, p. 224.

103. *Was Christ Both God and Man? Fourth in the Series of Fundamentalist-Modernist Debates Between Rev. John Roach Straton . . . and Rev. Charles Francis Potter . . .* , pp. 11–24, 66–75.

104. *Ibid.*, pp. 25–63, 77–100.

105. Potter, *Preacher and I*, p. 227.

106. Straton, *Fighting the Devil*, p. ii.

107. Charles B. Driscoll, "A Voice Crying in the Wilderness," *The New McClure's*, Nov. 1928, p. 28; Straton, *Fighting the Devil*, p. ii; *The New York Herald Tribune*, Oct. 30, 1929.

108. Straton, *Menace of Immorality*, p. 173.

109. *Ibid.*, p. 200.

110. *Ibid.*, p. 188.

111. Part of Straton's showmanship was his critical analysis of various leaders. He called Clarence Darrow "a big bluffer . . . who had a wicked personality and didn't know much law." Al Smith was "a good cheap truck-driver type of bar-room politician." Straton saw William Jennings Bryan as "one of the noblest souls that ever lived," and Calvin Coolidge as "an excellent average nominal president." Straton termed Nietzsche "the devil in human form" and said of Nicholas Murray Butler: "That man ought to be in jail. I would lock him up if I had my way, and Fosdick with him. They are too dangerous to be at large."

112. Potter, *Preacher and I*, p. 236.

113. *The New York Herald Tribune*, Oct. 30, 1929. For a fuller discussion of the "rural mentality," see Carter, *The Twenties in America*, pp. 80–81.

Chapter Four. William Bell Riley, Organizational Fundamentalist

1. For accounts of this confrontation, see John Pollock, *Billy Graham, The Authorized Biography*, pp. 42–43; Stanley High, *Billy Graham: The Personal Story of the Man, His Message, and His Mission*, pp. 144–145; Curtis Mitchell, *Billy Graham: The Making of a Crusader*, pp. 232–233; *The* (Northwestern) *Scroll*, 1952, p. 18. Pollock has Riley using I Kings, ch. 19, where Elijah casts his mantle upon Elisha.

2. Riley, who first met Graham at a Youth for Christ rally in Minneapolis in 1944, had asked him earlier to assume the presidency of Northwestern

Schools. Previously Graham had declined or had postponed an answer while awaiting "divine guidance."

3. Mitchell, *Making of a Crusader*, p. 231.

4. Robert Sheldon McBirnie, "Basic Issues in the Fundamentalism of William Bell Riley" (unpublished doctoral dissertation, State University of Iowa, 1952), p. 132 ("ablest leader" and "inclusive fellowship" quotes); Cole, *History of Fundamentalism*, p. 325 ("ablest executive" quote).

5. *The Watchman-Examiner*, Dec. 11, 1947, p. 1236; Richard V. Clearwaters, "The Passing of Dr. W. B. Riley," *The Watchman-Examiner*, Jan. 1, 1948, p. 10 ("Martin Luther" quote); John R. Rice, "Dr. W. B. Riley, Evangelist," *The Northwestern Pilot*, Jan. 1948, p. 120 (Spurgeon reference).

6. Harry A. Ironside, "Dr. W. B. Riley, Defender of the Faith," *The Northwestern Pilot*, Jan. 1948, p. 119.

7. Only a few works of an academic nature have been written on Riley's life. These include three unpublished doctoral dissertations: McBirnie's (n. 4, above); Lloyd B. Hull, "A Rhetorical Study of the Preaching of William Bell Riley" (Wayne State University, 1960); and Ferenc M. Szasz, "Three Fundamentalist Leaders: The Roles of William Bell Riley, John Roach Straton, and William Jennings Bryan in the Fundamentalist-Modernist Controversy" (University of Rochester, 1969). Professor Szasz used some of the material in his dissertation for his article "William B. Riley and the Fight Against Teaching of Evolution in Minnesota," in *Minnesota History*, Spring 1969, pp. 201–216. The book by Riley's second wife is basically adulatory in nature. Furthermore, Riley himself wrote the preface and first chapter and probably revised other portions. Marie Acomb Riley, *The Dynamic of a Dream: The Life Story of Dr. William B. Riley*.

The author read extensively in Riley's papers at Northwestern College (although little of his correspondence remains), attended services at the First Baptist Church of Minneapolis, and interviewed the following persons: Dr. Curtis B. Akenson, Riley's ministerial successor; Mrs. Evalyn Camp, a longtime member of Riley's congregation; George M. Wilson, vice-president of Billy Graham Evangelistic Association; William B. Berntsen, president of Northwestern College; Dr. Alton G. Snyder, at that time minister of First Baptist Church, St. Paul; and the late Marie Acomb Riley.

8. W. B. Riley, "My Conversion to Christ," *The Watchman-Examiner*, May 6, 1943, p. 432; "Death of Dr. W. B. Riley," *The Watchman-Examiner*, Dec. 18, 1947, p. 1259. Riley's father had felt the call to preach at the age of thirty-two but resisted because of a large family and a lack of education. Thereafter he had the feeling of being "out of God's will." Psychologically, this factor may have had a strong influence on his son's choice of profession.

9. The early pastorates were Carrolton, Kentucky (1883–1886); New Albany, Indiana (1887–1888); Lafayette, Indiana (1888–1891); and Bloomington, Illinois (1891–1893). Previously (1881–1883), Riley acted as supply preacher at North Madison, Indiana, and Warsaw, Kentucky.

10. Riley also averred that the professors at Southern Baptist Seminary were "fundamental believers" with the important exception that they did not hold to premillennial views.

Riley first met Moody in 1887, when the layman-evangelist conducted a series of meetings in Louisville, Kentucky. Moody's tabernacle was built on the seminary grounds and the student body, of which Riley was a member, organized itself for personal work under the evangelist's direction. Two years later Riley secured Moody for a union meeting in Lafayette, Indiana, where Riley's church was used for the services. Riley also saw much of the urban evangelist in Chicago at the time of the World's Fair Campaign in the early 1890's. He was impressed by the forcefulness of Moody's prayers, the simplicity and directness of his speech, and his remarkable faith. Ironically, the broad and tolerant spirit of Moody did not appear to make a corresponding impact on Riley.

11. Marie Riley, *Dynamic of a Dream*, p. 58.

12. Riley's initial contact with liberal religious leaders came during his pastorate of the mission church in Chicago. While attending the weekly meeting of Baptist ministers, he clashed with George Burnham Foster and William Rainey Harper of the University of Chicago.

13. W. B. Riley, *Ten Burning Questions*, p. 42.

14. W. B. Riley, *Ten Sermons on the Greater Doctrines of Scripture*, pp. 14–17.

15. *Ibid.*, p. 4; Riley, *Ten Burning Questions*, p. 42; W. B. Riley, *Inspiration or Evolution* p. 22.

16. W. B. Riley, "The College vs. Christianity," *Religious Herald*, April 28, 1921. Riley did not appear to be perfectly consistent in his espousal of the verbal inerrancy of the Bible. As late as 1929, in a debate with Harry Rimmer, Riley took the affirmative side of the question: "Resolved, that the Creative Days of Genesis were Aeons, not Solar Days." See undated pamphlet, *A Debate*, published by Research Science Bureau, Duluth, Minnesota.

17. McBirnie, "Basic Issues," p. 57.

18. Riley, *Inspiration or Evolution*, p. 18.

19. W. B. Riley, "Seminaries and a Statement of Faith," *The Watchman-Examiner*, Jan. 2, 1919, p. 11. W. B. Riley, "Fundamentalism and the Faith of the Baptists," *The Watchman-Examiner*, Aug. 25, 1921, pp. 1087–1088. *The Literary Digest*, June 25, 1927.

20. These beliefs and interpretations, of course, were not new with Riley. He had been influenced in part by the New Hampshire Confession of Faith, which provided the doctrinal background for the statement of faith adopted by professors at Southern Baptist Theological Seminary. Riley's book *Ten Sermons on the Great Doctrines of Scripture* followed the outline of this same confession.

21. W. B. Riley, "The Meditations of an Old Man," *The Northwestern Pilot*, Jan. 1948, p. 114. (Published posthumously.)

22. Riley, *Ten Burning Questions*, pp. 108 ff.

23. *Ibid.*, pp. 112–121.

24. W. B. Riley, *The Perennial Revival: A Plea for Evangelism*, 3d ed., revised (American Baptist Publication Society, 1933), p. 239.

25. A kingdom, not a democracy, was the ideal form of government in Riley's mind. He believed that democracy was in the experimental stage and could neither be accepted as a solution for all political problems nor defended as a demonstrated success (the millions of minds represent a low intellectual level). Hope rests, however, in a divine kingdom under the benevolent rule of Jesus, God's king. See Riley, *Ten Burning Questions*, pp. 184–186.

26. W. B. Riley, *The Evolution of the Kingdom*, pp. 11–12, 172–178. Other indications that he believed were signs of the imminency of Jesus' return included the worldliness of the church and the many earthquakes of the previous fifty years.

27. *Ibid.*, pp. 142–152.

28. Marie Riley, *Dynamic of a Dream*, p. 68; Riley, *Perennial Revival* (3d ed., revised), pp. 169–183.

29. Marie Riley, *Dynamic of a Dream*, p. 74.

30. *Ibid.*, p. 76.

31. *Ibid.*, p. 87.

32. A study of the records of Trinity Church by Mark S. Ketcham of the United Theological Seminary, New Brighton, Minnesota, indicates that additional factors, beyond those cited in the Riley biography, may have been at work in the division between Riley and "the minority." These include doctrinal differences and what some felt was a violation of Baptist church polity (the refusal of First Baptist Church to call a mutual council which in turn led to the calling of an ex parte council by "the minority"). The doctrinal differences dealt in part with Riley's preaching of the imminency of Christ's second coming, his belief in divine healing, and his qualified support of J. A. Dowie, founder of a fundamentalist-premillenarian, communal theocracy established at Zion City, Illinois, in 1896. Ketcham minimizes the pew-rental aspect of the controversy, because he could find no evidence of rented pews in the Trinity records, although a pew could be assigned on request. Ketcham's unpublished paper, "An Investigation of the Causes for the Separation of Trinity Baptist Church from First Baptist Church, Minneapolis, Minnesota, in 1903," was produced for a course in historical theology taught by Ernest R. Sandeen.

33. Letter of Riley to his congregation, March 1907. Riley Papers.

34. W. B. Riley, "Sunday Night at the Sanctuary or the Picture Show?" *Baptist World*, Feb. 5, 1917, p. 5.

35. Riley, *Perennial Revival*, *in toto;* quote, pp. 117–118.

36. Riley claimed that these books were not a commentary but rather an exposition of the text. Such a series was consistent with the distrust by fundamentalists of denominational and interdenominational Sunday school

commentaries where supposedly liberal theological influences had made their inroads.

37. Marie Riley, *Dynamic of a Dream*, pp. 179, 181.

38. For a discussion of evangelism in American life, see William G. McLoughlin, *Modern Revivalism: Charles Grandison Finney to Billy Graham*. In the revivalistic tradition, Riley was especially fond of Reuben Archer Torrey and J. Wilbur Chapman. Riley expanded his remarks about Unitarianism into a book: *The Blight of Unitarianism* (L. W. Camp, 1926).

39. *Seattle Post-Intelligencer*, Jan. 23, 1913.

40. *Ibid.*

41. Szasz, "Three Fundamentalist Leaders," p. 88.

42. Marie Riley, *Dynamic of a Dream*, pp. 173–177.

43. Riley, *Perennial Revival*, p. 233.

44. *Ibid.*, pp. 205–209.

45. Riley, *Perennial Revival*, pp. 236–237.

46. Szasz, "Three Fundamentalist Leaders," p. 92.

47. Marie Riley, *Dynamic of a Dream*, pp. 60–61.

48. Riley, *Ten Burning Questions*, pp. 127–128, 147–157; Roy L. Smith, comp., *The Minneapolis Pulpit*, p. 72. In this collection of sermons by ministers of Minneapolis, the one preached by Riley dealt with illegitimacy. He drew the attention of his audience with the bluntness of one of his opening statements: "What greater blow can strike the life of a lad than to begin it as a bastard."

49. *Minneapolis Journal*, Jan. 11, 1926, p. 17; *The Baptist*, Feb. 6, 1932, pp. 177–178; W. B. Riley, *The Philosophies of Father Coughlin*, pp. 22, 24, 28–40; *The Watchman-Examiner*, Feb. 13, 1936, p. 165. Riley's proof text for capital punishment was Gen. 9:6: "Whoso sheddeth man's blood, by man shall his blood be shed: for in the image of God made he man." Riley also suggested the "advertising" of criminals through the newspapers, believing that such publicity, joined with the moral support of the public, would shame them from their misdeeds.

50. Marie Riley, *Dynamic of a Dream*, pp. 61–62; Szasz, "Three Fundamentalist Leaders," pp. 84–85. For Riley's convictions on Communism, see *Ten Burning Questions*, pp. 167 ff.; *Philosophies of Father Coughlin*, pp. 41–58; and Marie Riley's *Dynamic of a Dream*, pp. 188–191. He assailed Communism, especially in the 1930's, because of its deliberate rejection of God and the Scriptures and its glorification of brute power. He believed there were multitudes of Soviet emissaries in this country, including thousands of professors in the universities and liberal clergymen in the churches. Despite the dangers of Communism, Riley saw in it the "falling away" necessary to the fulfillment of prophecy.

51. Riley, *Philosophies of Father Coughlin*, pp. 32, 35.

52. *Ibid.*, p. 33.

53. Gatewood, ed., *Controversy in the Twenties*, p. 20.

54. Riley, *Ten Burning Questions*, p. 52.

55. Riley, *Inspiration or Evolution*, pp. 10, 51, 76.

56. Gatewood, ed., *Controversy in the Twenties*, p. 22.

57. For a monograph on Riley's battle against evolution in Minnesota, see Szasz, "William B. Riley and the Fight Against Teaching of Evolution in Minnesota," pp. 201–216.

58. Marie Riley, *Dynamic of a Dream*, p. 106.

59. W. B. Riley, "Bryan, The Great Commoner and Christian." Sermon preached Aug. 2, 1925, shortly after Bryan's death. Riley Papers.

60. Marie Riley, *Dynamic of a Dream*, pp. 103–107.

61. Cole, *History of Fundamentalism*, p. 313. Cole points out that Riley approved the antievolution bill because, in his judgment, it was fair and constitutional, met a popular demand, did not restrict scientific research, and was the evangelicals' only means of redress for their grievances.

62. Marie Riley, *Dynamic of a Dream*, p. 107.

63. Other advocates of evolution with whom Riley clashed in public debate included Prof. Edwin A. Burt and Prof. Henry Holmes, chairmen of the Departments of Philosophy at the University of Chicago and Swarthmore College respectively; Prof. J. B. McCabe, "a noted rationalist of the Old World"; and Dr. Birkhead, prominent Unitarian clergyman from Kansas City.

64. Undated, untitled newspaper article. Riley Papers, Scrapbook 35.

65. *The Truth Seeker*, July 18, 1925; *Christian Fundamentals in School and Church*, Oct.–Dec. 1925, p. 10; *Minneapolis Star*, Nov. 18, 1925, p. 5.

66. Riley, *Inspiration or Evolution*, pp. 150, 174, 253–272.

67. *Ibid.*, pp. 164–179, 257.

68. W. B. Riley, "A Document of Decision," *The Northwestern Pilot*, April 1947, p. 199.

69. *Minneapolis Tribune*, Aug. 4, 1908, p. 10.

70. W. B. Riley, "Shall Northern Baptists Automatically Exclude Ultra-Conservatives?" *The Watchman-Examiner*, May 11, 1922, p. 589.

71. *The Watchman-Examiner*, July 1, 1920, p. 840.

72. *The Watchman-Examiner*, July 7, 1921, pp. 835, 841. Riley wrote in the June 4, 1921, issue of *The Baptist*, p. 577, that "the Baptist denomination will be stronger in spirit the day that those who have quit our faith are refused our fellowship also. And if they will not voluntarily quit it, then . . . let us take the sanitary course of self-cleaning and begin by disinfecting our schools."

73. *The Watchman-Examiner*, June 29, 1922, pp. 814–816.

74. *The Watchman-Examiner*, May 8, 1924, p. 578.

75. Cole, *History of Fundamentalism*, p. 74.

76. *Ibid.*, p. 81 (quote).

77. Riley, *Inspiration or Evolution*, pp. 257–260.

78. Sandeen, *Roots of Fundamentalism*, p. 243; Marie Riley, *Dynamic of a*

Dream, p. 122. Those present included John Campbell, William Evans, W. H. Griffith Thomas, Robert M. Russell, H. Wyse Jones, and Charles Alexander. Stewart G. Cole also has A. C. Dixon present, although this is doubted by Ernest Sandeen (*Roots of Fundamentalism,* p. 243).

79. W. B. Riley, "The Great Divide, or Christ and the Present Crisis," *God Hath Spoken,* p. 27. Riley also believed that the first meeting of the WCFA brought within prospect the fulfillment of Biblical teaching, declaring that now "men shall come from the east, . . . the west, . . . the north, . . . the south, and shall sit down in the Kingdom with Abraham, Isaac, and Jacob." Whom he equated with the patriarchs is not clear.

80. Sandeen, *Roots of Fundamentalism,* p. 243.

81. *Christian Fundamentals in School and Church,* July–Sept. 1920, p. 374. The gradation of membership and the annual fee proved to be sources of criticism.

82. The original board of directors consisted of Riley, A. S. Johnson, Arthur I. Brown, Harry Rimmer, J. Frank Norris, Leander S. Keyser, Marion M. Hull, George Washburn, Gerald B. Winrod, W. H. Hilker, Samuel Miller, John Brown, H. U. Roop, William McCarrell, L. W. Munhall, T. T. Shields, and a Professor Campbell.

83. Szasz, "Three Fundamentalist Leaders," p. 159.

84. Gatewood, ed., *Controversy in the Twenties,* p. 36.

85. For the list of these institutions (most of them Bible schools or Bible institutes), see *The Christian Fundamentalist,* July 1930, pp. 26–28. These schools included the Northwestern Bible and Missionary Training School, Minneapolis, Minnesota; The Bible Institute of Los Angeles; Providence Bible Institute, Providence, Rhode Island; Bob Jones College (then at Lynn Haven, Florida); Asbury College, Wilmore, Kentucky; Juniata College, Huntingdon, Pennsylvania; Houghton College, Houghton, New York; and Eastern Baptist Seminary, Philadelphia, Pennsylvania.

86. Robert T. Handy, "The American Scene," *Twentieth Century Christianity,* ed. by Bishop Stephen Neill, p. 194.

87. *The Christian Fundamentalist,* June 1939, p. 207.

88. Szasz, "Three Fundamentalist Leaders," p. 195. Riley broke with Norris in 1927 when the latter changed the name of his paper from *The Searchlight* to *The Fundamentalist*—a move intended to make his publication appear to be the official organ of the World's Christian Fundamentals Association. (See n. 96 of Chapter Two, above.) In 1941, Riley described Norris as "a moral leper and the most inordinate liar living. [There is] no crime he has not committed—murder included." See Roy, *Apostles of Discord,* p. 354.

89. Cole, *History of Fundamentalism,* pp. 311–313.

90. W. B. Riley, "Is Quitting the Sign of Courage?" Sermon in Riley Papers.

91. W. B. Riley, *Pastoral Problems,* pp. 21–23; W. B. Riley, "Favor for the

Forum," *The Watchman-Examiner*, April 29, 1937; W. B. Riley, "Baptist Polity Versus Autocracy," *The Watchman-Examiner*, April 27, 1944, p. 401.

92. W. B. Riley, "Northern Baptists, A Bipartisan Convention," *The Watchman-Examiner*, Feb. 22, 1945, p. 180.

93. Marie Riley, *Dynamic of a Dream*, p. 136.

94. W. B. Riley, "The Foreign Board Controversy," *The Watchman-Examiner*, Nov. 25, 1943, pp. 1131–1132.

95. *Yearbook of the American Baptist Convention*, 1951, p. 83.

96. For the complete text of Riley's letter, see "Editor-in-Chief Resigns Life Membership in N.B.C.," *The Northwestern Pilot*, June 1947, p. 275, and *The Baptist Bulletin*, June 1947, p. 8.

97. Szasz, "Three Fundamentalist Leaders," p. 78.

98. The New Testament Association of Independent Baptist Churches was formed at Indianapolis on June 10, 1966, with twenty-seven churches in the chartering group. Today, some fifty churches belong to this body, including the Fourth Baptist Church and the Plymouth Baptist Church of Minneapolis. Its seminary is the Central Baptist Theological Seminary of Minneapolis of which Richard V. Clearwaters was the founder. This Association broke with the Conservative Baptist Association of America, believing the latter had compromised its stand on the Word of God, supported ecumenical evangelism (e.g., Billy Graham Crusades), and unwisely placed $1,200,000 on the stock market. Doctrinally, the Association is fundamentalist in its stance, with special stress on the absolute independence of the local church. It also believes in sanctification, but not eradication, and rejects the speaking in tongues as a sign of either regeneration or sanctification. See B. Myron Cedarholm, "Why a New Association of Churches Is Needed," *Central Testimony*, Nov.–Dec. 1967; "The Confession of Faith of the New Testament Association of Independent Baptist Churches" (n.p., n.d.); and a pamphlet, *The New Testament Association of Independent Baptist Churches* (n.p., n.d.).

99. Interview with William B. Berntsen, president of Northwestern College, June 4, 1971.

100. William G. McLoughlin, *Billy Graham: Revivalist in a Secular Age*, pp. 19, 225, 227.

101. Billy Graham to C. Allyn Russell, Aug. 16, 1971. Letter in author's possession.

102. McBirnie, "Basic Issues," p. 134.

103. Gasper, *The Fundamentalist Movement*, pp. 21–37.

104. W. J. Lhamon, "A Study of Fundamentalism," *The Christian*, Nov. 5, 1926, p. 4.

Chapter Five. J. C. Massee, Moderate Fundamentalist

1. To the author's knowledge, no previous article or book had been written about J. C. Massee prior to the original publication of this chapter. Material

for this chapter was gleaned from Massee's personal papers; unpublished genealogical information about the Massee and Bryan families gathered by Mrs. Drew Massee of Marshallville, Georgia; personal interviews with members of Massee's family; and various secondary sources. Members of Massee's family who gave their full cooperation to the project included a son, Logan Massee, Wilbraham, Massachusetts; a son and daughter-in-law, Mr. and Mrs. Drew Massee, Marshallville, Georgia; and Massee's third wife, Mrs. Edna Blair Massee; a son, Dr. Joseph C. Massee; and a daughter, Ms. Marjorie Massee, all of Atlanta, Georgia.

2. It is uncertain why Massee was named Jasper Cortenus. Jasper was the name of a Biblical stone as well as that of a well-known black preacher. Massee's oldest sister had a close friend called Cortenus. It is certain that Massee preferred to be called simply J. C. Massee.

3. The Primitive Baptists were hyper-Calvinists who protested against man-made efforts to evangelize, to carry on missionary activity, and to organize religious groups, including Sunday schools and associations of churches. They practiced the ordinance of foot washing, normally opposed the use of instrumental music in their churches as being unscriptural, and did not believe in the necessity of a theological education for their ministers. Because conversion, from their viewpoint, was entirely an act of God, they sought to avoid emotionalism, although they were proponents of evangelism. Massee's grandparents, Needham and Sara Massee, were both Primitive Baptists. For several years Massee's parents drove to Culloden, Georgia, to attend Sunday services in a Primitive Baptist church. They joined the Marshallville Baptist Church (then known as the Greenwood Baptist Church) in 1848. Shortly thereafter this church became a member of the Southern Baptist Convention. Robert George Torbet, *A History of the Baptists*, pp. 278–280; Frank S. Mead, *Handbook of Denominations in the United States* (1951), p. 36; author's correspondence with Mrs. Drew Massee, Dec. 1968.

4. J. C. Massee, "My Mother's Legacy," *The Watchman-Examiner*, 1935 (no further date). Massee Papers.

5. Massee married three times. His first wife, Mrs. Sally Shepherd Stuart of Abbeville, Georgia, was a twenty-four-year-old widow with one child, who became his bride in Dec. 1893. His second wife, Mary Olla Oliver of Kissimmee, Florida, was the twenty-year-old daughter of a businessman who represented Osceola County in the state legislature. She lived until 1932, although an invalid the last twenty years of her life. Massee's final marriage, in 1935, was to Edna Blair, former dean of "Bethany Girls," at Winona Lake, Indiana, with Homer Rodeheaver as best man.

6. William A. Mueller, *A History of Southern Baptist Theological Seminary*, p. 155.

7. *Ibid.*, p. 161.

8. J. C. Massee, "Gathering Storms." Unpublished article written late in 1962. Massee Papers.

9. When Massee was not rehired in 1942, at the age of seventy-one, student

petitions asked for his reinstatement. Copies were sent to Massee, one of them containing a postscript declaring, "It is the consensus of the student body that your successor is a complete failure." Student petition addressed to Charles S. Walton, chairman, Board of Trustees, Feb. 20, 1941; "Herb" Rumford to Massee, Oct. 2, 1942. Massee Papers.

10. Massee to R. S. Beal, July 22, 1946. Massee Papers.

11. J. C. Massee, *The Ten Greatest Christian Doctrines*, p. 52.

12. J. C. Massee, *Revival Sermons*, p. 9.

13. *The* (Boston) *Post*, March 10, 1922.

14. *The Watchman-Examiner*, June 23, 1921, p. 791.

15. J. C. Massee, *The Second Coming*, esp. Ch. 5; Princeton Theology held to a strict doctrine of predestination, the inspiration and inerrancy of the Scriptures, and placed what Lefferts A. Loetscher has called "a startling confidence in the competence of human reasoning powers" as its methodological ideal even though God is, in some respects, incomprehensible. Lefferts A. Loetscher, *The Broadening Church: A Study of Theological Issues in the Presbyterian Church Since 1869*, pp. 21–25. The Council at Chalcedon defined Jesus as the God-man, having two natures—one human, one divine—in a single personality without fusion. Sabellianism taught that Jesus possessed only one divine essence.

16. J. C. Massee, "I Found God," p. 4. Unpublished sermon in possession of Marjorie Massee.

17. *The Watchman-Examiner*, March 16, 1922, p. 332.

18. *The Boston Traveler*, Jan. 6, 1923.

19. *The* (Toronto) *Globe*, undated newspaper clipping. Massee Papers.

20. In 1677, Solomon Stoddard, pastor of the Congregational Church at Northampton, Massachusetts, and grandfather of Jonathan Edwards, allowed unconverted church members to partake of Communion because it might serve as a means of conversion. Years later, Edwards, who succeeded his grandfather, saw the Lord's Supper as a "confessing ordinance," and sought to restrict it to professing Christians who were members of the visible church. This was a principal cause of disharmony between Edwards and his congregation and, joined with his rejection of the Half-Way Covenant, eventually led to his dismissal.

21. *The Boston Globe*, April 8, 1929.

22. Massee, *Ten Greatest Doctrines*, p. 95.

23. J. C. Massee, "The Challenge of the Kingdom of Heaven," p. 3. Unpublished sermon, Massee Papers; undated newspaper clipping from *The* (Toronto) *Globe*, Masseee Papers.

24. *The* (Raleigh) *News and Observer*, Sept. 2, 1903. Early in his life Massee was taught to regard the black person with respect. One day, when Massee and his mother were riding down Marshallville's only street in a surrey, they met a group of Negro youngsters. "Good morning, children," said Mrs. Massee. "They are niggers," whispered the boy. The mother glared

at him and spoke emphatically, "They are children!" The truth learned from that experience led Massee to his first major controversy in the pastoral ministry as described. Interview with Marjorie Massee and Mrs. Edna Blair Massee, Sept. 11, 1968, Atlanta, Georgia.

25. *The* (Raleigh) *News and Observer*, Sept. 4, 1903.

26. *Ibid.*, Sept. 6, 1903. Massee's account of this controversy is found in an unpublished and untitled article. Massee Papers. Fifty years after the controversy, Massee learned through a mutual friend that shortly before his death Josephus Daniels expressed greater regret for what he had done to Massee in Raleigh than for any other deed in his life.

27. Massee, reflecting the social standards of many of his generation raised in the South, once told a class at Eastern Baptist Seminary that he would be willing to preach to Negroes at any time, but that he would refuse to eat with them. Norman Maring to C. Allyn Russell, Dec. 17, 1969.

28. Edward John Carnell, "Fundamentalism," in *A Handbook of Christian Theology*, ed. by Marvin Halverson, p. 152.

29. In a sermon preached many times, entitled "Should Girls Smoke?" Massee graphically proclaimed that inhaling arsenic (he believed cigarette paper was bleached with it) inflamed the mucous membranes, thickened them, and made it impossible for oxygen to reach the lungs. The consequence was that impure blood was carried by the veins and arteries into the heart and went up into the brain as well. Massee thought this caused a debasing of the judgment, an inflaming of the imagination, the arousal of unholy desires, and accomplished a deadly reaction on physical health. Then, with a flourish which frequently drew applause as well as laughter, Massee would say: "Girls, if you must smoke in this world, smoke a pipe." In the same sermon Massee pointed out that he and his assistant at Raleigh went into every "lawless" house in the city preaching the gospel where they found many a woman sober as regards liquor, but in every instance addicted to Coca-Cola and cigarettes. J. C. Massee, "Should Girls Smoke?" Sermon preached at Tremont Temple, March 22, 1925. Massee Papers.

30. *The* (Toronto) *Globe*, undated newspaper clipping. Massee Papers.

31. Untitled and undated newspaper clipping. Massee Papers. Massee, however, used pledge cards, as we have seen, in his evangelistic campaigns.

32. See *The* (Raleigh) *News and Observer*, March 15–20, 1908, for published letters in this correspondence.

33. J. C. Massee, *The Gospel in the Ten Commandments*, pp. 105, 109. See also *The Mansfield* (Ohio) *Shield*, March 11, 1903; *The Lowell* (Massachusetts) *Courier*, April 16, 1920; *The Watchman-Examiner*, Jan. 29, 1931.

34. J. C. Massee, "Companionship with Christ," pp. 6–7. Unpublished sermon in possession of Marjorie Massee.

35. *Ibid.*, p. 7.

36. Sam Smith, "Preachers You Hear on the Radio," *The* (Boston) *Post*, ca. 1924. Undated newspaper clipping. Massee Papers.

37. *The* (Boston) *Post*, March 3, 1922.

38. Massee, *Gospel in the Ten Commandments*, p. 9; J. C. Massee, "What I Would Do If I Were the Devil." Unpublished sermon in possession of Marjorie Massee.

39. Massee's services were broadcast over WNAC, Boston.

40. Undated newspaper clipping. *The* (Boston) *Post*. Massee Papers.

41. Others in the academic procession included President Nathan R. Wood of Gordon College; President Everett C. Herrick of Newton Theological School; Dr. Hugh H. Heath, executive secretary of the Massachusetts Baptist Convention; and Leonard Rhodes, senior deacon of the host church, who presided at the occasion.

42. *The* (Brooklyn) *Daily Eagle*, Feb. 13, 1920.

43. "Baptist Fundamentalism." Pamphlet in Dargon-Carver Library, Nashville, Tennessee, cited by R. Quinn Pugh, "J. C. Massee, Minister of Christ," *Baptist History and Heritage*, Oct. 1971, p. 236.

44. J. C. Massee, "Fundamentalists and the Northern Convention," *The Watchman-Examiner*, May 17, 1923, p. 619.

45. *The Watchman-Examiner*, May 20, 1920, p. 652.

46. *Ibid.*

47. Eschatological questions did not enter into any of the discussions at Buffalo. The conservatives were united in their belief in the second coming of Christ, but differed markedly among themselves on the millennial question. Curtis Lee Laws, "Convention Sidelights," *The Watchman-Examiner*, July 1, 1920.

48. *The Watchman-Examiner*, July 1, 1920, p. 840.

49. Those suggested were F. M. Goodchild, I. Carpenter, J. W. Brougher, Henry Bond, W. B. Riley, J. J. Ross, C. R. Brock, Edward S. Clinch, and A. K. DeBlois.

50. *The Watchman-Examiner*, July 1, 1920, p. 843. The committee suggested by the Fundamentalist Federation was accepted, although a vacancy was created when W. B. Riley declined to serve because of his close association with his own school, and for reasons unknown Clinch and Ross were later replaced by F. W. Sweet and M. J. Twomey.

51. At Buffalo, Massee also opposed a subsidy of $25,000 which had been proposed to strengthen the work of *The Baptist*, the convention's newspaper. He dramatically moved that *The Baptist* be sold to the highest bidder, because he objected to an official organ based on the ground of denominational loyalty. His motion was lost, however, because many could see no difference between denominational ownership and the control of educational institutions, on the one hand, and a denominationally owned and controlled newspaper, on the other hand.

52. *The Watchman-Examiner*, July 1, 1920, p. 845.

53. J. C. Massee, "Gathering Storms." Some endeavored to rationalize the convention of 1920 as contributing to Christian unity, meaning a polarization

of one or both sides. Others condemned it as the most intense exhibition of bad feeling in the history of the denomination. As Straton spoke at the fundamentals conference, President Evans of Crozer Seminary said to Massee: "Call him down, Massee. He is ruining your cause." Massee replied: "I know it, Doctor, but we are Baptists and every man has a right to be heard in his own way." This undercuts the claim of John W. Bradbury that "the Conference was conducted in an atmosphere of great reverence, and solemn, high culture." *Foundations*, Jan. 1962, p. 55.

54. J. C. Massee, "The Churches and the Schools," *The Watchman-Examiner*, March 17, 1921, pp. 335–337. Massee conceded that Baptist liberty accorded every man the right to believe what he pleased. But he added that Baptist honesty, sanity, and permanence forbade any man to teach in Baptist schools and churches any creeds and theories out of harmony with historic Baptist belief.

55. J. C. Massee, "An Answer to the Board of Education," *The Watchman-Examiner*, June 16, 1921, p. 752.

56. *The Watchman-Examiner*, July 7, 1921, pp. 835, 841.

57. *Ibid.*, June 30, 1921, pp. 805, 811–813; Jan. 17, 1924, p. 82; also correspondence by Massee with R. S. Beal, July 22, 1946. Massee Papers.

58. Helen Barrett Montgomery, "The Columbia Conference," *The Watchman-Examiner*, Feb. 16, 1922, p. 208.

59. *The Watchman-Examiner*, July 27, 1922, p. 946.

60. Massee, "Gathering Storms," pp. 7, 9. Massee's position on a creed is a perplexing one. Normally he favored a confession of faith that should never be required as a test of fellowship. Yet in 1928 he advocated that every church ought to have a creed that should be known, understood, and accepted by each member of the church. This would embrace the church's conviction about the character of the gospel message, the manner of life of the Christian, the method of church finance, the purpose of the labors of the church, and the basis of association with other religious bodies. (J. C. Massee, "The Matter of a Creed," *The Watchman-Examiner*, May 19, 1938, p. 543.) One gains the impression that when Liberalism was a threat, he leaned in the direction of a creed; when ultrafundamentalism was a threat, he stressed freedom and personal interpretation of the Scriptures.

61. *The Watchman-Examiner*, June 29, 1922, pp. 814–815.

62. *Ibid.*, July 27, 1922, p. 955; Handy, "Fundamentalism and Modernism in Perspective," *Religion in Life*, p. 390.

63. *The Watchman-Examiner*, May 18, 1922, p. 623.

64. Curtis Lee Laws wrote: "We send out missionaries not to relieve the body, not to educate the mind, but to save souls. All else is secondary." *The Watchman-Examiner*, Aug. 24, 1922.

65. *Ibid.*

66. *Ibid.*, July 5, 1923, p. 841.

67. *Ibid.*, Jan. 17, 1924, p. 82. Straton's group had been complaining that

there were non-Baptists teaching in missionary schools in foreign countries. A representative of the Board responded by explaining that it was difficult to secure an orthodox Baptist in China to teach a subject such as Chinese classics.

68. *Ibid.*, June 12, 1924, p. 749.

69. *Ibid.*, p. 761.

70. *Ibid.*, May 1, 1924, p. 566.

71. *Ibid.*, June 12, 1924, p. 736.

72. Furniss, *Fundamentalist Controversy*, p. 115.

73. *Ibid.*, p. 116.

74. *The Watchman-Examiner*, Feb. 11, 1926, p. 181. The sympathetic *Watchman-Examiner* gave as the sole reason for Massee's resignation the press of heavy duties at Tremont Temple.

75. Massee, "Gathering Storms," p. 5.

76. Undated correspondence between Massee and W. W. Adams, 1962. Massee Papers.

77. Massee to James M. Gray, president of Moody Bible Institute, June 29, 1926. Massee Papers.

78. Massee, "Gathering Storms," p. 5.

79. *The Baptist*, June 3, 1926, pp. 691–694.

80. *The Watchman-Examiner*, June 3, 1926.

81. Cole, *History of Fundamentalism*, pp. 80–81.

82. *Ibid.*

83. *Ibid.*

84. Apparently there was little love lost between Pierce and Massee. Upon reading Massee's article on the Modernist-Fundamentalist Controversy in *The Chronicle*, Pierce wrote Massee: "I read your article in the Chronical *[sic.]*, such as it was."

85. G. K. Longmore to C. Allyn Russell, March 3, 1970.

86. Untitled newspaper clippping in scrapbook by Mrs. Cross, 1950, American Baptist Historical Society.

87. *Ibid.*

88. J. C. Massee, "The Thirty Years' War," *The Chronicle*, April 1954, pp. 106–116.

89. *Ibid.*, pp. 110–111.

90. *Ibid.*, p. 115.

91. *Ibid.*, p. 116.

92. Massee to R. S. Beal, July 22, 1946. Massee Papers.

93. Sandeen, "Historical Interpretation," p. 83.

94. Richard Hofstadter, *Anti-Intellectualism in American Life*, p. 7.

95. Stevick, *Beyond Fundamentalism*, p. 23.

96. Neo-orthodox Christianity is a reaffirmation of historic Christian doctrines, with such changes as seem mandatory as a result of modern scholarship. Neo-evangelicalism represents a type of mystical supernatural-

ism that purportedly gives greater attention to Biblical criticism and a social interpretation of the gospel than does Fundamentalism.

97. Carnell, "Fundamentalism," in Halverson, ed., *Handbook of Christian Theology*, p. 143.

98. Massee to Will H. Houghton, president of Moody Bible Institute, May 2, 1944. Massee Papers.

Chapter Six. J. Gresham Machen, Scholarly Fundamentalist

1. The major work is Ned B. Stonehouse, *J. Gresham Machen, A Biographical Memoir*. Stonehouse studied under Machen at Princeton Seminary and was one of the original faculty members at Westminster. When Machen died, Stonehouse succeeded him as professor of New Testament. Other helpful secondary sources are Loetscher, *The Broadening Church: A Study of Theological Issues in the Presbyterian Church Since 1869;* Lefferts A. Loetscher, "Machen, John Gresham," *Dictionary of American Biography*, Vol. XI, Supplement Two, ed. by Robert L. Schuyler, pp. 411–412; and Edwin H. Rian, *The Presbyterian Conflict*. Two doctoral dissertations have centered on Machen's thought: Dallas Roark, "J. Gresham Machen and His Desire to Maintain a Doctrinally True Presbyterian Church" (State University of Iowa, 1963); and William D. Livingstone, "The Princeton Apologetic as Exemplified by the Work of Benjamin B. Warfield and J. Gresham Machen: A Study in American Theology, 1880–1930" (Yale University, 1948). A portion of Roark's study was published as a two-part article in the *Journal of Presbyterian History*, June 1965, pp. 124–138, and Sept. 1965, pp. 174–181.

Primary sources for Machen's life and thought center in his personal papers which are kept at Westminster Theological Seminary, Philadelphia (Chestnut Hill), Pennsylvania. Among the finer primary sources is an article by Machen, "Christianity in Conflict," in *Contemporary American Theology: Theological Autobiographies*, ed. by Vergilius Ferm, Vol. I, pp. 243–274.

2. Charles Hodge (1797–1878) was the chief theologian of Old School Presbyterianism. He believed in and taught a federal theology, the verbal inspiration of the Bible, the salvation of infants, and a covenant of grace which is universal but becomes efficacious only in the elect who are given by the Father to the Son. Benjamin B. Warfield (1851–1921) continued this emphasis, stressing the Reformed beliefs and adding a new rigidity to the doctrine of Scriptural inspiration, that is, the limitation of inerrancy to the original (and now lost) Biblical manuscripts.

3. Machen was concerned that his name be pronounced correctly. It was "May-chen" with the accent on the first syllable, the "May" being pronounced like the fifth month of the year and the "ch" like the "ch" in "chin." The division of syllables in his Christian name came between the "s" and the "h,"

thereby being pronounced "Gres-ham," not "Gresh-am." Machen to Braman
B. Adams, July 7, 1925. Machen Papers. At the time of his birth, Machen's
mother was twenty-three years of age, and his father was forty-five.

4. Machen, "Christianity in Conflict," p. 246.

5. Stonehouse, *Memoir*, p. 33.

6. *Ibid.*, pp. 29–30.

7. *Ibid.*, p. 72.

8. Machen, "Christianity in Conflict," p. 249. Machen's statement may
have been better evidence of his pride in adult years than that of Biblical
knowledge in his youth. Or it might have been disdain for the kind of
theological education given seminarians at the time of writing, 1932.

9. Machen to his mother, Feb. 16, 1921, as quoted in Stonehouse, *Memoir*,
p. 310.

10. Machen's doctoral degrees were honorary ones from Hampden-Sydney
College in 1921 and Wheaton College (Illinois) in 1928.

11. Machen, "Christianity in Conflict," p. 256. Also see Stonehouse,
Memoir, Ch. 5.

12. Machen, "Christianity in Conflict," p. 263.

13. *Ibid.*

14. In his tome on the virgin birth, Machen argued that there was a firm
and well-formulated belief in that birth which dated from the early years of
the second century and that the denials of the virgin birth, which appeared in
the same century, were probably based more on philosophical or dogmatic
presuppositions than on genuine historical tradition. J. Gresham Machen,
The Virgin Birth of Christ, p. 43.

15. During his year abroad, Machen bicycled over 630 miles in Germany
alone. Stonehouse, *Memoir*, p. 92.

16. *Ibid.*, p. 155.

17. The reference of Machen about Warfield was contained in a letter to
his mother, Feb. 16, 1921, as quoted in Stonehouse, *Memoir*, p. 310; the quote
about his mother was contained in Machen's last letter to her, dated Oct. 11,
1931, as found in Stonehouse, *Memoir*, p. 467.

18. The letters of Machen's mother to him are a part of the Machen
Papers.

19. Loetscher, "Machen, John Gresham," *DAB*, Vol. XI, Supplement Two,
p. 412.

20. Machen quoted Warfield as saying that Reformed theology was not
just one kind of Christianity as over against other kinds, but it was just
Christianity as over against more or less serious departures from Christianity. One may see here the seed of Machen's later attitude toward Protestant
Liberalism. Machen to H. McAllister Griffiths, July 19, 1925. Machen Papers.

21. J. Gresham Machen, *The Christian Faith in the Modern World*, pp. 63,
66.

22. J. Gresham Machen, "Religion and Fact," *The Real Issue*, April 15,
1924, p. 5.

23. J. Gresham Machen, "History and Faith," *Princeton Theological Review*, July 1915, p. 2.

24. J. Gresham Machen, *Christianity and Liberalism*, pp. 69–70.

25. *Ibid.*, p. 26.

26. "A Debate: Is the Teaching of Harry Emerson Fosdick Opposed to the Christian Religion?" Undated article from unknown publication in Machen scrapbook. Machen Papers.

27. Machen, *Christianity and Liberalism*, pp. 126–128.

28. *Ibid.*, pp. 73–74. See also Charles Hodge, *Systematic Theology*, Vol. I (Wm. B. Eerdmans Publishing Company, 1940), pp. 156–157. For a further explanation of Machen's views on the Scriptures, see "The Modern Use of the Bible" (review of Fosdick's book of the same name), *Princeton Theological Review*, Jan. 1925, pp. 66–81.

29. *The Presbyterian Guardian*, Nov. 14, 1936, p. 42.

30. Machen, *Christianity and Liberalism*, pp. 48–49.

31. Machen to Peter Stam, Jr., Nov. 28, 1930. Machen Papers.

32. The Pauline reference is I Tim. 5:23. Machen's theological and ecclesiastical enemies used his stand on alcohol in an endeavor to discredit him during the later days of church conflict. Machen went to the extent of verifying that the Machen family had no stockholdings in the beverage companies.

33. Stonehouse, *Memoir*, p. 85.

34. Machen to F. E. Robinson, Esq., June 25, 1927. Machen Papers. Also found in *The Presbyterian*, July 7, 1927, p. 8.

35. Machen, *Christianity and Liberalism*, pp. 6–7; J. Gresham Machen, "Is Christianity True?" *The Bible Today*, May 1923, p. 197. Machen consistently referred to the liberals as "the alienists."

36. Machen, *Christianity and Liberalism*, p. 7.

37. *Ibid., passim.*

38. *Ibid.*, pp. 80–112.

39. Machen, "History and Faith," p. 7.

40. *Ibid.*, p. 8.

41. *Ibid.*, pp. 8, 11.

42. Machen, *Christian Faith in the Modern World*, p. 204.

43. Machen, *Christianity and Liberalism*, pp. 159–160, 166.

44. J. Gresham Machen, "Does Christianity Obstruct Social Progress?" *Survey Graphic*, July 1924, p. 425; Machen, *Christianity and Liberalism*, p. 11.

45. J. Gresham Machen, "The So-called Child Labor Amendment," *The Presbyterian*, Jan. 22, 1925, p. 6; interview with Paul Woolley, May 26, 1972.

46. Machen, "Does Christianity Obstruct Social Progress?" p. 426.

47. *Ibid.*; J. Gresham Machen, "The Church in the War," *The Presbyterian*, May 29, 1919, p. 10.

48. Machen to G. H. Hospers, Dec. 27, 1924. Machen Papers.

49. J. Gresham Machen, "Christianity and Culture," *Princeton Theological Review*, Jan. 1913, as summarized in Loetscher, *Broadening Church*, p. 192.

50. Machen to the Hon. J. R. Ramsen, Jan. 3, 1918. Machen Papers. Also published in *The Congressional Record*, Jan. 10, 1918.

51. *Ibid.* In 1925 Machen regretted the giving of positions of responsibility on denominational boards to unordained persons—namely, women—who "have for the most part been hostile, through ignorance or otherwise, to the witness-bearing of our church."

52. Machen, *Christianity and Liberalism*, p. 13.

53. Stonehouse, *Memoir*, p. 402.

54. *Joint Hearings Before the Committee on Education and Labor, United States Senate, and The Committee on Education, House of Representatives, Sixty-ninth Congress* . . . Feb. 24–26, 1926 (Government Printing Office, 1926), p. 104 (complete argument, pp. 95–104). Also see J. Gresham Machen, "Shall We Have a Federal Department of Education?" *The Woman Patriot*, Feb. 15, 1926.

55. *The New York Times*, June 7, 1926; also, interview with Paul Woolley, May 26, 1972.

56. *The New Republic*, Dec. 31, 1924; Machen, "The So-called Child Labor Amendment," p. 6.

57. Machen to H. M. Rehasky, Sept. 10, 1925, Machen Papers; Machen to Clarence H. Lee, Dec. 15, 1924, Machen Papers; *Trenton Sunday Times-Advertiser*, Jan. 25, 1925.

58. *The New York Herald Tribune*, Dec. 7, 1925.

59. *The New York Times*, Sept. 18, 1925.

60. *Ibid.* After summarizing first the position of the honor fraternity and then the reasons for Machen's opposition to their decision, the editor of the *Baltimore Evening Sun* commented: "All of which goes to prove that this is, indeed and despite everything, A Wonderful World." The *Baltimore Evening Sun*, Oct. 7, 1925.

61. *The New York Times*, Feb. 18, 1925. For other expressions of Machen's thought on this subject, see *The Bar Harbor* (Maine) *Times*, Jan. 20, 1925; Machen to Robert Underwood Johnson, March 2, 1925. Machen Papers.

62. *The New York Herald Tribune*, Dec. 28, 1930.

63. Interview with Paul Woolley, May 26, 1972.

64. Machen, who was a contemporary of Walter Rauschenbusch (1861–1918), for thirty-seven years, placed no hope whatsoever in the Golden Rule for the improvement of society because he believed that rule was not of universal application but addressed only to the disciples of Jesus. "Help a drunkard to get rid of his evil habit, and you will soon come to distrust the modern interpretation of the Golden Rule. The trouble is that the drunkard's companions apply the rule only too well; they do unto him exactly what they would have him do unto them—by buying him a drink. The Golden Rule becomes a powerful obstacle in the way of moral advance." Machen, *Christianity and Liberalism*, p. 37.

65. New England Theology was much more Arminian in its emphasis than Calvinism. Nathaniel Taylor, its leading proponent, taught that men were free to repent and virtually promised that they would be saved if they did. Moreover, men could improve their lives and the lives of those around them, as both a prelude to and a testimony of conversion.

66. Clifton E. Olmstead, *History of Religion in the United States*, pp. 312–313.

67. The arrangement of a Baptist serving as an associate minister in a Presbyterian pulpit was an early, deliberate experiment in ecumenism. Machen was especially critical of Fosdick. He wrote on one occasion: "Dr. Fosdick teaches exactly what was taught fifty years ago by the avowed opponents of Christianity, the only difference is that he is ethically far inferior to them, since they did not try to combat, by false pretenses, the faith of a creedal Church from within." Machen to Joseph H. Barton, Jan. 1, 1925. Machen Papers. For Fosdick's account of his struggle with Fundamentalism, see Fosdick, *The Living of These Days*, Ch. VII.

68. Loetscher, *Broadening Church*, p. 98.

69. Rian, *Presbyterian Conflict*, pp. 20–22.

70. *Ibid.*, p. 42. The Auburn Affirmation was called by that name because the secretary of the committee that prepared the statement was from Auburn Seminary in Auburn, New York. Its official title was "An Affirmation Designed to Safeguard the Unity and Liberty of the Presbyterian Church in the U.S.A."

71. *Minutes of the General Assembly of the Presbyterian Church in the U.S.A, 1925*, Part I, p. 88.

72. *Minutes of the General Assembly of the Presbyterian Church in the U.S.A, 1926*, Part I, p. 78.

73. Furniss, *Fundamentalist Controversy*, p. 189; Loetscher, *Broadening Church*, p. 138; *The Presbyterian*, June 10, 1926.

74. Machen to Reid Dickson, March 10, 1925. Machen Papers.

75. Loetscher, *Broadening Church*, p. 142.

76. The faculty "minority" according to Lefferts A. Loetscher during the years of controversy consisted of J. Ross Stevenson, Charles R. Erdman, F. W. Loetscher, and J. Ritchie Smith. Loetscher, *Broadening Church*, p. 139. Machen wrote a friend that "the real anti-evangelical machine at the Seminary consists of Dr. Stevenson, Dr. Davis [John D. Davis, professor of Oriental and Old Testament literature], Mr. Martin, and Dr. Erdman." He indicated that Dr. Ritchie Smith and Dr. Loetscher voted the same way, although adding "I do not quite put Dr. Loetscher in all respects in the same category." Machen to Reid Dickson, March 10, 1925. Machen Papers. The conflict between Machen and Erdman, professor of practical theology, was a natural one since Machen looked disparagingly upon the "practical" studies as reflecting a "drab utilitarianism."

77. Ruth Rouse and Stephen C. Neill, *A History of the Ecumenical Movement, 1517–1948* (The Westminster Press, 1967), pp. 445–446.

78. *The Presbyterian,* June 10, 1920, pp. 7–8; *The Presbyterian,* March 17, 1921, p. 26. Machen to Robert Atkinson, June 5, 1925. Machen Papers.

79. Stonehouse, *Memoir,* pp. 313–314; Machen to Reid Dickson, March 30, 1925. Machen Papers.

80. *The New York Herald,* Jan. 7, 1924.

81. *The Packet,* July 12, 1924.

82. *Ibid.* For correspondence on the Machen-Van Dyke fiasco, see *The New York Times,* Jan. 5, 1924; *The Newark Evening News,* Jan. 5, 1924; *The Presbyterian,* Feb. 12, 1925.

83. Loetscher, *Broadening Church,* p. 140.

84. Machen to Reid Dickson, April 10, 1925, Machen Papers; *The Presbyterian,* April 23, 1925, p. 16; pamphlet (undated) by Joseph A. Schofield, Jr., *A Misapprehension Corrected,* Machen Papers; *The Presbyterian,* Oct. 20, 1927; *Christian Work,* May 16, 1925.

85. Loetscher, *Broadening Church,* p. 151.

86. The holding up of Machen's appointment was a most unusual step and indicated the depth of the division at Princeton. Stevenson declared that Machen was "not temperamentally fitted for the position." *The Baltimore Sun,* Nov. 22, 1926; *The Presbyterian,* Aug. 19, 1926.

87. *The Presbyterian,* June 10, 1926.

88. *Minutes of the General Assembly of the Presbyterian Church in the U.S.A., 1927,* Part I, pp. 131–133.

89. *The New York Sun,* Sept. 30, 1927.

90. *Minutes of the General Assembly of the Presbyterian Church in the U.S.A., 1928,* Part I, p. 246. By the new arrangement, the hiring, promotion, and dismissal of faculty members was left entirely to the judgment of the Board of Trustees. The approval of the General Assembly was no longer required.

91. Machen to Theron Lee, May 29, 1925, Machen Papers; Loetscher, *Broadening Church,* p. 119; *Christian Work,* May 16, 1925, p. 628.

92. Perhaps more significant than those who left Princeton for Westminster were those who did not. One of these, William Park Armstrong, professor of New Testament, a staunch conservative, had been Machen's longtime personal friend.

93. *Catalogue of Westminster Theological Seminary,* Philadelphia, 1929–1930, pp. 10–11.

94. The faculty was constituted as follows: Robert Dick Wilson, professor of Semitic Philology and Old Testament Criticism; J. Gresham Machen, professor of New Testament; Oswald T. Allis, professor of Old Testament History and Exegesis; Cornelius Van Til, professor of Apologetics; R. B. Kuiper, professor of Systematic Theology; Ned B. Stonehouse, instructor in New Testament; Paul Woolley, instructor in Church History; and Allan A. MacRae, instructor in Semitic Philology.

95. Stonehouse, *Memoir,* pp. 452–453.

96. *The New York Times*, Sept. 26, 1929.

97. Machen wrote in 1934 to his fundamentalist colleague William Bell Riley: "The primary evidence against the Board of Foreign Missions of the Presbyterian Church in the U.S.A. seems to me to lie not among the missionaries, but right here at home at 156 Fifth Avenue." Machen to William Bell Riley, Dec. 17, 1934. Machen Papers. Ironically, the Independent Board that Machen had founded was taken over by Independents rather than Presbyterians. Machen was ousted as president. This was a hard blow to him, the shock of which may have lessened his will to live. Dallas M. Roark, "J. Gresham Machen: The Doctrinally True Presbyterian Church," *Journal of Presbyterian History*, June 1965, pp. 137–138.

98. Clarence E. Macartney, *The Making of a Minister*, p. 188. Rian, *Presbyterian Conflict*, Chs. VI–VIII.

99. Rian, *Presbyterian Conflict*, p. 234.

100. Macartney, *Making of a Minister*, p. 188.

101. Interview with Paul Woolley, May 26, 1972; Rian, *Presbyterian Conflict*, pp. 235–243. Machen's devotion to Presbyterianism cannot be overstressed. In 1927 he declined to accept the presidency of Bryan Memorial University because, in part, he was loath to relinquish distinctively Presbyterian work. Machen to F. E. Robinson, Esq., *The Presbyterian*, July 7, 1927.

102. Rian, *Presbyterian Conflict*, p. 243.

103. *The Presbyterian Guardian*, June 26, 1937, as quoted in Rian, *Presbyterian Conflict*, p. 243.

104. Jorstad, *Politics of Doomsday*, p. 33.

105. Clarence E. Macartney believed that Machen's death was not as untimely as it may have appeared. "Had he lived, he would have seen the seminary which he founded split with faction, and the Board of Missions and the Orthodox Church . . . falling far short of what he had planned and expected. His true monument is not in these institutions or societies, but in the inspiration he left behind him of his courageous, devout, and highly intellectual witness to the 'grand particularities' of the Christian faith." Macartney, *Making of a Minister*, p. 189.

106. At the time of Machen's death the Orthodox Presbyterian Church (then known as the Presbyterian Church of America) was only six months old. It had no buildings of its own, as the Presbyterian Church in the U.S.A. was claiming title to all of the real property. It was holding its worship services in rented halls and auditoriums which were not adequate or appropriate for funeral services. It was unthinkable to hold the service in a building of the Presbyterian Church in the U.S.A. because that church was actively pursuing a suit in the civil courts about the name of the new church and was hostile to it in every way. Paul Woolley to C. Allyn Russell, Aug. 24, 1972.

107. Loetscher, *Broadening Church*, p. 117.

108. An example of Machen's extremism as well as an illustration of his

false caricature of Liberalism is found in a letter to a friend: "Every sermon of his [Harry Emerson Fosdick's] and every book is passionately opposed to the Christian religion root and branch. I do not think that any one . . . would be deceived by the Christian terminology which Dr. Fosdick uses. . . . Dr. Fosdick is passionately opposed to the whole notion of the holiness of God, the sinfulness of man, the authority of the Bible, the deity of our Lord, and the redeeming significance of the Cross." Machen to Joseph H. Barton, Jan. 1, 1925. Machen Papers. Even so, Furniss believed that Machen's invectives were not as "savage" as those of other fundamentalists. Furniss, *Fundamentalist Controversy*, p. 128.

109. Illustrative of such varying interpreters are Caspar Wistar Hodge, Machen's colleague at Princeton; an unnamed Presbyterian denominational leader; and Dallas M. Roark, professor of religion at Wayland Baptist College, Plainview, Texas. Hodge referred to Machen as "the greatest theologian in the English-speaking world" and "the greatest leader of the whole cause of evangelical Christianity." The denominational official thought of Machen as a man of "temperamental idiosyncrasies." Roark concludes that "Machen's doctrine of the church went beyond the [Calvinistic] norms that he accepted and treasured." Stonehouse, *Memoir*, preface; Cole, *History of Fundamentalism*, p. 126; Roark, "J. Gresham Machen," *Journal of Presbyterian History*, Sept. 1965, p. 181.

110. Sandeen, *Roots of Fundamentalism*, p. 257.

111. *Ibid.*

112. Stonehouse, *Memoir*, p. 499.

113. Loetscher, *Broadening Church*, p. 139.

114. About 160 students attend Westminster Seminary today, a majority of whom come from Presbyterian, Reformed, and Baptist backgrounds. The Orthodox Presbyterian Church in 1974 was comprised of 123 churches with a total membership of 14,871, including 205 ordained clergymen. *Yearbook of American and Canadian Churches, 1974*, ed. by Constant H. Jacquet, Jr. (Abingdon Press, 1974), p. 76.

Chapter Seven. William Jennings Bryan, Statesman-Fundamentalist

1. The primary sources for this chapter have included Bryan's books plus his personal papers. Secondary sources dealing with Bryan's life include Paolo E. Coletta, *William Jennings Bryan*, 3 vols.; Paul W. Glad, ed., *William Jennings Bryan, A Profile;* Paxton Hibben, *The Peerless Leader, William Jennings Bryan;* Louis W. Koenig, *Bryan, A Political Biography of William Jennings Bryan,* Lawrence W. Levine, *Defender of the Faith, William Jennings Bryan: The Last Decade, 1915–1925;* and Charles M. Wilson, *The Commoner, William Jennings Bryan* (Doubleday & Company, Inc., 1970).

2. The first known Bryan to settle in the United States was William Smith Bryan, who came to Glouchester County, Virginia, in 1650. "William Jennings Bryan: Biographical Notes, His Speeches, Letters and Other Writings," enlarged and ed. by Grace Dexter Bryan, Dec. 10, 1941, p. 2. Typescript. Bryan Papers. Hereafter referred to as Grace D. Bryan, "Biographical Notes."

3. Koenig, *Bryan*, p. 178.

4. William Jennings Bryan, *The First Battle: A Story of the Campaign of 1896*, p. 206. Koenig points out that while Bryan's address was a silver speech, it was ingeniously unspecific. "His words were a fabric of catchy but vacuous expressions; rich in cadenced appeals to an audience in which emotion, rather than reason, reigned. Midway in the uproar which followed Bryan's speech, Altgeld [the governor of Illinois], turned to Clarence Darrow and asked . . . 'I have been thinking over Bryan's speech. What did he say, anyhow?' " Koenig, *Bryan*, p. 199.

5. Koenig, *Bryan*, pp. 251–252. For other statistical analyses of the campaign of 1896, see Bryan, *The First Battle*, pp. 607, 611; William Jennings Bryan, *The Memoirs of William Jennings Bryan, By Himself and His Wife, Mary Baird Bryan*, p. 267 (hereafter referred to as *Memoirs*); T. Harry Williams, Richard N. Current, and Frank Freidel, *A History of the United States*, Vol. II, *Since 1865*, p. 230. Bryan was the first of several authors to point out that the election was so close that a properly distributed change of less than 25,000 votes in six key states would have given the Democrats a majority in the electoral college.

6. In a letter written during the course of the campaign of 1908, President Theodore Roosevelt said: "Of course I do not dare in public to express my real opinion of Bryan. He is a kindly man and well-meaning in a weak way. . . . But he is the cheapest fakir we have ever proposed for President." S. E. Forman, *Our Republic*, p. 724.

7. Originally, the Nebraska delegation was pledged to Clark. When the New York contingent, however, gave its support to Clark, Bryan felt justified in switching to Wilson, declaring that he would not give encouragement to any man who had the backing of the New York crowd. Bryan believed the latter group was dominated by the monied interests of Wall Street and that any candidate who had such support was not a true progressive and had no chance to win. *Memoirs*, pp. 180–183.

8. A further disagreement between Bryan and Wilson concerned the matter of neutral ships carrying ammunition to a belligerent nation. Bryan opposed such a policy, believing that it was contrary to the spirit of neutrality. For his views, Bryan was dubbed a pacifist, pro-German, and disloyal to his own country. Nevertheless, when the United States entered the war Bryan offered his services as a private in the Army.

9. Bryan desired such a constitutional change so that control by either the President, the Senate, or the House, would not ensure defeat of a proposed

amendment. *The Washington Herald*, Dec. 7, 1916; Grace D. Bryan, "Biographical Notes," p. 305.

10. Grace D. Bryan, "Biographical Notes," p. 388. Bryan's first recorded advocacy of peace through international arbitration appeared in an editorial in *The Commoner*, Feb. 17, 1905.

11. "Prohibition Address by Hon. William Jennings Bryan" (Government Printing Office, 1916), p. 11. Pamphlet. Bryan Papers.

12. William Jennings Bryan, untitled eleven-page handwritten speech on temperance, ca. 1883–1885, p. 11. Bryan Papers.

13. William Jennings Bryan, "Why Abstain?" Address delivered at Philadelphia, March 15, 1915, auspices of the National Abstainers Union, pp. 1–8. Pamphlet. Bryan Papers. In late nineteenth- and early twentieth-century America, "temperance" had come to mean total abstinence.

14. Szasz, "Three Fundamentalist Leaders," p. 187.

15. Bryan, *Memoirs*, p. 351.

16. Bryan, "Prohibition Address," p. 11.

17. William Jennings Bryan, *In His Image*, p. 216. In this country the Eighteenth Amendment passed Congress in 1917; was ratified in 1919, and became law in 1920.

18. *Ibid.*, p. 17.

19. Koenig, *Bryan*, p. 449.

20. William Jennings Bryan, "The Race Problem," *The Commoner*, Oct. 2, 1903, p. 1.

21. *Ibid.*

22. *Ibid.*, Aug. 21, 1903, p. 1. In 1924, Bryan led a successful movement at the Democratic National Convention against condemning the Ku Klux Klan by name. He believed that the Klan did not need the "advertisement" that such a motion would bring; the Roman Catholic Church did not need political aid with its rich spiritual heritage; furthermore, neither his party nor the Christian church needed the division such a resolution would bring. William Jennings Bryan, "Religious Liberty." Speech, Democratic National Convention, New York City, June 28, 1924. Pamphlet. Bryan Papers.

23. William Jennings Bryan, *Shall Christianity Remain Christian? Seven Questions in Dispute*, p. 16.

24. Bryan, *In His Image*, p. 39.

25. *Ibid.*, p. 58.

26. *Ibid.*, p. 30.

27. William Jennings Bryan, *The Prince of Peace*, as found in Grace D. Bryan, "Biographical Notes," p. 269.

28. William Jennings Bryan, "They Have Taken Away My Lord." Sermon, Bethany Presbyterian Church, March 17, 1925. Printed abstract. Bryan Papers.

29. Bryan, *In His Image*, p. 32.

30. Szasz, "Three Fundamentalist Leaders," p. 187.

31. Bryan, *Seven Questions*, preface.

32. Bryan, *In His Image*, pp. 144–145, 190, 230.

33. *Ibid.*, p. 158.

34. William Jennings Bryan, "Perfection." Handwritten essay, Oct. 23, 1880. Bryan Papers.

35. Bryan, *In His Image*, p. 259.

36. *Ibid.* Despite his high regard for man Bryan still believed in original sin, declaring that no one would doubt the doctrine if he studied (human) nature and then analyzed himself.

37. William Jennings Bryan, "Graduating Address," June 1888 (school not indicated), in Grace D. Bryan, "Biographical Notes," p. 21.

38. Bryan, *In His Image*, p. 233.

39. Grace D. Bryan, "Biographical Notes," p. 382.

40. Bryan, *In His Image*, pp. 121–134.

41. *Ibid.*, pp. 121–122.

42. Bryan, *Memoirs*, p. 513.

43. Bryan, *In His Image*, p. 264.

44. *Ibid.*, p. 189.

45. Harry P. Harrison and Karl Detzer, *Culture Under Canvas: The Story of Tent Chautauqua*, p. 156.

46. Coletta, *William Jennings Bryan*, Vol. I, p. 7.

47. Bryan, *Memoirs*, p. 27.

48. *Ibid.*, pp. 10–11.

49. Alice Vaughan, "Memorials to William Jennings Bryan, at his birthplace, Salem" (DAR, Isaac Hull Chapter, Salem, Illinois, Feb. 1931), I. Bryan Papers.

50. Bryan, *Memoirs*, p. 11.

51. Coletta, *William Jennings Bryan*, Vol. I.

52. Grace D. Bryan, "Biographical Notes," p. 9.

53. Bryan, *Memoirs*, p. 17. In older years Bryan justified his choice of a legal career above that of the ministry by a Biblical proof text (Prov. 21:3): "To do justice and judgment is more acceptable to the LORD than sacrifice."

54. At the age of forty-four, Bryan's father bought a 500-acre farm about a mile northwest of Salem and built "a mansion there which was the showplace of Marion County." Paolo Coletta commented: "The Judge [Bryan's father] might call himself a commoner and often speak on the 'laboring and toiling masses,' yet by the time he retired from the bench in 1872 he was as close to being an aristocrat as rural conditions permitted. Few families in Salem owned 500 acres unencumbered, hired Negro servants, used silver at table, and had a piano in the parlor." Coletta, *William Jennings Bryan*, Vol. I, pp. 3, 5.

55. Grace D. Bryan, "Biographical Notes," p. 7.

56. Bryan, *Memoirs*, p. 501. Bryan applied the Biblical teaching of love rather than force in several instances. When the *Lusitania* was sunk, Bryan

thought that a commission should be set up to investigate the matter, with the understanding that it would have a year to reach a decision. Wilson and his cabinet, however, were opposed to such a method. Rather than dispatch a note that Wilson had drafted to Germany, and that he was sure would result in war, Bryan resigned his position as Secretary of State. On another occasion, Bryan, as Secretary of State, led the United States in declining to recognize the Huerta Government in Mexico in 1913 because it had come to power by force.

57. *Ibid.*, p. 204. Populism refers to a party or cause supported by the people. In American political history the Populist (People's) Party was formed in 1891. It advocated an increase of the currency, free coinage of silver, public ownership and operation of railroads and telegraphs, an income tax, and limitation in ownership of land. Its members were called Populists.

58. Clarence E. Macartney, *Six Kings of the American Pulpit*, p. 207.

59. Coletta, *William Jennings Bryan*, Vol. III, pp. 188–191.

60. Bryan caused an uproar at the Democratic Convention of 1912 by proposing that his party declare itself opposed to the nomination of any candidate for president "who is the representative of or under obligation to J. Pierpont Morgan, Thomas R. Ryan, August Belmont, or any other member of the privilege-hunting and favor-seeking class." Mrs. Bryan claimed that the state of excitement was such that one delegate offered $25,000 to anyone who would kill her husband. Bryan, *Memoirs*, pp. 174–177.

61. Bryan, *In His Image*, p. 156.

62. Bryan, *Memoirs*, p. 452.

63. Szasz, "Three Fundamentalist Leaders," p. 102.

64. *Ibid.*, p. 103.

65. The increased time that Bryan gave to religious interests in his later years is reflected in his books and the dates of their publication: *Heart to Heart Appeals* (1917); *The First Commandment* (ca. 1919); *The Bible and Its Enemies* (1920); *In His Image* (1922); *Orthodox Christianity Versus Modernism* (1923); *Famous Figures of the Old Testament* (ca. 1923); *Shall Christianity Remain Christian? Seven Questions in Dispute* (1924); *Christ and His Companions: Famous Figures of the New Testament* (ca. 1925); *Memoirs* (1925).

66. Bryan, "They Have Taken Away My Lord." Sermon delivered at Bethany Presbyterian Church, Philadelphia, March 17, 1925. Bryan Papers.

67. Bryan, *Seven Questions*, p. 18.

68. *Ibid.*, p. 25.

69. William Jennings Bryan, "It Is Written." Address at the Southern Bible Conference, Miami, Florida, Feb. 17, 1924, p. 7. Pamphlet. Bryan Papers.

70. Bryan, *In His Image*, p. 80.

71. *Ibid.*, p. 91.

72. *Ibid.*, p. 120.

73. *Ibid.*, p. 106.

74. Bryan, *In His Image*, pp. 40–46.

75. William Jennings Bryan, "Billy Sunday and His Work," *The Commoner*, Dec. 1916, p. 102. Bryan believed that revivals awakened church members, brought a new religious force into the community, and tended to bring the churches into a new spirit of cooperation. Of Billy Sunday, Bryan agreed that his manner was dramatic and his language undignified but asserted that the important thing was that he communicated with his listeners.

76. Allyn K. Foster, "A Communication," *The Christian Century*, June 15, 1922, p. 755.

77. Norman F. Furniss, *The Fundamentalist Controversy, 1918–1931* (The Shoe String Press, Inc., Archon Books, 1963), p. 133.

78. Koenig, *Bryan*, p. 630.

79. *Ibid.* Consistent with his opposition to the extreme fundamentalists, Bryan rejected in 1920 the document known as *The Protocols of the Learned Elders of Zion* which maliciously and falsely pictured the Jew as the arch troublemaker of the world. Bryan branded the work a spurious product of an enemy of the Jewish people and proceeded to indicate the many prominent Jews whom he counted as intimate friends. William Jennings Bryan, "The Protocols," *The Commoner*, Dec. 1920.

80. Koenig, *Bryan*, p. 631.

81. Bryan, "They Have Taken Away My Lord," p. 10.

82. *Ibid.*, p. 13.

83. For monographs on the Scopes Trial, see John T. Scopes and James Presley, *Center of the Storm: Memoirs of John T. Scopes;* Ray Ginger, *Six Days or Forever? Tennessee v. John Thomas Scopes;* Leslie Henri Allen, ed. and comp., *Bryan and Darrow at Dayton;* Jerry R. Tompkins, ed., *D-Days at Dayton: Reflections on the Scopes Trial;* Ferenc M. Szasz, "The Scopes Trial in Perspective," *Tennessee Historical Quarterly*, Fall 1971.

84. W. B. Mann to Bryan, July 6, 1925. Bryan Papers.

85. Dudley Field Malone, "Comments on the Scopes Trial," p. 9. Nine-page summary (several pages missing). Bryan Papers.

86. Levine, *Defender of the Faith*, p. 346.

87. Koenig, *Bryan*, p. 646.

88. Bryan, *In His Image*, p. 13.

89. Bryan to Howard A. Kelly, June 22, 1925. Bryan Papers.

90. J. Frank Norris to Bryan, June 3, 1925. Bryan Papers.

91. James M. Gray to Bryan, June 22, 1925. Bryan Papers.

92. P. H. Welshimer to Bryan, June 23, 1925. Bryan Papers.

93. Alfred W. McCann to Bryan, June 30, 1925. Bryan Papers. These letters are but samples of a larger correspondence from fundamentalist leaders. It is possible that the fundamentalist leaders failed to see the importance of the trial or, more likely, felt unable to defend their position when confronted directly by evolutionists.

94. Ahlstrom, *Religious History*, p. 879.

95. Macartney, *Six Kings of the American Pulpit*, p. 200; *The Christian Century*, May 31, 1923; Bryan, *Memoirs*, p. 493.

96. *The Vintage Mencken*, compiled by Alistair Cooke, p. 164.

97. Charles S. Thomas to J. T. Scopes, June 26, 1925; Charles S. Thomas to Bryan, June 27, 1925. Bryan Papers.

98. Williams, Current, and Freidel, *History of the United States*, Vol. II, *Since 1865*, p. 226.

99. Scopes and Presley, *Center of the Storm*, p. 217.

100. The reference to the Federal Council of Churches is found in Szasz, "Three Fundamentalist Leaders," p. 182. Bryan spoke for the YMCA, and the YWCA, the Epworth League, the Christian Endeavor organization, to many Protestant denominations, to Catholics, and to Jews. His wife once said to him that it seemed strange that all denominations seemed so pleased to have him speak. "I should think it would be easy to give offence." Bryan replied: "The underlying truth of all religions is the same. One can discuss these great principles before any audience and in the presentation each one recognizes his own belief."

101. William Jennings Bryan, "Peace and Prohibition," p. 14. Speech delivered at Democratic National Convention, San Francisco, July 2, 1920. Pamphlet. Bryan Papers.

102. Szasz, "Three Fundamentalist Leaders," p. 182. Bryan is an exception to Furniss' judgment that the fundamentalist movement was characterized by violence in thought and language. Furniss, *The Fundamentalist Controversy*, p. 36.

103. Bryan, *Memoirs*, p. 556.

Chapter Eight. Clarence E. Macartney, Preacher-Fundamentalist

1. Conservative tendencies have been prominent in recent years among Presbyterians as indicated by diminished enthusiasm for the Consultation on Church Union, the defeat of Eugene Carson Blake as Moderator of The United Presbyterian Church in the U.S.A., separatist tendencies within the Presbyterian Church in the United States (southern), retreat on social action, and a renewed emphasis on the local church, with less attention given to denominational concerns.

2. Dean M. Kelley, *Why Conservative Churches Are Growing* (Harper & Row, Publishers, Inc., 1972).

3. Clarence Edward Macartney, *The Making of a Minister: The Autobiography of Clarence E. Macartney*, ed. by J. Clyde Henry. A number of unpublished theses and dissertations have been written about Macartney. These invariably deal, however, with his homiletical abilities and contributions and devote little attention to the role he played in ecclesiastical affairs,

less attention to his theology, and least attention to his social attitudes. One of the best Ph.D. dissertations is by Harry Eugene Farra, chairman of the Speech Department, Geneva College: "The Rhetoric of Reverend Clarence Edward Macartney: A Man Under Authority" (Pennsylvania State University, 1970).

4. The primary sources for this study have been articles and books written by Macartney, plus his personal papers. The author also checked the correspondence between Macartney and J. Gresham Machen in the Machen Papers at Westminster Theological Seminary, Chestnut Hill, Pennsylvania. In addition, several interviews were conducted with people who knew Macartney, including G. Hall Todd, one of Macartney's successors as minister of the Arch Street Presbyterian Church, Philadelphia. Finally, the author attended a service of worship in the First Presbyterian Church of Pittsburgh to catch the spirit of the congregation where Macartney served his longest pastorate.

5. Clarence E. Macartney, following the lead of his older brother, J. Robertson Macartney, changed the spelling of his last name from McCartney. Other members of the family kept the original spelling, consequently the variation which the reader will notice in this chapter.

6. Macartney's father met his future wife while studying in Scotland. Her wealthy father was greatly opposed to the marriage. After a ten-year courtship by the devoted couple, however, he gave his reluctant consent.

7. Frank S. Mead, *Handbook of Denominations in the United States* (1951), pp. 155–156.

8. Macartney, *Making of a Minister*, p. 48.

9. The interplay between culture and religion was manifested early in the McCartney family. One Sunday, the president of the college was preaching an eschatological sermon in the local Reformed Presbyterian Church to which the McCartneys belonged. Macartney's sister, in reminiscing about this experience, wrote: "The devil was a very real person to us children. I can [still] see tall Dr. H. H. George as with appropriate gesture he roared out, 'Satan will be kicked out of the universe and chained!' We were sure these chains were to be forged by the Keystone Driller Co. (of Beaver Falls)." Wilhelmina Guerard, "Clarence Macartney Biographical Notes." Typed manuscript (n.d.), p. 12. Macartney Papers.

10. Clarence E. Macartney, "Looking Backward and Looking Forward." Address delivered at the fiftieth reunion of the class of 1901 at the University of Wisconsin, June 1951, pp. 3–4. Macartney Papers. Macartney knew Turner, although he took no courses from him since the latter was on leave of absence during much of Macartney's time at Wisconsin.

11. When Macartney placed a close second in the contest, largely because of one judge who scored him sixth and last in manuscript, the future senator (LaFollette) said to the disappointed contestant: "Macartney, the judge who gave you a last place was either a fool or a knave." *Ibid.*, p. 6.

12. Guerard, "Biographical Notes," p. 32.

13. *Ibid.*, p. 35.

14. Macartney, *Making of a Minister*, p. 120.

15. Macartney never considered his continuing interest in history and literature as a "hobby," but rather an integral part of his ministry, adding richness to his stock of illustrations. Macartney considered hobbies a sign of intellectual weakness!

16. Macartney's bachelorhood sometimes provided occasion for jesting remarks, especially by theological opponents, including members of his own family. Once when the air was charged with tension at a meeting of the General Assembly at Baltimore in 1926, Macartney's brother, Albert, said: "Clarence is all right, friends. The only trouble is he is not married. If that old bachelor would get married he would not have much time to look after other people's theology (laughter and applause)." Edgar DeWitt Jones, *American Preachers of Today*, p. 182.

The Napoleonic theme in Macartney's life is a fascinating one for those interested in psychoanalysis. Macartney, who in some ways looked like the Corsican leader, visited the tomb of Napoleon in France, kept a bust of Napoleon in his office in Pittsburgh, and wrote a book entitled *The Bonapartes in America*. His sister wrote that from his early days Macartney had and kept a Napoleonic complex. Farra, "The Rhetoric of . . . Macartney," fn. 48. On one occasion, Macartney told G. Hall Todd that he perceived in his own profile a likeness to Julius Caesar. Interview with G. Hall Todd, Jan. 16, 1974.

17. Macartney had personal contact with prominent political leaders, including Presidents McKinley, Cleveland, and Wilson; with leaders of the arts such as John Philip Sousa and John Masefield; with men of business, among them John Wanamaker; and with many religious personalities ranging from General William Booth to Congressman-Clergyman Adam Clayton Powell, Jr.

18. The source of this statement is G. Hall Todd, who attended Macartney's funeral. Interview, June 14, 1973.

19. Macartney preached regularly at Sunday morning and evening services, at the noon meeting for men on Tuesdays, and at the midweek service on Wednesday evenings.

20. Macartney, as a preacher, possessed weaknesses as well as strengths. These included frequent repetition, excessive spiritualizing, rambling comments, improbable imaginative descriptions, occasional disregard of the Biblical context, and false generalizations, such as "evangelical preaching is the answer for all our church problems." Richard D. Lucas, "The Preaching of Clarence E. Macartney." Unpublished Th.D. dissertation, Southern Baptist Theological Seminary, 1959, pp. 158–165.

21. W. J. Larkin, "C. E. Macartney: Champion of the Faith," *Moody Monthly*, Jan. 1973, p. 49.

22. The title "Come Before Winter" was an expression purportedly by Paul from Rome urging Timothy in Ephesus to visit him before winter set in when navigation would be difficult. (II Tim. 4:21.)

23. Russell H. Conwell, founder of Baptist Temple in Philadelphia, out of which grew Temple University, delivered his popular lecture, "Acres of Diamonds," some six thousand times between the years 1868 and 1913. It was an appeal for individuals to seek money and to use it wisely.

24. Clarence E. Macartney, "Come Before Winter," *First Church Pulpit*. Undated sermon, pamphlet form, pp. 19–20. Macartney Papers.

25. Farra, "The Rhetoric of . . . Macartney," p. 127.

26. The Tuesday noon meetings usually consisted of eating a cafeteria luncheon, singing familiar hymns, listening to a large male chorus, and hearing a ten- to fifteen-minute address by Macartney. Offerings were not taken.

27. An analysis in 1946 of those who attended the Tuesday noon meetings in Pittsburgh revealed that the largest percentage came from Presbyterian ranks. The Methodists ran a poor second, followed by Lutherans, Episcopalians, Baptists, and members of smaller denominations. By business and profession, the largest groupings were insurance salesmen and executives, railroad officials, steel company employees, and employees of banks in the city. Also included were thirty-eight attorneys and twenty-four ministers. *Year Book of the First Presbyterian Church, Pittsburgh, 1946* (pages unnumbered). Macartney Papers.

28. Farra, "The Rhetoric of . . . Macartney," p. 217. Macartney's congregations averaged one hundred new members each year of his pastoral leadership.

29. The statistics are found in *Minutes of the General Assembly of the Presbyterian Church in the U.S.A.* for the corresponding years. The source for the Sunday evening statistics at Philadelphia is *The Presbyterian*, Nov. 18, 1943, p. 4. In addition to the numerical strength of his churches, near the end of his ministry Macartney was reaching 50,000 homes through his radio broadcasts and his publishers had sold nearly a half million copies of his books. Farra, "The Rhetoric of . . . Macartney," pp. 204–205.

30. Macartney, *Making of a Minister*, p. 198.

31. The expression within quotations is from Farra, "The Rhetoric of . . . Macartney," p. 217. Professor Farra adds that Macartney's triumph through monologues could be expected of a man who subscribed to a fixed and unchangeable kind of truth that was not open to question.

32. Princeton Theology held to a strict doctrine of predestination, the inspiration and the inerrancy of the Scriptures, and placed what Lefferts A. Loetscher has called "a startling confidence in the competence of human reasoning powers" as its methodological ideal even though God is, in some respects, incomprehensible. Doctrinally, Princeton Theology owed much to the founder of the seminary, Archibald Alexander of Virginia, who in turn

relied heavily on the seventeenth-century scholasticism of Francois Turretin, a defender of Genevan orthodoxy. For an excellent description of Princeton Theology, see Loetscher, *Broadening Church*, pp. 21–25.

33. Edward H. Roberts to Macartney, July 2, 1953. Macartney Papers.

34. *The Pittsburgh Press*, April 1, 1927.

35. *The Pittsburgh Post*, April 4, 1927.

36. Clarence E. Macartney, *Twelve Great Questions About Christ*, Ch. VI; Clarence E. Macartney, "Warm Hearts and Steady Faith," *The Christian Century*, March 8, 1939.

37. Clarence E. Macartney, *The Greatest Men of the Bible*, p. 161.

38. Archibald A. Hodge and Benjamin B. Warfield, "Inspiration," *Presbyterian Review*, Vol. II (1881), p. 238, as quoted in H. Shelton Smith, Robert T. Handy, and Lefferts A. Loetscher, eds., *American Christianity: An Historical Interpretation with Representative Documents*, Vol. II, *1820–1960*, p. 332.

39. Sandeen, *Roots of Fundamentalism*, pp. 118–131. Sandeen points out that "the Princeton doctrine of inspiration was characterized by a concentration upon external verifications to the neglect of the internal . . . [while] . . . the emphasis in the *Westminster Confession* is, though judicially balanced, decidedly in favor of internal proofs." Also, Sandeen indicates that while the Princeton theologians came to limit inerrancy to the original documents, the Westminster Confession of Faith speaks of the providence of God which keeps the Scriptures "pure in all ages."

40. Macartney to G. A. Johnston Ross, March 24, 1924, Macartney Papers; Macartney, "The Authority of the Holy Scriptures," *Princeton Theological Review*, Vol. XXIII (1925), p. 389.

41. Luke 24:44: "And he [Jesus] said unto them, These are the words which I spake unto you, while I was yet with you, that all things must be fulfilled, which were written in the law of Moses, and in the prophets, and in the psalms, concerning me."

42. Clarence E. Macartney, "The Tomorrow of Protestantism." Excerpts of address delivered at the First Commencement of Westminster Theological Seminary, Philadelphia, *First Church* (Pittsburgh) *Life*, n.d. (presumably 1930), p. 11.

43. Deut. 29:29.

44. Clarence E. Macartney, *Great Interviews of Jesus*, p. 168.

45. Two-page untitled and undated typed statement by Macartney. Macartney Papers.

46. The fundamentalists with whom Macartney kept close company included Maitland Alexander, J. Gresham Machen, and William Jennings Bryan, whom Macartney called "the greatest Christian layman of his age" and "the greatest lay preacher in the history of America." Macartney, *Six Kings of the American Pulpit* (1942; Books for Libraries Press, 1971), p. 200.

47. Clarence E. Macartney, "The Second Coming of Christ," *The Watchman-Examiner*, Feb. 17, 1949, p. 156; Clarence E. Macartney, *Things*

Most Surely Believed: A Series of Sermons on the Apostles' Creed, pp. 102–115; Clarence Edward Macartney, "The Second Coming of Christ," undated sermon, pamphlet form, preached at First Presbyterian Church, Pittsburgh, Macartney Papers; Clarence Edward Macartney, "Shall Unbelief Win? A Reply to Dr. Fosdick," pp. 16–17.

48. Macartney, "Warm Hearts and Steady Faith," p. 317.

49. *Ibid.*

50. Clarence Edward Macartney, *The Greatest Texts of the Bible*, p. 5.

51. Walter Rauschenbusch, *A Theology for the Social Gospel* (The Macmillan Company, 1917), p. 7.

52. Clarence E. Macartney, "Is America on the Road to Ruin?" Sermon preached at the First Presbyterian Church, Pittsburgh, Jan. 28, 1945, and printed in pamphlet form. Macartney Papers.

53. H. D. Hough, "Prince of the American Pulpit." Unpublished B.D. thesis, Western Theological Seminary, 1952, p. 15.

54. In addition to the salary arrangement, the church at Pittsburgh agreed to contribute 10 percent of Macartney's salary to a pension fund for him rather than the usual 7.5 percent, and it also promised him a vacation of two months. Contract entitled "Call for a Pastor," dated Jan. 31, 1927. Macartney Papers.

55. *The New York Times*, Sept. 27, 1927; *The Philadelphia Inquirer*, April 30, 1931; Macartney, "Is America on the Road to Ruin?"

56. Clarence E. Macartney, "Birth Control and the Presbyterian Church." Three-page typed comment, 1927 (no further date), p. 3. Macartney Papers. Macartney added emotionally: "Should the recommendations of many Protestant ministers today be followed, it will come to this . . . after a second or third child has been brought into the home by the physician, the Protestant minister will be summoned to strangle it, so that the firstborn will have a chance to go to college."

57. Macartney, *Making of a Minister*, p. 150.

58. Undated newspaper clipping, *The Pittsburgh Post*. Macartney Papers.

59. Macartney, *Making of a Minister*, p. 17. The source is J. Clyde Henry.

60. Clarence Edward Macartney, *The Faith Once Delivered*, p. 142. Macartney had in mind Gen. 9:6, "Whoso sheddeth man's blood, by man shall his blood be shed: for in the image of God made he man."

61. Undated, untitled newspaper clipping summarizing a sermon Macartney preached at Arch Street Presbyterian Church, Philadelphia. Macartney Papers.

62. While Macartney's sermons did not deal with racial matters, he did seek the admission of a young black, Irwin W. Underhill, to Princeton Seminary in the 1920's. Macartney encountered considerable difficulty before eventually gaining Underhill's acceptance. Interview with G. Hall Todd, Jan. 16, 1974.

63. Macartney, *Making of a Minister*, p. 153.

64. Clarence E. Macartney, "In the Year of '97," *Bulletin of the University of Denver*, Jan. 10, 1941; undated, untitled newspaper clipping, Macartney Papers.

65. By political affiliation, Macartney was a Republican who on occasion voted for a Democratic presidential candidate. The Philadelphia banker, George Stevenson, a staunch Republican, and a member of the Arch Street Presbyterian Church, Philadelphia, once proposed Macartney for membership in the Union League. The club was a Republican stronghold, formed during the Civil War in support of the Union cause. "But I couldn't belong," said the pastor, "I voted for Woodrow Wilson." The shocked Stevenson surveyed Macartney from head to foot. "Young man," he said firmly, "I assumed you must at some time have sinned, but never, never that deeply." *The* (Philadelphia) *Evening Bulletin*, Sept. 26, 1932.

66. Macartney's "training" in nationalism was reflected in one experience while he was a student at the University of Denver. Macartney and his brother attended Sunday evening services in Denver at the Central Presbyterian Church where James E. Sentz was the minister. On their way to church one evening, the two young men saw a bulletin posted in the window of the *Rocky Mountain News* stating that Commodore [later Admiral] Dewey had fought and sunk the Spanish fleet in Manila Bay. Upon reaching the church, they passed the word on to Dr. Sentz. After the opening doxology, the clergyman said to his congregation: "I have just been informed that the Spanish fleet is at the bottom of Manila Bay. Let us stand and sing 'The Star-spangled Banner.'" Macartney, *Making of a Minister*, pp. 96–97.

67. Two-page typed summary, "Remarks by Dr. Clarence E. Macartney at the Public Prayer Service for Victory and Peace, conducted from the Street Pulpit of the First Presbyterian Church, Pittsburgh, Pennsylvania, June 6, 1944." Macartney Papers.

68. Clarence E. Macartney, "A Good Soldier of Jesus Christ," *The Watchman-Examiner*, Aug. 2, 1945, p. 747.

69. Macartney, "Warm Hearts and Steady Faith," p. 317.

70. Clarence E. Macartney, "The Teaching of Ethics in the Public Schools." Printed pamphlet, n.d. Macartney Papers.

71. Macartney, "Is America on the Road to Ruin?"

72. Fosdick, *Living of These Days*, p. 173.

73. Fosdick was indebted to Prof. William Newton Clarke of Colgate University for this distinction between the forms and the abiding experiences and the teachings they attempted to express. *Ibid.*, p. 65.

74. *Ibid.*, p. 146.

75. Macartney's mother once said to him: "Can't you leave poor Fosdick alone?" "No, I'll not leave him alone," Macartney answered with vehemence. "The Presbyterian Church is committed to a body of doctrines; and the doctrine would be endangered if ministers were not subject to the discipline of their denomination." Guerard, "Biographical Notes," p. 59. On another

occasion, Macartney said: "If they [the liberals] wish to attack our fortress, let them take off our uniform and withdraw from our citadel." Clarence E. Macartney, "Precious Memories Center in the Old Home," *The Presbyterian*, March 26, 1925.

76. *Ibid.*

77. Fosdick, *Living of These Days*, p. 176. It should be noted that opposition to Fosdick came, not from the church he served in New York City, but from conservative Presbyterians in the larger denomination.

78. *Ibid.*, p. 146.

79. Undated, untitled newspaper clipping in display case in Macartney Room, Geneva College.

80. An analysis of the voting shows that Macartney's greatest support came from Pennsylvania, Maryland, West Virginia, Kansas, Oklahoma, and California. *The* (Philadelphia) *Evening Bulletin*, May 22, 1924.

81. Clarence E. Macartney, "The State of the Church," *Princeton Theological Review*, April 1925, p. 182.

82. J. Gresham Machen to Macartney, Feb. 6, 1926. Machen Papers.

83. Macartney to J. Gresham Machen, Sept. 27, 1927. Machen Papers.

84. *The Presbyterian Banner*, June 6, 1929; *Minutes of the General Assembly*, 1929, as quoted in Loetscher, *Broadening Church*.

85. Minutes of the Board of Trustees, Westminster Theological Seminary, Jan. 7, 1936. Machen Papers. This tension between denominational loyalty and a desire for an ecumenical fellowship has been one characteristic of Protestantism throughout its history in America.

86. *Christianity Today*, Feb. 1936.

87. Macartney's loyalty to his denomination may have been motivated in part by practical consequences, that is, the need to keep his position where he could continue to preach effectively.

88. Macartney, "Warm Hearts and Steady Faith," p. 317. Despite his hope in this regard, Macartney was not an ecumenist, fearing that ecumenism would come at the cost of doctrinal sacrifice. He quoted approvingly a London clergyman who told how the movements toward church unity amounted to giving up various distinguishing doctrines until finally two churches agreed to unite on the general proposition of the truth of the multiplication table. Illustrative of Macartney's hesitancy to associate with theological liberals was his refusal to become a contributor to *The Interpreter's Bible*. He declined, believing that his affiliation with other writers not adhering to his orthodox views might imply his approval of those views and classify him as a theological liberal. Interview with G. Hall Todd, Jan. 16, 1974.

89. Farra, "The Rhetoric of . . . Macartney," p. 217.

90. Wilbur M. Smith to Macartney, May 16, 1933. Macartney Papers. Smith, at the time, was minister of the Presbyterian Church in Coatesville, Pennsylvania. Later he became a faculty member at Moody Bible Institute (1938) and then at Fuller Theological Seminary (1947).

Chapter Nine. Voices in Perspective

1. George W. Dollar divides contemporary fundamentalists into three groups: the militant, the moderate, and the modified. He refers to T. T. Shields, William Bell Riley, J. Frank Norris, and John Roach Straton as the prima donnas of the second generation of fundamentalists. J. Gresham Machen is interpreted as an "orthodox ally" of the fundamentalists rather than as a fundamentalist himself. Dollar, *History of Fundamentalism*, pp. 105–143, 173–183, 282–289.

2. Edward John Carnell, *The Case for Orthodox Theology*, p. 115.

3. In 1975, the experts of the World Health Organization recommended that countries introduce sweeping legislative changes to control cigarette smoking in order to improve health and prolong life. In the United States, the same year, federal and state agencies were seeking to help nine million recognized alcoholics.

4. Carnell, *Orthodox Theology*, p. 121.

5. Smith, Handy, and Loetscher, eds., *American Christianity*, Vol. II, p. 250.

6. Roy, *Apostles of Discord*, preface.

7. Erik H. Erikson, professor of human development and lecturer on psychiatry at Harvard University, is a leading figure in the field of psychoanalysis. He is known for psychoanalytical biographies of Luther and Gandhi.

8. Carnell, *Orthodox Theology*, p. 124. For another critical analysis of Fundamentalism, see L. Harold DeWolf, *Present Trends in Christian Thought*, Ch. 3.

A SELECTIVE
BIBLIOGRAPHY
Selectively Annotated

The following is a listing of the primary and
secondary sources used in the preparation of this book.

I. Primary Sources

A. Personal Papers

1. Beaver Falls, Pennsylvania. McCartney Library, Geneva College.
Personal Papers of Clarence E. Macartney.

The variation in the spelling of Macartney is correct. See Ch. Eight,
n. 5. These papers are particularly rich in sermonic material,
carefully arranged, but are light on correspondence that deals with
the Modernist-Fundamentalist Controversy.

2. Nashville, Tennessee. Dargan-Carver Library. Personal Papers of
J. Frank Norris, including correspondence covering the years
1927–1952. Owned by the Southern Baptist Convention. Permission
has kindly been given by the Historical Commission of the Southern
Baptist Convention to quote from these papers.

The papers have been microfilmed (twenty-seven reels). They
reflect correspondence, clippings, and records of the fundamentalist
movement from the 1920's into the post-World War II years. Topics
include the Al Smith–Herbert Hoover presidential campaign of
1928; the evolution issue, especially as it pertained to Baylor
University; Norris' charges of Communist sympathies against noted
American churchmen; and Norris' standing controversy with non-
fundamentalist Baptists. Excellent source material with broad-
ranging correspondence.

3. Philadelphia, Pennsylvania (Chestnut Hill). Westminster Theological Seminary. Personal Papers of J. Gresham Machen.

The finest collection of personal papers of a fundamentalist leader, in most instances carefully cataloged. Machen's correspondence, except that with his mother, is arranged yearly in alphabetical order. Substantial correspondence with other fundamentalists.

4. Rochester, New York. American Baptist Historical Society. Personal Papers of J. C. Massee.

The Massee Papers contain eleven archive boxes of material. Strong on sermons in manuscript form; weak on correspondence in the 1920's.

5. Rochester, New York. American Baptist Historical Society. Personal Papers of John Roach Straton.

A great deal of material, but disappointing in the absence of correspondence at the height of the theological struggle. Good for articles, newspaper clippings, and sermons that reflect Straton's thought.

6. Roseville, Minnesota. Northwestern College. Personal Papers of William Bell Riley.

Numerous scrapbooks, books, sermons, journals, yearbooks of Northwestern Schools, and memorabilia. Light on correspondence.

7. Washington, D.C. Library of Congress, Division of Manuscripts. Personal Papers of William Jennings Bryan.

These papers contain some 18,000 items, spanning the years 1877–1940, with nearly one third relating to the presidential campaign of 1896 and the greater part of the remainder dated between 1913 and 1925. Correspondence prior to 1890 and that in the period between 1901 and 1913 is very light. Excellent material on the Scopes Trial.

B. Books

Allen, Leslie Henri, ed. and comp. *Bryan and Darrow at Dayton: The Record and Documents of the "Bible-Evolution" Trial.* A. Lee and Company, 1925; Russell & Russell, Inc., 1967.

American Christianity: An Historical Interpretation with Representative Documents. 2 vols. (Vol. I, *1607–1820;* Vol. II, *1820–1960*). Edited by H. Shelton Smith, Robert T. Handy, and Lefferts A. Loetscher. Charles Scribner's Sons, 1960; 1963.

An excellent sourcebook. Vol. II contains a portion of Fosdick's famous sermon, "Shall the Fundamentalists Win?"

Bryan, William Jennings. *The First Battle: A Story of the Campaign of 1896.* W. B. Conkey Company, 1896.

Contains a collection of speeches by Bryan and a biographical sketch of Bryan by his wife.

———. *The Prince of Peace.* Funk & Wagnalls Company, 1915.

An address delivered at numerous Chautauquas and YMCA and other religious meetings in the United States and at Tokyo, Manila, Bombay, Cairo, Jerusalem, Montreal, and Toronto.

———. *Heart to Heart Appeals: Speeches Delivered 1890–1916.* Fleming H. Revell Company, 1917.

See remarks on "Religion" and "The Liquor Question." Other topics are primarily political in nature.

———. *The First Commandment.* N.p., ca. 1919.

———. *In His Image.* Fleming H. Revell Company, 1922.

By 1924, this book was in its tenth edition.

———. *Orthodox Christianity Versus Modernism.* Fleming H. Revell Company, 1923.

———. *Famous Figures of the Old Testament.* Fleming H. Revell Company, ca. 1923.

A collection of Bible Talks by Bryan, delivered to his Sunday school class in Miami.

———. *Shall Christianity Remain Christian? Seven Questions in Dispute.* Fleming H. Revell Company, 1924.

Contents: The Inspiration of the Bible; The Deity of Christ; The Virgin Birth; The Blood Atonement; The Bodily Resurrection of Jesus; The Miracles of Our Lord; The Origin of Man. This is a series Bryan had written for the *Sunday School Times.*

———. *Christ and His Companions: Famous Figures of the New Testament.* Fleming H. Revell Company, ca. 1925.

A collection of Bryan's Bible Talks.

———. *The Memoirs of William Jennings Bryan, By Himself and His Wife, Mary Baird Bryan.* John C. Winston Company, 1925.

At the time of his death, Bryan had completed about two fifths of the manuscript. Mrs. Bryan completed the work with the help of friends and relatives. The result is an overly sympathetic volume.

Campbell, Robert, ed. *Spectrum of Protestant Beliefs.* Bruce Publishing Company, 1968.

Bob Jones, Jr., represents the fundamentalist spectrum of Protestantism in setting forth his beliefs on a variety of religious, theological, and social subjects.

Entzminger, Louis. *The J. Frank Norris I Have Known for Thirty-four Years.* N.p., n.d.

An adulatory work.

Fosdick, Harry Emerson. *The Living of These Days: An Autobiography.* Harper & Brothers, 1956.

See Ch. 7 for "The Fundamentalist Controversy." Fosdick pictures himself as having been raked by both sides: the fundamentalists on one hand, and the radical liberals on the other. Other excellent chapters are "Winds of Doctrine" and "Ideas That Have Used Me."

Jones, Edgar DeWitt. *American Preachers of Today.* The Bobbs-Merrill Company, Inc., 1933.

Contains a chapter on Macartney.

Macartney, Clarence Edward Noble. *Twelve Great Questions About Christ.* Fleming H. Revell Company, 1923.

Foreword by J. Gresham Machen.

————. *Things Most Surely Believed: A Series of Sermons on the Apostles' Creed.* Cokesbury Press, 1930.

————. *The Great Men of the Bible.* Abingdon-Cokesbury Press, 1941.

————. *Six Kings of the American Pulpit.* The Westminster Press, 1942.

The "kings": George Whitefield; Matthew Simpson; Henry Ward Beecher; Phillips Brooks; T. DeWitt Talmage; William Jennings Bryan. An uncritical treatment.

————. *Great Interviews of Jesus.* Abingdon-Cokesbury Press, 1944.

Typical of Macartney's Biblical and biographical preaching.

————. *The Greatest Texts of the Bible.* Abingdon-Cokesbury Press, 1947.

————. *The Faith Once Delivered.* Abingdon-Cokesbury Press, 1952.

Especially helpful for an understanding of Macartney's doctrinal views.

——. *The Making of a Minister: The Autobiography of Clarence E. Macartney.* Edited by J. Clyde Henry. Channel Press, 1961.

Published posthumously. Not as strong on theology as one might wish.

Macartney, Clarence Edward Noble, and Dorrance, Gordon. *The Bonapartes in America.* Dorrance & Company, Inc., 1939.

Machen, John Gresham. *The Virgin Birth of Christ.* Harper & Brothers, 1930.

The Thomas Smyth Lectures delivered by Machen at Columbia Theological Seminary in 1927. Considered the finest tome in defense of the historicity of the virgin birth.

——. *The Christian Faith in the Modern World.* The Macmillan Company, 1936.

Originally a series of radio addresses given by Machen in 1933.

——. *Christianity and Liberalism.* The Presbyterian Guardian, 1940.

The classical Machen volume in which he declares that Christianity and Liberalism are two different entities.

Massee, J. C. *The Second Coming.* Philadelphia School of the Bible, 1919.

Massee affirms that the millennial kingdom will never evolve from the evil seed of an unregenerate humanity.

——. *The Gospel in the Ten Commandments.* Fleming H. Revell Company, 1923.

Expository sermons on each of the Ten Commandments.

——. *The Ten Greatest Christian Doctrines.* George H. Doran Company, 1925.

——. *Revival Sermons.* Fleming H. Revell Company, 1928.

Norris, John Franklyn. *The Gospel of Dynamite: Messages That Resulted in Over 700 Conversions. Delivered to the Largest Congregations in America, Including the Recent Sermon, The Fear of Death and How to Overcome It.* N.p., n.d.

The title reflects Norris' character.

——. *Infidelity Among Southern Baptists Endorsed by Highest Officials.* N.p., n.d.

Norris-Wallace Debate, Delivered in Forth Worth, Texas, November 5th, 6th, and 7th, 1934, (by) J. Frank Norris and Foy E. Wallace. The Fundamentalist Publishing Company, ca. 1935.

Norris, John Franklyn. *Inside History of First Baptist Church, Fort Worth; and Temple Baptist Church, Detroit. Life Story of Dr. J. Frank Norris.* N.p., n.d.

Potter, Charles F. *The Preacher and I: An Autobiography.* Crown Pubs., 1951.

"The Preacher" refers to John Roach Straton, Potter's erstwhile opponent in public debate. Valuable for a contrasting viewpoint.

Rauschenbusch, Walter. *Christianity and the Social Crisis.* The Macmillan Company, 1907.

The most important book by the ablest exponent of the Social Gospel. Contains specific suggestions as to how to realize the kingdom ("all humanity reorganized according to the will of God").

Riley, William Bell. *Ten Sermons on the Greater Doctrines of Scripture.* Leader Publishing Company, 1891.

———. *The Perennial Revival: A Plea for Evangelism.* Winona Publishing Company, 1904, 3d ed., revised, American Baptist Publication Society, 1933.

———. *The Evolution of the Kingdom.* (From serial issue in *Grace and Truth.*) C. C. Cook, 1913.

Contains what Riley believed is the Biblical order of millennial events and a section entitled "The Historical Ministry of Premillennarianism."

———. *Inspiration or Evolution.* 2d ed. Union Gospel Press, 1926.

———. *Ten Burning Questions.* Fleming H. Revell Company, 1932.

———. *The Philosophies of Father Coughlin. Four Sermons by W. B. Riley.* Zondervan Publishing House, 1935.

———. *Pastoral Problems.* Fleming H. Revell Company, ca. 1936.

Scopes, John T., and Presley, James. *Center of the Storm: Memoirs of John T. Scopes.* Holt, Rinehart & Winston, Inc., 1967.

Valuable for human-interest features.

Straton, John Roach. *The Salvation of Society and Other Addresses, Including a Series Reviewing the Fundamental Truths of Christianity.* Fleet-McGinley Company, ca. 1908.

Includes a series of addresses on what Straton believed were the fundamental truths of Christianity, e.g., "Will Christ Come Back Again?" pp. 207–216.

————. *The Scarlet Stain on the City and How to Wipe It Out.* First Baptist Church Men's League, ca. 1916. (Norfolk, Virginia.)

————. *The Menace of Immorality in Church and State: Messages of Wrath and Judgment.* George H. Doran Company, 1920.

————. *The Battle Over the Bible; First in the Series of Fundamentalist-Modernist Debates Between Rev. John Roach Straton . . . and Rev. Charles Francis Potter . . .* George H. Doran Company, 1924.

Good for content of the Straton-Potter debates.

————. *Evolution Versus Creation; Second in the Series of Fundamentalist-Modernist Debates Between Rev. John Roach Straton . . . and Rev. Charles Francis Potter . . .* George H. Doran Company, 1924.

————. *The Virgin Birth—Fact or Fiction? Third in the Series of Fundamentalist-Modernist Debates Between Rev. John Roach Straton . . . and Rev. Charles Francis Potter . . .* George H. Doran Company, 1924.

————. *Was Christ Both God and Man? Fourth in the Series of Fundamentalist-Modernist Debates Between Rev. John Roach Straton . . . and Rev. Charles Francis Potter . . .* George H. Doran Company, 1924.

————. *Divine Healing in Scripture and Life.* Christian Alliance Publishing Company, 1927.

Excellent for the views of one fundamentalist toward healing. A difficult book to secure.

————. *Fighting the Devil in Modern Babylon.* The Stratford Company, 1929.

Selected sermons by Straton in which he condemns the dance, the prizefight, the cinema, and religious modernism.

The Vintage Mencken, Alistair Cooke, compiler. Vintage Books, Inc., 1955.

Some material on Dayton and the Scopes Trial. The complete book enables one to catch Mencken's general spirit.

C. Articles

Bryan, William Jennings. "Perfection." Handwritten essay, Oct. 23, 1880. Bryan Papers.

———. "The Race Problem," *The Commoner*, Oct. 2, 1903.

———. "Billy Sunday and His Work," *The Commoner*, Dec. 1916.

Clearwaters, Richard V. "The Passing of Dr. W. B. Riley," *The Watchman-Examiner*, Jan. 1, 1948, pp. 10–11.

"Death of Dr. W. B. Riley," *The Watchman-Examiner*, Dec. 18, 1947, p. 1259.

Foster, Allyn K. "A Communication," *The Christian Century*, June 15, 1922.

Laws, Curtis Lee. "Convention Sidelights," *The Watchman-Examiner*, July 1, 1920, pp. 834–835.

Comments by the editor of *The Watchman-Examiner* upon the Northern Baptist Convention of 1920 held at Buffalo and the founding Conference on Baptist Fundamentals.

Macartney, Clarence Edward Noble. "Birth Control and the Presbyterian Church." Three-page typescript, 1927 (no further date). Macartney Papers.

———. "Shall Unbelief Win? A Reply to Dr. Fosdick." Wilber-Hanf, n.d. (1923).

———. "Precious Memories Center in the Old Home," *The Presbyterian*, March 26, 1925.

———. "The Authority of the Holy Scriptures." *Princeton Theological Review*, Vol. XXIII (1925), pp. 389–396.

———. "The State of the Church," *Princeton Theological Review*, April 1925, pp. 177–192.

———. "The Tomorrow of Protestantism," *First Church* (Pittsburgh) *Life*, n.d. (presumably 1930).

———. "Warm Hearts and Steady Faith," *The Christian Century*, March 8, 1939, pp. 315–319.

———. "In the Year of '97," *Bulletin of the University of Denver*, Jan. 10, 1941.

———. "A Good Soldier of Jesus Christ," *The Watchman-Examiner*, Aug. 2, 1945, pp. 746–747.

A plea to soldiers for moral courage in time of war.

———. "The Second Coming of Christ," *The Watchman-Examiner*, Feb. 17, 1949, pp. 156–157.

Macartney believes that the solution to the historical muddle is the return of Jesus. He denies the theory of invincible progress, but does not espouse specifically the premillennialist position.

Machen, J. Gresham. "Christianity and Culture," *Princeton Theological Review*, Jan. 1913.

―――. "History and Faith," *Princeton Theological Review*, July 1915.

―――. "The Church in the War," *The Presbyterian*, May 29, 1919.

―――. "Religion and Fact," *The Real Issue*, April 15, 1924.

―――. "Does Christianity Obstruct Social Progress?" *Survey Graphic*, July 1924.

―――. "The So-called Child Labor Amendment," *The Presbyterian*, Jan. 22, 1925.

―――. "Shall We Have a Federal Department of Education?" *The Woman Patriot*, Feb. 15, 1926.

―――. "Christianity in Conflict," *Contemporary American Theology: Theological Autobiographies*, Vol. I, ed. by Vergilius Ferm. Round Table Press, Inc., 1932, pp. 243–274.

Massee, J. C. "An Answer to the Board of Education," *The Watchman-Examiner*, June 16, 1921, pp. 752–753.

―――. "The Churches and the Schools," *The Watchman-Examiner*, March 17, 1921, pp. 335–337.

The Board of Education of the Northern Baptist Convention replied through its Executive Committee in an article entitled "The Churches and the Schools. A Reply to Dr. Massee by the Board of Education." *The Watchman-Examiner*, Vol. IX (1921), pp. 713–714. Massee responds to the response. J. C. Massee, "An Answer to the Board of Education," *The Watchman-Examiner*, Vol. IX (1921), pp. 752–753.

―――. "Fundamentalists and the Northern Convention," *The Watchman-Examiner*, May 17, 1923, pp. 619–620.

Includes a specific list of "accomplishments" brought about by the fundamentalists within the denomination.

―――. "Gathering Storms." Unpublished article written late in 1962. Massee Papers.

―――. "My Mother's Legacy," *The Watchman-Examiner*, 1935 (no further date). Massee Papers.

————. "The Thirty Years' War," *The Chronicle*, April 1954, pp. 106–116.

Montgomery, Helen Barrett. "The Columbia Conference," *The Watchman-Examiner*, Feb. 16, 1922.

Norris, J. Frank. " 'Americanism': An Address to the Texas Legislature." Seminary Bible and Book House, 1949.

Riley, William Bell. "Sunday Night at the Sanctuary or the Picture Show?" *Baptist World*, Feb. 5, 1917.

————. "Seminaries and a Statement of Faith," *The Watchman-Examiner*, Jan. 2, 1919, pp. 11–12.

————. "The Great Divide, or Christ and the Present Crisis," *God Hath Spoken*. Bible Conference Committee, 1919.

————. "Fundamentalism and the Faith of the Baptists," *The Watchman-Examiner*, Aug. 25, 1921, pp. 1087–1088.

Riley answers an "attack" on the fundamentalists by the denominational publication *The Baptist*.

————. "Shall Northern Baptists Automatically Exclude Ultra-Conservatives?" *The Watchman-Examiner*, May 11, 1922, pp. 589–590.

Riley claims that ministers have found themselves dropped from committee rolls and ignored in associational assemblies. He declares that such actions are a disregard of the inviolable autonomy of the local church and a forgetting of the occasion and intent of associations.

————. "Favor for the Forum," *The Watchman-Examiner*, April 29, 1937, pp. 498–499.

Riley favors the discussion of the controversial issues of the day in *The Watchman-Examiner*.

————. "My Conversion to Christ," *The Watchman-Examiner*, May 6, 1943, pp. 431–432.

Riley writes of his conversion at the age of seventeen in Dallasburg, Kentucky, and his call to the ministry in his twentieth year.

————. "The Foreign Board Controversy," *The Watchman-Examiner*, Nov. 25, 1943, pp. 1131–1132.

————. "Northern Baptists, A Bipartisan Convention," *The Watchman-Examiner*, Feb. 22, 1945, pp. 180–182.

Riley suggests that for elective offices, especially at the level of the state conventions, at least two sets of candidates should be presented by the nominating committee.

――――. "Baptist Polity Versus Autocracy," *The Watchman-Examiner*, April 27, 1944, pp. 401–402.

――――. "A Document of Decision," *The Northwestern Pilot*, April 1947.

――――. "The Meditations of an Old Man," *The Northwestern Pilot*, Jan. 1948, p. 114.

Straton, John Roach, "Does the Bible Forbid Women to Preach and Pray in Public?" Religious Literature Department, Calvary Baptist Church, n.d.

――――. "Licensing the Liquor Traffic, A Wrong and Wise Policy." Essay written while Executive Secretary, Social Service Commission, Baltimore, Maryland, 1913. Straton Papers.

――――. "The Truth About Calvary of New York," *The Religious Herald*, Nov. 10, 1921.

――――. "Religious Authority and the Lawless Dr. Fosdick," *The Faith Fundamentalist*, Dec. 28, 1924, pp. 1–9.

――――. "What's Wrong with the World?" *The Faith (Fundamentalist)*, March 15, 1925.

――――. "A Life-Changing Business," *The Christian Herald*, Dec. 28, 1929.

Published posthumously.

Editorial. "And, Now, It Is Dr. Straton," *Religious Herald*, July 1, 1926.

Walker, Stanley. "The Meshuggah of Manhattan," *The New Yorker*, April 16, 1927, pp. 25–27.

D. Sermons and Pamphlets

Bryan, William Jennings. "Why Abstain?" Address delivered at Philadelphia, March 15, 1915, auspices of the National Abstainers Union. Pamphlet. Bryan Papers.

――――. "It Is Written." Address at the Southern Bible Conference, Miami, Florida, Feb. 17, 1924. Bryan Papers.

――――. "They Have Taken Away My Lord." Printed abstract of

sermon preached at Bethany Presbyterian Church, Philadelphia, March 17, 1925. Bryan Papers.

Macartney, Clarence Edward Noble. "Come Before Winter." Sermon printed in pamphlet form, n.d. Macartney Papers.

———. "The Teaching of Ethics in the Public Schools." Printed pamphlet, n.d. Macartney Papers.

———. "The Tomorrow of Protestantism." Excerpts of address delivered at the First Commencement of Westminster Theological Seminary, Philadelphia. *First Church* (Pittsburgh) *Life*, n.d. (1930).

———. "The Second Coming of Christ." Undated sermon preached at First Presbyterian Church, Pittsburgh. Macartney Papers.

———. "Looking Backward and Looking Forward." Address delivered at the fiftieth reunion of the class of 1901 at the University of Wisconsin, June 1951. Typed. Macartney Papers.

Malone, Dudley Field. "Comments on the Scopes Trial." Nine-page summary (several pages missing). Bryan Papers.

Massee, J. C. "What I Would Do If I Were the Devil." Unpublished sermon in possession of Marjorie Massee, n.d.

———. "Companionship with Christ." Unpublished sermon in possession of Marjorie Massee, n.d.

———. "The Challenge of the Kingdom of Heaven." Unpublished sermon, n.d. Massee Papers.

Riley, William Bell. "Is Quitting the Sign of Courage?" Sermon in Riley Papers.

———. "Bryan, The Great Commoner and Christian." Sermon preached Aug. 2, 1925. Riley Papers.

Straton, John Roach. "Our American House Divided Against Itself: The Menace of White Ku Kluxism, Green Sectarianism, Yellow Journalism, and General Blackguardianism." Sermon preached Dec. 3, 1922. Straton Papers.

———. "Can New York Handle the Jewish and Catholic Questions in the More Excellent Way?" Sermon preached Dec. 17, 1922.

———. "How to Fight the Negroes, the Foreigners, the Catholics, and the Jews—The More Excellent Way." Sermon preached Dec. 17, 1922. Straton Papers.

A Debate. Duluth, Minnesota: Research Science Bureau, n.d. Pamphlet. Riley Papers.

E. Interviews by C. Allyn Russell

J. Frank Norris, Jr.; Rev. Omer Ritchie; Rev. Homer Ritchie; Dr. Hillyer H. Straton. Dr. Curtis B. Akenson; Mrs. Evalyn Camp; Dr. George M. Wilson; Dr. William B. Berntsen; Dr. Alton G. Snyder; Mrs. Marie Acomb Riley. Mr. Logan Massee; Mr. and Mrs. Drew Massee; Mrs. Edna Blair Massee; Dr. Joseph C. Massee; Marjorie Massee. Dr. Paul Woolley and Dr. G. Hall Todd.

F. Miscellaneous

Bryan, Grace Dexter. "William Jennings Bryan: Biographical Notes, His Speeches, Letters and Other Writings." Typescript, n.d. Bryan Papers.

Guerard, Wilhelmina. "Clarence Macartney Biographical Notes." Typescript, n.d. Macartney Papers.

Who Was Who in America, 1897–1942, Vol. I. Charles Scribner's Sons, 1942. 4th printing, 1960.

II. Secondary Sources

A. Books

Ahlstrom, Sydney E. *A Religious History of the American People.* Yale University Press, 1972.

National Book Award for 1972. Superb overview of religion in America.

Allen, Frederick Lewis. *Only Yesterday: An Informal History of the Nineteen Twenties.* Harper & Brothers, 1931.

Good for a general description of society in the 1920's. Light on religious analysis.

Bailey, K. K. *Southern White Protestantism in the Twentieth Century.* Harper & Row, Publishers, Inc., 1962.

Excellent monograph on religion in the South.

Broyles, J. Allen. *The John Birch Society: Anatomy of a Protest.* Beacon Press, Inc., 1964.

Helpful as it relates to J. Frank Norris, who led John Birch to his religious conversion.

Carnell, Edward John. *The Case for Orthodox Theology.* The Westminster Press, 1959.

A valuable book with an excellent critique of Fundamentalism (Chapter 8). Carnell believes that Fundamentalism is Orthodoxy gone cultic.

Carter, Paul A. *The Twenties in America.* The Thomas Y. Crowell Company, 1968.

A scholarly treatise in The Crowell American History Series.

Cole, Stewart G. *The History of Fundamentalism.* Richard R. Smith, Inc., 1931.

An older work that still has merit. A good "contemporary" bibliography. Little attention to the controversy over evolution.

Coletta, Paolo E. *William Jennings Bryan,* 3 vols. University of Nebraska Press, 1964–1969. (Vol. I, *Political Evangelist: 1860–1908;* Vol. II, *Progressive Politician and Moral Statesman, 1900–1915;* Vol. III, *Political Puritan, 1915–1925.*)

The most thorough of the academic works on Bryan. Volume III has been particularly helpful to this study. This is the way history should be written.

Dawson, Joseph Martin. *A Century with Texas Baptists.* The Broadman Press, 1947.

Dawson's volumes are important for their knowledge of Texas Baptists in general and J. Frank Norris in particular.

———. *A Thousand Months to Remember: An Autobiography.* Baylor University Press, 1964.

DeWolf, L. Harold. *Present Trends in Christian Thought.* Association Press, 1960.

Provides a good critical analysis of the strengths and weaknesses of Fundamentalism.

Dollar, George W. *A History of Fundamentalism in America.* Bob Jones University Press, 1973.

Good for factual information about various fundamentalist groups but highly opinionated from the ultraconservative standpoint. Dollar's understanding of Liberalism is superficial and there is constant sermonizing from the standpoint of militant Fundamentalism. Its helpful biographical index must be checked occasionally for errors of fact. Extremely critical of evangelicals such as Billy Graham and Harold John Ockenga.

Forman, S. E. *Our Republic.* D. Appleton-Century Company, Inc., 1937.

Furniss, Norman F. *The Fundamentalist Controversy, 1918–1931.* Yale University Press, 1954.

For many years the authoritative book on the Modernist-Fundamentalist struggle. In time, its limitations and inaccuracies caused it to be viewed in a more realistic light. It is heavy on the religious struggle in the various denominations. However, there is little theological analysis and the presentation is weighted from the liberal side.

Gasper, Louis. *The Fundamentalist Movement.* The Hague: Mouton & Co., 1963.

Traces the developments within the organized fundamentalist movement in American Protestant Christianity from 1930 to date of publication. In that sense, continues the account begun by Norman F. Furniss but covers a later period and concentrates heavily on ecumenical evangelicalism, i.e., the National Association of Evangelicals and the American Council of Christian Churches. Largely factual; light on interpretation.

Gatewood, Willard B., Jr., ed. *Controversy in the Twenties: Fundamentalism, Modernism, and Evolution.* Vanderbilt University Press, 1969.

A highly commendable sourcebook with thoughtful introductions and a valuable bibliography on secondary sources (pp. 444–452). Concentrates on the struggle over evolution.

Gaustad, Edwin S., ed. *The Rise of Adventism: Religion and Society in Mid-nineteenth-Century America.* Harper & Row, Publishers, Inc., 1974.

Scholarly lectures delivered at the University Church, Loma Linda University, Loma Linda, California.

Ginger, Ray. *Six Days or Forever? Tennessee v. John Thomas Scopes.* Beacon Press, Inc., 1958.

Many scholars consider this volume, which probes into the psychological and sociological milieu of the Scopes Trial, the most able account of the events at Dayton.

Glad, Paul W., ed. *William Jennings Bryan, A Profile.* Hill & Wang, Inc., 1968.

An important work on Bryan in the American Profile Series. Bibliographical notes, pp. 245–248.

Harrison, Harry P., and Detzer, Karl. *Culture Under Canvas: The Story of Tent Chautauqua.* Hastings House, Publishers, Inc., 1958.

Sheds light on one aspect of Bryan's career.

Hibben, Paxton. *The Peerless Leader, William Jennings Bryan.* Farrar & Rinehart, Inc., 1929.

An older work, with an introduction by Charles A. Beard.

High, Stanley. *Billy Graham: The Personal Story of the Man, His Message, and His Mission.* McGraw-Hill Book Co., Inc., 1956.

Not a helpful book.

Hill, Samuel S., Jr. *Southern Churches in Crisis.* Beacon Press, Inc., 1966.

Excellent overview of the problems confronting southern churches.

Hofstadter, Richard. *Anti-Intellectualism in American Life.* Random House, Inc., 1962.

A classic in academic historiography on a particular theme. See especially pp. 117–136 for a critique of Fundamentalism.

James, Powhatan W. *George W. Truett: A Biography.* The Macmillan Company, 1945.

Significant for what it does not say about J. Frank Norris.

Jorstad, Erling. *The Politics of Doomsday: Fundamentalists of the Far Right.* Abingdon Press, 1970.

An academically respectable treatise which shows how four individuals and their programs have created "the politics of doomsday": Carl McIntire, Billy James Hargis, Edgar C. Bundy, and Verne P. Kaub.

Koenig, Louis W. *Bryan, A Political Biography of William Jennings Bryan.* G. P. Putnam's Sons, Inc., 1971.

A superbly written book, with helpful information on Bryan's religion, despite the emphasis on the political. A fine bibliography, pp. 705–719.

Levine, Lawrence W. *Defender of the Faith, William Jennings Bryan: The Last Decade, 1915–1925.* Oxford University Press, 1965.

Important to an understanding of Bryan and his faith.

Lipphard, William B. *Fifty Years an Editor.* Judson Press, 1963.

Valuable for Lipphard's knowledge of Straton and the Foreign Mission Controversy among the Northern Baptists.

Loetscher, Lefferts A. *The Broadening Church: A Study of Theological Issues in the Presbyterian Church Since 1869.* University of Pennsylvania Press, 1954.

Excellent for material on Machen and Macartney as well as providing a scholarly background for the struggle within the Presbyterian ranks between liberals and fundamentalists. Thoughtful interpretations.

McLoughlin, William G. *Billy Graham: Revivalist in a Secular Age.* The Ronald Press Co., 1960.

From an academic standpoint, the finest of the biographies of Graham. Gives attention to Graham's social, political, and religious views.

————. *Modern Revivalism: Charles Grandison Finney to Billy Graham.* The Ronald Press Co., 1959.

The best of the general treatments on American revivalism.

Mead, Frank S. *Handbook of Denominations in the United States.* Abingdon-Cokesbury Press, 1951.

Merrill, William Pierson. *Liberal Christianity.* Harper & Brothers, 1925.

Reflects liberal position contemporary to the conflict.

Mitchell, Curtis. *Billy Graham: The Making of a Crusader.* Chilton Company, 1966.

Overly sympathetic to Graham. Lacks documentation, index, and bibliography.

Moore, Edmund A. *A Catholic Runs for President: The Campaign of 1928.* The Ronald Press Co., 1956.

Used for insights into Norris' role in 1928.

Mueller, William A. *A History of Southern Baptist Theological Seminary.* The Broadman Press, 1959.

Scholarly treatise on the institution at which several of the leaders of Fundamentalism were trained.

O'Connor, Richard. *The First Hurrah: A Biography of Alfred E. Smith.* G. P. Putnam's Sons, Inc., 1970.

Helpful in trying to understand the opposition of Norris and Straton to Smith.

Olmstead, Clifton E. *History of Religion in the United States.* Prentice-Hall, Inc., 1960.

An encyclopedia-like treatment.

Peel, Roy V., and Donnelly, Thomas C. *The 1928 Campaign: An Analysis*. Farrar & Rinehart, Inc., 1931.

Again, used in the attempt to understand Norris.

Pollock, John. *Billy Graham, The Authorized Biography*. McGraw-Hill Book Co., Inc., 1966.

Lacking in critical evaluation of Graham, as one would expect of an authorized treatment. This book, which was probably a response to McLoughlin's work of 1960, emphasizes the nature of Graham's opposition. An index and a brief note as to sources, but no documentation.

Rian, Edwin H. *The Presbyterian Conflict*. Wm. B. Eerdmans Publishing Company, 1940.

An important book on the theological struggle among the Presbyterians, although sympathetic to the more conservative side.

Riley, Marie Acomb. *The Dynamic of a Dream: The Life Story of Dr. William B. Riley*. Wm. B. Eerdmans Publishing Company, 1938.

Of minimal help academically, but of value because of some human interest insights, as one would expect of Riley's wife.

Roy, Ralph Lord. *Apostles of Discord: A Study of Organized Bigotry and Disruption on the Fringes of Protestantism*. Beacon Press, Inc., 1953.

Somewhat on the sensational side, but contains helpful information on Norris and Riley.

———. *Communism and the Churches*. Harcourt, Brace and Company, Inc., 1960.

Used sparingly.

Sandeen, Ernest R. *The Roots of Fundamentalism: British and American Millenarianism, 1800–1930*. The University of Chicago Press, 1970.

A bold, thorough, and valuable work, although the content seems to fit the second half of the title better than the first. An important bibliography, pp. 285–310.

Silva, Ruth C. *Rum, Religion, and Votes: 1928 Re-examined*. Pennsylvania State University Press, 1962.

An important second look at 1928. Relates to the endeavor to interpret Norris and Straton.

Smith, Roy L., comp. *The Minneapolis Pulpit.* Fleming H. Revell Company, 1929.

Contains one of Riley's sermons.

Stevick, Daniel B. *Beyond Fundamentalism.* John Knox Press, 1964.

Incisively critical of Fundamentalism.

Stonehouse, Ned B. *J. Gresham Machen, A Biographical Memoir.* Wm. B. Eerdmans Publishing Company, 1954.

Stonehouse was Machen's intimate friend and associate for over seven years, eventually succeeding him as professor of New Testament, Westminster Theological Seminary, Philadelphia. This is, therefore, an adulatory book which abounds in too many lengthy, direct quotations. Documentation leaves something to be desired. It remains, however, an important source on Machen until someone writes a better volume.

Tatum, E. Ray. *Conquest or Failure? A Biography of J. Frank Norris.* Baptist Historical Foundation, 1966.

Tatum's biography stresses Norris' devotion to his mother, his emphasis on sensationalism and the driving desire for statistical successes. The book is hindered by too much stress on narrative description, historical inaccuracies, glaring typographical and spelling errors, the lack of mention of Norris' death, and the absence of a concluding evaluation. The work is also "thin" on the division in Norris' church at Detroit.

Tompkins, Jerry R., ed. *D-Days at Dayton: Reflections on the Scopes Trial.* Louisiana State University Press, 1965.

The chapters comprise a symposium by a variety of individuals who were either directly or indirectly associated with the Scopes Trial, including John Thomas Scopes, H. L. Mencken, and John Dillenberger.

Torbet, Robert George. *A History of the Baptists.* Judson Press, 1950.

The finest of the histories of the Baptists, with outstanding annotated bibliography.

Tuveson, Ernest Lee. *Redeemer Nation: The Idea of America's Millennial Role.* The University of Chicago Press, 1968.

This is a valuable, thought-provoking work in which the author distinguishes between pessimistic and optimistic (progressivist) millennialists. Tuveson feels that in the nineteenth century there were two "ideas of progress," not one. Also important for definitions of millennialists, millenarians, premillennialists, and postmillennialists.

Williams, T. Harry; Current, Richard N.; and Freidel, Frank. *A History of the United States*, Vol. II, *Since 1865*. Alfred A. Knopf, Inc., 1965.

Helpful for factual information—in a textbook context.

B. Articles

Carnell, Edward John. "Fundamentalism," in *A Handbook of Christian Theology*, Marvin Halverson, ed. Meridian Books, Inc., 1958. Pp. 142–143.

Driscoll, Charles B. "A Voice Crying in the Wilderness," *The New McClure's*, Nov. 1928, pp. 28 ff.

A good, contemporary article on Straton.

Handy, Robert T. "Fundamentalism and Modernism in Perspective," *Religion in Life*, Vol. XXIV (1955), pp. 381–394.

Handy sees the Modernist-Fundamentalist struggle in terms of the conflict between faith and reason. Handy was also one of the first to recognize that the distinguishing mark of Fundamentalism is as much an attitude as a belief or set of beliefs.

———. "The American Scene," *Twentieth Century Christianity*, ed. by Bishop Stephen Neill. Doubleday and Company, Inc., 1963.

A brief survey of American religion in this century.

Hofstadter, Richard. "Could a Protestant Have Beaten Hoover in 1928?" *The Reporter*, March 17, 1960, pp. 31–32.

A pertinent question by a scholar of national reputation.

Holmes, John Haynes. "Straton, John Roach," *Dictionary of American Biography*, Dumas Malone, ed. Charles Scribner's Sons, 1936. Vol. XVIII, pp. 125–126.

An excellent article, factually correct. Contains incisive comments by Straton's Unitarian contemporary in New York City at the Community Church.

Ironside, Harry A. "Dr. W. B. Riley, Defender of the Faith," *Northwestern Pilot*, Jan. 1948, pp. 119 ff.

Ironside's tribute at Riley's Memorial Service.

Larkin, W. J. "C. E. Macartney: Champion of the Faith," *Moody Monthly*, Jan. 1973.

Not helpful academically.

Lhamon, W. J. "A Study of Fundamentalism," *The Christian*, Nov. 5, 1926.

An article critical of Fundamentalism at the height of the theological tensions.

Loetscher, Lefferts A. "Machen, John Gresham," *Dictionary of American Biography*, Vol. XI, Supplement Two, Robert L. Schuyler, ed. Charles Scribner's Sons, 1958. Pp. 411–412.

The best of the briefer articles on Machen. Fair, factually correct, concise.

Marsden, George M. "Defining Fundamentalism," *Christian Scholar's Review*, Winter 1971, pp. 141–151.

Marsden acknowledges the importance of the millenarian backgrounds to Fundamentalism but sees other contributing factors, such as nineteenth-century evangelical Protestantism, revivalism, the erosion of Protestant culture, and opposition to modernism. The article essentially is a criticism of Sandeen's thesis set forth in his book of the previous year.

Moore, James Benedict. "The Sources of Elmer Gantry," *The New Republic*, Aug. 8, 1960, pp. 17–18.

Of significance in the sense that Straton and Norris may have provided some of the "inspiration" for *Elmer Gantry*.

Pugh, R. Quinn. "J. C. Massee, Minister of Christ," *Baptist History and Heritage*, Oct. 1971, pp. 233–239, 249.

Borders on the devotional rather than the academic, although there are one or two good quotations from Massee.

Rice, John R. "Dr. W. B. Riley, Evangelist," *Northwestern Pilot*, Jan. 1948.

Rice's tribute at Riley's Memorial Service.

Roark, Dallas M. "J. Gresham Machen: The Doctrinally True Presbyterian Church," *Journal of Presbyterian History*, June 1965, pp. 134–138; Sept. 1965, pp. 174–181.

A condensation in two installments of Roark's doctoral dissertation.

Russell, C. Allyn. "J. C. Massee, Unique Fundamentalist," *Foundations*, Oct.–Dec. 1969, pp. 330–356.

———. "John Roach Straton, Accusative Case," *Foundations*, Jan.–March 1970, pp. 44–72.

———. "J. Frank Norris: Violent Fundamentalist," *Southwestern Historical Quarterly*, Jan. 1972, pp. 271–302.

———. "William Bell Riley: Architect of Fundamentalism," *Minnesota History*, Spring 1972, pp. 14–30.

Winner of the Solon J. Buck award for the best article to appear in *Minnesota History* in 1972.

———. "J. Gresham Machen: Scholarly Fundamentalist," *Journal of Presbyterian History*, Spring 1973, pp. 40–69.

———. "Clarence E. Macartney: Fundamentalist Prince of the Pulpit," *Journal of Presbyterian History*, Spring 1974, pp. 33–58.

———. "William Jennings Bryan: Statesman-Fundamentalist," *Journal of Presbyterian History*, Summer 1975, pp. 93–117.

Sandeen, Ernest R. "Toward a Historical Interpretation of the Origins of Fundamentalism," *Church History*, March 1967, pp. 66–83.

Sandeen challenges the idea that Fundamentalism was "an agrarian protest movement centered in the South."

———. "Fundamentalism and American Identity." *The Sixties: Radical Change in American Religion, The Annals of the American Academy of Political and Social Science*, Jan. 1970, pp. 56–65.

A thought-provoking article which argues that Fundamentalism lives in symbiotic relationship with other forms of religion and with cultural trends, leading the fundamentalist, paradoxically, to affirm both his despair over the world and his identification with much of the world's culture.

———. "Defining Fundamentalism: A Reply to Professor Marsden," *Christian Scholar's Review*, Spring 1971, pp. 227–233.

Sandeen maintains his thesis that British and American millenarianism provide the major source for Fundamentalism.

Straton, Hillyer H. "John Roach Straton: Prophet of Social Righteousness: Three Decades of Protestant Activism," *Foundations*, Jan. 1962, pp. 17–38.

The article that influenced Walter Ross Peterson and a few others to think of John Roach Straton as a social prophet. It appears that Hillyer H. Straton is interpreting his father's ministry very selectively.

———. "The Straton-Brady Debate on the Theatre," *Encounter*, Autumn 1965, pp. 452–460.

A period piece from the 1920's.

———. "John Roach Straton and the Ku Klux Klan," *Andover-Newton Quarterly*, Nov. 1968, pp. 124–134.

The son of John Roach Straton seeks to justify his father's association with "The Supreme Kingdom," a Klan-related organization. He feels that in some instances his father was misunderstood by sections of the press. Of his father, Hillyer H. Straton writes: "He was naïve but . . . not grasping. His passion was to proclaim God's truth in a turbulent time to the people of the America that he loved with devotion and he stood ready to do it at great personal cost." Despite the son's defense, some unanswered questions remain.

Straton, Hillyer H., and Szasz, Ferenc M. "The Reverend John Roach Straton and the Presidential Campaign of 1928," *New York History*, April 1968, pp. 200–217.

An illustrated article of interest which depicts the role that John Roach Straton played in opposing Alfred E. Smith.

Szasz, Ferenc M. "William B. Riley and the Fight Against Teaching of Evolution in Minnesota," *Minnesota History*, Spring 1969, pp. 201–216.

An award-winning article depicting Riley's antievolution role in his home state. Fine use of primary sources.

———. "The Scopes Trial in Perspective," *Tennessee Historical Quarterly*, Fall 1971.

Szasz is of the opinion that the role of the Scopes Trial in the Modernist-Fundamentalist conflict has been overemphasized.

———. "John Roach Straton: Baptist Fundamentalist in an Age of Change, 1875–1929," *The Quarterly Review: A Survey of Southern Baptist Progress*, April–June 1974.

An excellent article reflecting Szasz's abilities for critical evaluation as well as his knowledge of Straton and his times.

Taylor, W. S. "Norris, John Franklyn," *Encyclopedia of Southern Baptists*. 2 vols. The Broadman Press, 1958. Vol. II, p. 983.

A measured, factually correct, article by a southern (and Southern) Baptist about a fellow southern Baptist and a former Southern Baptist.

C. Dissertations and Theses

1. Ph.D. Dissertations

Farra, Harry Eugene. "The Rhetoric of Reverend Clarence Edward Macartney: A Man Under Authority," Pennsylvania State University, 1970.

The finest of the dissertations and theses on Macartney, carefully written and thoroughly researched.

Hull, Lloyd B. "A Rhetorical Study of the Preaching of William Bell Riley." Wayne State University, 1960.

Views Machen primarily as a homiletician.

Livingstone, William D. "The Princeton Apologetic as Exemplified by the Work of Benjamin B. Warfield and J. Gresham Machen: A Study in American Theology, 1880–1930." Yale University, 1948.

Important to an understanding of Machen's theology.

McBirnie, Robert Sheldon. "Basic Issues in the Fundamentalism of William Bell Riley." State University of Iowa, 1952.

A good dissertation with helpful bibliography (pp. 145–149; 158–165). McBirnie declares Riley to be "the ablest leader of orthodox reaction during the early part of the twentieth century."

Peterson, Walter Ross. "John Roach Straton: Portrait of a Fundamentalist Preacher." Boston University Graduate School, 1965.

Contains excellent primary sources, although the author gives Straton too much credit as a social reformer.

Roark, Dallas. "J. Gresham Machen and His Desire to Maintain a Doctrinally True Presbyterian Church." State University of Iowa, 1963.

A commendable work. A portion of it was later published in two installments in *Journal of Presbyterian History*.

Szasz, Ferenc M. "Three Fundamentalist Leaders: The Roles of William Bell Riley, John Roach Straton, and William Jennings Bryan in the Fundamentalist-Modernist Controversy." The University of Rochester, 1969.

A superb dissertation, factually correct, excellent sources, plausible interpretations.

2. Others

Bouldin, D. G. "The J. M. Dawson–J. F. Norris Controversy: A Reflection of the Fundamentalist Controversy Among Texas Baptists." Master's thesis, Baylor University, 1960.

The best of the theses (and dissertations) related to Norris.

Burlinson, B. E. "The Ecclesiology and Strategy of J. Frank Norris, from 1919 to 1950." Master's thesis, Baylor University, 1960.

Connolly, Kenneth. "The Preaching of J. Frank Norris." Master's thesis, The University of Nebraska, 1960.

Considers Norris primarily from a homiletical standpoint.

Hough, H. D. "Prince of the American Pulpit." B.D. thesis, Western Theological Seminary, 1952.

Macartney is the prince to whom Hough refers.

Lucas, Richard D. "The Preaching of Clarence E. Macartney." Th.D. dissertation, Southern Baptist Theological Seminary, 1959.

Another consideration of a fundamentalist leader from a homiletical perspective.

Ritchie, Homer. "The Life and Career of J. Frank Norris." Master's thesis, Texas Christian University, 1967.

The greatest value of this thesis is that it is written by one who knew Norris well and who eventually succeeded him as minister of the First Baptist Church at Fort Worth. In numerous places it provides firsthand insights, although it tends to be uncritical.

Terre-Blanche, Henry S. "The Life of J. Frank Norris." Th.M. thesis, Dallas Theological Seminary, 1966.

INDEX